HENRIK IBSEN

was born of well-to-do parents at Skien, a small Norwegian coastal town, on March 20, 1828. In 1836 his father went bankrupt, and the family was reduced to near poverty. At the age of fifteen, he was apprenticed to an apothecary in Grimstad. In 1850 Ibsen went to Christiania—present-day Oslo—as a student, with the hope of becoming a doctor. On the strength of his first two plays, he was appointed "theater-poet" to the new Bergen National Theater, where he wrote five conventional romantic and historical dramas and absorbed the elements of his craft. In 1857 he was called to the directorship of the financially unsound Christiania Norwegian Theater, which failed in 1862. In 1864, exhausted and enraged by the frustration of his efforts toward a national drama and theater, he quit Norway for what became twenty-seven years of voluntary exile abroad. In Italy he wrote the volcanic *Brand* (1866), which made his reputation and secured him a poet's stipend from the government. Its companion piece, the phantasmagoric *Peer Gynt,* followed in 1867, then the immense double play, *Emperor and Galilean* (1873), expressing his philosophy of civilization. Meanwhile, having moved to Germany, Ibsen had been searching for a new style. With *The Pillars of Society* he found it; this became the first of twelve plays, appearing at two-year intervals, that confirmed his international standing as the foremost dramatist of his age. In 1900 Ibsen suffered the first of several strokes that incapacitated him. He died in Oslo on May 23, 1906.

HENRIK IBSEN

Four Major Plays

Volume I

A Doll House
The Wild Duck
Hedda Gabler
The Master Builder

In New Translations with a Foreword
by ROLF FJELDE

A SIGNET CLASSIC

SIGNET CLASSIC
Published by the Penguin Group
Penguin Putnam Inc., 375 Hudson Street,
New York, New York 10014, U.S.A.
Penguin Books Ltd, 27 Wrights Lane,
London W8 5TZ, England
Penguin Books Australia Ltd, Ringwood,
Victoria, Australia
Penguin Books Canada Ltd, 10 Alcorn Avenue,
Toronto, Ontario, Canada M4V 3B2
Penguin Books (N.Z.) Ltd, 182—190 Wairau Road,
Auckland 10, New Zealand

Penguin Books Ltd, Registered Offices:
Harmondsworth, Middlesex, England

Published by Signet Classic, an imprint of Dutton NAL,
a member of Penguin Putnam Inc.

First Signet Classic Printing, January, 1965
43 42 41 40 39 38 37 36 35

 REGISTERED TRADEMARK—MARCA REGISTRADA

Library of Congress Catalog Card Number: 91-068441

Printed in the United States of America

TO THOSE MANY ACTORS, DIRECTORS AND DESIGNERS WHO
HAVE GIVEN THESE TEXTS WINGS ON STAGE

CONTENTS

FOREWORD

To be a poet is, most of all, to see.
Ibsen

It is one of those happy accidents of literary history that Henrik Ibsen's career as a dramatist neatly coincides with the latter half of the nineteenth century, from *Catiline* (1850) to *When We Dead Awaken* (1899). Master builder that he was, one fleetingly suspects him of planning it that way, before filing the observation away as no more than a useful mnemonic. If, however, we withhold our impatient cataloging to delve a bit further in chronology, we may begin to wonder if Ibsen was not, in this respect, curiously accident-prone, with all the implications of an underlying pattern that the phrase connotes. For it also is a striking fact that there is a definite division at the center of that fifty-year career, the plays of the first twenty-five years sharing one group of properties, and those of the final twenty-five sharing another. *Emperor and Galilean,* the last play of the first series, appeared in 1873; *Pillars of Society,* the first play of the second series, appeared in 1877—which places a hypothetical dividing line, again neatly, right where it ought to be, in 1875.

The nature of the properties apportioned by these various boundary lines can perhaps best be brought out in terms of a metaphor, one that Ibsen himself introduces in possibly the most autobiographical of the later plays, the metaphor of architecture. Imagine Ibsen, not simply as the master builder, but as an errant town planner, proceeding down the main street of his life, raising the edifices of his plays

as inner necessity and occasion dictate. The resulting town,
like Budapest, has two parts: an Old Quarter and a New.
If we traverse this town from beginning to end, observing,
as the planner desired we should, not merely the individual
architectural details, but the total order and interrelation of
the buildings, its two sections come clearly into view. The
salient feature of the Old Quarter, we soon decide, is its
diversity of styles; we pass first a Roman villa, then several
gnarled stave churches, moated towers and archaic guild-
halls in the Viking manner, interspersed with a ruined
cabaret, a rustic summerhouse and a wittily ornamented
honeymoon hotel. Indifferent as the construction sometimes
is, the variety gluts the eye; and there are more imposing
works to come: two large ducal palaces, one austere and
forbidding, but impressively powerful in conception, the
other baroque and spaciously fantastic, with pennants flying; beyond these a small clapboard civic information booth;
then a vast Romanesque cathedral with, like Chartres, two
contrasting, unequal spires. Next we cross a brief arid open
space, the width of a couple of vacant lots, and suddenly
arrive in what appears to be a model town of virtually iden-
tical row houses that extend to the city line. The dimensions, the basic floor plans, the somber coloring of the
facades in this New Quarter seem hardly to vary from structure to structure; they look uniformly respectable and re-
strained. Only on closer acquaintance does one notice faint
carvings of coiled serpents on the lintels, or ghosts that seem
to materialize at the windows, or, on entrance, that the
cellars are dark and swarming with secret life, and the attics
are filled with long-forgotten things that nevertheless main-
tain their mysterious hold on the occupants below as they
move restlessly about from room to meticulously furnished
room.

With a writer as reticent as Ibsen, one can never really
know what inner compulsions brought about the change
from the milieu of *St. John's Eve, The Vikings at Helgeland*
and *Love's Comedy* to that of *A Doll House, The Wild
Duck* and *Hedda Gabler*. Many explanations have been offered, and a combination of many is certainly in order. It
is the undue emphasis on one or another exclusively that
has given rise to those still current oversimplifications, those

convenient labels, that misrepresent the stylistic unity of the later plays.

There is, for example, the conversion-to-naturalism theory that finds supporting evidence in Ibsen's angry response to the critical reception of *Peer Gynt*: "My book *is* poetry. And if it is not, then it shall be. The conception of poetry in our country, in Norway, shall be made to conform to my book. . . . If it is to be war, then let it be war! If I am no poet, then I have nothing to lose. I shall try my luck as a photographer." From this perspective, the later plays are a series of naturalistic photographs, literal and exact exposures of the social lies and corruptions of the time, leading to Yeats' dismissal of Ibsen as a writer for clever journalists. But it is difficult to believe that a born poet, having persisted against odds for forty years, in a momentary pique at his critics, decides to turn the theater with all its possibilities into a living tabloid. The Ibsen of the later plays is not the Scandinavian Zola of *Thérèse Raquin*—though one still can find him categorized in text books under the heading of Naturalism.

Another theory proposes that Ibsen, in his lifelong search for his true vocation as a writer, had it precipitated for him by the Danish critic Georg Brandes, in his famous dictum that "what is alive in modern literature shows in its capacity to submit problems to debate." Brandes' *Main Currents of Nineteenth Century Literature* (Part 1, 1872) obviously had a catalytic effect on Ibsen's creative development, as witness the fact, noted by Brian Downs, that "all Ibsen's poetry after 1875 could be written on a single sheet of notepaper." Its attack on the cultural nostalgia and idealizing aestheticism of the dominant romantic school reinforced Ibsen's own evolving thought, which already had accepted Kierkegaard's position that, of the three stages on life's way, the purely aesthetic was the lowest and least defensible. And yet if the romantic milieu of the early verse plays and historical dramas no longer seemed artistically habitable, Ibsen's rich imagination could not move on to a theater dedicated simply to ideas and utilitarian realism. Unlike Bernard Shaw, he was not by temperament a debater, a dialectician of the platform—and his inability to find satisfaction in this role marks one of the differences between their dramatic worlds: Shaw, in his plays, is interested in human beings insofar as they express ideas, whereas Ibsen is interested in ideas insofar as they are expressions of human beings.

Ibsen's dilemma was acute; he had, on the one hand, an outmoded technique, or array of techniques, which he could no longer employ with conviction, and, on the other, a restrictive blueprint for future writing which offered no freedom to his expansive imagination. According to the second of our theoretic simplifications, wherein the shift from poetry to prose is more like turning off a faucet than a painful diminishment of being, Ibsen himself shot the lyric Pegasus that had served him so well in *Brand* and *Peer Gynt* and became the pedestrian Social Dramatist. It is this approach that has given rise to the mistaken impression that Ibsen devoted his later years to writing a series of problem plays. Leaving aside the question of whether the problem play is a legitimate genre—it would seem to be more a function of content than of form—it is precisely the fact that Ibsen did *not* write problem plays that gives his drama its lasting fascination. It was rather his disciples who wrote the problem plays, about such matters as slum landlords or prison conditions or war profiteering—and their work soon exhausts our interest; whereas Ibsen concerned himself with writing plays that, among other things, pose problems, just as he explored social dimensions of existence without becoming a Social Dramatist and adapted naturalistic innovations without becoming a Naturalist.

If so many of the standard clichés about the later Ibsen dramas turn out to be superficial and inadequate, what then, we may ask, is the common substratum of these works? Considerations of intent, though tantalizing, soon lose their focus in the minutiae of biography and prove unproductive. We know, for instance, that shortly before the crucial dividing line in Ibsen's literary development, he evinced a strong determination to make himself over, that he altered his manner of dress, his appearance, even his handwriting from what previously had been casual and bohemian to what now became formal, elegant and correct, as if hoping that a revision in the outer man would evoke an inner transformation—but any attempt to locate an overriding motive behind these changes results at best in a study of the psychology of creativity, rather than a clearer understanding of the works themselves.

It is not the question *why* the stylistic shift, but *how* it was brought about, that leads to the unity of structure and texture that binds these twelve plays into one cycle. Before an artist can transcend the limitations of his present self, he has to figure out how, technically, he is going to accomplish his growth; until that quite specific, practical discovery is made, he is dealing with nothing more than his insubstantial aspirations. It is in Ibsen's workshop, hidden in the weeds of those apparently vacant lots between the two dissimilar milieus of style, that one can perhaps find the kernel of growth, the clue to a pattern of twenty-five years.

In July 1874, after a decade abroad during which the decisive battles of his artistic life had been fought and won, Ibsen returned for a visit to Norway. Accepted and welcomed now as a great national dramatist, he nevertheless experienced his return chiefly as a bitter reminder of the toll the long years of struggle had taken, an exacerbation of scarred emotions from old defeats that had brought him to the verge of despair and self-destruction. From the hour he sailed up the Christiania Fjord, he wrote, "I felt a weight settling down on my chest, a feeling of actual physical oppression. And this feeling lasted all the while I was at home" —except for one day he might have added. On September 10, a delegation of students marched with flags and music to his lodgings to give him a testimony of their admiration and affection. A song specially composed in his honor was sung. The occasion touched him deeply, and for once he dropped the gruff and ironic public mask to open his innermost feelings, so much so that his brief response has been gratefully raided by commentators ever since—and not least the remarks defining his chosen vocation. "What is it," he said, "to be a poet? It was a long time before I realized that to be a poet is, most of all, to see; but mark well, to see in such a way that what is seen is perceived by his audience just as the poet saw it."

To be a poet is to see. One can easily imagine, with the evidence at hand of the plays from *Pillars of Society* to *When We Dead Awaken,* Ibsen himself seeing, gaining a glimpse, a germinal hint, at about this time, of the solution to the dilemma facing him after his enormous and exhausting effort toward "that positive philosophy of life which the critics have demanded of me" monumentalized

in *Emperor and Galilean.* If indeed the poetry of conventional verse drama—the rich legacy of Shakespeare depleted
to a near bankrupt romanticism—now had to be sacrificed
to the plain truth that realism sought, as Brandes' strictures
implied, perhaps another poetry was waiting to be discovered underground, under the surfaces of ordinary life. Already, in his youthful poem, "The Miner," Ibsen had
seemingly anticipated a quest into the depths: "Downward
I must break my way till I hear the ore-stones ring . . . in
the deep is peace, peace and desolation from eternity; break
me the way, my heavy hammer, to the hidden mystery's
heart." In the hidden laws and interrelationships within life
itself was an inexhaustible source of poetry in the theater,
with respect to which rhyme and meter could be considered
as merely the outward, collateral evidence; the essential
problem was to see these truths and then find the means,
dramaturgically, to project them in concrete instances, ex-
emplary cases, so that the audience could not fail, propor-
tionate to their capacity for insight, to see the same.

As he elaborated the act of seeing into a practical dramatic technique, Ibsen, it would seem, came to recognize it
under three main aspects, which—when fused into one effective instrument and modified to the needs of each consec-
utive project—produced that unity of structure and texture
which has been the object of our search. In this threefold
method, to see, first of all, is to visualize. The most valuable
description of this phase of composition was given by Ibsen
to the Munich editor Georg Conrad, after it had proved
itself in practice several times: "Before I write down one
word, I have to have the character in mind through and
through. I must penetrate into the last wrinkle of his soul.
I always proceed from the individual; the stage setting, the
dramatic ensemble, all that comes naturally and does not
cause me any worry, as soon as I am certain of the individual in every aspect of his humanity. But I have to have his
exterior in mind also, down to the last button, how he
stands and walks, how he conducts himself, what his voice
sounds like. Then I do not let him go until his fate is
fulfilled."

Ibsen was capable of exercising this power of evoking the
physical presence of his characters with an intensity that
verged at times on hallucination; he once told his wife that

Nora had appeared to him that morning, wearing a blue dress, and at other occasions would give periodic reports on her changes of apparel. Such insistence on realizing general truths through the most scrupulously detailed particulars, "down to the last button," is no surprise to anyone who has seen examples of the costume designs meticulously rendered by Ibsen when he was stage manager for the Bergen theater. These, along with other reproductions of his art works, have been assembled by Otto Lous Mohr in an illuminating volume titled *Henrik Ibsen as a Painter*. Here we learn that, until approximately his thirty-fifth year, Ibsen had considerable ambitions as a painter, that he worked fairly consistently in a variety of media, and that it was only the repeated and strenuous urging of his wife that turned the balance and concentrated his energies in the field of dramatic writing. His extensive, if curtailed, experience in the graphic arts was hardly wasted, however, as the wealth of carefully selected, thematically significant visual detail in the later plays amply demonstrates. In fact, it is exactly this use of apt visual suggestion that became one of Ibsen's chief means of reintroducing the poetic richness of implication eliminated, in large measure, from the verbal text, as has been persuasively argued by John Northam in his indispensable study, *Ibsen's Dramatic Method*. (Northam's discussion of method and Maurice Valency's of the meaning of the subject matter serve the same essential function in clarifying the scope of Ibsen's dramatic art as, comparably, G. Wilson Knight's investigation of Shakespeare's method of compressing his thought into the modulating tensions between key archetypal images, or Theodore Spencer's and E. M. W. Tillyard's documentation of how Shakespeare's apparent awareness of the crumbling triple order of the Elizabethan world-picture stretched his tragic heroes on a cosmic rack.)

On a primary level, then, the Ibsen play can be regarded as a structure of successive visualizations, derived out of an intimate knowledge of the individual seen in all the concrete immediacy and humanity of his being. But this individual, this basic self on which so much depends, could never become theatrically interesting, dynamically motivated, enmeshed in a complex action, were it not for another, a second aspect of seeing: namely, that to see is to perceive relationships. It is here, in composition, that the individual—Nora, for example, or Hedda, or Solness—inevitably acquired a context, a place in a dramatic ensemble, a suitable stage setting; and also here, in interpretation, that the audience is called upon to follow a much more involved order of perceptions. They must perceive, first, through the translucent glass of the dialogue, the stress of relationships, tensions, dissonances within the self, described by Ibsen at one point as "the struggle which all serious-minded human beings have to wage with themselves to bring their lives into harmony with their convictions. For the different spiritual functions do not develop evenly and abreast of each other in any one human being . . . hence the conflict within the individual." Not only are there the spiritual conflicts, those matters that trouble the conscience, the stored furnishings of the attic in our earlier figure, but there is also—by virtue of what has often been remarked in Ibsen's work: his extraordinary, pre-Freudian sensitivity to unconscious pressures behind the conscious mind—the relationship of motives and conflicts bred in the troll-dark cellar, with all its swarming, secret, importunate life.

Beyond the self, too, there is a network of relationships to be perceived and appraised: the shifting pattern of the various characters' reactions to each other. In a letter to Sophie Reimers, an actress preparing for a production of *Rosmersholm*, Ibsen emphasized the need to see the individual as decipherable not solely by himself, but also in a social context: "the only piece of advice I can give you is to read the whole play over and over again and carefully observe what the other persons say about Rebecca. In earlier times our actors often committed the great mistake of studying their parts in isolation, without paying sufficient regard to the character's position in and connection with the whole work." The characters, in other words, must be construed as viewing each other through varying degrees of subjective distortion, while at the same time making certain valid discernments; and it is out of this amalgam of truth and illusion, which we are invited to evaluate, that they act and react.

Equally important in this passage of advice is the premise which gives us our final set of significant relationships, the assumption that, on this second level of seeing, the unit of measure is no longer the individual, but the whole play.

Thus the self, as its nature is explored and its destiny fulfilled, is related, not merely to its own inner traits and pressures, or to those embodied in the characters around it, but
to the total environment realized in the given work—that
image of the inanimate world defined by the properties, the
décor of the various stage settings, even those reflections of
a larger world evoked within the frame of the action. In
this last regard, Francis Fergusson has observed that beyond
the cramped and gaslit parlor on which the curtain rises,
there often seems to be, in an Ibsen play, a sense of the
immense void of the primeval European wilderness. For all
their self-preoccupying, civilized, middle-class concerns, the
characters are never very far from some quickening reminder of the green pine forests of the mountain uplands,
the black waters of the fjords, or the silent, drifting depths
of the sea. Modern man, though he has shut himself snugly
up in four-walled urban or suburban insulation, is still in
the midst of nature; it is around him and in him; and no
matter how he may try to ignore it, this marrow of his
physical being stirs in his consciousness as intimations of an
older, fiercer life of sagalike simplicity.

But that facet of the inanimate world which soon strikes
one as Ibsen's special province, made by him into a distinctive contribution to dramatic technique, is comprehended in
the relationship of the individual character to his "personal
props." Hedda's pistols, for instance, or Nora's macaroons,
have a more active role than they might in, say, a Chekhov
play, where each would serve as the exact, cohering particular at the hub of a multitude of general impressions, as the
fragmented mind of Chebutykin is mirrored in the clock he
shatters. Ibsen's objects have, of course, this value; but beyond it, they seem to liberate and implement the personali-
ties and vital energies of the characters, even to the point
of acquiring a kind of latent force, a mana of their own.
What exhibits power in the theater frequently proves to
have deep, primordial roots, so that one can find both rele-
vant and enlightening here a statement made in another
connection by Theodore Gaster in his notes for *The New
Golden Bough*: "What is really involved would seem to be
the primitive notion of what we may call *the extended self*.
The primitive believes that the self, or identity, of a person
is not limited to his physical being, but embraces also every-

thing associated with it and everything that can evoke his presence in another person's mind." Some intuitive grasp on Ibsen's part of this notion of the extended self, of the individual as a field of force entering into and appropriating certain personally expressive objects to fulfill its ends, appears to be the principle underlying much of the use of symbols in the plays. A similar intuitive grasp of the same principle ought to give the reader or the playgoer a livelier sense of the degree to which Ibsen has succeeded in transforming the apparently neutral trappings of the realistic stage into highly charged ingredients in a spiritual action, to which no element of the *mise en scène* is finally unrelated.

Such a sense is crucial to an understanding of these plays, for it is this transformation which gave Ibsen the solution to his dilemma regarding the place of poetry in the realistic theater. Just as visual suggestion provided the counterpart of imagery, so it was his discovery that, without manifestly violating the realistic convention, he could turn the contents of the stage itself, and all their intricate relationships, into large-scale metaphors for psychological states and spiritual conditions. Thus the costumes, properties, lighting and décor became the diction of a new kind of dramatic poetry, the vocabulary of a vision of the human situation whose full dimensions could bear comparison with Shakespeare's traditional medieval system of correspondences between microcosm and macrocosm, the little world of the individual and the majestic moral order of the cosmos.

As a sensitive observer of the iconoclastic latter nineteenth century, the era of Darwin, Huxley, Marx, Hartmann and Nietzsche, Ibsen did not find available to him even such sparse reference to a reassuring, all-containing cosmic order as Goethe could still make at the start of the century in the Prologue to *Faust*. Intellectual and scientific innovations and displacements had come too thick and fast to sustain even the remnants of that traditional belief in the universe as an intelligible structure of ascending hierarchies in which every entity had its place and divinely ordained purpose, that total synthesis of material fact and moral value which was the greatest achievement and bequest of the medieval mind, articulated in all its clarity and sublimity in the magnificent architectonics of Dante's *Divine Comedy*. If the stability of that order had, either apparently or in reality, vanished, then the ultimate ground of meaning—that ground which furnished the support of any poetry that was more than a mindless celebration of the obvious—was profoundly called in question. At times the somber coloring of the later plays seems wholly a product of this feeling that the foundations of a whole civilization have dissolved, and humanity is adrift. As Ibsen put it in a note for one of his plays, catching both sides of the imbalance: "The keynote is to be: The prolific growth of our intellectual life, in literature, arts, etc.—and in contrast to this: all of mankind gone astray."

At other times, however, it appeared to him that the ground of meaning persisted in another form: not in the immutable cosmic order out of which the old absolutes had come, but within what was flowing, changing, relative — namely, history. To an aspiring young writer, he wrote in 1879 that "an extensive knowledge of history is indispensable to a modern author, for without it he is incapable of judging his age, his contemporaries and their motives and actions, except in the most incomplete and superficial manner." Both the theories of Darwin and the conversion of the seventeenth-century scientific revolution into the spectacular advances of nineteenth-century technology suggested that ultimate meaning was an *evolving* order, a process, not a timeless system. In *The Birth of Tragedy* a few years previous, Nietzsche had accused the villain of the piece, Socrates, of murdering the ecstatic Dionysian spirit of tragedy with the cool, clear, rational, optimistic unfolding of his dialectic. Ostensibly the setting was Periclean Athens; actually it was nineteenth-century Europe, the villain was positivistic science, and the culture hero who would bring back the ancient grandeur was to be Wagner, tragedy reborn from the spirit of music. Ibsen now offered another alternative: tragedy reborn from the spirit of history. By what means? Through cultivation of the third, last and most important mode of seeing, whereby the poet becomes the seer, and to see means to prophesy.

From his earliest years, Ibsen was apparently drawn to identify his life with the prophet's role. Of the sixty or more of his art works that survive, there is only one having a religious subject. Painted in 1845 when Ibsen was a solitary, seventeen-year-old apothecary's apprentice in the town of

Grimstad, it depicts, in rather crude and cloudy outline, a winged angel descending from a brightly illuminated sky toward a bearded man, kneeling or sitting, almost swallowed and lost in a dark, enveloping landscape; the painting is titled, "The Prophet Elijah under a juniper tree in the wilderness, I Kings, 19,5." The text referred to reads: "And he lay down and slept under a juniper tree; and behold, an angel touched him, and said to him, 'Arise and eat.' " What is there in this passage, we wonder, that Ibsen should want to paint it? Enigmatic by itself, it can be at least partially resolved in context. Elijah, earliest of the prophets and the model of his type, is likewise a solitary man. In a fury of wrath, when "the hand of the Lord" is on him, he slays a multitude of the false prophets of Baal; yet shortly after, when Jezebel, the queen, sends a message threatening his life, he is terrified and takes flight. Thus Elijah exemplifies an ambivalence that constantly recurs among the biblical prophets: in his natural person, he is lonely, introspective, timid, an outcast—like Ibsen in Grimstad—but gripped by his larger purpose, he has the courage of lions to accomplish works of might. The verse immediately preceding the one in question describes the prophet in the former attitude, that of abasement: "But he himself went a day's journey into the wilderness, and came and sat down under a juniper tree; and he asked that he might die, saying, 'It is enough now, O Lord, take away my life; for I am no better than my fathers.' " For Ibsen, it was less than a year afterwards, in 1846, that a liaison which became one of the crises of his life resulted in his illegitimate child, born to a servant girl ten years his senior; he contributed to the support of this child through fifteen years of his harshest struggles. One could well argue that this experience of abasement returns to haunt the later plays in multiple guises, in motifs of the suppressed and guilty secret (as in *The Wild Duck*), the traumatic awakening (in *A Doll House*), the lost or abandoned child (in *Hedda Gabler* and *The Master Builder*)— and, by so arguing, again risk losing focus in the merely biographical. Or, reviewing the premonitory painting, one could speculate: was it an accident—or part of a pattern? For the painted scene now emerges as a prototypal moment of restoration and renewal, the descent of inspiration, strength and purpose to the figure of the poet as seer, al-

most obliterated in his personal wilderness. It is after this
turning point, in the biblical account, that Elijah journeys
on to a cave, the entrance to the hidden mystery's heart;
and from here the word of the Lord guides him to an understanding of the true nature of divine being, not as tempest,
earthquake or fire, but as a still small voice. It is no surprise, then, that after twenty-five years of varied experi-
ments in the theater, Ibsen concentrates the whole of his
knowledge, the sum of his art, on a cycle of works that, in
one way or another, are all plays of the still small voice,
tracing the destinies of rebels and outcasts, radical protes-
tants, defenders and martyrs of conscience, probers for
truth, broken pioneers of a new faith evolving out of the
unfinished life of the spirit.

The figure of the prophet finds repeated incarnations
throughout the various dramas. There is the satiric scorn
reserved for the false prophet in *Peer Gynt,* who uses his
presumed powers of insight merely to exploit; Eilert
Løvborg can be thought of as another variant of the role.
The most portentous of these embodiments of prophecy,
however, is that of Maximus in *Emperor and Galilean.* It is
Maximus who gives the young Julian that vision of the future for which, in time, as the Apostate, he will die. Ibsen's
ten-act, two-part play bears the subtitle, "a world-historical
drama"; it is, as Wilson Knight observes, the one great
dramatic statement we have of the central conflict in West-
ern civilization; "all history is before us, turning on the one,
axial, problem." As Maximus envisions that conflict, there
are, in the West, two worlds that are dying and one as yet
powerless to be born. Just as there are in the Athens of
Julian's time two roads, one which leads to the university
and one to the church, and a third road which leads out
from town toward Eleusis, toward the great mystery, so
there are two empires, the first founded on the tree of
knowledge, the second on the tree of the cross—and the
third empire to come, "the empire of the great mystery, the
empire which shall be founded on the tree of knowledge
and the tree of the cross together, because it hates and loves
them both . . ." In other words, there is the empire of
Greco-Roman paganism with its worship of philosophy and/
or sensuous beauty, and the empire of Christianity, with its
worship of the Saviour, the pale Galilean—and the empire

of those for whom "the time is near," those who will "not need to die to live as gods on earth," the "twin-natured" ones who, by willing the new synthesis through self-realization, will comprehend and pass beyond the values of both Emperor and Galilean, as the child is lost in the youth and the youth is lost in the man, "but neither the child nor the youth is lost." It is this toward which the history of man is tending, and this for which his true heroes are born. As Maximus declares: "There is *one* who always returns at certain intervals in the life of the human race. He is like a rider breaking in a wild horse in the enclosure. Time and again it throws him. Soon the rider is in the saddle again, each time more confident, more skilled; but *down* he had to come in his various forms up to this very day. . . . Who knows how often he has walked among us, unrecognized by any man?"

"From the cross on which you pin your hopes, I will build a ladder for him you do not know," says Julian later, alluding to this prophetically revealed, perennially dying and reborn hero who is the vehicle of humanity-to-come. Climbing the rungs of that ladder, he intimates, the pioneers of the race will leave behind the child and the youth, the warring pagan humanistic and Christian theocentric dispensations and enter a realm that values, not hedonism, but a compassionate joy; not suffering, but a seasoned fulfillment; a realm in which the divine principle worthy of worship will be found within the self. The actual ladder that Ibsen built, however—the rungs of which were his later plays—was of a different order. It could never have been fashioned without this vision; but it was, by prior necessity, a ladder downwards. It descended into the darkness for which Ibsen had such a strong and gifted affinity—the darkness of those unacknowledged mixed motives and ambiguous feelings, those human corruptions, lies and self-evasions, that would first have to be clearly seen and eradicated before the Third Empire could come about.

Georg Brandes, in the literary study that affected Ibsen so deeply, had written that, "looked at from the historical point of view, a book, even though it may be a perfect, complete work of art, is only a piece cut out of an endlessly continuous web." The largest unit of measure, then, in the ranks of seeing is the world-spirit working itself out through

the innumerable, apparently chaotic currents and crosscur-
rents of history. Once this is intuited as the background
of the plays, then the tightly controlled, intensive dramatic
actions, the skirmishes by which small plots of ground are
lost or won, disclose their full implication of meaning. Thus
it is, for instance, as Maurice Valency notes, that the domestic clash in *A Doll House* comes to imply "the corre-
spondence of the family quarrel with the dialectic of history
on every plane of the social structure down to the individual
soul." It is in this dimension of relationships as well that
the play represents "a kind of dramatic metaphor, a play of
symbols, a conceit. The opposition of irreconcilable view-
points which brings about the dissolution of this union is
then seen to be a reflection of the vast conflict which is
bringing about a readjustment of social relations on every
level. The only possible reconciliation of spiritual entities
which are here displayed in opposition must be, accordingly,
in terms of that synthesis which will, in its largest aspect,
result in the Third Empire." What is true of *A Doll House*
also applies in kind to the subsequent plays; all the dead
and wounded on this many-sectored battleground of values
lie stretched in one direction, like shattered signposts pointing toward the world to be.

To summarize the main lines of our inquiry, then: as a
dramatic poet intent on remaining himself, in possession of
the poet's fluid range of reference, while managing to function under the restrictive conditions of the modern realistic
stage, Ibsen decided, at about the midpoint of his career,
to concentrate his work around a way of seeing, deceptively
photographic on the surface, actually a complex fusion of
perspectives, which then became his dramatic method. The
practical success and productive versatility of this method
led to what emerged as the typical pattern of the later Ibsen
drama, which could be described as a meticulously concrete
visualization of individuals realized within a contemporary
setting which the audience is induced to see and see into
until its manifold relationships become an expansive dramatic metaphor that conveys, at its ultimate extension, the
total situation of these individuals within, spatially, the pri-
mal immensity of nature, largely closed out and offstage,
and, temporally, a changing, evolving historical context with

a latent inner core of meaning, against which the fates of the characters are etched like prophecies.

After this brief survey of the master builder's working methods, it remains only to appreciate and enjoy the landmarks of his art at firsthand. That suggests an approach, both in reading and viewing, somewhere between the strain of trying to encompass all the meanings at once—and the impoverishment of ignoring or denying their presence. For the meanings assuredly are present and have to be reckoned with—much to the irritation of those skeptics who fail to recognize that the complexity and subtlety of a first-rate mind in the arts can be equivalent to the same complexity and subtlety when expressed in quantum mechanics or set theory; and that part of the subtlety of that mind in the art of the theater consists in disguising its musings as forthright speech. Henry James, a comparable artist who tried repeatedly but never could manage that theatrical feat, caught the ulterior quality of Ibsen's accomplishment in describing his appeal to actors: "The opportunity that he gives them is almost always to do the deep and delicate thing—the sort of chance that, in proportion as they are intelligent, they are most on the look out for." The deep and delicate thing—rightly it can only be appreciated, as Ibsen has indicated, by experiencing the play over and over again. A major play, like a great symphony or string quartet, needs several exposures under varied interpretations before it begins to release its secrets. And ultimately its stature, like beauty, will depend wholly on the eye and mind of the beholder, on the degree of that self-realization in the audience that Ibsen sought so ardently and resourcefully to develop through the challenge of his demanding art. With this central purpose of the dramatist in mind, of raising questions rather than giving answers, I would leave the plays to present their own issues in terms of the method described above, were it not for the interference of a few venerable misreadings that, by sufferance in each instance, have almost become traditions themselves.

When the troubled applause died away, and the first audience for Ibsen's *A Doll House* rose to their somewhat unsteady feet and filed up the aisles, no one among them could have known that he had participated, four days before

Christmas of 1879, in the birth of modern drama. The long view is a privilege reserved for posterity, whereas the shaken spectators in Copenhagen's Royal Theater, still reverberating with the slam of that historic door, had other, more immediate concerns to cope with.

They had been held, for one thing, by a sequence of vivid dramatic images that had drawn them insidiously, moment by moment, scene by scene, to an abrupt, intolerable conclusion. Their heroine had gone from her lilting entrance, a slender, vulnerable creature of macaroons and Christmas toys, to her final departure, a remorselessly independent figure wreathed in a funereal shawl. All that occurred in between remained to tease the mind with questions. How could she do such a thing, leave home and husband and children after eight years of marriage? Was she justified? Would she return the next day? How could her character change so suddenly? And what was that character, to start with? Had they been deceived in their assumptions? Were they perhaps deceived in reality, right now? As they went their many separate ways back to homes grown appreciably more perilous, the audience was induced to ponder the matrix of causes that had shaped the heroine's past and the network of involvements that wove about her present. And, as they pondered and discussed and argued and brooded, it seemed increasingly apparent to them—in Scandinavia and Germany and England and France and throughout Europe and America—that something incalculable had shifted, had altered, never to be the same again, that, as Bernard Shaw put it, "Nora's revolt is the end of a chapter in human history."

As this reconstruction of the widening circles of contemporary response implies, it is with *A Doll House* that Ibsen's dramatic method comes into its own and its practical success is assured. But Shaw's highly vocal part in that response makes clear where the emphasis has fallen and where attention has been too narrowly directed. If there is one cliché I could choose to wish away—as I could with each of these four dramas—one stereotype worth shattering to help liberate the living play from the revered Dramatic Classic, it would be the tired notion that this is a feminist play, and that we have done our duty as playgoers when we have followed gallant Nora through her struggle for her rights.

Perhaps the fault lies in the title. There is certainly no
sound justification for perpetuating the awkward and blindly
traditional misnomer of *A Doll's House*: the house is not
Nora's, as the possessive implies; the familiar children's toy
is called a doll house; and one can make a reasonable sup-
position that Ibsen, intending an ironic modern contrast to
the heroic ring of the house of Atreus or Cadmus, at least
partially includes Torvald with Nora in the original title, *Et
Dukkehjem*, for the two of them at the play's opening are
still posing like the little marzipan bride and groom atop
the wedding cake.

In the preliminary notes to what he first subtitled "A
Modern Tragedy," Ibsen makes clear from the start his assumption that the fall of the house of Helmer desolates both
parties. "There are two kinds of spiritual law," he writes,
"two kinds of conscience, one in man and another, altogether different, in woman. They do not understand each
other. . . ." The superstructure of Torvald's conscience, his
sense of right and wrong, is founded on the formulation:
"the most important thing is that *I* be a success; all else will
follow from that." Nora's moral sense, on the other hand,
is that "the most important thing is that *we* live in, and out
of, the truth of our feelings; all else will follow from that."
What is at stake is nothing less than the respective defini-
tions that the society allows of a man and a woman. And
because Ibsen lives in a universe where essences are no
longer given a priori, out of a fixed, eternal order, out of
some Platonic idea of man and woman, but rather in a
flowing process where selves are chiefly defined by the
choices they make, the unenlightened struggle of Torvald
and Nora to define themselves along separate paths inevitably brings them into conflict. It is crucial, however, to note
that whereas the play begins with Nora, and in time Torvald
appears, after the action has run its course Nora withdraws,
and the play ends with Torvald. The balance is significant.
Moreover, the situation of Torvald at the conclusion is, if
anything, more pathetic; his bland, commonsensical, self-
righteous attempt to establish his authority has failed, and,
although Nora has been strengthened by facing up to at
least a glimpse of the truth, Torvald has had love pulled
from under his feet while, by the nature of his conventional

code, he has hardly an inkling of what he can possibly have done that was wrong.

Once we realize that the crux of the play is not primarily an individual, but a relationship—the modern middle-class conception of marriage—we are in a position to see both why Ibsen did, then, concentrate on the character of Nora and also the skill with which he uses the other relationships of the play to develop and amplify her situation. His interest centers on Nora because, in her own terms, she internalizes the conflict, which Ibsen designates in his notes as "natural feeling on the one hand and belief in authority on the other." Authority, she believes, is something located outside herself, first in her father, then in Torvald, little realizing that Torvald is likewise and more subtly the puppet of others' expectations, namely of his co-workers at the bank and, in a larger sense, of public opinion, of what *they* will think. Both are dolls—a doll being a thing in a human shape without the hard-won, distinctively human attributes.

In the marvelous design of the action, Ibsen shows Nora painfully acquiring those attributes, in effect recapitulating the development of the race as she moves from, metaphorically, the role of a little animal, a lark, a squirrel, to a newborn human self with something of the tragic sense of life. In the parallel relationship with Krogstad, she discovers a visible embodiment of the horror of degradation ahead of her, since it was "nothing more and nothing worse" that he did which poisoned his home and caused Torvald and society in general to reject him; and simultaneously in the relationship with Rank, crippled in body as she sees herself crippled in conscience, she finds the strength to die alone, if necessary. And, in a carefully modulated antithesis, Krogstad and Mrs. Linde, the two who have known the darkness outside, move into the light, the warmth of the home, together, at the same time that Torvald and Nora move apart, out of the "sunlit happiness" of their union into the harsh instruction of that same darkness. Structurally, the play is a wonder; and thematically, far from being dated, it is only beginning to communicate its relevance.

The stereotype that interferes probably more than any other with an appreciation of *The Wild Duck* may also be an oblique consequence of the title. Since the play, unlike most of the Ibsen dramas, lacks any one single character that dominates attention and stirs conjecture, the audience's curiosity passes by default to the meaning of the wild duck itself, which then becomes one of those Ibsen symbols that have a way, in discussion, of detaching themselves from the text and flying around like ectoplasm. Who is the wild duck? Hjalmar? Old Ekdal? Both? Hedvig? The entire Ekdal family? All the characters? Modern civilized man? And in each connection, in what sense? These are legitimate questions; the action invites them; yet one can soon reach Gina's point of exasperation with all the fuss made over that sacred duck —or else lose in riddles the primary emotional response that James Joyce honored when he wrote of the play that "one can only brood upon it as upon a personal woe."

Ibsen takes no sides on Gina's being right or wrong. Life is prosaic and matter-of-fact, exacting of us only a simple and responsible effort toward some understanding of each other, and, at the same time, something mysterious and haunting beyond anything we ever dreamed: it is part of the greatness of the play that it maintains both perspectives. Both are converged in the prismatic symbol of life that crowns the play, the once wounded, now rather pampered, reacclimated household pet and, as Hedvig observes, the creature of unknown origin whom nobody really knows. A crown, however, is only the emblem of power; and to locate the peculiar force of the play, the audience might do better by examining its substantial underpinnings in, particularly, the use of the settings. Act I, in Werle's study, presents us with a view of those on top in society, those who, through clear-sighted, tough-minded realism, manipulate their way into control, along with their retainers and sycophants. The remaining four acts are devoted to those on the bottom, those who are the manipulated and controlled. And yet the actual setting is elevated, a garret studio under a skylight. In this ambiguous play of illusion and reality, it is the fantasies of the poor that exalt them in the only victories they know, and if those compensating fantasies are left alone, who is to declare for sure the losers from the winners? Right from the start, moreover, in that most contemplative room in Werle's house where Hjalmar and Gregers reencounter each other, the keynote is struck, as Northam observes, in the fact that the prevailing light cast by the lampshades is green, the green of nature, the green of the cut forests that take revenge, the green of the depths of the sea. And now we can understand why no single character dominates our attention; none of them, individually, is strong enough to. All the characters that reside in the divided setting of the last four acts, with its practical foreground for eating, arguing and doing business, suggestive of the conscious mind, and its more remote, cavernous inner room full of diminished remnants of the natural world, like the unconscious mind—all have gone down, like the wounded wild duck, into the undertow of life. *The Wild Duck* is a drowned world; once we grasp this basic metaphor of the play and enter into it imaginatively, we can freely explore the channels of the deep, where the lost voyagers rest suspended, nearly weightless, beyond salvage, in their timeless dream.

In the case of *Hedda Gabler* there is no problem regarding the lack of a commanding personality to arouse curiosity and speculation. The vivid, anguished, dangerous character of Hedda has long impressed actresses and audiences alike as tinder enough to ignite the play—so much so that she constantly threatens to become her own stereotype. Too often in the theater, and perhaps in the reader's mind's eye, there are Heddas that pace like caged tigresses, Heddas that glide like hooded cobras, Aztec Heddas made to cut out hearts— that would immediately have sent George Tesman fleeing into breathless, terrorstricken exile in the stacks of the *Bibliothèque nationale*.

Such conceptions are false to the text in two ways: they violate the deep and delicate art of Ibsen's portraiture of the individual, and, by magnifying Hedda, they distort the balanced ensemble of the whole play which composes its ultimate meaning. Like the play itself, Hedda is one of the most complex creations Ibsen ever shaped. Far from being simply a vampire, a *belle dame sans merci,* she is, as James noted, "infinitely perverse," but also, as on reconsideration he was prompted to add, "various and sinuous and graceful, complicated and natural; she suffers, she struggles, she is human, and by that fact exposed to a dozen interpretations." Or as Valency describes her, she is "neither good nor evil . . . both creative and destructive, idealistic and selfish, noble and despicable . . . a bundle of unresolved tendencies, a human being in process of development, conditioned by heredity, limited by environment, capable of anything, and striking out blindly in search of fulfillment." She is the woman, Shaw stated, that most men of any experience have at some time encountered, whose temperament may have fascinated and challenged them, and whom they have been fortunate enough, through some inner check, not to marry. Unlike the wily, overcalculating Brack or the unstable Løvborg, however, George Tesman, bluff, good-natured, unseeing, is the fool who rushes in to claim this dubious prize—perhaps, with her inflated expectations, the one match she should hope to aspire to if, like the wild duck, she could once acclimatize herself. But under the icy exterior, a rage burns too strongly in Hedda, shown visually by her many associations with the stove and with fire, climaxing in the burning of the manuscript—a rage not, like that more moderate desire in the counterbalancing portrait of Nora, to live her own life, but rather to live someone else's life vicariously, to form it, control it, use it as both a means of self-fulfillment and a weapon for striking back.

Again Ibsen employs the tested device of the significantly divided stage—but this time the inner room is cramped and confined, dominated by the painting of the late General Gabler, just as Hedda is dominated by her father, not her husband, as the play's title makes clear: still Hedda Gabler, not Tesman. Into this room, her sanctuary, she brings her piano, her connection with the Dionysian energies she longs toward, the expressive instrument of the wild dance she merely plays rather than enacts, like her stronger, healthier counterpart, Nora. With her covert fixation on vine leaves and orgies, it is the Dionysian spirit Hedda wants to bring out in Løvborg, who ironically has already known it to excess in the company of the "chaste" goddess, Mlle. Diana. Thus Hedda is attempting what Julian failed in: escape from the constraints of the pale Galilean by turning back into an illusion of pagan freedom.

But Hedda's doomed enterprise takes on full meaning only if her milieu is completely conveyed in both its human density and limitation. Like most of Ibsen's later masterpieces, the play is chamber music, calling for virtuosi in every part. As Halvdan Koht has noted, two well-delineated worlds are brought here into conflict, with a spectrum of individuals to represent each: on one side of Hedda, the solid, respectable, bourgeois establishment, warmhearted, decent, complacent, dull—Mrs. Elvsted and the whole house of Tesman; and to the other side of Hedda, a world of spiritual unrest, morally unstable, full of ambivalent potentialities, whose alternatives are embodied in Løvborg and Brack. And of these, inseparable from Hedda in the overall meaning, is Løvborg; for with the Swiss watch workmanship of this masterful play, Ibsen shifts the focus of his dramatic concern. Man's ills—moral, psychological, spiritual—are no longer diagnosed toward the Third Empire to come; instead he embarks on a series of explorations-in-depth of thwarted genius, of exceptionally gifted men, in other words, of what mankind is capable of, not in some remote synthesis, but now.

Eilert Løvborg stands in the shadow of his nemesis, Hedda; but the second of these exceptional individuals, Halvard Solness, stands boldly in the foreground of his play, *The Master Builder*. Here, once again, Ibsen's thought shows its tendency to develop through mutually correcting antitheses. Just as Hedda's character and situation offered several wry contrasts to Nora's, so in this play we find what seem to be a number of inverse analogies to *The Wild Duck*. The earlier work was a study of lack of ambition, whereas here we have ambition to excess; thus the former was appropriately a play of the submarine depths, while the latter is a play of vertiginous heights, of mountains, towers and the spirit world. The theme is made visible from the very start: as the servants in *The Wild Duck* were shown masking the direct light in the study with the soothing and flattering obscurity of the green shades, so *The Master Builder* begins with an exhausted man gasping for breath, for oxygen, because he cannot drive himself to work any longer. Later we learn, of other characters, that Dr. Herdal met Hilda first at a mountain lodge; that, in turn, Hilda has met Mrs. Solness before at a sanatorium, also presumably high in the mountains; and that her initial, indelible image of Solness is of him wreathing the top of a church tower. Throughout the play, as Herdal remarks, Hilda is dressed for mountain climbing. Thus everything here is altitude and the outreaching of the self, culminating in the sense that Solness is, or believes he is, in touch with superhuman powers, occult

beings, the helpers and servers, the troll within, the god he
speaks to from the pinnacle of his achievement.

The last of these traditional stereotypes that need to be
broken, then, is the idea that we are still on the level terrain
of what are frequently, but never quite accurately, described
as the "social dramas." The action looms larger than profes-
sional or marital ethics; and Solness cannot be imagined or
impersonated—as he sometimes is—as if he were as clipped
and tidy as an eighteenth-century deist or an Ivy League
lawyer. On the contrary, this is a man who is smoldering,
elemental, hypnotic—and only if he is seen as such are his
genius and his accomplishment credible. Kaja thinks of him
as a god and goes down on her knees before him in rapt
adoration. She has much in her of the masochistic slave,
but what she sees is not all distortion. Her seeming idolatry
is in the nature of a defining tribute to one who, more and
more as the drama progresses, takes on the immemorial
role of the sacred king whose fate it is to undergo ritual
sacrifice at the height of his powers on a marked day—here
at the autumnal equinox—so that the energies of the tribe
may find release and renewal, an impression that is strik-
ingly reinforced when, in the last act, the young king, Ragnar, brings to the old king, Solness, that ambiguous symbol
of victory and death, the ribboned wreath.

Again Ibsen uses setting to give heightened feeling and
dimension to what might otherwise too easily pass as no
more than a foolish infatuation of September with May. In
the three acts of the drama we move progressively from
the master builder's workroom, with its inner near-duplicate
augmenting the impression of a confined, lifelong dedication
to conceiving, planning and constructing architectural possibilities for the lives of others; through the domestic setting
of the builder's own living room, ironically blighted now
and uninhabitable, hopefully to be exchanged for a new
dwelling free from ghosts of the past; to the final setting
where that hope is dashed, and yet where, in the presence
of the community and the openness of nature, of the glowing sunset sky and the tranquil air where castles were never
meant to rise, death is transfigured into something larger
than itself, bitter, yet inevitable and strangely right. In this
play Ibsen perhaps came closest to writing the modern trag-

edy, inexorable, emotionally moving and possessed of a true catharsis.

There is so much more to say about the play—or perhaps leave unsaid and simply appreciate. One could speak of those brief emanations of insight, so frequent in Ibsen's late plays, that body forth in a few lines of dialogue some truth from the hidden recesses of the mind or the outer limits of perception, turning luminescently under the surface of the text, then disappearing. Or of the remarkable characterization of Hilda, so mercurially alive, so aggressively enchanting, Eve before the apple. Or even the vexed question of the autobiographical content of the play—though here it is well to avoid that literalminded misunderstanding of the imagination that believes that an author writes his life in his works; rather he writes exaggerated tendencies of that life, extensions of it, apprehensions and potentialities within which he trues his course.

Still, Ibsen would not want any of these questions left unraised. Not the denial nor the simplification of experience, but the seeing into it from every angle of perspective, was his goal. The word often used to characterize his formal, elegant and correct demeanor after the midpoint of his career applies as well to that manner of seeing: circumspection became both his way of life and his mode of vision. And this circumspection he set to a purpose: not to lull—nor merely shock—the bourgeoisie, not to lecture the proletariat, but to instigate human beings into existence, to dare each individual to think, to feel, to question, to live, to inherit the best of himself in his own time and place. And to realize that purpose, he chose the ancient and everchanging art form of the drama, where the complexity of life perpetually happens now before one's eyes and where its laws and possibilities can always be probed and reproduced in fresh combinations that become, in their greatest triumphs, the poet's truth.

A NOTE ON THESE TRANSLATIONS

In writing to a would-be American translator of his plays, Ibsen stipulated that "I consider it most important that the dialogue in the translations be kept as close to ordinary, everyday speech as possible. All turns of speech and inflections that belong only in books must be very carefully avoided in plays, especially in plays like mine, which aim at making the reader or spectator feel that during the reading or performance he is actually experiencing a piece of real life. . . ." And elsewhere, as a more general observation on the subject: "I believe that a translator should employ the style which the original author would have used if he had written in the language of those who are to read him in translation."

In spite of these clear directives, Ibsen translation, even down to the present day, has too frequently suffered from a stiff and hobbled diction—or, certainly no better, a cavalier freedom that has cut or padded the text. William Archer is probably the wrong foot on which all this error started out. Everyone stands in his debt for the yeoman service he rendered in first bringing Ibsen over complete into English, yet he had an uncommonly dull ear for verbal nuance and the spare, biblical simplicity of Ibsen's prose rhythms. For instance, there are no verb contractions in the Dano-Norwegian of the original, a native characteristic of the language; brought over literally into English, this trait results in such constructions as "I had not better return with you to the croft then, Nils, had I?"—a kind of artificial patois, a stage-Norwegian dialect distinctive enough to merit being dubbed "Old High Ibsenese." This, while Henry James, Ibsen's contemporary, was writing dialogue full of contractions, much of which has the fluidity of good modern conversation.

As to violations of the original on the side of liberty-become license, it seems to me no part of the translator's business to cut set descriptions, stage directions, and certainly not dialogue. What a director may choose to alter or ignore is at his own responsibility and risk; it is the translator's job to convey, to the best of his ability, the text, the whole text and nothing but the text. Occasionally he is forced to make small changes that give him an inward wrench, but this is merely facing the fact that it is sometimes preferable to reach for, hopefully, an inspired equivalent drawn from the background of his own culture than to render an expression or allusion verbatim out of misguided scholarship.

Similarly, when one encounters speeches in an Ibsen translation that run half again as long, or longer, than their counterparts in the original, one suspects that the translator has again overstepped his rather closely drawn circle of freedom. Otto Jespersen's classic example of the English "First come, first served" for the Danish *"Den der kommer først til mølle, faar først malet"*—four words for nine—probably marks an extremity of contrast; but it lies in the nature of the languages that an English translation will regularly run shorter and more concise than the text in Norwegian or Danish.

One technical point: in a letter to the Swedish director, August Lindberg, Ibsen emphasized that the description of the stage picture and the actors' entrances and exits were "arranged from the point of view of the audience and not from that of the actor. I arrange everything as I visualize it while writing it down." In order that the reader may more easily follow that visualization, as Ibsen hoped he would, I have not changed his directions to the stage left, stage right orientation standard in American plays; but the reversal should be made in production.

ROLF FJELDE

A NOTE ON THE REVISED EDITION

Over the sizable span of years since these translations first appeared in print, they have enjoyed hundreds of productions at all levels of the American theater, from Broadway and regional repertory to college and high school, as well as television and radio. These productions comprise a living testimony that Henrik Ibsen, the leading playwright of the nineteenth century, retains a tenacious hold on the imaginations and sensibilities of contemporary audiences. Among the many sources of his major plays' perennial appeal, characters as centrally vital as Nora and Torvald Helmer, Hjalmar Ekdal and Gregers Werle, Hedda Gabler and Eilert Løvborg, Hilda Wangel and Halvard Solness, will continue to challenge gifted actors, directors, and designers to realize their distinctive passions, unfolding psychologies, and prophetic fates in vivid theatrical terms.

A translator of classic drama whose author has wide currency is doubly fortunate. First, he has ample opportunity to study and restudy the works themselves on stage in differing interpretations and changing cultural contexts. Secondly, his words are regularly put to the acid test of public scrutiny. If he has prepared his text properly, nearly the entirety feels and reads right, and represents the very best he can do. There remain, however, those occasional lapses which afflict him as he follows the score of his solutions against the actuality of performance: the optimal wording that stubbornly resisted him before, the tardily discovered typo, the inadvertently dropped minor stage direction, the rare but galling gaffe in interpreting the original. As a result, he starts keeping a conscience-file of revisions toward the day that a new edition will, he fondly hopes, Finally Get It Right.

Improvements stem in good part from a sum of inner artistic discernments, but also from a medley of authoritative sources without, and appropriately so: the translator's fictive world, unlike most writing, is not his own to shape. An event from family history, a chanced-on critical article, a post-rehearsal conversation, a question raised by a university guest lecturer may isolate and clarify what needs to be reworked. *The Wild Duck* and *A Doll House,* in that order, were the plays in which I first sought to express Ibsen's subtle, dramatically charged prose-poetry in the medium of American common speech. I received several fruitful suggestions, and was especially grateful for two sets of close queries, one from John Bettenbender and Thomas Van Laan for a production of *The Wild Duck* at the Douglass College Little Theater at Rutgers, and the other from Bernard Dukore for a staging of *A Doll House* at the Kennedy Theater in Hawaii. And lately, for this revision, Prof. Einar Haugen of Harvard and his wife Eva, distinguished Scandinavicists both, fine-combed all four plays line by line for any significant discrepancies between the Norwegian and English, further enhancing this volume.

Ibsen's presence in the theater, an amalgam of all the presences of his individually defined and crafted characters, is as unique and indispensable today as ever. It blends an evocative surface of particularized facts and recognizable behaviors with a substrate of the most profound and universal human con-

cerns. The more a searching mind is devoted to the understanding of Ibsen's complexly intermeshed art, the more that
art responds, opening depth upon depth to reward it.

The poet Rilke, addressing Ibsen in his imagination, caught
the essence of the plays when he observed: "Your blood drove
you, not to form, not to speak, but to reveal." Every one of
Ibsen's major plays strives, through the life struggles of its
protagonists, to reveal a healing wholeness. The sole road
toward that revelation, in action after dramatic action, is the
quest for and progressive engagement with truth in all its
forms: its varied amplitude, its necessary pain, its dismantling
of illusion and repression, its recovery of unclouded insight,
its liberating strength.

For my part, I can only trust that this quartet of masterpieces, now newly emended to approach still closer the wholeness of their respective truths, will help introduce countless
more to the master spirit behind them. Ibsen's art and thought
have so much yet to convey to us.

ROLF FJELDE
New York City
July 1991

SELECTED BIBLIOGRAPHY

HENRIK IBSEN: THE MAJOR PLAYS

Catiline   (1850)
The Burial Mound   (1850)
Norma   (1851)
St. John's Eve   (1853)
Lady Inger of Ostraat   (1855)
The Feast at Solhaug   (1856)
Olaf Liljekrans   (1857)
The Vikings at Helgeland   (1858)
Love's Comedy   (1862)
The Pretenders   (1863)
Brand   (1866)
Peer Gynt   (1867)
The League of Youth   (1869)
Emperor and Galilean   (1873)
Pillars of Society   (1877)
A Doll House   (1879)
Ghosts   (1881)
An Enemy of the People   (1882)
The Wild Duck   (1884)
Rosmersholm   (1886)
The Lady from the Sea   (1888)
Hedda Gabler   (1890)
The Master Builder   (1892)
Little Eyolf   (1894)
John Gabriel Borkman   (1896)
When We Dead Awaken   (1899)

SELECTED BIBLIOGRAPHY

Bentley, Eric. *The Playwright As Thinker*. New York: Harcourt Brace, 1987 (1946).

Chamberlain, John. *Ibsen: The Open Vision*. London: Athlone Press Ltd., 1982.

Downs, Brian W. *Ibsen: The Intellectual Background*. Cambridge: Cambridge University Press, 1948.

Durbach, Errol. *'Ibsen the Romantic*.' Athens, Ga.: University of Georgia Press, 1982.

Egan, Michael. *Ibsen, The Critical Heritage*. Boston: Routledge and Kegan Paul, 1972.

Fjelde, Rolf, ed. *Ibsen, A Collection of Critical Essays*. Englewood Cliffs, N.J.: Prentice Hall, 1965.

Haugen, Einar. *Ibsen's Drama*. Minneapolis: University of Minnesota Press, 1979.

Ibsen, Henrik. *The Oxford Ibsen*. Vols. V-VII. Ed. and tr. James W. McFarlane, et al. New York: Oxford University Press, 1960–77.

———, *The Complete Major Prose Plays*. Tr. and introd. Rolf Fjelde. New York: New American Library, 1978.

———, *Letters and Speeches*. Ed. Evert Sprinchorn. New York: Hill and Wang, 1964.

Holtan, Orley I. *Mythic Patterns in Ibsen's Last Plays*. Minneapolis: University of Minnesota Press, 1970.

Johnston, Brian. *The Ibsen Cycle*. University Park, Penn.: Pennsylvania State University Press, 1992 (1975).

———, *Text and Supertext in Ibsen's Drama*. University Park, Penn.: Pennsylvania State University Press, 1989.

Koht, Halvdan. *Life of Ibsen*. Tr. and ed. Einar Haugen and A.E. Santiello. New York: Benjamin Blom Inc., 1971.

Knight, G. Wilson, *Henrik Ibsen*. New York: Grove Press Inc., 1962.

Meyer, Michael. *Ibsen: A Biography*. Garden City, N.Y.: Doubleday, 1971.

Northam, John. *Ibsen's Dramatic Method*. London: Faber and Faber, 1953.

Salomé, Lou. *Ibsen's Heroines*. Ed. and tr. Siegfried Mandel. Redding Ridge, Conn.: Black Swan Books, 1985 (1892).

Schanke, Robert A. *Ibsen in America: A Century of Change*. Metuchen, N.J.: Scarecrow Press, Inc., 1988.

Shafer, Yvonne, ed. *Approaches to Teaching Ibsen's* A Doll House. New York: The Modern Language Association of America, 1985.

Shaw, G.B. *The Quintessence of Ibsenism*. New York: Hill and Wang, 1957 (1913).

Valency, Maurice. *The Flower and the Castle*. New York: Schocken, 1982 (1963).

Weigand, Hermann J. *The Modern Ibsen*. New York: E.P. Dutton, 1960 (1925).

A DOLL HOUSE

THE CHARACTERS

TORVALD HELMER, a lawyer
NORA, his wife
DR. RANK
MRS. LINDE
NILS KROGSTAD, a bank clerk
THE HELMERS' THREE SMALL CHILDREN
ANNE-MARIE, their nurse
HELENE, a maid
A DELIVERY BOY

The action takes place in HELMER'S *residence.*

ACT ONE

A comfortable room, tastefully but not expensively furnished. A door to the right in the back wall leads to the entryway; another to the left leads to HELMER's *study. Between these doors, a piano. Midway in the left-hand wall a door, and farther down a window. Near the window a round table with an armchair and a small sofa. In the right-hand wall, toward the rear, a door, and nearer the foreground a porcelain stove with two armchairs and a rocking chair beside it. Between the stove and the side door, a small table. Engravings on the walls. An etagère with china figures and other small art objects; a small bookcase with richly bound books; the floor carpeted; a fire burning in the stove. It is a winter day.*

A bell rings in the entryway; shortly after we hear the door being unlocked. NORA *comes into the room, humming happily to herself; she is wearing street clothes and carries an armload of packages, which she puts down on the table to the right. She has left the hall door open; and through it a* DELIVERY BOY *is seen, holding a Christmas tree and a basket, which he gives to the* MAID *who let them in.*

NORA.   Hide the tree well, Helene. The children mustn't get a glimpse of it till this evening, after it's trimmed. (*To the* DELIVERY BOY, *taking out her purse.*) How much?

DELIVERY BOY.   Fifty, ma'am.

NORA.   There's a crown. No, keep the change. (*The* BOY *thanks her and leaves.* NORA *shuts the door. She laughs softly to herself while taking off her street things. Drawing a bag of macaroons from her pocket, she eats a couple, then steals over and listens at her husband's study door.*) Yes, he's home. (*Hums again as she moves to the table right.*)

HELMER (*from the study*).   Is that my little lark twittering out there?

NORA (*busy opening some packages*).   Yes, it is.

HELMER.   Is that my squirrel rummaging around?

43

NORA. Yes!

HELMER. When did my squirrel get in?

NORA. Just now. (*Putting the macaroon bag in her pocket and wiping her mouth.*) Do come in, Torvald, and see what I've bought.

HELMER. Can't be disturbed. (*After a moment he opens the door and peers in, pen in hand.*) Bought, you say? All that there? Has the little spendthrift been out throwing money around again?

NORA. Oh, but Torvald, this year we really should let ourselves go a bit. It's the first Christmas we haven't had to economize.

HELMER. But you know we can't go squandering.

NORA. Oh yes, Torvald, we can squander a little now. Can't we? Just a tiny, wee bit. Now that you've got a big salary and are going to make piles and piles of money.

HELMER. Yes—starting New Year's. But then it's a full three months till the raise comes through.

NORA. Pooh! We can borrow that long.

HELMER. Nora! (*Goes over and playfully takes her by the ear.*) Are your scatterbrains off again? What if today I borrowed a thousand crowns, and you squandered them over Christmas week, and then on New Year's Eve a roof tile fell on my head, and I lay there—

NORA (*putting her hand on his mouth*). Oh! Don't say such things!

HELMER. Yes, but what if it happened—then what?

NORA. If anything so awful happened, then it just wouldn't matter if I had debts or not.

HELMER. Well, but the people I'd borrowed from?

NORA. Them? Who cares about them! They're strangers.

HELMER. Nora, Nora, how like a woman! No, but seriously, Nora, you know what I think about that. No debts! Never borrow! Something of freedom's lost—and something of beauty, too—from a home that's founded on borrowing and debt. We've made a brave stand up to now, the two of us; and we'll go right on like that the little while we have to.

NORA (*going toward the stove*). Yes, whatever you say, Torvald.

HELMER (*following her*). Now, now, the little lark's

wings mustn't droop. Come on, don't be a sulky squirrel. (*Taking out his wallet.*) Nora, guess what I have here.

NORA (*turning quickly*).   Money!

HELMER.   There, see. (*Hands her some notes.*) Good Lord, I know how costs go up in a house at Christmastime.

NORA.   Ten—twenty—thirty—forty. Oh, thank you, Torvald; I can manage no end on this.

HELMER.   You really will have to.

NORA.   Oh yes, I promise I will! But come here so I can show you everything I bought. And so cheap! Look, new clothes for Ivar here—and a sword. Here a horse and a trumpet for Bob. And a doll and a doll's bed here for Emmy; they're nothing much, but she'll tear them to bits in no time anyway. And here I have dress material and handkerchiefs for the maids. Old Anne-Marie really deserves something more.

HELMER.   And what's in that package there?

NORA (*with a cry*).   Torvald, no! You can't see that till tonight!

HELMER.   I see. But tell me now, you little prodigal, what have you thought of for yourself?

NORA.   For myself? Oh, I don't want anything at all.

HELMER.   Of course you do. Tell me just what—within reason—you'd most like to have.

NORA.   I honestly don't know. Oh, listen, Torvald—

HELMER.   Well?

NORA (*fumbling at his coat buttons, without looking at him*).   If you want to give me something, then maybe you could—you could—

HELMER.   Come on, out with it.

NORA (*hurriedly*).   You could give me money, Torvald. No more than you think you can spare; then one of these days I'll buy something with it.

HELMER.   But Nora—

NORA.   Oh, please, Torvald darling, do that! I beg you, please. Then I could hang the bills in pretty gilt paper on the Christmas tree. Wouldn't that be fun?

HELMER.   What are those little birds called that always fly through their fortunes?

NORA.   Oh yes, spendthrifts; I know all that. But let's do as I say, Torvald; then I'll have time to decide what I really need most. That's very sensible, isn't it?

HELMER (*smiling*). Yes, very—that is, if you actually hung onto the money I give you, and you actually used it to buy yourself something. But it goes for the house and for all sorts of foolish things, and then I only have to lay out some more.

NORA. Oh, but Torvald—

HELMER. Don't deny it, my dear little Nora. (*Putting his arm around her waist.*) Spendthrifts are sweet, but they use up a frightful amount of money. It's incredible what it costs a man to feed such birds.

NORA. Oh, how can you say that! Really, I save everything I can.

HELMER (*laughing*). Yes, that's the truth. Everything you can. But that's nothing at all.

NORA (*humming, with a smile of quiet satisfaction*). Hm, if you only knew what expenses we larks and squirrels have, Torvald.

HELMER. You're an odd little one. Exactly the way your father was. You're never at a loss for scaring up money; but the moment you have it, it runs right out through your fingers; you never know what you've done with it. Well, one takes you as you are. It's deep in your blood. Yes, these things are hereditary, Nora.

NORA. Ah, I could wish I'd inherited many of Papa's qualities.

HELMER. And I couldn't wish you anything but just what you are, my sweet little lark. But wait; it seems to me you have a very—what should I call it?—a very suspicious look today—

NORA. I do?

HELMER. You certainly do. Look me straight in the eye.

NORA (*looking at him*). Well?

HELMER (*shaking an admonitory finger*). Surely my sweet tooth hasn't been running riot in town today, has she?

NORA. No. Why do you imagine that?

HELMER. My sweet tooth really didn't make a little detour through the confectioner's?

NORA. No, I assure you, Torvald—

HELMER. Hasn't nibbled some pastry?

NORA. No, not at all.

HELMER. Not even munched a macaroon or two?

NORA. No, Torvald, I assure you, really—

HELMER.   There, there now. Of course I'm only joking.

NORA (*going to the table, right*).   You know I could never think of going against you.

HELMER.   No, I understand that; and you *have* given me your word. (*Going over to her.*) Well, you keep your little Christmas secrets to yourself, Nora darling. I expect they'll come to light this evening, when the tree is lit.

NORA.   Did you remember to ask Dr. Rank?

HELMER.   No. But there's no need for that; it's assumed he'll be dining with us. All the same, I'll ask him when he stops by here this morning. I've ordered some fine wine. Nora, you can't imagine how I'm looking forward to this evening.

NORA.   So am I. And what fun for the children, Torvald!

HELMER.   Ah, it's so gratifying to know that one's gotten a safe, secure job, and with a comfortable salary. It's a great satisfaction, isn't it?

NORA.   Oh, it's wonderful!

HELMER.   Remember last Christmas? Three whole weeks before, you shut yourself in every evening till long after midnight, making flowers for the Christmas tree, and all the other decorations to surprise us. Ugh, that was the dullest time I've ever lived through.

NORA.   It wasn't at all dull for me.

HELMER (*smiling*).   But the outcome *was* pretty sorry, Nora.

NORA.   Oh, don't tease me with that again. How could I help it that the cat came in and tore everything to shreds.

HELMER.   No, poor thing, you certainly couldn't. You wanted so much to please us all, and that's what counts. But it's just as well that the hard times are past.

NORA.   Yes, it's really wonderful.

HELMER.   Now I don't have to sit here alone, boring myself, and you don't have to tire your precious eyes and your fair little delicate hands—

NORA (*clapping her hands*).   No, is it really true, Torvald, I don't have to? Oh, how wonderfully lovely to hear! (*Taking his arm.*) Now I'll tell you just how I've thought we should plan things. Right after Christmas—(*The doorbell rings.*) Oh, the bell. (*Straightening the room up a bit.*) Somebody would have to come. What a bore!

HELMER.   I'm not at home to visitors, don't forget.

MAID (*from the hall doorway*). Ma'am, a lady to see you—

NORA. All right, let her come in.

MAID (*to* HELMER). And the doctor's just come too.

HELMER. Did he go right to my study?

MAID. Yes, he did.

> (HELMER *goes into his room. The* MAID *shows in* MRS. LINDE, *dressed in traveling clothes, and shuts the door after her.*)

MRS. LINDE (*in a dispirited and somewhat hesitant voice*). Hello, Nora.

NORA. (*uncertain*). Hello—

MRS. LINDE. You don't recognize me.

NORA. No, I don't know—but wait, I think—(*Exclaiming.*) What! Kristine! Is it really you?

MRS. LINDE. Yes, it's me.

NORA. Kristine! To think I didn't recognize you. But then, how could I? (*More quietly.*) How you've changed, Kristine!

MRS. LINDE. Yes, no doubt I have. In nine—ten long years.

NORA. Is it so long since we met! Yes, it's all of that. Oh, these last eight years have been a happy time, believe me. And so now you've come in to town, too. Made the long trip in the winter. That took courage.

MRS. LINDE. I just got here by ship this morning.

NORA. To enjoy yourself over Christmas, of course. Oh, how lovely! Yes, enjoy ourselves, we'll do that. But take your coat off. You're not still cold? (*Helping her.*) There now, let's get cozy here by the stove. No, the easy chair there! I'll take the rocker here. (*Seizing her hands.*) Yes, now you have your old look again; it was only in that first moment. You're a bit more pale, Kristine—and maybe a bit thinner.

MRS. LINDE. And much, much older, Nora.

NORA. Yes, perhaps a bit older; a tiny, tiny bit; not much at all. (*Stopping short; suddenly serious.*) Oh, but thoughtless me, to sit here, chattering away. Sweet, good Kristine, can you forgive me?

MRS. LINDE. What do you mean, Nora?

NORA (*softly*). Poor Kristine, you've become a widow.

MRS. LINDE.   Yes, three years ago.

NORA.   Oh, I knew it, of course; I read it in the papers. Oh, Kristine, you must believe me; I often thought of writing you then, but I kept postponing it, and something always interfered.

MRS. LINDE.   Nora dear, I understand completely.

NORA.   No, it was awful of me, Kristine. You poor thing, how much you must have gone through. And he left you nothing?

MRS. LINDE.   No.

NORA.   And no children?

MRS. LINDE.   No.

NORA.   Nothing at all, then?

MRS. LINDE.   Not even a sense of loss to feed on.

NORA (*looking incredulously at her*).   But Kristine, how could that be?

MRS. LINDE (*smiling wearily and stroking Nora's hair*).   Oh, sometimes it happens, Nora.

NORA.   So completely alone. How terribly hard that must be for you. I have three lovely children. You can't see them now; they're out with the maid. But now you must tell me everything—

MRS. LINDE.   No, no, no, tell me about yourself.

NORA.   No, you begin. Today I don't want to be selfish. I want to think only of you today. But there *is* something I must tell you. Did you hear of the wonderful luck we had recently?

MRS. LINDE.   No, what's that?

NORA.   My husband's been made manager in the bank, just think!

MRS. LINDE.   Your husband? How marvelous!

NORA.   Isn't it? Being a lawyer is such an uncertain living, you know, especially if one won't touch any cases that aren't clean and decent. And of course Torvald would never do that, and I'm with him completely there. Oh, we're simply delighted, believe me! He'll join the bank right after New Year's and start getting a huge salary and lots of commissions. From now on we can live quite differently—just as we want. Oh, Kristine, I feel so light and happy! Won't it be lovely to have stacks of money and not a care in the world?

MRS. LINDE. Well, anyway, it would be lovely to have enough for necessities.

NORA. No, not just for necessities, but stacks and stacks of money!

MRS. LINDE (*smiling*). Nora, Nora, aren't you sensible yet? Back in school you were such a free spender.

NORA (*with a quiet laugh*). Yes, that's what Torvald still says. (*Shaking her finger.*) But "Nora, Nora" isn't as silly as you all think. Really, we've been in no position for me to go squandering. We've had to work, both of us.

MRS. LINDE. You too?

NORA. Yes, at odd jobs—needlework, crocheting, embroidery, and such—(*Casually.*) and other things too. You remember that Torvald left the department when we were married? There was no chance of promotion in his office, and of course he needed to earn more money. But that first year he drove himself terribly. He took on all kinds of extra work that kept him going morning and night. It wore him down, and then he fell deathly ill. The doctors said it was essential for him to travel south.

MRS. LINDE. Yes, didn't you spend a whole year in Italy?

NORA. That's right. It wasn't easy to get away, you know. Ivar had just been born. But of course we had to go. Oh, that was a beautiful trip, and it saved Torvald's life. But it cost an awful lot of money, Kristine.

MRS. LINDE. I can well imagine.

NORA. Four thousand, eight hundred crowns it cost. That's really a lot of money.

MRS. LINDE. But it's lucky you had it when you needed it.

NORA. Well, as it was, we got it from Papa.

MRS. LINDE. I see. It was just about the time your father died.

NORA. Yes, just about then. And, you know, I couldn't make that trip out to nurse him. I had to stay here, expecting Ivar any moment, and with my poor sick Torvald to care for. Dearest Papa, I never saw him again, Kristine. Oh, that was the worst time I've known in all my marriage.

MRS. LINDE. I know how you loved him. And then you went off to Italy?

NORA. Yes. We had the means now, and the doctors urged us. So we left a month after.

MRS. LINDE. And your husband came back completely cured?

NORA. Sound as a drum!

MRS. LINDE. But—the doctor?

NORA. Who?

MRS. LINDE. I thought the maid said he was a doctor, the man who came in with me.

NORA. Yes, that was Dr. Rank—but he's not making a sick call. He's our closest friend, and he stops by at least once a day. No, Torvald hasn't had a sick moment since, and the children are fit and strong, and I am, too. (*Jumping up and clapping her hands.*) Oh, dear God, Kristine, what a lovely thing to live and be happy! But how disgusting of me—I'm talking of nothing but my own affairs. (*Sits on a stool close by* KRISTINE, *arms resting across her knees.*) Oh, don't be angry with me! Tell me, is it really true that you weren't in love with your husband? Why did you marry him, then?

MRS. LINDE. My mother was still alive, but bedridden and helpless—and I had my two younger brothers to look after. In all conscience, I didn't think I could turn him down.

NORA. No, you were right there. But was he rich at the time?

MRS. LINDE. He was very well off, I'd say. But the business was shaky, Nora. When he died, it all fell apart, and nothing was left.

NORA. And then—?

MRS. LINDE. Yes, so I had to scrape up a living with a little shop and a little teaching and whatever else I could find. The last three years have been like one endless workday without a rest for me. Now it's over, Nora. My poor mother doesn't need me, for she's passed on. Nor the boys, either; they're working now and can take care of themselves.

NORA. How free you must feel—

MRS. LINDE. No—only unspeakably empty. Nothing to live for now. (*Standing up anxiously.*) That's why I couldn't take it any longer out in that desolate hole. Maybe here it'll be easier to find something to do and keep my mind occupied. If I could only be lucky enough to get a steady job, some office work—

NORA.   Oh, but Kristine, that's so dreadfully tiring, and you already look so tired. It would be much better for you if you could go off to a spa.

MRS. LINDE (*going toward the window*).   I have no father to give me travel money, Nora.

NORA (*rising*).   Oh, don't be angry with me.

MRS. LINDE (*going to her*).   Nora dear, don't you be angry with me. The worst of my kind of situation is all the bitterness that's stored away. No one to work for, and yet you're always having to snap up your opportunities. You have to live; and so you grow selfish. When you told me the happy change in your lot, do you know I was delighted less for your sakes than for mine?

NORA.   How so? Oh, I see. You think maybe Torvald could do something for you.

MRS. LINDE.   Yes, that's what I thought.

NORA.   And he will, Kristine! Just leave it to me; I'll bring it up so delicately—find something attractive to humor him with. Oh, I'm so eager to help you.

MRS. LINDE.   How very kind of you, Nora, to be so concerned over me—doubly kind, considering you really know so little of life's burdens yourself.

NORA.   I—? I know so little—?

MRS. LINDE (*smiling*).   Well, my heavens—a little needlework and such—Nora, you're just a child.

NORA (*tossing her head and pacing the floor*).   You don't have to act so superior.

MRS. LINDE.   Oh?

NORA.   You're just like the others. You all think I'm incapable of anything serious—

MRS. LINDE.   Come now—

NORA.   That I've never had to face the raw world.

MRS. LINDE.   Nora dear, you've just been telling me all your troubles.

NORA.   Hm! Trivia! (*Quietly.*) I haven't told you the big thing.

MRS. LINDE.   Big thing? What do you mean?

NORA.   You look down on me so, Kristine, but you shouldn't. You're proud that you worked so long and hard for your mother.

MRS. LINDE. I don't look down on a soul. But it *is* true: I'm proud—and happy, too—to think it was given to me to make my mother's last days almost free of care.

NORA. And you're also proud thinking of what you've done for your brothers.

MRS. LINDE. I feel I've a right to be.

NORA. I agree. But listen to this, Kristine—I've also got something to be proud and happy for.

MRS. LINDE. I don't doubt it. But whatever do you mean?

NORA. Not so loud. What if Torvald heard! He mustn't, not for anything in the world. Nobody must know, Kristine. No one but you.

MRS. LINDE. But what is it, then?

NORA. Come here. (*Drawing her down beside her on the sofa.*) It's true—I've also got something to be proud and happy for. I'm the one who saved Torvald's life.

MRS. LINDE. Saved—? Saved how?

NORA. I told you about the trip to Italy. Torvald never would have lived if he hadn't gone south—

MRS. LINDE. Of course; your father gave you the means—

NORA (*smiling*). That's what Torvald and all the rest think, but—

MRS. LINDE. But—?

NORA. Papa didn't give us a pin. I was the one who raised the money.

MRS. LINDE. You? That whole amount?

NORA. Four thousand, eight hundred crowns. What do you say to that?

MRS. LINDE. But Nora, how was it possible? Did you win the lottery?

NORA (*disdainfully*). The lottery? Pooh! No art to that.

MRS. LINDE. But where did you get it from then?

NORA (*humming, with a mysterious smile*). Hmm, tra-la-la-la.

MRS. LINDE. Because you couldn't have borrowed it.

NORA. No? Why not?

MRS. LINDE. A wife can't borrow without her husband's consent.

NORA (*tossing her head*). Oh, but a wife with a little business sense, a wife who knows how to manage—

MRS. LINDE.   Nora, I simply don't understand—

NORA.   You don't have to. Whoever said I *borrowed* the money? I could have gotten it other ways. (*Throwing herself back on the sofa.*) I could have gotten it from some admirer or other. After all, a girl with my ravishing appeal—

MRS. LINDE.   You lunatic.

NORA.   I'll bet you're eaten up with curiosity, Kristine.

MRS. LINDE.   Now listen here, Nora—you haven't done something indiscreet?

NORA (*sitting up again*).   Is it indiscreet to save your husband's life?

MRS. LINDE.   I think it's indiscreet that without his knowledge you—

NORA.   But that's the point: he mustn't know! My Lord, can't you understand? He mustn't ever know the close call he had. It was to *me* the doctors came to say his life was in danger—that nothing could save him but a stay in the south. Didn't I try strategy then! I began talking about how lovely it would be for me to travel abroad like other young wives; I begged and I cried; I told him please to remember my condition, to be kind and indulge me; and then I dropped a hint that he could easily take out a loan. But at that, Kristine, he nearly exploded. He said I was frivolous, and it was his duty as man of the house not to indulge me in whims and fancies—as I think he called them. Aha, I thought, now you'll just have to be saved—and that's when I saw my chance.

MRS. LINDE.   And your father never told Torvald the money wasn't from him?

NORA.   No, never. Papa died right about then. I'd considered bringing him into my secret and begging him never to tell. But he was too sick at the time—and then, sadly, it didn't matter.

MRS. LINDE.   And you've never confided in your husband since?

NORA.   For heaven's sake, no! Are you serious? He's so strict on that subject. Besides—Torvald, with all his masculine pride—how painfully humiliating for him if he ever found out he was in debt to me. That would just ruin our relationship. Our beautiful, happy home would never be the same.

MRS. LINDE.   Won't you ever tell him?

NORA (*thoughtfully, half smiling*). Yes—maybe sometime, years from now, when I'm no longer so attractive. Don't laugh! I only mean when Torvald loves me less than now, when he stops enjoying my dancing and dressing up and reciting for him. Then it might be wise to have something in reserve—(*Breaking off.*) How ridiculous! That'll never happen—Well, Kristine, what do you think of my big secret? I'm capable of something too, hm? You can imagine, of course, how this thing hangs over me. It really hasn't been easy meeting the payments on time. Listen, in the business world there's what they call quarterly interest and what they call amortization, and these are always so terribly hard to manage. I've had to skimp a little here and there, wherever I could, you know. I could hardly save anything from my house allowance, because Torvald has to live well. I couldn't let the children go poorly dressed; whatever I got for them, I felt I had to use up completely—the darlings!

MRS. LINDE. Poor Nora, so it had to come out of your own budget, then?

NORA. Yes, of course. But then it really was up to me, too. Every time Torvald gave me money for new clothes and such, I never used more than half; always bought the simplest, cheapest outfits. It was a godsend that everything looks so well on me that Torvald never noticed. But it did weigh me down at times, Kristine. It *is* such a joy to wear fine things. You understand.

MRS. LINDE. Oh, of course.

NORA. And then I found other ways of making money. Last winter I was lucky enough to get a lot of copying to do. I locked myself in and sat writing every evening till late in the night. Ah, I was tired so often, dead tired. But still it was wonderful fun, sitting and working like that, earning money. It was almost like being a man.

MRS. LINDE. But how much have you paid off this way so far?

NORA. That's hard to say, exactly. These accounts, you know, aren't easy to figure. I only know that I've paid out all I could scrape together. Time and again I haven't known where to turn. (*Smiling.*) Then I'd sit here dreaming of a rich old gentleman who had fallen in love with me—

MRS. LINDE. What! Who is he?

NORA. Oh, really! And that he'd died, and when his will

was opened, there in big letters it said, "All my fortune shall be paid over in cash, immediately, to that enchanting Mrs. Nora Helmer."

MRS. LINDE. But Nora dear—who *was* this gentleman?

NORA. Good Lord, can't you understand? The old man never existed; that was only something I'd dream up time and again whenever I was at my wits' end for money. But it makes no difference now; the old fossil can go where he pleases for all I care; I don't need him or his will—because now I'm free. (*Jumping up.*) Oh, how lovely to think of that, Kristine! Carefree! To know you're carefree, utterly carefree; to be able to romp and play with the children, and to keep up a beautiful, charming home—everything just the way Torvald likes it! And think, spring is coming, with big blue skies. Maybe we can travel a little then. Maybe I'll see the ocean again. Oh yes, it *is* so marvelous to live and be happy!

(*The front doorbell rings.*)

MRS. LINDE (*rising*). There's the bell. It's probably best that I go.

NORA. No, stay. No one's expected. It must be for Torvald.

MAID (*from the hall doorway*). Excuse me, ma'am—there's a gentleman here to see Mr. Helmer, but I didn't know—since the doctor's with him—

NORA. Who is the gentleman?

KROGSTAD (*from the doorway*). It's me, Mrs. Helmer.

(MRS. LINDE *starts and turns away toward the window.*)

NORA (*stepping toward him, tense, her voice a whisper*). You? What is it? Why do you want to speak to my husband?

KROGSTAD. Bank business—after a fashion. I have a small job in the investment bank, and I hear now your husband is going to be our chief—

NORA. In other words, it's—

KROGSTAD. Just dry business, Mrs. Helmer. Nothing but that.

NORA. Yes, then please be good enough to step into the

study. (*She nods indifferently as she sees him out by the hall door, then returns and begins stirring up the stove.*)

MRS. LINDE.   Nora—who was that man?

NORA.   That was a Mr. Krogstad—a lawyer.

MRS. LINDE.   Then it really was him.

NORA.   Do you know that person?

MRS. LINDE.   I did once—many years ago. For a time he was a law clerk in our town.

NORA.   Yes, he's been that.

MRS. LINDE.   How he's changed.

NORA.   I understand he had a very unhappy marriage.

MRS. LINDE.   He's a widower now?

NORA.   With a number of children. There now, it's burning. (*She closes the stove door and moves the rocker a bit to one side.*)

MRS. LINDE.   They say he has a hand in all kinds of business.

NORA.   Oh? That may be true; I wouldn't know. But let's not think about business. It's so dull.

(DR. RANK *enters from* HELMER'S *study.*)

RANK (*still in the doorway*).   No, no, really—I don't want to intrude, I'd just as soon talk a little while with your wife. (*Shuts the door, then notices* MRS. LINDE.) Oh, beg pardon. I'm intruding here too.

NORA.   No, not at all. (*Introducing him.*) Dr. Rank, Mrs. Linde.

RANK.   Well now, that's a name much heard in this house. I believe I passed the lady on the stairs as I came.

MRS. LINDE.   Yes, I take the stairs very slowly. They're rather hard on me.

RANK.   Uh-hm, some touch of internal weakness?

MRS. LINDE.   More overexertion, I'd say.

RANK.   Nothing else? Then you're probably here in town to rest up in a round of parties?

MRS. LINDE.   I'm here to look for work.

RANK.   Is that the best cure for overexertion?

MRS. LINDE.   One has to live, Doctor.

RANK.   Yes, there's a common prejudice to that effect.

NORA.   Oh, come on, Dr. Rank—you really do want to live yourself.

RANK.   Yes, I really do. Wretched as I am, I'll gladly

prolong my torment indefinitely. All my patients feel like that. And it's quite the same, too, with the morally sick. Right at this moment there's one of those moral invalids in there with Helmer—

MRS. LINDE (*softly*).   Ah!

NORA.   Who do you mean?

RANK.   Oh, it's a lawyer, Krogstad, a type you wouldn't know. His character is rotten to the root—but even he began chattering all-importantly about how he had to *live.*

NORA.   Oh? What did he want to talk to Torvald about?

RANK.   I really don't know. I only heard something about the bank.

NORA.   I didn't know that Krog—that this man Krogstad had anything to do with the bank.

RANK.   Yes, he's gotten some kind of berth down there. (*To* MRS. LINDE.)   I don't know if you also have, in your neck of the woods, a type of person who scuttles about breathlessly, sniffing out hints of moral corruption, and then maneuvers his victim into some sort of key position where he can keep an eye on him. It's the healthy these days that are out in the cold.

MRS. LINDE.   All the same, it's the sick who most need to be taken in.

RANK (*with a shrug*).   Yes, there we have it. That's the concept that's turning society into a sanatorium.

(NORA, *lost in her thoughts, breaks out into quiet laughter and claps her hands.*)

RANK.   Why do you laugh at that? Do you have any real idea of what society is?

NORA.   What do I care about dreary old society? I was laughing at something quite different—something terribly funny. Tell me, Doctor—is everyone who works in the bank dependent now on Torvald?

RANK.   Is that what you find so terribly funny?

NORA (*smiling and humming*).   Never mind, never mind! (*Pacing the floor.*) Yes, that's really immensely amusing: that we—that Torvald has so much power now over all those people. (*Taking the bag out of her pocket.*) Dr. Rank, a little macaroon on that?

RANK.   See here, macaroons! I thought they were contraband here.

NORA. Yes, but these are some that Kristine gave me.

MRS. LINDE. What? I—?

NORA. Now, now, don't be afraid. You couldn't possibly know that Torvald had forbidden them. You see, he's worried they'll ruin my teeth. But hmp! Just this once! Isn't that so, Dr. Rank? Help yourself! (*Puts a macaroon in his mouth.*) And you too, Kristine. And I'll also have one, only a little one—or two, at the most. (*Walking about again.*) Now I'm really tremendously happy. Now there's just one last thing in the world that I have an enormous desire to do.

RANK. Well! And what's that?

NORA. It's something I have such a consuming desire to say so Torvald could hear.

RANK. And why can't you say it?

NORA. I don't dare. It's quite shocking.

MRS. LINDE. Shocking?

RANK. Well, then it isn't advisable. But in front of us you certainly can. What do you have such a desire to say so Torvald could hear?

NORA. I have such a huge desire to say—to hell and be damned!

RANK. Are you crazy?

MRS. LINDE. My goodness, Nora!

RANK. Go on, say it. Here he is.

NORA (*hiding the macaroon bag*). Shh, shh, shh!

(HELMER *comes in from his study, hat in hand, overcoat over his arm.*)

NORA (*going toward him*). Well, Torvald dear, are you through with him?

HELMER. Yes, he just left.

NORA. Let me introduce you—this is Kristine, who's arrived here in town.

HELMER. Kristine—? I'm sorry, but I don't know—

NORA. Mrs. Linde, Torvald dear. Mrs. Kristine Linde.

HELMER. Of course. A childhood friend of my wife's, no doubt?

MRS. LINDE. Yes, we knew each other in those days.

NORA. And just think, she made the long trip down here in order to talk with you.

HELMER. What's this?

MRS. LINDE.   Well, not exactly—

NORA.   You see, Kristine is remarkably clever in office work, and so she's terribly eager to come under a capable man's supervision and add more to what she already knows—

HELMER.   Very wise, Mrs. Linde.

NORA.   And then when she heard that you'd become a bank manager—the story was wired out to the papers—then she came in as fast as she could and— Really, Torvald, for my sake you can do a little something for Kristine, can't you?

HELMER.   Yes, it's not at all impossible. Mrs. Linde, I suppose you're a widow?

MRS. LINDE.   Yes.

HELMER.   Any experience in office work?

MRS. LINDE.   Yes, a good deal.

HELMER.   Well, it's quite likely that I can make an opening for you—

NORA (*clapping her hands*).   You see, you see!

HELMER.   You've come at a lucky moment, Mrs. Linde.

MRS. LINDE.   Oh, how can I thank you?

HELMER.   Not necessary. (*Putting his overcoat on.*) But today you'll have to excuse me—

RANK.   Wait, I'll go with you. (*He fetches his coat from the hall and warms it at the stove.*)

NORA.   Don't stay out long, dear.

HELMER.   An hour; no more.

NORA.   Are you going too, Kristine?

MRS. LINDE (*putting on her winter garments*).   Yes, I have to see about a room now.

HELMER.   Then perhaps we can all walk together.

NORA (*helping her*).   What a shame we're so cramped here, but it's quite impossible for us to—

MRS. LINDE.   Oh, don't even think of it! Good-bye, Nora dear, and thanks for everything.

NORA.   Good-bye for now. Of course you'll be back this evening. And you too, Dr. Rank. What? If you're well enough? Oh, you've got to be! Wrap up tight now.

(*In a ripple of small talk the company moves out into the hall; children's voices are heard outside on the steps.*)

NORA. There they are! There they are! (*She runs to open the door. The children come in with their nurse,* ANNE-MARIE.) Come in, come in! (*Bends down and kisses them.*) Oh, you darlings—! Look at them, Kristine. Aren't they lovely!

RANK. No loitering in the draft here.

HELMER. Come, Mrs. Linde—this place is unbearable now for anyone but mothers.

> (DR. RANK, HELMER, *and* MRS. LINDE *go down the stairs.* ANNE-MARIE *goes into the living room with the children.* NORA *follows, after closing the hall door.*)

NORA. How fresh and strong you look. Oh, such red cheeks you have! Like apples and roses. (*The children interrupt her throughout the following.*) And it was so much fun? That's wonderful. Really? You pulled both Emmy and Bob on the sled? Imagine, all together! Yes, you're a clever boy, Ivar. Oh, let me hold her a bit, Anne-Marie. My sweet little doll baby! (*Takes the smallest from the nurse and dances with her.*) Yes, yes, Mama will dance with Bob as well. What? Did you throw snowballs? Oh, if I'd only been there! No, don't bother, Anne-Marie—I'll undress them myself. Oh yes, let me. It's such fun. Go in and rest; you look half frozen. There's hot coffee waiting for you on the stove. (*The nurse goes into the room to the left.* NORA *takes the children's winter things off, throwing them about, while the children talk to her all at once.*) Is that so? A big dog chased you? But it didn't bite? No, dogs never bite little, lovely doll babies. Don't peek in the packages, Ivar! What is it? Yes, wouldn't you like to know. No, no, it's an ugly something. Well? Shall we play? What shall we play? Hide-and-seek? Yes, let's play hide-and-seek. Bob must hide first. I must? Yes, let me hide first. (*Laughing and shouting, she and the children play in and out of the living room and the adjoining room to the right. At last* NORA *hides under the table. The children come storming in, search, but cannot find her, then hear her muffled laughter, dash over to the table, lift the cloth up and find her. Wild shouting. She creeps forward as if to scare them. More shouts. Meanwhile, a knock at the hall door; no one has noticed it. Now the door half opens, and* KROGSTAD *appears. He waits a moment; the game goes on.*)

KROGSTAD.   Beg pardon, Mrs. Helmer—

NORA (*with a strangled cry, turning and scrambling to her knees*).   Oh! What do you want?

KROGSTAD.   Excuse me. The outer door was ajar; it must be someone forgot to shut it—

NORA (*rising*).   My husband isn't home, Mr. Krogstad.

KROGSTAD.   I know that.

NORA.   Yes—then what do you want here?

KROGSTAD.   A word with you.

NORA.   With—? (*To the children, quietly.*) Go in to Anne-Marie. What? No, the strange man won't hurt Mama. When he's gone, we'll play some more. (*She leads the children into the room to the left and shuts the door after them. Then, tense and nervous:*) You want to speak to me?

KROGSTAD.   Yes, I want to.

NORA.   Today? But it's not yet the first of the month—

KROGSTAD.   No, it's Christmas Eve. It's going to be up to you how merry a Christmas you have.

NORA.   What is it you want? Today I absolutely can't—

KROGSTAD.   We won't talk about that till later. This is something else. You do have a moment to spare, I suppose?

NORA.   Oh yes, of course—I do, except—

KROGSTAD.   Good. I was sitting over at Olsen's Restaurant when I saw your husband go down the street—

NORA.   Yes?

KROGSTAD.   With a lady.

NORA.   Yes. So?

KROGSTAD.   If you'll pardon my asking: wasn't that lady a Mrs. Linde?

NORA.   Yes.

KROGSTAD.   Just now come into town?

NORA.   Yes, today.

KROGSTAD.   She's a good friend of yours?

NORA.   Yes, she is. But I don't see—

KROGSTAD.   I also knew her once.

NORA.   I'm aware of that.

KROGSTAD.   Oh? You know all about it. I thought so. Well, then let me ask you short and sweet: is Mrs. Linde getting a job in the bank?

NORA.   What makes you think you can cross-examine

me, Mr. Krogstad—you, one of my husband's employees?
But since you ask, you might as well know—yes, Mrs.
Linde's going to be taken on at the bank. And I'm the one
who spoke for her, Mr. Krogstad. Now you know.

KROGSTAD. So I guessed right.

NORA (*pacing up and down*). Oh, one does have a tiny
bit of influence, I should hope. Just because I am a woman,
don't think it means that— When one has a subordinate
position, Mr. Krogstad, one really ought to be careful about
pushing somebody who—hm—

KROGSTAD. Who has influence?

NORA. That's right.

KROGSTAD (*in a different tone*). Mrs. Helmer, would
you be good enough to use your influence on my behalf?

NORA. What? What do you mean?

KROGSTAD. Would you please make sure that I keep
my subordinate position in the bank?

NORA. What does that mean? Who's thinking of taking
away your position?

KROGSTAD. Oh, don't play the innocent with me. I'm
quite aware that your friend would hardly relish the chance
of running into me again; and I'm also aware now whom I
can thank for being turned out.

NORA. But I promise you—

KROGSTAD. Yes, yes, yes, to the point: there's still time,
and I'm advising you to use your influence to prevent it.

NORA. But Mr. Krogstad, I have absolutely no
influence.

KROGSTAD. You haven't? I thought you were just saying—

NORA. You shouldn't take me so literally. I! How can
you believe that I have any such influence over my
husband?

KROGSTAD. Oh, I've known your husband from our student days. I don't think the great bank manager's more
steadfast than any other married man.

NORA. You speak insolently about my husband, and I'll
show you the door.

KROGSTAD. The lady has spirit.

NORA. I'm not afraid of you any longer. After New
Year's, I'll soon be done with the whole business.

KROGSTAD (*restraining himself*). Now listen to me, Mrs.

Helmer. If necessary, I'll fight for my little job in the bank as if it were life itself.

NORA.   Yes, so it seems.

KROGSTAD.   It's not just a matter of income; that's the least of it. It's something else— All right, out with it! Look, this is the thing. You know, just like all the others, of course, that once, a good many years ago, I did something rather rash.

NORA.   I've heard rumors to that effect.

KROGSTAD.   The case never got into court; but all the same, every door was closed in my face from then on. So I took up those various activities you know about. I had to grab hold somewhere; and I dare say I haven't been among the worst. But now I want to drop all that. My boys are growing up. For their sakes, I'll have to win back as much respect as possible here in town. That job in the bank was like the first rung in my ladder. And now your husband wants to kick me right back down in the mud again.

NORA.   But for heaven's sake, Mr. Krogstad, it's simply not in my power to help you.

KROGSTAD.   That's because you haven't the will to—but I have the means to make you.

NORA.   You certainly won't tell my husband that I owe you money?

KROGSTAD.   Hm—what if I told him that?

NORA.   That would be shameful of you. (*Nearly in tears.*) This secret—my joy and my pride—that he should learn it in such a crude and disgusting way—learn it from you. You'd expose me to the most horrible unpleasantness—

KROGSTAD.   Only unpleasantness?

NORA (*vehemently*).   But go on and try. It'll turn out the worse for you, because then my husband will really see what a crook you are, and then you'll *never* be able to hold your job.

KROGSTAD.   I asked if it was just domestic unpleasantness you were afraid of?

NORA.   If my husband finds out, then of course he'll pay what I owe at once, and then we'd be through with you for good.

KROGSTAD (*a step closer*).   Listen, Mrs. Helmer—you've either got a very bad memory, or else no head at all for business. I'd better put you a little more in touch with the facts.

NORA.   What do you mean?

KROGSTAD.   When your husband was sick, you came to me for a loan of four thousand, eight hundred crowns.

NORA.   Where else could I go?

KROGSTAD.   I promised to get you that sum—

NORA.   And you got it.

KROGSTAD.   I promised to get you that sum, on certain conditions. You were so involved in your husband's illness, and so eager to finance your trip, that I guess you didn't think out all the details. It might just be a good idea to remind you. I promised you the money on the strength of a note I drew up.

NORA.   Yes, and that I signed.

KROGSTAD.   Right. But at the bottom I added some lines for your father to guarantee the loan. He was supposed to sign down there.

NORA.   Supposed to? He did sign.

KROGSTAD.   I left the date blank. In other words, your father would have dated his signature himself. Do you remember that?

NORA.   Yes, I think—

KROGSTAD.   Then I gave you the note for you to mail to your father. Isn't that so?

NORA.   Yes.

KROGSTAD.   And naturally you sent it at once—because only some five, six days later you brought me the note, properly signed. And with that, the money was yours.

NORA.   Well, then; I've made my payments regularly, haven't I?

KROGSTAD.   More or less. But—getting back to the point—those were hard times for you then, Mrs. Helmer.

NORA.   Yes, they were.

KROGSTAD.   Your father was very ill, I believe.

NORA.   He was near the end.

KROGSTAD.   He died soon after?

NORA.   Yes.

KROGSTAD.   Tell me, Mrs. Helmer, do you happen to recall the date of your father's death? The day of the month, I mean.

NORA.   Papa died the twenty-ninth of September.

KROGSTAD. That's quite correct; I've already looked into that. And now we come to a curious thing—(*Taking out a paper.*) which I simply cannot comprehend.

NORA. Curious thing? I don't know—

KROGSTAD. This is the curious thing: that your father co-signed the note for your loan three days after his death.

NORA. How——? I don't understand.

KROGSTAD. Your father died the twenty-ninth of September. But look. Here your father dated his signature October second. Isn't that curious, Mrs. Helmer? (NORA *is silent.*) Can you explain it to me? (NORA *remains silent.*) It's also remarkable that the words "October second" and the year aren't written in your father's hand, but rather in one that I think I know. Well, it's easy to understand. Your father forgot perhaps to date his signature, and then someone or other added it, a bit sloppily, before anyone knew of his death. There's nothing wrong in that. It all comes down to the signature. And there's no question about *that,* Mrs. Helmer. It really *was* your father who signed his own name here, wasn't it?

NORA (*after a short silence, throwing her head back and looking defiantly at him*). No, it wasn't. *I* signed Papa's name.

KROGSTAD. Wait, now—are you fully aware that this is a dangerous confession?

NORA. Why? You'll soon get your money.

KROGSTAD. Let me ask you a question—why didn't you send the paper to your father?

NORA. That was impossible. Papa was so sick. If I'd asked him for his signature, I also would have had to tell him what the money was for. But I couldn't tell him, sick as he was, that my husband's life was in danger. That was just impossible.

KROGSTAD. Then it would have been better if you'd given up the trip abroad.

NORA. I couldn't possibly. The trip was to save my husband's life. I couldn't give that up.

KROGSTAD. But didn't you ever consider that this was a fraud against me?

NORA. I couldn't let myself be bothered by that. You weren't any concern of mine. I couldn't stand you, with all those cold complications you made, even though you knew how badly off my husband was.

KROGSTAD. Mrs. Helmer, obviously you haven't the vaguest idea of what you've involved yourself in. But I can tell you this: it was nothing more and nothing worse that I once did—and it wrecked my whole reputation.

NORA. You? Do you expect me to believe that you ever acted bravely to save your wife's life?

KROGSTAD. Laws don't inquire into motives.

NORA. Then they must be very poor laws.

KROGSTAD. Poor or not—if I introduce this paper in court, you'll be judged according to law.

NORA. This I refuse to believe. A daughter hasn't a right to protect her dying father from anxiety and care? A wife hasn't a right to save her husband's life? I don't know much about laws, but I'm sure that somewhere in the books these things are allowed. And you don't know anything about it—you who practice the law? You must be an awful lawyer, Mr. Krogstad.

KROGSTAD. Could be. But business—the kind of business we two are mixed up in—don't you think I know about that? All right. Do what you want now. But I'm telling you *this*: if I get shoved down a second time, you're going to keep me company. (*He bows and goes out through the hall.*)

NORA (*pensive for a moment, then tossing her head*). Oh, really! Trying to frighten me! I'm not so silly as all that. (*Begins gathering up the children's clothes, but soon stops.*) But—? No, but that's impossible! I did it out of love.

THE CHILDREN (*in the doorway, left*). Mama, that strange man's gone out the door.

NORA. Yes, yes, I know it. But don't tell anyone about the strange man. Do you hear? Not even Papa!

THE CHILDREN. No, Mama. But now will you play again?

NORA. No, not now.

THE CHILDREN. Oh, but Mama, you promised.

NORA. Yes, but I can't now. Go inside; I have too much to do. Go in, go in, my sweet darlings. (*She herds them gently back in the room and shuts the door after them. Settling on the sofa, she takes up a piece of embroidery and makes some stitches, but soon stops abruptly.*) No! (*Throws*

the work aside, rises, goes to the hall door and calls out.)
Helene! Let me have the tree in here. (*Goes to the table, left, opens the table drawer, and stops again.*) No, but that's utterly impossible!

MAID (*with the Christmas tree*). Where should I put it, ma'am?

NORA. There. The middle of the floor.

MAID. Should I bring anything else?

NORA. No, thanks. I have what I need.

(*The* MAID, *who has set the tree down, goes out.*)

NORA (*absorbed in trimming the tree*). Candles here— and flowers here. That terrible creature! Talk, talk, talk! There's nothing to it at all. The tree's going to be lovely. I'll do anything to please you, Torvald. I'll sing for you, dance for you—

(HELMER *comes in from the hall, with a sheaf of papers under his arm.*)

NORA. Oh! You're back so soon?

HELMER. Yes. Has anyone been here?

NORA. Here? No.

HELMER. That's odd. I saw Krogstad leaving the front door.

NORA. So? Oh yes, that's true. Krogstad was here a moment.

HELMER. Nora, I can see by your face that he's been here, begging you to put in a good word for him.

NORA. Yes.

HELMER. And it was supposed to seem like your own idea? You were to hide it from me that he'd been here. He asked you that, too, didn't he?

NORA. Yes, Torvald, but—

HELMER. Nora, Nora, and you could fall for that? Talk with that sort of person and promise him anything? And then in the bargain, tell me an untruth.

NORA. An untruth—?

HELMER. Didn't you say that no one had been here? (*Wagging his finger.*) My little songbird must never do that again. A songbird needs a clean beak to warble with. No false notes. (*Putting his arm about her waist.*) That's the way it should be, isn't it? Yes, I'm sure of it. (*Releasing her.*) And so, enough of that. (*Sitting by the stove.*) Ah, how snug and cozy it is here. (*Leafing among his papers.*)

NORA (*busy with the tree, after a short pause*). Torvald!

HELMER. Yes.

NORA. I'm so much looking forward to the Stenborgs' costume party, day after tomorrow.

HELMER. And I can't wait to see what you'll surprise me with.

NORA. Oh, that stupid business!

HELMER. What?

NORA. I can't find anything that's right. Everything seems so ridiculous, so inane.

HELMER. So my little Nora's come to *that* recognition?

NORA (*going behind his chair, her arms resting on its back*). Are you very busy, Torvald?

HELMER. Oh—

NORA. What papers are those?

HELMER. Bank matters.

NORA. Already?

HELMER. I've gotten full authority from the retiring management to make all necessary changes in personnel and procedure. I'll need Christmas week for that. I want to have everything in order by New Year's.

NORA. So that was the reason this poor Krogstad—

HELMER. Hm.

NORA (*still leaning on the chair and slowly stroking the nape of his neck*). If you weren't so very busy, I would have asked you an enormous favor, Torvald.

HELMER. Let's hear. What is it?

NORA. You know, there isn't anyone who has your good taste—and I want so much to look well at the costume party. Torvald, couldn't you take over and decide what I should be and plan my costume?

HELMER. Ah, is my stubborn little creature calling for a lifeguard?

NORA. Yes, Torvald, I can't get anywhere without your help.

HELMER. All right—I'll think it over. We'll hit on something.

NORA. Oh, how sweet of you. (*Goes to the tree again. Pause.*) Aren't the red flowers pretty—? But tell me, was it really such a crime that this Krogstad committed?

HELMER. Forgery. Do you have any idea what that means?

NORA. Couldn't he have done it out of need?

HELMER. Yes, or thoughtlessness, like so many others. I'm not so heartless that I'd condemn a man categorically for just one mistake.

NORA. No, of course not, Torvald!

HELMER. Plenty of men have redeemed themselves by openly confessing their crimes and taking their punishment.

NORA. Punishment—?

HELMER. But now Krogstad didn't go that way. He got himself out by sharp practices, and that's the real cause of his moral breakdown.

NORA. Do you really think that would—?

HELMER. Just imagine how a man with that sort of guilt in him has to lie and cheat and deceive on all sides, has to wear a mask even with the nearest and dearest he has, even with his own wife and children. And with the children, Nora—that's where it's most horrible.

NORA. Why?

HELMER. Because that kind of atmosphere of lies infects the whole life of a home. Every breath the children take in is filled with the germs of something degenerate.

NORA (*coming closer behind him*). Are you sure of that?

HELMER. Oh, I've seen it often enough as a lawyer. Almost everyone who goes bad early in life has a mother who's a chronic liar.

NORA. Why just—the mother?

HELMER. It's usually the mother's influence that's dominant, but the father's works in the same way, of course. Every lawyer is quite familiar with it. And still this Krogstad's been going home year in, year out, poisoning his own children with lies and pretense; that's why I call him morally lost. (*Reaching his hands out toward her.*) So my sweet little Nora must promise me never to plead his cause. Your hand on it. Come, come, what's this? Give me your hand. There, now. All settled. I can tell you it'd be impossible for me to work alongside of him. I literally feel physically revolted when I'm anywhere near such a person.

NORA (*withdraws her hand and goes to the other side of the Christmas tree*). How hot it is here! And I've got so much to do.

HELMER (*getting up and gathering his papers*). Yes, and I have to think about getting some of these read through before dinner. I'll think about your costume, too. And something to hang on the tree in gilt paper, I may even see about that. (*Putting his hand on her head.*) Oh you, my darling little songbird. (*He goes into his study and closes the door after him.*)

NORA (*softly, after a silence*). Oh, really! it isn't so. It's impossible. It must be impossible.

ANNE-MARIE (*in the doorway, left*). The children are begging so hard to come in to Mama.

NORA. No, no, no, don't let them in to me! You stay with them, Anne-Marie.

ANNE-MARIE. Of course, ma'am. (*Closes the door.*)

NORA (*pale with terror*). Hurt my children—! Poison my home? (*A moment's pause; then she tosses her head.*) That's not true. Never. Never in all the world.

ACT TWO

Same room. In the corner by the piano the Christmas tree now stands stripped of ornament, burned-down candle stubs on its ragged branches. NORA's *outdoor clothes lie on the sofa.* NORA, *alone in the room, moves restlessly about; at last she stops at the sofa and picks up her coat.*

NORA (*dropping the coat again*). Someone's coming! (*Goes toward the door, listens.*) No—there's no one. Of course—nobody's coming today, Christmas Day—or tomorrow, either. But maybe—(*Opens the door and looks out.*) No, nothing in the mailbox. Quite empty. (*Coming forward.*) What nonsense! He won't do anything serious. Nothing terrible could happen. It's impossible. Why, I have three small children.

(ANNE-MARIE, *with a large carton, comes in from the room to the left.*)

ANNE-MARIE. Well, at last I found the box with the masquerade clothes.

NORA. Thanks. Put it on the table.

ANNE-MARIE (*does so*). But they're all pretty much of a mess.

NORA. Ahh! I'd love to rip them in a million pieces!

ANNE-MARIE. Oh, mercy, they can be fixed right up. Just a little patience.

NORA. Yes, I'll go get Mrs. Linde to help me.

ANNE-MARIE. Out again now? In this nasty weather? Miss Nora will catch cold—get sick.

NORA. Oh, worse things could happen— How are the children?

ANNE-MARIE. The poor mites are playing with their Christmas presents, but—

NORA. Do they ask for me much?

ANNE-MARIE. They're so used to having Mama around, you know.

72

NORA.   Yes, but Anne-Marie, I *can't* be together with them as much as I was.

ANNE-MARIE.   Well, small children get used to anything.

NORA.   You think so? Do you think they'd forget their mother if she was gone for good?

ANNE-MARIE.   Oh, mercy—gone for good!

NORA.   Wait, tell me, Anne-Marie—I've wondered so often—how could you ever have the heart to give your child over to strangers?

ANNE-MARIE.   But I had to, you know, to become little Nora's nurse.

NORA.   Yes, but how could you *do* it?

ANNE-MARIE.   When I could get such a good place? A girl who's poor and who's gotten in trouble is glad enough for that. Because that slippery fish, he didn't do a thing for me, you know.

NORA.   But your daughter's surely forgotten you.

ANNE-MARIE.   Oh, she certainly has not. She's written to me, both when she was confirmed and when she was married.

NORA (*clasping her about the neck*).   You old Anne-Marie, you were a good mother for me when I was little.

ANNE-MARIE.   Poor little Nora, with no other mother but me.

NORA.   And if the babies didn't have one, then I know that you'd— What silly talk! (*Opening the carton.*) Go in to them. Now I'll have to— Tomorrow you can see how lovely I'll look.

ANNE-MARIE.   Oh, there won't be anyone at the party as lovely as Miss Nora. (*She goes off into the room, left.*)

NORA (*begins unpacking the box, but soon throws it aside*).   Oh, if I dared to go out. If only nobody would come. If only nothing would happen here while I'm out. What craziness—nobody's coming. Just don't think. This muff—needs a brushing. Beautiful gloves, beautiful gloves. Let it go. Let it go! One, two, three, four, five, six— (*With a cry.*) Oh, there they are! (*Poises to move toward the door, but remains irresolutely standing.* MRS. LINDE *enters from the hall, where she has removed her street clothes.*)

NORA.   Oh, it's you, Kristine. There's no one else out there? How good that you've come.

MRS. LINDE.   I hear you were up asking for me.

NORA. Yes, I just stopped by. There's something you really can help me with. Let's get settled on the sofa. Look, there's going to be a costume party tomorrow evening at the Stenborgs' right above us, and now Torvald wants me to go as a Neapolitan peasant girl and dance the tarantella that I learned in Capri.

MRS. LINDE. Really, are you giving a whole performance?

NORA. Torvald says yes, I should. See, here's the dress. Torvald had it made for me down there; but now it's all so tattered that I just don't know—

MRS. LINDE. Oh, we'll fix that up in no time. It's nothing more than the trimmings—they're a bit loose here and there. Needle and thread? Good, now we have what we need.

NORA. Oh, how sweet of you!

MRS. LINDE (*sewing*). So you'll be in disguise tomorrow, Nora. You know what? I'll stop by then for a moment and have a look at you all dressed up. But listen, I've absolutely forgotten to thank you for that pleasant evening yesterday.

NORA (*getting up and walking about*). I don't think it was as pleasant as usual yesterday. You should have come to town a bit sooner, Kristine— Yes, Torvald really knows how to give a home elegance and charm.

MRS. LINDE. And you do, too, if you ask me. You're not your father's daughter for nothing. But tell me, is Dr. Rank always so depressed as he was yesterday?

NORA. No, that was quite unusual. But he does suffer from a serious illness—tuberculosis of the spine, poor man. You know, his father was a disgusting thing who kept mistresses and so on—and that's why the son's been sickly from birth.

MRS. LINDE (*lets her sewing fall to her lap*). But my dearest Nora, how do you know about such things?

NORA (*walking more jauntily*). Hmp! When you've had three children, then you've had a few visits from—from women who know something of medicine, and they tell you this and that.

MRS. LINDE (*resumes sewing; a short pause*). Does Dr. Rank come here every day?

NORA. Every blessed day. He's Torvald's best friend from childhood, and *my* good friend, too. Dr. Rank almost belongs to this house.

MRS. LINDE. But tell me—is he quite sincere? I mean, doesn't he rather enjoy flattering people?

NORA. Just the opposite. Why do you think that?

MRS. LINDE. When you introduced us yesterday, he claimed that he'd often heard my name in this house; but later I noticed that your husband hadn't the slightest idea who I really was. So how could Dr. Rank—?

NORA. But it's all true, Kristine. You see, Torvald loves me beyond words, and, as he puts it, he'd like to keep me all to himself. For a long time he'd almost be jealous if I even mentioned any of my old friends back home. So of course I dropped that. But with Dr. Rank I talk a lot about such things, because he likes hearing about them.

MRS. LINDE. Now listen, Nora; in many ways you're still like a child. I'm a good deal older than you, with a little more experience. I'll tell you something: you ought to put an end to all this with Dr. Rank.

NORA. What should I put an end to?

MRS. LINDE. Both parts of it, I think. Yesterday you said something about a rich admirer who'd provide you with money—

NORA. Yes, one who doesn't exist—worse luck. So?

MRS. LINDE. Is Dr. Rank well off?

NORA. Yes, he is.

MRS. LINDE. With no dependents?

NORA. No, no one. But—

MRS. LINDE. And he's over here every day?

NORA. Yes, I told you that.

MRS. LINDE. How can a man of such refinement be so grasping?

NORA. I don't follow you at all.

MRS. LINDE. Now don't try to hide it, Nora. You think I can't guess who loaned you the forty-eight hundred crowns?

NORA. Are you out of your mind? How could you think such a thing! A friend of ours, who comes here every single day. What an intolerable situation that would have been!

MRS. LINDE. Then it really wasn't him.

NORA. No, absolutely not. It never even crossed my mind for a moment— And he had nothing to lend in those days; his inheritance came later.

MRS. LINDE. Well, I think that was a stroke of luck for you, Nora dear.

NORA. No, it never would have occurred to me to ask Dr. Rank— Still, I'm quite sure that if I had asked him—

MRS. LINDE. Which you won't, of course.

NORA. No, of course not. I can't see that I'd ever need to. But I'm quite positive that if I talked to Dr. Rank—

MRS. LINDE. Behind your husband's back?

NORA. I've got to clear up this other thing; *that's* also behind his back. I've *got* to clear it all up.

MRS. LINDE. Yes, I was saying that yesterday, but—

NORA (*pacing up and down*). A man handles these problems so much better than a woman—

MRS. LINDE. One's husband does, yes.

NORA. Nonsense. (*Stopping.*) When you pay everything you owe, then you get your note back, right?

MRS. LINDE. Yes, naturally.

NORA. And can rip it into a million pieces and burn it up—that filthy scrap of paper!

MRS. LINDE (*looking hard at her, laying her sewing aside, and rising slowly*). Nora, you're hiding something from me.

NORA. You can see it in my face?

MRS. LINDE. Something's happened to you since yesterday morning. Nora, what is it?

NORA (*hurrying toward her*). Kristine! (*Listening.*) Shh! Torvald's home. Look, go in with the children a while. Torvald can't bear all this snipping and stitching. Let Anne-Marie help you.

MRS. LINDE (*gathering up some of the things*). All right, but I'm not leaving here until we've talked this out. (*She disappears into the room, left, as* TORVALD *enters from the hall.*)

NORA. Oh, how I've been waiting for you, Torvald dear.

HELMER. Was that the dressmaker?

NORA. No, that was Kristine. She's helping me fix up my costume. You know, it's going to be quite attractive.

HELMER. Yes, wasn't that a bright idea I had?

NORA. Brilliant! But then wasn't I good as well to give in to you?

HELMER (*taking her under the chin*). Good—because you give in to your husband's judgment? All right, you little goose, I know you didn't mean it like that. But I won't disturb you. You'll want to have a fitting, I suppose.

NORA. And you'll be working?

HELMER. Yes. (*Indicating a bundle of papers.*) See. I've been down to the bank. (*Starts toward his study.*)

NORA. Torvald.

HELMER (*stops*). Yes.

NORA. If your little squirrel begged you, with all her heart and soul, for something—?

HELMER. What's that?

NORA. Then would you do it?

HELMER. First, naturally, I'd have to know what it was.

NORA. Your squirrel would scamper about and do tricks, if you'd only be sweet and give in.

HELMER. Out with it.

NORA. Your lark would be singing high and low in every room—

HELMER. Come on, she does that anyway.

NORA. I'd be a wood nymph and dance for you in the moonlight.

HELMER. Nora—don't tell me it's that same business from this morning?

NORA (*coming closer*). Yes, Torvald, I beg you, please!

HELMER. And you actually have the nerve to drag that up again?

NORA. Yes, yes, you've got to give in to me; you *have* to let Krogstad keep his job in the bank.

HELMER. My dear Nora, I've slated his job for Mrs. Linde.

NORA. That's awfully kind of you. But you could just fire another clerk instead of Krogstad.

HELMER. This is the most incredible stubbornness! Because you go and give an impulsive promise to speak up for him, I'm expected to—

NORA. That's not the reason, Torvald. It's for your own sake. That man does writing for the worst papers; you said it yourself. He could do you any amount of harm. I'm scared to death of him—

HELMER. Ah, I understand. It's the old memories haunting you.

NORA. What do you mean by that?

HELMER. Of course, you're thinking about your father.

NORA. Yes, all right. Just remember how those nasty gossips wrote in the papers about Papa and slandered him so cruelly. I think they'd have had him dismissed if the department hadn't sent you up to investigate, and if you hadn't been so kind and helpful toward him.

HELMER. My dear Nora, there's a notable difference between your father and me. Your father's official career was hardly above reproach. But mine is; and I hope it'll stay that way as long as I hold my position.

NORA. Oh, who can ever tell what vicious minds can invent? We could be so snug and happy now in our quiet, carefree home—you and I and the children, Torvald! That's why I'm pleading with you so—

HELMER. And just by pleading for him you make it impossible for me to keep him on. It's already known at the bank that I'm firing Krogstad. What if it's rumored around now that the new bank manager was vetoed by his wife—

NORA. Yes, what then—?

HELMER. Oh yes—as long as our little bundle of stubbornness gets her way—! I should go and make myself ridiculous in front of the whole office—give people the idea I can be swayed by all kinds of outside pressure. Oh, you can bet I'd feel the effects of that soon enough! Besides—there's something that rules Krogstad right out at the bank as long as I'm the manager.

NORA. What's that?

HELMER. His moral failings I could maybe overlook if I had to—

NORA. Yes, Torvald, why not?

HELMER. And I hear he's quite efficient on the job. But he was a crony of mine back in my teens—one of those rash friendships that crop up again and again to embarrass you later in life. Well, I might as well say it straight out: we're on a first-name basis. And that tactless fool makes no effort at all to hide it in front of others. Quite the contrary—he thinks that entitles him to take a familiar air around me, and so every other second he comes booming out with his "Yes, Torvald!" and "Sure thing, Torvald!" I tell you, it's been excruciating for me. He's out to make my position in the bank unbearable.

NORA. Torvald, you can't be serious about all this.

HELMER. Oh no? Why not?

NORA. Because these are such petty considerations.

HELMER. What are you saying? Petty? You think I'm petty!

NORA. No, just the opposite, Torvald dear. That's exactly why—

HELMER. Never mind. You call my motives petty; then I might as well be just that. Petty! All right! We'll put a stop to this for good. (*Goes to the hall door and calls.*) Helene!

NORA. What do you want?

HELMER (*searching among his papers*). A decision. (*The* MAID *comes in.*) Look here; take this letter; go out with it at once. Get hold of a messenger and have him deliver it. Quick now. It's already addressed. Wait, here's some money.

MAID. Yes, sir. (*She leaves with the letter.*)

HELMER (*straightening his papers*). There, now, little Miss Willful.

NORA (*breathlessly*). Torvald, what was that letter?

HELMER. Krogstad's notice.

NORA. Call it back, Torvald! There's still time. Oh, Torvald, call it back! Do it for my sake—for your sake, for the children's sake! Do you hear, Torvald; do it! You don't know how this can harm us.

HELMER. Too late.

NORA. Yes, too late.

HELMER. Nora dear, I can forgive you this panic, even though basically you're insulting me. Yes, you are! Or isn't it an insult to think that *I* should be afraid of a courtroom hack's revenge? But I forgive you anyway, because this shows so beautifully how much you love me. (*Takes her in his arms.*) This is the way it should be, my darling Nora. Whatever comes, you'll see: when it really counts, I have strength and courage enough as a man to take on the whole weight myself.

NORA (*terrified*). What do you mean by that?

HELMER. The whole weight, I said.

NORA (*resolutely*). No, never in all the world.

HELMER. Good. So we'll share it, Nora, as man and wife. That's as it should be. (*Fondling her.*) Are you happy now? There, there, there—not these frightened dove's eyes. It's nothing at all but empty fantasies— Now you should run through your tarantella and practice your tambourine. I'll go to the inner office and shut both doors, so I won't hear a thing; you can make all the noise you like. (*Turning in the doorway.*) And when Rank comes, just tell him where he can find me. (*He nods to her and goes with his papers into the study, closing the door.*)

NORA (*standing as though rooted, dazed with fright, in a whisper*). He really could do it. He will do it. He'll do it in spite of everything. No, not that, never, never! Anything but that! Escape! A way out— (*The doorbell rings.*) Dr. Rank! Anything but that! *Anything*, whatever it is! (*Her hands pass over her face, smoothing it; she pulls herself together, goes over and opens the hall door.* DR. RANK *stands outside, hanging his fur coat up. During the following scene, it begins getting dark.*)

NORA. Hello, Dr. Rank. I recognized your ring. But you mustn't go in to Torvald yet; I believe he's working.

RANK. And you?

NORA. For you, I always have time to spare—you know that. (*He has entered, and she shuts the door after him.*)

RANK. Many thanks. I'll make use of that time while I can.

NORA. What do you mean by that? While you can?

RANK. Does that disturb you?

NORA. Well, it's such an odd phrase. Is anything going to happen?

RANK. What's going to happen is what I've been expecting so long—but I honestly didn't think it would come so soon.

NORA (*gripping his arm*). What is it you've found out? Dr. Rank, you have to tell me!

RANK (*sitting by the stove*). I'm going downhill fast. There's nothing to be done about it.

NORA (*breathing easier*). Is it you—then—?

RANK. Who else? There's no point in lying to one's self. I'm the most miserable of all my patients, Mrs. Helmer. These past few days I've been auditing my internal accounts. Bankrupt! Within a month I'll probably be laid out and rotting in the churchyard.

NORA. Oh, what a horrible thing to say.

RANK. The thing itself is horrible. But the worst of it is all the other horror before it's over. There's only one final examination left; when I'm finished with that, I'll know about when my disintegration will begin. There's something I want to say. Helmer with his sensitivity has such a sharp distaste for anything ugly. I don't want him near my sickroom.

NORA.   Oh, but Dr. Rank—

RANK.   I won't have him in there. Under no condition. I'll lock my door to him— As soon as I'm completely sure of the worst, I'll send you my calling card marked with a black cross, and you'll know then the wreck has started to come apart.

NORA.   No, today you're completely unreasonable. And I wanted you so much to be in a really good humor.

RANK.   With death up my sleeve? And then to suffer this way for somebody else's sins. Is there any justice in that? And in every single family, in some way or another, this inevitable retribution of nature goes on—

NORA (*her hands pressed over her ears*).   Oh, stuff! Please—cheer up!

RANK.   Yes, I'd just as soon laugh at it all. My poor, innocent spine, serving time for my father's wild army days.

NORA (*by the table, left*).   He was so infatuated with asparagus tips and *pâté de foie gras*, wasn't that it?

RANK.   Yes—and with truffles.

NORA.   Truffles, yes. And then with oysters, I suppose?

RANK.   Yes, tons of oysters, naturally.

NORA.   And then the port and champagne to go with it. It's so sad that all these delectable things have to strike at our bones.

RANK.   Especially when they strike at the unhappy bones that never shared in the fun.

NORA.   Ah, that's the saddest of all.

RANK (*looks searchingly at her*).   Hm.

NORA (*after a moment*).   Why did you smile?

RANK.   No, it was you who laughed.

NORA.   No, it was you who smiled, Dr. Rank!

RANK (*getting up*).   You're even a bigger tease than I'd thought.

NORA.   I'm full of crazy ideas today.

RANK.   That's obvious.

NORA (*putting both hands on his shoulders*).   Dear, dear Dr. Rank, you'll never die for Torvald and me.

RANK. Oh, that loss you'll easily get over. Those who go away are soon forgotten.

NORA (*looks fearfully at him*). You believe that?

RANK. One makes new connections, and then—

NORA. Who makes new connections?

RANK. Both you and Torvald will when I'm gone. I'd say you're well under way already. What was that Mrs. Linde doing here last evening?

NORA. Oh, come—you can't be jealous of poor Kristine?

RANK. Oh yes, I am. She'll be my successor here in the house. When I'm down under, that woman will probably—

NORA. Shh! Not so loud. She's right in there.

RANK. Today as well. So you see.

NORA. Only to sew on my dress. Good gracious, how unreasonable you are. (*Sitting on the sofa.*) Be nice now, Dr. Rank. Tomorrow you'll see how beautifully I'll dance; and you can imagine then that I'm dancing only for you— yes, and of course for Torvald, too—that's understood. (*Takes various items out of the carton.*) Dr. Rank, sit over here and I'll show you something.

RANK (*sitting*). What's that?

NORA. Look here. Look.

RANK. Silk stockings.

NORA. Flesh-colored. Aren't they lovely? Now it's so dark here, but tomorrow— No, no, no, just look at the feet. Oh well, you might as well look at the rest.

RANK. Hm—

NORA. Why do you look so critical? Don't you believe they'll fit?

RANK. I've never had any chance to form an opinion on that.

NORA (*glancing at him a moment*). Shame on you. (*Hits him lightly on the ear with the stockings.*) That's for you. (*Puts them away again.*)

RANK. And what other splendors am I going to see now?

NORA. Not the least bit more, because you've been naughty. (*She hums a little and rummages among her things.*)

RANK (*after a short silence*). When I sit here together with you like this, completely easy and open, then I don't know—I simply can't imagine—whatever would have become of me if I'd never come into this house.

NORA (*smiling*). Yes, I really think you feel completely at home with us.

RANK (*more quietly, staring straight ahead*). And then to have to go away from it all—

NORA. Nonsense, you're not going away.

RANK (*his voice unchanged*). —and not even be able to leave some poor show of gratitude behind, scarcely a fleeting regret—no more than a vacant place that anyone can fill.

NORA. And if I asked you now for—? No—

RANK. For what?

NORA. For a great proof of your friendship—

RANK. Yes, yes?

NORA. No, I mean—for an exceptionally big favor—

RANK. Would you really, for once, make me so happy?

NORA. Oh, you haven't the vaguest idea what it is.

RANK. All right, then tell me.

NORA. No, but I can't, Dr. Rank—it's all out of reason. It's advice and help, too—and a favor—

RANK. So much the better. I can't fathom what you're hinting at. Just speak out. Don't you trust me?

NORA. Of course. More than anyone else. You're my best and truest friend, I'm sure. That's why I want to talk to you. All right, then, Dr. Rank: there's something you can help me prevent. You know how deeply, how inexpressibly dearly Torvald loves me; he'd never hesitate a second to give up his life for me.

RANK (*leaning toward her*). Nora—do you think he's the only one—

NORA (*with a slight start*). Who—?

RANK. Who'd gladly give up his life for you.

NORA (*heavily*). I see.

RANK. I swore to myself you should know this before I'm gone. I'll never find a better chance. Yes, Nora, now you know. And also you know now that you can trust me beyond anyone else.

NORA (*rising, slowly and calmly*). Let me by.

RANK (*making room for her, but still sitting*). Nora—

NORA (*in the hall doorway*). Helene, bring the lamp in.

(*Goes over to the stove.*) Ah, dear Dr. Rank, that was really mean of you.

RANK (*getting up*). That I've loved you just as deeply as somebody else? Was *that* mean?

NORA. No, but that you came out and told me. That was quite unnecessary—

RANK. What do you mean? Have you known—?

(*The* MAID *comes in with the lamp, sets it on the table, and goes out again.*)

RANK. Nora—Mrs. Helmer—I'm asking you: have you known about it?

NORA. Oh, how can I tell what I know or don't know? Really, I don't know what to say— Why did you have to be so clumsy, Dr. Rank! Everything was so good.

RANK. Well, in any case, you now have the knowledge that my body and soul are at your command. So won't you speak out?

NORA (*looking at him*). After that?

RANK. Please, just let me know what it is.

NORA. You can't know anything now.

RANK. I have to. You mustn't punish me like this. Give me the chance to do whatever is humanly possible for you.

NORA. Now there's nothing you can do for me. Besides, actually, I don't need any help. You'll see—it's only my fantasies. That's what it is. Of course! (*Sits in the rocker, looks at him, and smiles.*) What a nice one you are, Dr. Rank. Aren't you a little bit ashamed, now that the lamp is here?

RANK. No, not exactly. But perhaps I'd better go—for good?

NORA. No, you certainly can't do that. You must come here just as you always have. You know Torvald can't do without you.

RANK. Yes, but *you*?

NORA. Oh, I think it's always such fun whenever you come here.

RANK. That's precisely what threw me off. You're a mystery to me. So many times I've felt you'd almost rather be with me than with Helmer.

NORA. Yes—you see, there are some people that one

loves most and other people that one would almost prefer being with.

RANK. Yes, there's something to that.

NORA. When I was back home, of course I loved Papa most. But I always thought it was so much fun when I could sneak down to the maids' quarters, because they never tried to improve me, and it was always so amusing, the way they talked to each other.

RANK. Aha, so it's *their* place that I've filled.

NORA (*jumping up and going to him*). Oh, dear, sweet Dr. Rank, that's not what I meant at all. But you can understand that with Torvald it's just the same as with Papa—

(*The* MAID *enters from the hall.*)

MAID. Ma'am—please! (*She whispers to* NORA *and hands her a calling card.*)

NORA (*glancing at the card.*) Ah! (*Slips it into her pocket.*)

RANK. Anything wrong?

NORA. No, no, not at all. It's only some—it's my new dress—

RANK. Really? But—there's your dress.

NORA. Oh, that. But this is another one—I ordered it—Torvald mustn't know—

RANK. Ah, now we have the big secret.

NORA. That's right. Just go in with him—he's back in the inner study. Keep him there for a while—

RANK. Don't worry. He won't get away. (*Goes into the study.*)

NORA (*to the* MAID). And he's standing waiting in the kitchen?

MAID. Yes, he came up by the back stairs.

NORA. But didn't you tell him somebody was here?

MAID. Yes, but that didn't do any good.

NORA. He won't leave?

MAID. No, he won't go till he's talked with you, ma'am.

NORA. Let him come in, then—but quietly. Helene, don't breathe a word about this. It's a surprise for my husband.

MAID. Yes, yes, I understand— (*Goes out.*)

NORA. This horror—it's going to happen. No, no, no, it can't happen, it mustn't. (*She goes and bolts* HELMER'*s door. The* MAID *opens the hall door for* KROGSTAD *and shuts it behind him. He is dressed for travel in a fur coat, boots, and a fur cap.*)

NORA (*going toward him*). Talk softly. My husband's home.

KROGSTAD. Who cares?

NORA. What do you want?

KROGSTAD. Some information.

NORA. Hurry up, then.. What is it?

KROGSTAD. You know, of course, that I got my notice.

NORA. I couldn't prevent it, Mr. Krogstad. I fought for you to the bitter end, but nothing worked.

KROGSTAD. Does your husband's love for you run so thin? He knows everything I can expose you to, and all the same he dares to—

NORA. How can you imagine he knows anything about this?

KROGSTAD. Ah, no—I can't imagine it either, now. It's not at all like my fine Torvald Helmer to have so much guts—

NORA. Mr. Krogstad, I demand respect for my husband!

KROGSTAD. Why, of course—all due respect. But since the lady's keeping it so carefully hidden, may I presume to ask if you're also a bit better informed than yesterday about what you've actually done?

NORA. More than you ever could teach me.

KROGSTAD. Yes, I *am* such an awful lawyer.

NORA. What is it you want from me?

KROGSTAD. Just a glimpse of how you are, Mrs. Helmer. I've been thinking about you all day long. Even a bill collector, an ambulance chaser, a—well, a type like me also has a little of what they call a heart, you know.

NORA. Then show it. Think of my children.

KROGSTAD. Did you or your husband ever think of mine? But never mind. I simply wanted to tell you that you don't need to take this thing too seriously. For the present, I'm not proceeding with any action.

NORA. Oh no, really! Well—I knew that.

KROGSTAD. Everything can be settled in a friendly spirit. It doesn't have to get around town at all; it can stay just among us three.

NORA. My husband must never know anything of this.

KROGSTAD. How can you manage that? Perhaps you can pay me the balance?

NORA. No, not right now.

KROGSTAD. Or you know some way of raising the money in a day or two?

NORA. No way that I'm willing to use.

KROGSTAD. Well, it wouldn't have done you any good, anyway. If you stood in front of me with a fistful of bills, you still couldn't buy your signature back.

NORA. Then tell me what you're going to do with it.

KROGSTAD. I'll just hold onto it—keep it on file. There's no outsider who'll even get wind of it. So if you've been thinking of taking some desperate step—

NORA. I have.

KROGSTAD. Been thinking of running away from home—

NORA. I have!

KROGSTAD. Or even of something worse—

NORA. How could you guess that?

KROGSTAD. You can drop those thoughts.

NORA. How could you guess I was thinking of *that*?

KROGSTAD. Most of us think about *that* at first. I thought about it too, but I discovered I hadn't the courage—

NORA (*lifelessly*). I don't either.

KROGSTAD (*relieved*). That's true, you haven't the courage? You too?

NORA. I don't have it—I don't have it.

KROGSTAD. It would be terribly stupid, anyway. After that first storm at home blows out, why, then— I have here in my pocket a letter for your husband—

NORA. Telling everything?

KROGSTAD. As charitably as possible.

NORA (*quickly*). He mustn't ever get that letter. Tear it up. I'll find some way to get money.

KROGSTAD. Beg pardon, Mrs. Helmer, but I think I just told you—

NORA. Oh, I don't mean the money I owe you. Let me know how much you want from my husband, and I'll manage it.

KROGSTAD. I don't want any money from your husband.

NORA. What do you want, then?

KROGSTAD. I'll tell you what. I want to recoup, Mrs. Helmer; I want to get on in the world—and there's where your husband can help me. For a year and a half I've kept myself clean of anything disreputable—all that time struggling with the worst conditions; but I was satisfied, working my way up step by step. Now I've been written right off, and I'm just not in the mood to come crawling back. I tell you, I want to move on. I want to get back in the bank—in a better position. Your husband can set up a job for me—

NORA. He'll never do that!

KROGSTAD. He'll do it. I know him. He won't dare breathe a word of protest. And once I'm in there together with him, you just wait and see! Inside of a year, I'll be the manager's right-hand man. It'll be Nils Krogstad, not Torvald Helmer, who runs the bank.

NORA. You'll never see the day!

KROGSTAD. Maybe you think you can—

NORA. I have the courage now—for *that*.

KROGSTAD. Oh, you don't scare me. A smart, spoiled lady like you—

NORA. You'll see; you'll see!

KROGSTAD. Under the ice, maybe? Down in the freezing, coal-black water? There, till you float up in the spring, ugly, unrecognizable, with your hair falling out—

NORA. You don't frighten me.

KROGSTAD. Nor do you frighten me. One doesn't do these things, Mrs. Helmer. Besides, what good would it be? I'd still have him safe in my pocket.

NORA. Afterwards? When I'm no longer—?

KROGSTAD. Are you forgetting that *I'll* be in control then over your final reputation? (NORA *stands speechless, staring at him.*) Good; now I've warned you. Don't do anything stupid. When Helmer's read my letter, I'll be waiting for his reply. And bear in mind that it's your husband himself who's forced me back to my old ways. I'll never forgive him for that. Good-bye, Mrs. Helmer. (*He goes out through the hall.*)

NORA (*goes to the hall door, opens it a crack, and listens*). He's gone. Didn't leave the letter. Oh no, no, that's impossible too! (*Opening the door more and more.*) What's that? He's standing outside—not going downstairs. He's thinking it over? Maybe he'll—? (*A letter falls in the mailbox; then* KROGSTAD'*s footsteps are heard, dying away down a flight of stairs.* NORA *gives a muffled cry and runs over toward the sofa table. A short pause.*) In the mailbox. (*Slips warily over to the hall door.*) It's lying there. Torvald, Torvald—now we're lost!

MRS. LINDE (*entering with the costume from the room, left*). There now, I can't see anything else to mend. Perhaps you'd like to try—

NORA (*in a hoarse whisper*). Kristine, come here.

MRS. LINDE (*tossing the dress on the sofa*). What's wrong? You look upset.

NORA. Come here. See that letter? *There!* Look—through the glass in the mailbox.

MRS. LINDE. Yes, yes, I see it.

NORA. That letter's from Krogstad—

MRS. LINDE. Nora—it's Krogstad who loaned you the money!

NORA. Yes, and now Torvald will find out everything.

MRS. LINDE. Believe me, Nora, it's best for both of you.

NORA. There's more you don't know. I forged a name.

MRS. LINDE. But for heaven's sake—?

NORA. I only want to tell you that, Kristine, so that you can be my witness.

MRS. LINDE. Witness? Why should I—?

NORA. If I should go out of my mind—it could easily happen—

MRS. LINDE. Nora!

NORA. Or anything else occurred—so I couldn't be present here—

MRS. LINDE. Nora, Nora, you aren't yourself at all!

NORA. And someone should try to take on the whole weight, all of the guilt, you follow me—

MRS. LINDE. Yes, of course, but why do you think—?

NORA. Then you're the witness that it isn't true, Kristine. I'm very much myself; my mind right now is perfectly clear; and I'm telling you: nobody else has known about this; I alone did everything. Remember that.

MRS. LINDE. I will. But I don't understand all this.

NORA. Oh, how could you ever understand it? It's the miracle now that's going to take place.

MRS. LINDE. The miracle?

NORA. Yes, the miracle. But it's so awful, Kristine. It mustn't take place, not for anything in the world.

MRS. LINDE. I'm going right over and talk with Krogstad.

NORA. Don't go near him; he'll do you some terrible harm!

MRS. LINDE. There was a time once when he'd gladly have done anything for me.

NORA. He?

MRS. LINDE. Where does he live?

NORA. Oh, how do I know? Yes. (*Searches in her pocket.*) Here's his card. But the letter, the letter—!

HELMER (*from the study, knocking on the door*). Nora!

NORA (*with a cry of fear*). Oh! What is it? What do you want?

HELMER. Now, now, don't be so frightened. We're not coming in. You locked the door—are you trying on the dress?

NORA. Yes, I'm trying it. I'll look just beautiful, Torvald.

MRS. LINDE (*who has read the card*). He's living right around the corner.

NORA. Yes, but what's the use? We're lost. The letter's in the box.

MRS. LINDE. And your husband has the key?

NORA. Yes, always.

MRS. LINDE. Krogstad can ask for his letter back unread; he can find some excuse—

NORA. But it's just this time that Torvald usually—

MRS. LINDE. Stall him. Keep him in there. I'll be back as quick as I can. (*She hurries out through the hall entrance.*)

NORA (*goes to* HELMER'*s door, opens it, and peers in*). Torvald!

HELMER (*from the inner study*). Well—does one dare set foot in one's own living room at last? Come on, Rank, now we'll get a look— (*In the doorway.*) But what's this?

NORA. What, Torvald dear?

HELMER. Rank had me expecting some grand masquerade.

RANK (*in the doorway*). That was my impression, but I must have been wrong.

NORA. No one can admire me in my splendor—not till tomorrow.

HELMER. But Nora dear, you look so exhausted. Have you practiced too hard?

NORA. No, I haven't practiced at all yet.

HELMER. You know, it's necessary—

NORA. Oh, it's absolutely necessary, Torvald. But I can't get anywhere without your help. I've forgotten the whole thing completely.

HELMER. Ah, we'll soon take care of that.

NORA. Yes, take care of me, Torvald, please! Promise me that? Oh, I'm so nervous. That big party— You must give up everything this evening for me. No business—don't even touch your pen. Yes? Dear Torvald, promise?

HELMER. It's a promise. Tonight I'm totally at your service—you little helpless thing. Hm—but first there's one thing I want to— (*Goes toward the hall door.*)

NORA. What are you looking for?

HELMER. Just to see if there's any mail.

NORA. No, no, don't do that, Torvald!

HELMER. Now what?

NORA. Torvald, please. There isn't any.

HELMER. Let me look, though. (*Starts out.* NORA, *at the piano, strikes the first notes of the tarantella.* HELMER, *at the door, stops.*) Aha!

NORA. I can't dance tomorrow if I don't practice with you.

HELMER (*going over to her*). Nora dear, are you really so frightened?

NORA. Yes, so terribly frightened. Let me practice right now; there's still time before dinner. Oh, sit down and play for me, Torvald. Direct me. Teach me, the way you always have.

HELMER. Gladly, if it's what you want. (*Sits at the piano.*)

NORA (*snatches the tambourine up from the box, then a long, varicolored shawl, which she hurriedly throws around herself, whereupon she springs forward and cries out:*) Play for me now! Now I'll dance!

(HELMER *plays and* NORA *dances.* RANK *stands behind* HELMER *at the piano and looks on.*)

HELMER (*as he plays*). Slower. Slow down.

NORA. Can't change it.

HELMER. Not so violent, Nora!

NORA. Has to be just like this.

HELMER (*stopping*).   No, no, that won't do at all.

NORA (*laughing and swinging her tambourine*).   Isn't that what I told you?

RANK.   Let me play for her.

HELMER (*getting up*).   Yes, go on. I can teach her more easily then.

> (RANK *sits at the piano and plays;* NORA *dances more and more wildly.* HELMER *has stationed himself by the stove and repeatedly gives her directions; she seems not to hear them; her hair loosens and falls over her shoulders; she does not notice, but goes on dancing.* MRS. LINDE *enters.*)

MRS. LINDE (*standing dumbfounded at the door*).   Ah—!

NORA (*still dancing*).   See what fun, Kristine!

HELMER.   But Nora darling, you dance as if your life were at stake.

NORA.   And it is.

HELMER.   Rank, stop! This is pure madness. Stop it, I say!

> (RANK *breaks off playing, and* NORA *halts abruptly*).

HELMER (*going over to her*).   I never would have believed it. You've forgotten everything I taught you.

NORA (*throwing away the tambourine*).   You see for yourself.

HELMER.   Well, there's certainly room for instruction here.

NORA.   Yes, you see how important it is. You've got to teach me to the very last minute. Promise me that, Torvald?

HELMER.   You can be sure of that.

NORA.   You mustn't, either today or tomorrow, think about anything else but me; you mustn't open any letters— or the mailbox—

HELMER.   Ah, it's still the fear of that man—

NORA.   Oh yes, yes, that too.

HELMER.   Nora, it's written all over you—there's already a letter from him out there.

NORA.   I don't know. I guess so. But you mustn't read such things now; there mustn't be anything ugly between us before it's all over.

RANK (*quietly to* HELMER).   You shouldn't deny her.

HELMER (*putting his arm around her*). The child can have her way. But tomorrow night, after you've danced—

NORA.   Then you'll be free.

MAID (*in the doorway, right*).   Ma'am, dinner is served.

NORA.   We'll be wanting champagne, Helene.

MAID.   Very good, ma'am. (*Goes out.*)

HELMER.   So—a regular banquet, hm?

NORA.   Yes, a banquet—champagne till daybreak! (*Calling out.*) And some macaroons, Helene. Heaps of them— just this once.

HELMER (*taking her hands*).   Now, now, now—no hysterics. Be my own little lark again.

NORA.   Oh, I will soon enough. But go on in—and you, Dr. Rank. Kristine, help me put up my hair.

RANK (*whispering, as they go*).   It's not a case of—something on the way, is it?

HELMER.   Oh, of course not. It's nothing more than this childish anxiety I was telling you about. (*They go out, right.*)

NORA.   Well?

MRS. LINDE.   Left town.

NORA.   I could see by your face.

MRS. LINDE.   He'll be home tomorrow evening. I wrote him a note.

NORA.   You shouldn't have. Don't try to stop anything now. After all, it's a wonderful joy, this waiting here for the miracle.

MRS. LINDE.   What is it you're waiting for?

NORA.   Oh, you can't understand that. Go in to them; I'll be along in a moment.

> (MRS. LINDE *goes into the dining room.* NORA *stands a short while as if composing herself; then she looks at her watch.*)

NORA.   Five. Seven hours to midnight. Twenty-four hours to the midnight after, and then the tarantella's done. Seven and twenty-four? Thirty-one hours to live.

HELMER (*in the doorway, right*).   What's become of the little lark?

NORA (*going toward him with open arms*).   Here's your lark!

ACT THREE

Same scene. The table, with chairs around it, has been moved to the center of the room. A lamp on the table is lit. The hall door stands open. Dance music drifts down from the floor above. MRS. LINDE *sits at the table, absently paging through a book, trying to read, but apparently unable to focus her thoughts. Once or twice she pauses, tensely listening for a sound at the outer entrance.*

MRS. LINDE (*glancing at her watch*). Not yet—and there's hardly any time left. If only he's not—(*Listening again.*) Ah, there he is. (*She goes out in the hall and cautiously opens the outer door. Quiet footsteps are heard on the stairs. She whispers:*) Come in. Nobody's here.

KROGSTAD (*in the doorway*). I found a note from you at home. What's this all about?

MRS. LINDE. I just *had* to talk to you.

KROGSTAD. Oh? And it just *had* to be here in this house?

MRS. LINDE. At my place it was impossible; my room hasn't a private entrance. Come in; we're all alone. The maid's asleep, and the Helmers are at the dance upstairs.

KROGSTAD (*entering the room*). Well, well, the Helmers are dancing tonight? Really?

MRS. LINDE. Yes, why not?

KROGSTAD. How true—why not?

MRS. LINDE. All right, Krogstad, let's talk.

KROGSTAD. Do we two have anything more to talk about?

MRS. LINDE. We have a great deal to talk about.

KROGSTAD. I wouldn't have thought so.

MRS. LINDE. No, because you've never understood me, really.

KROGSTAD. Was there anything more to understand—except what's all too common in life? A heartless woman throws over a man the moment a better catch comes by.

MRS. LINDE. You think I'm so thoroughly heartless? You think I broke it off lightly?

KROGSTAD.   Didn't you?

MRS. LINDE.   Nils—is that what you really thought?

KROGSTAD.   If you cared, then why did you write me the way you did?

MRS. LINDE.   What else could I do? If I had to break off with you, then it was my obligation as well to root out everything you felt for me.

KROGSTAD (*wringing his hands*).   So that was it. And this—all this, simply for money!

MRS. LINDE.   Don't forget I had a helpless mother and two small brothers. We couldn't wait for you, Nils; you had such a long road ahead of you then.

KROGSTAD.   That may be; but you still hadn't the right to abandon me for somebody else's sake.

MRS. LINDE.   Yes—I don't know. So many, many times I've asked myself if I did have that right.

KROGSTAD (*more softly*).   When I lost you, it was as if all the solid ground dissolved from under my feet. Look at me; I'm a half-drowned man now, hanging onto a wreck.

MRS. LINDE.   Help may be near.

KROGSTAD.   It was near—but then you came and blocked it off.

MRS. LINDE.   Without my knowing it, Nils. Today for the first time I learned that it's you I'm replacing at the bank.

KROGSTAD.   All right—I believe you. But now that you know, will you step aside?

MRS. LINDE.   No, because that wouldn't benefit you in the slightest.

KROGSTAD.   Not "benefit" me, hm! I'd step aside anyway.

MRS. LINDE.   I've learned to be realistic. Life and hard, bitter necessity have taught me that.

KROGSTAD.   And life's taught me never to trust fine phrases.

MRS. LINDE.   Then life's taught you a very sound thing. But you do have to trust in actions, don't you?

KROGSTAD.   What does that mean?

MRS. LINDE.   You said you were hanging on like a half-drowned man to a wreck.

KROGSTAD.   I've good reason to say that.

MRS. LINDE.   I'm also like a half-drowned woman on a wreck. No one to care about, and no one to care for.

KROGSTAD.   You made your choice.

MRS. LINDE.   There wasn't any choice then.

KROGSTAD.   So—what of it?

MRS. LINDE.   Nils, if only we two shipwrecked people could reach across to each other.

KROGSTAD.   What are you saying?

MRS. LINDE.   Two on one wreck are at least better off than each on his own.

KROGSTAD.   Kristine!

MRS. LINDE.   Why do you think I came into town?

KROGSTAD.   Did you really have some thought of me?

MRS. LINDE.   I have to work to go on living. All my born days, as long as I can remember, I've worked, and it's been my best and my only joy. But now I'm completely alone in the world, so terribly lost and forsaken. To work for yourself—there's no joy in that. Nils, give me something—someone to work for.

KROGSTAD.   I don't believe all this. It's just some hysterical feminine urge to go out and make a noble sacrifice.

MRS. LINDE.   Have you ever found me to be hysterical?

KROGSTAD.   Can you honestly mean this? Tell me—do you know everything about my past?

MRS. LINDE.   Yes.

KROGSTAD.   And you know what they think I'm worth around here.

MRS. LINDE.   From what you were saying before, it would seem that with me you could have been another person.

KROGSTAD.   I'm positive of that.

MRS. LINDE.   Couldn't it happen still?

KROGSTAD.   Kristine—you're saying this in all seriousness? Yes, you are! I can see it in you. And do you really have the courage, then—?

MRS. LINDE.   I need to have someone to care for; and your children need a mother. We both need each other. Nils, I have faith that you're good at heart—I'll risk everything together with you.

KROGSTAD (*gripping her hands*).   Kristine, thank you, thank you— Now I know I can win back a place in their eyes. Yes—but I forgot—

MRS. LINDE (*listening*).   Shh! The tarantella. Go now! Go on!

KROGSTAD.   Why? What is it?

MRS. LINDE.   Hear the dance up there? When that's over, they'll be coming down.

KROGSTAD.   Oh, then I'll go. But—it's all pointless. Of course, you don't know the move I made against the Helmers.

MRS. LINDE.   Yes, Nils, I know.

KROGSTAD.   And all the same, you have the courage to—?

MRS. LINDE.   I know how far despair can drive a man like you.

KROGSTAD.   Oh, if I only could take it all back.

MRS. LINDE.   You easily could—your letter's still lying in the mailbox.

KROGSTAD.   Are you sure of that?

MRS. LINDE.   Positive. But—

KROGSTAD (*looks at her searchingly*).   Is that the meaning of it, then? You'll save your friend at any price. Tell me straight out. Is that it?

MRS. LINDE.   Nils—anyone who's sold herself for somebody else once isn't going to do it again.

KROGSTAD.   I'll demand my letter back.

MRS. LINDE.   No, no.

KROGSTAD.   Yes, of course. I'll stay here till Helmer comes down; I'll tell him to give me my letter again—that it only involves my dismissal—that he shouldn't read it—

MRS. LINDE.   No, Nils, don't call the letter back.

KROGSTAD.   But wasn't that exactly why you wrote me to come here?

MRS. LINDE.   Yes, in that first panic. But it's been a whole day and night since then, and in that time I've seen such incredible things in this house. Helmer's got to learn everything; this dreadful secret has to be aired; those two have to come to a full understanding; all these lies and evasions can't go on.

KROGSTAD.   Well, then, if you want to chance it. But at least there's one thing I can do, and do right away—

MRS. LINDE (*listening*).   Go now, go, quick! The dance is over. We're not safe another second.

KROGSTAD.   I'll wait for you downstairs.

MRS. LINDE.   Yes, please do; take me home.

KROGSTAD.   I can't believe it; I've never been so happy.

(*He leaves by way of the outer door; the door between the room and the hall stays open.*)

MRS. LINDE (*straightening up a bit and getting together her street clothes*). How different now! How different! Someone to work for, to live for—a home to build. Well, it is worth the try! Oh, if they'd only come! (*Listening.*) Ah, there they are. Bundle up. (*She picks up her hat and coat.* NORA*'s and* HELMER*'s voices can be heard outside; a key turns in the lock, and* HELMER *brings* NORA *into the hall almost by force. She is wearing the Italian costume with a large black shawl about her; he has on evening dress, with a black domino open over it.*)

NORA (*struggling in the doorway*). No, no, no, not inside! I'm going up again. I don't want to leave so soon.

HELMER. But Nora dear—

NORA. Oh, I beg you, please, Torvald. From the bottom of my heart, *please*—only an hour more!

HELMER. Not a single minute, Nora darling. You know our agreement. Come on, in we go; you'll catch cold out here. (*In spite of her resistance, he gently draws her into the room.*)

MRS. LINDE. Good evening.

NORA. Kristine!

HELMER. Why, Mrs. Linde—are you here so late?

MRS. LINDE. Yes, I'm sorry, but I did want to see Nora in costume.

NORA. Have you been sitting here, waiting for me?

MRS. LINDE. Yes. I'm afraid I wasn't here early enough; you were already upstairs; and then I thought I really couldn't leave without seeing you.

HELMER (*removing* NORA*'s shawl*). Yes, take a good look. She's worth looking at, I can tell you that, Mrs. Linde. Isn't she lovely?

MRS. LINDE. Yes, I should say—

HELMER. A dream of loveliness, isn't she? That's what everyone thought at the party, too. But she's horribly stubborn—this sweet little thing. What's to be done with her? Can you imagine, I almost had to use force to pry her away.

NORA. Oh, Torvald, you're going to regret you didn't indulge me, even for just a half hour more.

HELMER. There, you see. She danced her tarantella and got a tumultuous hand—which was well earned, although the performance may have been a bit too naturalistic—I mean it rather overstepped the proprieties of art. But never mind—what's important is, she made a success, an overwhelming success. You think I could let her stay on after that and spoil the effect? Oh no; I took my lovely little Capri girl—my capricious little Capri girl, I should say—took her under my arm; one quick tour of the ballroom, a nod to one and all, and then—as they say in novels—the beautiful vision disappeared. An exit should always be effective, Mrs. Linde, but that's what I can't get Nora to grasp. Phew, it's hot in here. (*Flings the domino on a chair and opens the door to his room.*) Why's it dark in here? Oh yes, of course. Excuse me. (*He goes in and lights a couple of candles.*)

NORA (*in a sharp, breathless whisper*). So?

MRS. LINDE (*quietly*). I talked with him.

NORA. And—?

MRS. LINDE. Nora—you must tell your husband everything.

NORA (*dully*). I knew it.

MRS. LINDE. You've got nothing to fear from Krogstad, but you have to speak out.

NORA. I won't.

MRS. LINDE. Then the letter will.

NORA. Thanks, Kristine. I know now what's to be done. Shh!

HELMER (*reentering*). Well, then, Mrs. Linde—have you admired her?

MRS. LINDE. Yes, and now I'll say good night.

HELMER. Oh, come, so soon? Is this yours, this knitting?

MRS. LINDE. Yes, thanks. I nearly forgot it.

HELMER. Do you knit, then?

MRS. LINDE. Oh yes.

HELMER. You know what? You should embroider instead.

MRS. LINDE. Really? Why?

HELMER. Yes, because it's a lot prettier. See here, one holds the embroidery so, in the left hand, and then one guides the needle with the right—so—in an easy, sweeping curve—right?

MRS. LINDE. Yes, I guess that's—

HELMER. But, on the other hand, knitting—it can never be anything but ugly. Look, see here, the arms tucked in, the knitting needles going up and down—there's something Chinese about it. Ah, that was really a glorious champagne they served.

MRS. LINDE.   Yes, good night, Nora, and don't be stubborn anymore.

HELMER.   Well put, Mrs. Linde!

MRS. LINDE.   Good night, Mr. Helmer.

HELMER (*accompanying her to the door*).   Good night, good night. I hope you get home all right. I'd be very happy to—but you don't have far to go. Good night, good night. (*She leaves. He shuts the door after her and returns.*) There, now, at last we got her out the door. She's a deadly bore, that creature.

NORA.   Aren't you pretty tired, Torvald?

HELMER.   No, not a bit.

NORA.   You're not sleepy?

HELMER.   Not at all. On the contrary, I'm feeling quite exhilarated. But you? Yes, you really look tired and sleepy.

NORA.   Yes, I'm very tired. Soon now I'll sleep.

HELMER.   See! You see! I was right all along that we shouldn't stay longer.

NORA.   Whatever you do is always right.

HELMER (*kissing her brow*).   Now my little lark's talking like a human being. But did you notice how lively Rank was tonight?

NORA.   Oh, was he? I didn't get to speak with him.

HELMER.   I scarcely did either, but it's a long time since I've seen him in such high spirits. (*Gazes at her a moment, then comes nearer her.*) Hm—it's marvelous, though, to be back home again—to be completely alone with you. Oh, you bewitchingly lovely young woman!

NORA.   Torvald, don't look at me like that!

HELMER.   Why shouldn't I look at my dearest possession? At all that loveliness that's mine, mine alone, completely mine?

NORA (*moving around to the other side of the table*). You mustn't talk to me that way tonight.

HELMER (*following her*).   The tarantella is still in your blood, I can see—and it makes you even more enticing. Listen. The guests are beginning to go. (*Dropping his voice.*) Nora—it'll soon be quiet through this whole house.

NORA.   Yes, I hope so.

HELMER.   You do, don't you, my love? Do you realize—when I'm out at a party like this with you—do you know why I talk to you so little, and keep such a distance away; just send you a stolen look now and then—you know why I do it? It's because I'm imagining then that you're my secret darling, my secret young bride-to-be, and that no one suspects there's anything between us.

NORA.   Yes, yes; oh, yes, I know you're always thinking of me.

HELMER.   And then when we leave and I place the shawl over those fine young rounded shoulders—over that wonderful curving neck—then I pretend that you're my young bride, that we're just coming from the wedding, that for the first time I'm bringing you into my house—that for the first time I'm alone with you—completely alone with you, your trembling young beauty! All this evening I've longed for nothing but you. When I saw you turn and sway in the tarantella—my blood was pounding till I couldn't stand it—that's why I brought you down here so early—

NORA.   Go away, Torvald! Leave me alone. I don't want all this.

HELMER.   What do you mean? Nora, you're teasing me. You will, won't you? Aren't I your husband—?

(*A knock at the outside door.*)

NORA (*startled*).   What's that?

HELMER (*going toward the hall*).   Who is it?

RANK (*outside*).   It's me. May I come in a moment?

HELMER (*with quiet irritation*).   Oh, what does he want now? (*Aloud.*) Hold on. (*Goes and opens the door.*) Oh, how nice that you didn't just pass us by!

RANK.   I thought I heard your voice, and then I wanted so badly to have a look in. (*Lightly glancing about.*) Ah, me, these old familiar haunts. You have it snug and cozy in here, you two.

HELMER.   You seemed to be having it pretty cozy upstairs, too.

RANK.   Absolutely. Why shouldn't I? Why not take in everything in life? As much as you can, anyway, and as long as you can. The wine was superb—

HELMER.   The champagne especially.

RANK.   You noticed that too? It's amazing how much I could guzzle down.

NORA.   Torvald also drank a lot of champagne this evening.

RANK.   Oh?

NORA.   Yes, and that always makes him so entertaining.

RANK.   Well, why shouldn't one have a lively evening after a well-spent day?

HELMER.   Well spent? I'm afraid I can't claim that.

RANK (*slapping him on the back*).   But I can, you see!

NORA.   Dr. Rank, you must have done some scientific research today.

RANK.   Quite so.

HELMER.   Come now—little Nora talking about scientific research!

NORA.   And can I congratulate you on the results?

RANK.   Indeed you may.

NORA.   Then they were good?

RANK.   The best possible for both doctor and patient— certainty.

NORA (*quickly and searchingly*).   Certainty?

RANK.   Complete certainty. So don't I owe myself a lively evening afterwards?

NORA.   Yes, you're right, Dr. Rank.

HELMER.   I'm with you—just so long as you don't have to suffer for it in the morning.

RANK.   Well, one never gets something for nothing in life.

NORA.   Dr. Rank—are you very fond of masquerade parties?

RANK.   Yes, if there's a good array of odd disguises—

NORA.   Tell me, what should we two go as at the next masquerade?

HELMER.   You little featherhead—already thinking of the next!

RANK.   We two? I'll tell you what: you must go as Charmed Life—

HELMER.   Yes, but find a costume for *that*!

RANK.   Your wife can appear just as she looks every day.

HELMER.   That was nicely put. But don't you know what you're going to be?

RANK.   Yes, Helmer, I've made up my mind.

HELMER.   Well?

RANK.   At the next masquerade I'm going to be invisible.

HELMER.   That's a funny idea.

RANK.   They say there's a hat—black, huge—have you never heard of the hat that makes you invisible? You put it on, and then no one on earth can see you.

HELMER (*suppressing a smile*).   Ah, of course.

RANK.   But I'm quite forgetting what I came for. Helmer, give me a cigar, one of the dark Havanas.

HELMER.   With the greatest pleasure. (*Holds out his case.*)

RANK.   Thanks. (*Takes one and cuts off the tip.*)

NORA (*striking a match*).   Let me give you a light.

RANK.   Thank you. (*She holds the match for him; he lights the cigar.*) And now good-bye.

HELMER.   Good-bye, good-bye, old friend.

NORA.   Sleep well, Doctor.

RANK.   Thanks for that wish.

NORA.   Wish me the same.

RANK.   You? All right, if you like— Sleep well. And thanks for the light. (*He nods to them both and leaves.*)

HELMER (*his voice subdued*).   He's been drinking heavily.

NORA (*absently*).   Could be. (HELMER *takes his keys from his pocket and goes out in the hall.*) Torvald—what are you after?

HELMER.   Got to empty the mailbox; it's nearly full. There won't be room for the morning papers.

NORA.   Are you working tonight?

HELMER.   You know I'm not. Why—what's this? Someone's been at the lock.

NORA.   At the lock—?

HELMER.   Yes, I'm positive. What do you suppose—? I can't imagine one of the maids—? Here's a broken hairpin. Nora, it's yours—

NORA (*quickly*).   Then it must be the children—

HELMER.   You'd better break them of that. Hm, hm— well, opened it after all. (*Takes the contents out and calls into the kitchen.*) Helene! Helene, would you put out the lamp in the hall. (*He returns to the room, shutting the hall door, then displays the handful of mail.*) Look how it's piled up. (*Sorting it through.*) Now what's this?

NORA (*at the window*).   The letter! Oh, Torvald, no!

HELMER.   Two calling cards—from Rank.

NORA. From Dr. Rank?

HELMER (*examining them*). "Dr. Rank, Consulting Physician." They were on top. He must have dropped them in as he left.

NORA. Is there anything on them?

HELMER. There's a black cross over the name. See? That's a gruesome notion. He could almost be announcing his own death.

NORA. That's just what he's doing.

HELMER. What! You've heard something? Something he's told you?

NORA. Yes. That when those cards came, he'd be taking his leave of us. He'll shut himself in now and die.

HELMER. Ah, my poor friend! Of course I knew he wouldn't be here much longer. But so soon— And then to hide himself away like a wounded animal.

NORA. If it has to happen, then it's best it happens in silence—don't you think so, Torvald?

HELMER (*pacing up and down*). He'd grown right into our lives. I simply can't imagine him gone. He with his suffering and loneliness—like a dark cloud setting off our sunlit happiness. Well, maybe it's best this way. For him, at least. (*Standing still.*) And maybe for us too, Nora. Now we're thrown back on each other, completely. (*Embracing her.*) Oh you, my darling wife, how can I hold you close enough? You know what, Nora—time and again I've wished you were in some terrible danger, just so I could stake my life and soul and everything, for your sake.

NORA (*tearing herself away, her voice firm and decisive*). Now you must read your mail, Torvald.

HELMER. No, no, not tonight. I want to stay with you, dearest.

NORA. With a dying friend on your mind?

HELMER. You're right. We've both had a shock. There's ugliness between us—these thoughts of death and corruption. We'll have to get free of them first. Until then—we'll stay apart.

NORA (*clinging about his neck*). Torvald—good night! Good night!

HELMER (*kissing her on the forehead*). Good night, little songbird. Sleep well, Nora. I'll be reading my mail now. (*He takes the letters into his room and shuts the door after him.*)

NORA (*with bewildered glances, groping about, seizing* HELMER's *domino, throwing it around her, and speaking in short, hoarse, broken whispers*). Never see him again. Never, never. (*Putting her shawl over her head.*) Never see the children either—them, too. Never, never. Oh, the freezing black water! The depths—down— Oh, I wish it were over— He has it now; he's reading it—now. Oh no, no, not yet. Torvald, good-bye, you and the children— (*She starts for the hall; as she does,* HELMER *throws open his door and stands with an open letter in his hand.*)

HELMER.   Nora!

NORA (*screams*).   Oh—!

HELMER.   What is this? You know what's in this letter?

NORA.   Yes, I know. Let me go! Let me out!

HELMER (*holding her back*).   Where are you going?

NORA (*struggling to break loose*).   Don't try and save me, Torvald!

HELMER (*totters back*).   True! Then it's true what he writes? How horrible! No, no, it's impossible—it can't be true.

NORA.   It *is* true. I've loved you more than all this world.

HELMER.   Ah, none of your slippery tricks.

NORA (*taking one step toward him*).   Torvald—!

HELMER.   What *is* this you've blundered into!

NORA.   Just let me loose. You're not going to suffer for my sake. You're not going to take on my guilt.

HELMER.   No more playacting. (*Locks the hall door.*) You stay right here and give me a reckoning. You understand what you've done? Answer! You understand?

NORA (*looking squarely at him, her face hardening*). Yes. I'm beginning to understand everything now.

HELMER (*striding about*).   Oh, what an awful awakening! In all these eight years—she who was my pride and joy—a hypocrite, a liar—worse, worse—a criminal! How infinitely disgusting it all is! The shame! (NORA *says nothing and goes on looking straight at him. He stops in front of her.*) I should have suspected something of the kind. I should have known. All your father's flimsy values— Be still! All your father's flimsy values have come out in you. No religion, no morals, no sense of duty— Oh, how I'm punished for letting him off! I did it for your sake, and you repay me like this.

NORA.   Yes, like this.

HELMER. Now you've wrecked all my happiness—ruined my whole future. Oh, it's awful to think of. I'm in the hands of a totally unscrupulous man; he can do anything he wants with me, ask for anything, play with me like a puppet—and I can't breathe a word. I'll be swept down miserably into the depths on account of a featherbrained woman.

NORA. When I'm gone from this world, you'll be free.

HELMER. Oh, quit posing. Your father had a mess of those speeches too. What good would that ever do me if you were gone from this world, as you say? Not the slightest. He can still make the whole thing known; and if he does, I could be falsely suspected as your accomplice. They might even think that I was behind it—that I put you up to it. And all that I can thank you for—you that I've coddled the whole of our marriage. Can you see now what you've done to me?

NORA (*icily calm*). Yes.

HELMER. It's so incredible, I just can't grasp it. But we'll have to try and put things to rights. Take off the shawl. I said, take it off! I've got to appease him somehow or other. The thing has to be hushed up at any cost. And as for you and me, it's got to seem like everything between us is just as it was—to the outside world, that is. You'll go right on living in this house, of course. But you can't be allowed to bring up the children; I don't dare trust you with them— Oh, to have to say this to someone I've loved so much, and that I still—! Well, that's done with. From now on happiness doesn't matter; all that matters is saving the bits and pieces, the appearance—(*The doorbell rings.* HELMER *starts.*) What's that? And so late. Maybe the worst—? You think he'd—? Hide, Nora! Say you're sick. (NORA *remains standing motionless.* HELMER *goes and opens the door.*)

MAID (*half dressed, in the hall*). A letter for Mrs. Helmer.

HELMER. I'll take it. (*Snatches the letter and shuts the door.*) Yes, it's from him. You don't get it; I'm reading it myself.

NORA. Then read it.

HELMER (*by the lamp*). I hardly dare. We may be ruined, you and I. But—I've got to know. (*Rips open the letter, skims through a few lines, glances at an enclosure, then cries out joyfully.*) Nora! (NORA *looks inquiringly at him.*) Nora! Wait—better check it again— Yes, yes, it's true. I'm saved. Nora, I'm saved!

NORA. And I?

HELMER. You too, of course. We're both saved, both of us. Look. He's sent back your note. He says he's sorry and ashamed—that a happy development in his life—oh, who cares what he says! Nora, we're saved! No one can hurt you. Oh, Nora, Nora—but first, this ugliness all has to go. Let me see—(*Takes a look at the note.*) No, I don't want to see it; I want the whole thing to fade like a dream. (*Tears the note and both letters to pieces, throws them into the stove and watches them burn.*) There—now there's nothing left— He wrote that since Christmas Eve you— Oh, they must have been three terrible days for you, Nora.

NORA. I fought a hard fight in those three days.

HELMER. And suffered pain and saw no escape but— No, we're not going to dwell on anything unpleasant. We'll just be grateful and keep on repeating: it's over now, it's over! You hear me, Nora? You don't seem to realize—it's over. What's it mean—that frozen look? Oh, poor little Nora, I understand. You can't believe I've forgiven you. But I have, Nora; I swear I have. I know that what you did, you did out of love for me.

NORA. That's true.

HELMER. You loved me the way a wife ought to love her husband. It's simply the means that you couldn't judge. But you think I love you any the less for not knowing how to handle your affairs? No, no—just lean on me; I'll guide you and teach you. I wouldn't be a man if this feminine helplessness didn't make you twice as attractive to me. You mustn't mind those sharp words I said—that was all in the first confusion of thinking my world had collapsed. I've forgiven you, Nora; I swear I've forgiven you.

NORA. My thanks for your forgiveness. (*She goes out through the door, right.*)

HELMER. No, wait— (*Peers in.*) What are you doing in there?

NORA (*inside*). Getting out of my costume.

HELMER (*by the open door*). Yes, do that. Try to calm yourself and collect your thoughts again, my frightened little songbird. You can rest easy now; I've got wide wings to shelter you with. (*Walking about close by the door.*) How snug and nice our home is, Nora. You're safe here; I'll keep you like a hunted dove I've rescued out of a hawk's claws. I'll bring peace to your poor, shuddering heart. Gradually it'll happen, Nora; you'll see. Tomorrow all this will look different to you; then everything will be as it was. I won't have to go on repeating I forgive you; you'll feel it for yourself. How can you imagine I'd ever conceivably want to disown you—or even blame you in any way? Ah, you don't know a man's heart, Nora. For a man there's something indescribably sweet and satisfying in knowing he's forgiven his wife—and forgiven her out of a full and open heart. It's as if she belongs to him in two ways now: in a sense he's given her fresh into the world again, and she's become his wife and his child as well. From now on that's what you'll be to me—you little, bewildered, helpless thing. Don't be afraid of anything, Nora; just open your heart to me, and I'll be conscience and will to you both—(NORA *enters in her regular clothes.*) What's this? Not in bed? You've changed your dress?

NORA.   Yes, Torvald, I've changed my dress.

HELMER.   But why now, so late?

NORA.   Tonight I'm not sleeping.

HELMER.   But Nora dear—

NORA (*looking at her watch*). It's still not so very late. Sit down, Torvald; we have a lot to talk over. (*She sits at one side of the table.*)

HELMER.   Nora—what is this? That hard expression—

NORA.   Sit down. This'll take some time. I have a lot to say.

HELMER (*sitting at the table directly opposite her*).   You worry me, Nora. And I don't understand you.

NORA.   No, that's exactly it. You don't understand me. And I've never understood you either—until tonight. No, don't interrupt. You can just listen to what I say. We're closing out accounts, Torvald.

HELMER.   How do you mean that?

NORA (*after a short pause*).   Doesn't anything strike you about our sitting here like this?

HELMER.   What's that?

NORA.   We've been married now eight years. Doesn't it

occur to you that this is the first time we two, you and I, man and wife, have ever talked seriously together?

HELMER. What do you mean—seriously?

NORA. In eight whole years—longer even—right from our first acquaintance, we've never exchanged a serious word on any serious thing.

HELMER. You mean I should constantly go and involve you in problems you couldn't possibly help me with?

NORA. I'm not talking of problems. I'm saying that we've never sat down seriously together and tried to get to the bottom of anything.

HELMER. But dearest, what good would that ever do you?

NORA. That's the point right there: you've never understood me. I've been wronged greatly, Torvald—first by Papa, and then by you.

HELMER. What! By us—the two people who've loved you more than anyone else?

NORA (*shaking her head*). You never loved me. You've thought it fun to be in love with me, that's all.

HELMER. Nora, what a thing to say!

NORA. Yes, it's true now, Torvald. When I lived at home with Papa, he told me all his opinions, so I had the same ones too; or if they were different I hid them, since he wouldn't have cared for that. He used to call me his doll-child, and he played with me the way I played with my dolls. Then I came into your house—

HELMER. How can you speak of our marriage like that?

NORA (*unperturbed*). I mean, then I went from Papa's hands into yours. You arranged everything to your own taste, and so I got the same taste as you—or I pretended to; I can't remember. I guess a little of both, first one, then the other. Now when I look back, it seems as if I'd lived here like a beggar—just from hand to mouth. I've lived by doing tricks for you, Torvald. But that's the way you wanted it. It's a great sin what you and Papa did to me. You're to blame that nothing's become of me.

HELMER. Nora, how unfair and ungrateful you are! Haven't you been happy here?

NORA. No, never. I thought so—but I never have.

HELMER. Not—not happy!

NORA. No, only lighthearted. And you've always been so kind to me. But our home's been nothing but a playpen.

I've been your doll-wife here, just as at home I was Papa's doll-child. And in turn the children have been my dolls. I thought it was fun when you played with me, just as they thought it fun when I played with them. That's been our marriage, Torvald.

HELMER.   There's some truth in what you're saying—under all the raving exaggeration. But it'll all be different after this. Playtime's over; now for the schooling.

NORA.   Whose schooling—mine or the children's?

HELMER.   Both yours and the children's, dearest.

NORA.   Oh, Torvald, you're not the man to teach me to be a good wife to you.

HELMER.   And you can say that?

NORA.   And I—how am I equipped to bring up children?

HELMER.   Nora!

NORA.   Didn't you say a moment ago that that was no job to trust me with?

HELMER.   In a flare of temper! Why fasten on that?

NORA.   Yes, but you were so very right. I'm not up to the job. There's another job I have to do first. I have to try to educate myself. You can't help me with that. I've got to do it alone. And that's why I'm leaving you now.

HELMER (*jumping up*).   What's that?

NORA.   I have to stand completely alone, if I'm ever going to discover myself and the world out there. So I can't go on living with you.

HELMER.   Nora, Nora!

NORA.   I want to leave right away. Kristine should put me up for the night—

HELMER.   You're insane! You've no right! I forbid you!

NORA.   From here on, there's no use forbidding me anything. I'll take with me whatever is mine. I don't want a thing from you, either now or later.

HELMER.   What kind of madness is this!

NORA.   Tomorrow I'm going home—I mean, home where I came from. It'll be easier up there to find something to do.

HELMER.   Oh, you blind, incompetent child!

NORA.   I must learn to be competent, Torvald.

HELMER.   Abandon your home, your husband, your children! And you're not even thinking what people will say.

NORA.   I can't be concerned about that. I only know how essential this is.

HELMER. Oh, it's outrageous. So you'll run out like this on your most sacred duties.

NORA. What do you think are my most sacred duties?

HELMER. And I have to tell you that! Aren't they your duties to your husband and children?

NORA. I have other duties equally sacred.

HELMER. That isn't true. What duties are they?

NORA. Duties to myself.

HELMER. Before all else, you're a wife and a mother.

NORA. I don't believe in that anymore. I believe that, before all else, I'm a human being, no less than you—or anyway, I ought to try to become one. I know the majority thinks you're right, Torvald, and plenty of books agree with you, too. But I can't go on being satisfied with what the majority says, or what's written in books. I have to think over these things myself and try to understand them.

HELMER. Why can't you understand your place in your own home? On a point like that, isn't there one infallible guide? Where's your religion?

NORA. Oh, Torvald, I'm really not sure what religion is.

HELMER. What are you saying?

NORA. I only know what the minister said when I was confirmed. He said religion consisted of *this* and *that*. When I get free of my life here and on my own, I'll go into that problem too. I'll see if what the minister said was right, or, in any case, if it's right for me.

HELMER. A young woman your age shouldn't talk like that. If religion can't guide you, I can try to rouse your conscience. You do have some moral feeling? Or, tell me— has that gone too?

NORA. It's not easy to answer that, Torvald. I simply don't know. I'm all confused about these things. I just know I see them so differently from you. I find out, for one thing, that the law's not at all what I'd thought—but I can't get it through my head that the law is fair. A woman hasn't a right to protect her dying father or save her husband's life! I can't believe that.

HELMER. You talk like a child. You don't know anything of the world you live in.

NORA. No, I don't. But now I'll begin to learn for myself. I'll try to discover who's right, the world or I.

HELMER.   Nora, you're sick; you've got a fever. I almost think you're out of your head.

NORA.   I've never felt more clearheaded and sure in my life.

HELMER.   And—clearheaded and sure—you're leaving your husband and children?

NORA.   Yes.

HELMER.   Then there's only one possible reason.

NORA.   What?

HELMER.   You no longer love me.

NORA.   No. That's exactly it.

HELMER.   Nora! You can't be serious!

NORA.   Oh, this is so hard, Torvald—you've been so kind to me always. But I can't help it. I don't love you anymore.

HELMER (*struggling for composure*).   Are you also clearheaded and sure about that?

NORA.   Yes, completely. That's why I can't go on staying here.

HELMER.   Can you tell me what I did to lose your love?

NORA.   Yes, I can tell you. It was this evening when the miraculous thing didn't come—then I knew you weren't the man I'd imagined.

HELMER.   Be more explicit; I don't follow you.

NORA.   I've waited now so patiently eight long years—for, my Lord, I know miracles don't come every day. Then this crisis broke over me, and such a certainty filled me: *now* the miraculous event would occur. While Krogstad's letter was lying out there, I never for an instant dreamed that you could give in to his terms. I was so utterly sure you'd say to him: go on, tell your tale to the whole wide world. And when he'd done that—

HELMER.   Yes, what then? When I'd delivered my own wife into shame and disgrace—!

NORA.   When he'd done that, I was so utterly sure that you'd step forward, take the blame on yourself and say: I am the guilty one.

HELMER.   Nora—!

NORA.   You're thinking I'd never accept such a sacrifice from you? No, of course not. But what good would my protests be against you? That was the miracle I was waiting for, in terror and hope. And to stave that off, I would have taken my life.

HELMER.   I'd gladly work for you day and night, Nora—
and take on pain and deprivation. But there's no one who
gives up honor for love.

NORA.   Millions of women have done just that.

HELMER.   Oh, you think and talk like a silly child.

NORA.   Perhaps. But you neither think nor talk like the
man I could join myself to. When your big fright was over—
and it wasn't from any threat against me, only for what
might damage you—when all the danger was past, for you
it was just as if nothing had happened. I was exactly the
same, your little lark, your doll, that you'd have to handle
with double care now that I'd turned out so brittle and frail.
(*Gets up.*) Torvald—in that instant it dawned on me that
for eight years I've been living here with a stranger, and
that I'd even conceived three children—oh, I can't stand the
thought of it! I could tear myself to bits.

HELMER (*heavily*).   I see. There's a gulf that's opened
between us—that's clear. Oh, but Nora, can't we bridge it
somehow?

NORA.   The way I am now, I'm no wife for you.

HELMER.   I have the strength to make myself over.

NORA.   Maybe—if your doll gets taken away.

HELMER.   But to part! To part from you! No, Nora, no—
I can't imagine it.

NORA (*going out, right.*)   All the more reason why it has
to be. (*She reenters with her coat and a small overnight bag,
which she puts on a chair by the table.*)

HELMER.   Nora, Nora, not now! Wait till tomorrow.

NORA (*putting on her coat*).   I can't spend the night in a
strange man's room.

HELMER.   But couldn't we live here like brother and
sister—

NORA (*ties her hat on*).   You know very well how long
that would last. (*Throws her shawl about her.*) Good-bye,
Torvald. I won't look in on the children. I know they're in
better hands than mine. The way I am now, I'm no use to
them.

HELMER.   But someday, Nora—someday—?

NORA.   How can I tell? I haven't the least idea what'll
become of me.

HELMER.   But you're my wife; you are and you always
will be.

NORA. Listen, Torvald—I've heard that when a wife deserts her husband's house just as I'm doing, then the law frees him from all responsibility. In any case, I'm freeing you from being responsible. Don't feel yourself bound, any more than I will. There has to be absolute freedom for us both. Here, take your ring back. Give me mine.

HELMER. That too?

NORA. That too.

HELMER. There it is.

NORA. Good. Well, now it's all over. I'm putting the keys here. The maids know all about keeping up the house—better than I do. Tomorrow, after I've left town, Kristine will stop by to pack up everything that's mine from home. I'd like those things shipped up to me.

HELMER. Over! All over! Nora, won't you ever think about me?

NORA. I'm sure I'll think of you often, and about the children and the house here.

HELMER. May I write you?

NORA. No—never. You're not to do that.

HELMER. Oh, but let me send you—

NORA. Nothing. Nothing.

HELMER. Or help you if you need it.

NORA. No. I accept nothing from strangers.

HELMER. Nora—can I never be more than a stranger to you?

NORA (picking up the overnight bag). Ah, Torvald—it would take the greatest miracle of all—

HELMER. Tell me the greatest miracle!

NORA. You and I both would have to transform ourselves to the point that— Oh, Torvald, I've stopped believing in miracles.

HELMER. But I'll believe. Tell me! Transform ourselves to the point that—?

NORA. That our living together could be a true marriage. (She goes out down the hall.)

HELMER (sinks down on a chair by the door, face buried in his hands). Nora! Nora! (Looking about and rising.) Empty. She's gone. (A sudden hope leaps in him.) The greatest miracle—?

(From below, the sound of a door slamming shut.)

THE WILD DUCK

THE CHARACTERS

HAAKON WERLE, wholesale merchant and millowner
GREGERS WERLE, his son
OLD EKDAL
HJALMAR EKDAL, his son, a photographer
GINA EKDAL, Hjalmar's wife
HEDVIG, their daughter, aged fourteen
MRS. SØRBY, housekeeper for the elder Werle
RELLING, a doctor
MOLVIK, a former divinity student
GRAABERG, a bookkeeper
PETTERSEN, manservant to the elder Werle
JENSEN, a hired waiter
A FAT MAN
A BALD-HEADED MAN
A NEARSIGHTED MAN
SIX OTHER MEN, dinner guests at Werle's
OTHER HIRED SERVANTS

The first act takes place in WERLE's *house; the following four acts in* HJALMAR EKDAL's *studio.*

ACT ONE

At WERLE's *house. A richly and comfortably furnished study, with bookcases and upholstered furniture, a writing table, with papers and reports, in the middle of the floor, and green-shaded lamps softly illuminating the room. In the rear wall, open folding doors with curtains drawn back disclose a large, fashionable room, brightly lit by lamps and candelabra. In the right foreground of the study, a small private door leads to the offices. In the left foreground, a fireplace filled with glowing coals, and further back a double door to the dining room.*

WERLE's *manservant,* PETTERSEN, *in livery, and* JENSEN, *a hired waiter, in black, are straightening up the study. In the larger room two or three other hired waiters are moving about, putting things in order and lighting more candles. In from the dining room come laughter and the hum of many voices in conversation; a knife clinks upon a glass; silence; a toast is made; cries of "Bravo," and the hum of conversation resumes.*

PETTERSEN (*lighting a lamp by the fireplace and putting on the shade*). Ah, you hear that, Jensen. Now the old boy's up on his feet, proposing a long toast to Mrs. Sørby.

JENSEN (*moving an armchair forward*). Is it really true what people say, that there's something between them?

PETTERSEN. Lord knows.

JENSEN. I've heard he was a real goat in his day.

PETTERSEN. Could be.

JENSEN. But they say it's his son he's throwing this party for.

PETTERSEN. Yes. His son came home yesterday.

JENSEN. I never knew before that old Werle had any son.

PETTERSEN. Oh yes, he's got a son. But he spends all his time up at the works in Hoidal. He hasn't been in town all the years I've served in this house.

A HIRED WAITER (*in the door to the other room*). Say, Pettersen, there's an old guy here who—

PETTERSEN (*muttering*). What the hell—somebody coming now!

> (*Old* EKDAL *appears from the right through the inner room. He is dressed in a shabby overcoat with a high collar, woollen gloves, and in his hand, a cane and a fur cap; under his arm is a bundle wrapped in brown paper. He has a dirty, reddish-brown wig and a little gray moustache.*)

PETTERSEN (*going toward him*). Good Lord, what do *you* want in here?

EKDAL (*at the door*). Just have to get into the office, Pettersen.

PETTERSEN. The office closed an hour ago, and—

EKDAL. Heard that one at the door, boy. But Graaberg's still in there. Be nice, Pettersen, and let me slip in that way. (*Pointing toward the private entrance.*) I've gone that way before.

PETTERSEN. All right, go ahead, then. (*Opens the door.*) But don't forget now—take the regular way out; we have guests.

EKDAL. Got you—hmm! Thanks, Pettersen, good old pal! Thanks. (*To himself.*) Bonehead! (*He goes into the office;* PETTERSEN *shuts the door after him.*)

JENSEN. Is *he* on the office staff too?

PETTERSEN. No, he's just someone who does copying on the outside when it's needed. Still, in his time he was well up in the world, old Ekdal.

JENSEN. Yes, he looks like he's been a little of everything.

PETTERSEN. Oh yes. He was a lieutenant once, if you can imagine.

JENSEN. Go on—him a lieutenant!

PETTERSEN. So help me, he was. But then he went into the lumber business or something. They say he must have pulled some kind of dirty deal on the old man once, for the two of them were running the Hoidal works together then. Oh, I know good old Ekdal, all right. We've drunk many a schnapps and bottle of beer together over at Eriksen's.

JENSEN. He can't have much money for standing drinks.

PETTERSEN. My Lord, Jensen, you can bet it's me that

stands the drinks. I always say a person ought to act refined toward quality that's come down in life.

JENSEN.   Did he go bankrupt, then?

PETTERSEN.   No, worse than that. He was sent to jail.

JENSEN.   To jail!

PETTERSEN.   Or maybe it was the penitentiary. (*Listens.*) Hist! They're leaving the table.

> (*The dining room door is opened by a pair of servants inside.* MRS. SØRBY, *in conversation with two gentlemen, comes out. A moment later the rest of the guests follow, among them* WERLE. *Last of all come* HJALMAR EKDAL *and* GREGERS WERLE.)

MRS. SØRBY (*to the servant, in passing*).   Pettersen, will you have coffee served in the music room.

PETTERSEN.   Yes, Mrs. Sørby.

> (*She and the two gentlemen go into the inner room and exit to the right.* PETTERSEN *and* JENSEN *leave in the same way.*)

A FAT GUEST (*to a balding man*).   Phew! That dinner— that was a steep bit of work!

THE BALD-HEADED GUEST.   Oh, with a little good will a man can do wonders in three hours.

THE FAT GUEST.   Yes, but afterward, my dear fellow, afterward.

A THIRD GUEST.   I hear we can sample coffee and liqueur in the music room.

THE FAT GUEST.   Fine! Then perhaps Mrs. Sørby will play us a piece.

THE BALD-HEADED GUEST (*in an undertone*).   Just so Mrs. Sørby doesn't play us to pieces.

THE FAT GUEST.   Oh, now really, Berta wouldn't punish her old friends, would she? (*They laugh and enter the inner room.*)

WERLE (*in a low, depressed tone*).   I don't think anyone noticed it, Gregers.

GREGERS.   What?

WERLE.   Didn't you notice it either?

GREGERS.   What should I have noticed?

WERLE.   We were thirteen at the table.

GREGERS. Really? Were we thirteen?

WERLE (*with a glance at* HJALMAR EKDAL). Yes—our usual number is twelve. (*To the others.*) Be so kind, gentlemen.

(*He and those remaining, excepting* HJALMAR
and GREGERS, *go out to the rear and right.*)

HJALMAR (*who has heard the conversation*). You shouldn't have sent me the invitation, Gregers.

GREGERS. What! The party's supposed to be for *me*. And then I'm not supposed to have my best and only friend—

HJALMAR. But I don't think your father likes it. Ordinarily I never come to this house.

GREGERS. So I hear. But I had to see you and talk with you, for I'm sure to be leaving soon again. Yes, we two old classmates, we've certainly drifted a long way apart. You know, we haven't seen each other now in sixteen—seventeen years.

HJALMAR. Has it been so long?

GREGERS. Yes, all of that. Well, how have you been? You look well. You're almost becoming stout.

HJALMAR. Hm, stout is hardly the word, though I probably look more of a man than I did then.

GREGERS. Yes, you do. The outer man hasn't suffered.

HJALMAR (*in a gloomier tone*). Ah, but the inner man! Believe me, he has a different look. You know, of course, what misery we've been through, I and my family, since the last time the two of us met.

GREGERS (*dropping his voice*). How's it going for your father now?

HJALMAR. Oh, Gregers, let's not talk about that. My poor, unhappy father naturally lives at home with me. He's got no one else in the whole world to turn to. But this all is so terribly hard for me to talk about, you know. Tell me, instead, how you've found life up at the mill.

GREGERS. Marvelously solitary, that's what—with a good chance to mull over a great many things. Come on, let's be comfortable.

(*He sits in an armchair by the fire and urges*
HJALMAR *down into another by its side.*)

HJALMAR (*softly*). In any case, I'm grateful that you asked me here, Gregers, because it proves you no longer have anything against me.

GREGERS (*astonished*). How could you think that I had anything against you?

HJALMAR. In those first years you did.

GREGERS. Which first years?

HJALMAR. Right after that awful misfortune. And it was only natural you should. It was just by a hair that your own father escaped being dragged into this—oh, this ugly business.

GREGERS. And that's why I had it in for you? Whoever gave you that idea?

HJALMAR. I know you did, Gregers; it was your father himself who told me.

GREGERS (*startled*). Father! I see. Hm—is that why I never heard from you—not a single word?

HJALMAR. Yes.

GREGERS. Not even when you went out and became a photographer.

HJALMAR. Your father said it wasn't worth my writing you—about anything at all.

GREGERS (*looking straight ahead*). No, no, maybe he was right there— But tell me, Hjalmar—do you find yourself reasonably content with things as they are?

HJALMAR (*with a small sigh*). Oh, I suppose I do. What else can I say? At first, you can imagine, it was all rather strange for me. They were such very different circumstances I found myself in. But then everything else was so different, too. That immense, shattering misfortune for Father—the shame and the scandal, Gregers—

GREGERS (*shaken*). Yes, yes. Of course.

HJALMAR. I couldn't dream of going on with my studies; there wasn't a penny to spare. On the contrary, debts instead—mainly to your father, I think—

GREGERS. Hm—

HJALMAR. Anyway, I thought it was best to make a clean break—and cut all the old connections. It was your father especially who advised me to; and since he'd been so helpful to me—

GREGERS. He had?

HJALMAR. Yes, you knew that, didn't you? Where could

I get the money to learn photography and fit out a studio and establish myself? I can tell you, that all adds up.

GREGERS.   And all that Father paid for?

HJALMAR.   Yes, Gregers, didn't you know? I understood him to say that he'd written you about it.

GREGERS.   Not a word saying *he* was the one. Maybe he forgot. We've never exchanged anything but business letters. So that was Father, too—!

HJALMAR.   That's right. He never wanted people to know, but he was the one. And he was also the one who put me in a position to get married. Or perhaps—didn't you know that either?

GREGERS.   No, not at all. (*Gripping his arm.*) But Hjalmar, I can't tell you how all this delights me—and disturbs me. Perhaps I've been unfair to my father—in certain ways. Yes, for all this does show good-heartedness, doesn't it? It's almost a kind of conscience—

HJALMAR.   Conscience?

GREGERS.   Yes, or whatever you want to call it. No, I can't tell you how glad I am to hear this about my father. So you're married, then, Hjalmar. That's further than I'll ever go. Well, I hope you're happy as a married man?

HJALMAR.   Oh, absolutely. She's as capable and fine a wife as any man could wish for. And she's not entirely without culture, either.

GREGERS (*a bit surprised*).   No, I'm sure she's not.

HJALMAR.   No. Life is a teacher, you see. Associating with me every day—and then there are one or two gifted people who visit us regularly. I can tell you, you wouldn't recognize Gina now.

GREGERS.   Gina?

HJALMAR.   Yes, Gregers, had you forgotten her name is Gina?

GREGERS.   Whose name is Gina? I haven't the faintest idea—

HJALMAR.   But don't you remember, she was here in this very house a while—in service?

GREGERS (*looking at him*).   You mean Gina Hansen—?

HJALMAR.   Yes, of course. Gina Hansen.

GREGERS.   Who was housekeeper for us that last year of Mother's illness?

HJALMAR. Exactly. But my dear Gregers, I know for sure that your father wrote you about my marriage.

GREGERS (*who has gotten up*). Yes, of course he did. But not that— (*Walks about the floor.*) Yes, wait a minute— it may well be, now that I think of it. My father's letters are always so brief. (*Sits on chair arm.*) Listen, tell me, Hjalmar—this is interesting—how did you come to know Gina?—your wife, I mean.

HJALMAR. Oh, it was all very simple. Gina didn't stay long here in the house; there was so much confusion—your mother's sickness and all. It was more than Gina could stand, so she gave notice and left. That was the year before your mother died—or maybe it was the same year.

GREGERS. It was the same year. And I was up at the works at the time. But what then?

HJALMAR. Well, then Gina lived at home with her mother, a Mrs. Hansen, a very capable, hardworking woman who ran a little restaurant. She also had a room for rent, a very pleasant, comfortable room.

GREGERS. And you were lucky enough to find it?

HJALMAR. Yes. Actually it was your father who suggested it to me. And it was there, you see—there that I really got to know Gina.

GREGERS. And then your engagement followed?

HJALMAR. Yes. Young people fall in love so easily— hm—

GREGERS (*getting up and pacing about a little*). Tell me—when you became engaged—was it *then* that my father got you to—I mean, was it then that you started in learning photography?

HJALMAR. That's right. I wanted to get on and set up a home as soon as possible, and both your father and I decided that this photography idea was the most feasible one. And Gina thought so too. Yes, and you see, there was another inducement, a lucky break, in that Gina had already taken up retouching.

GREGERS. That worked out wonderfully all around.

HJALMAR (*pleased, getting up*). Yes, isn't that so? Don't you think it's worked out wonderfully all around?

GREGERS. Yes, I must say. My father has almost been a kind of providence to you.

HJALMAR (*with feeling*). He didn't abandon his old

friend's son in a time of need. You see, he does have a heart.

MRS. SØRBY (*entering with* WERLE *on her arm*).   No more nonsense, my dear Mr. Werle. You mustn't stay in there any longer, staring at all those lights; it's doing you no good.

WERLE (*freeing his arm from hers and passing his hand over his eyes*).   Yes, I guess you're right about that.

(PETTERSEN *and* JENSEN *enter with trays.*)

MRS. SØRBY (*to the guests in the other room*).   Gentlemen, please—if anyone wants a glass of punch, he must take the trouble to come in here.

THE FAT GUEST (*comes over to* MRS. SØRBY).   But really, is it true you've abolished our precious smoking privilege?

MRS. SØRBY.   Yes. Here in Mr. Werle's sanctum, it's forbidden.

THE BALD-HEADED GUEST.   When did you pass these drastic amendments to the cigar laws, Mrs. Sørby?

MRS. SØRBY.   After the last dinner—when there were certain persons here who let themselves exceed all limits.

THE BALD-HEADED GUEST.   And my dear Berta, one isn't permitted to exceed the limits, even a little bit?

MRS. SØRBY.   Not in any respect, Mr. Balle.

(*Most of the guests have gathered in the study;
the waiters are proffering glasses of punch.*)

WERLE (*to* HJALMAR, *over by a table*).   What is it you're poring over, Ekdal?

HJALMAR.   It's only an album, Mr. Werle.

THE BALD-HEADED GUEST (*who is wandering about*).   Ah, photographs! Yes, of course, that's just the thing for you.

THE FAT GUEST (*seated in an armchair*).   Haven't you brought along some of your own?

HJALMAR.   No, I haven't.

THE FAT GUEST.   You really should have. It's so good for the digestion to sit and look at pictures.

THE BALD-HEADED GUEST.   And then it always adds a morsel to the entertainment, you know.

A NEARSIGHTED GUEST.   And all contributions are gratefully received.

MRS. SØRBY.   These gentlemen mean that if one's invited for dinner, one must also work for the food, Mr. Ekdal.

THE FAT GUEST.   Where the larder's superior, *that* is pure joy.

THE BALD-HEADED GUEST.   My Lord, it's all in the struggle for existence—

MRS. SØRBY.   How right you are! (*They continue laughing and joking.*)

GREGERS (*quietly*).   You should talk with them, Hjalmar.

HJALMAR (*with a shrug*).   What could I talk about?

THE FAT GUEST.   Don't you think, Mr. Werle, that Tokay compares favorably as a healthful drink for the stomach?

WERLE (*by the fireplace*).   The Tokay you had today I can vouch for in any case; it's one of the very, very finest years. But you recognized that well enough.

THE FAT GUEST.   Yes, it had a remarkably delicate flavor.

HJALMAR (*tentatively*).   Is there some difference between the years?

THE FAT GUEST (*laughing*).   Oh, that's rich!

WERLE (*smiling*).   It certainly doesn't pay to offer you a noble wine.

THE BALD-HEADED GUEST.   Tokay wines are like photographs, Mr. Ekdal—sunshine is of the essence. Isn't that true?

HJALMAR.   Oh yes, light is very important.

MRS. SØRBY.   Exactly the same as with court officials—who push for their place in the sun too, I hear.

THE BALD-HEADED GUEST.   Ouch! That was a tired quip.

THE NEARSIGHTED GUEST.   The lady's performing—

THE FAT GUEST.   And at our expense. (*Frowning.*) Mrs. Sørby, Mrs. Sørby!

MRS. SØRBY.   Yes, but it certainly is true now that the years can vary enormously. The old vintages are the finest.

THE NEARSIGHTED GUEST.   Do you count me among the old ones?

MRS. SØRBY.   Oh, far from it.

THE BALD-HEADED GUEST.   Ha, you see! But what about me, Mrs. Sørby—?

THE FAT GUEST. Yes, and me! What years would you put us among?

MRS. SØRBY. I would put you all among the sweet years, gentlemen. (*She sips a glass of punch; the guests laugh and banter with her.*)

WERLE. Mrs. Sørby always finds a way out—when she wants to. Pass your glasses, gentlemen. Pettersen, take care of them. Gregers, I think we'll have a glass together. (GREGERS *does not stir.*) Won't you join us, Ekdal? I had no chance to remember you at the table.

> (GRAABERG, *the bookkeeper, peers out from the door to the offices.*)

GRAABERG. Beg pardon, Mr. Werle, but I can't get out.

WERLE. What, are you locked in again?

GRAABERG. Yes, and Flakstad's left with the keys—

WERLE. Well, then, go through here.

GRAABERG. But there's someone else—

WERLE. All right, all right, both of you. Don't be shy.

> (GRAABERG *and old* EKDAL *come out from the office.*)

WERLE (*involuntarily*). Oh no!

> (*The laughter and small talk die among the guests.* HJALMAR *starts at the sight of his father, sets down his glass, and turns away toward the fireplace.*)

EKDAL (*without looking up, but bowing slightly to each side and mumbling*). Door locked. Door locked. Beg your pardon. (*He and* GRAABERG *exit in back to the right.*)

WERLE (*between his teeth*). That damned Graaberg!

GREGERS (*with open mouth, staring at* HJALMAR). But it couldn't have been—!

THE FAT GUEST. What's going on? Who was that?

GREGERS. Oh, no one. Only the bookkeeper and somebody else.

THE NEARSIGHTED GUEST (*to* HJALMAR). Did *you* know him?

HJALMAR. I don't know—I didn't notice—

THE FAT GUEST (*getting up*). What in thunder's wrong? (*He goes over to some others, who are talking.*)

MRS. SØRBY (*whispering to the waiter*). Slip something to him outside, something really fine.

PETTERSEN (*nodding*). I'll see to it. (*He goes out.*)

GREGERS (*in a shocked undertone*). Then it really was him!

HJALMAR. Yes.

GREGERS. And yet you stood here and denied you knew him!

HJALMAR (*whispering fiercely*). But how could I—!

GREGERS. Be recognized by your father?

HJALMAR (*painfully*). Oh, if you were in my place, then—

(*The hushed conversations among the guests now mount into a forced joviality.*)

THE BALD-HEADED GUEST (*approaching* HJALMAR *and* GREGERS *amiably*). Ah ha! You over here, polishing up old memories from your student years? Well? Won't you smoke, Mr. Ekdal? Have a light? Oh, that's right, we're not supposed to—

HJALMAR. Thanks, I couldn't—

THE FAT GUEST. Haven't you got a neat little poem to recite for us, Mr. Ekdal? In times past you did that so nicely.

HJALMAR. I'm afraid I can't remember any.

THE FAT GUEST. Oh, that's a shame. Well, Balle, what can we find to do? (*The two men cross the floor into the other room and go out.*)

HJALMAR (*somberly*). Gregers—I'm going! When a man's felt a terrible blow from fate—you understand. Say good night to your father for me.

GREGERS. Yes, of course. Are you going straight home?

HJALMAR. Yes, why?

GREGERS. Well, I may pay you a visit later.

HJALMAR. No, you mustn't. Not to my home. My house is a sad one, Gregers—especially after a brilliant occasion like this. We can always meet somewhere in town.

MRS. SØRBY (*who has approached; in a low voice*). Are you going, Ekdal?

HJALMAR. Yes.

MRS. SØRBY. Greet Gina.

HJALMAR. Thank you.

MRS. SØRBY.   And tell her I'll stop by to see her one day soon.

HJALMAR.   Yes. Thanks. (*To* GREGERS.) Stay here. I'd rather disappear without any fuss. (*He strolls around the floor, then into the other room and out to the right.*)

MRS. SØRBY (*quietly to the waiter, who has returned*). Well, did the old man get something to take home?

PETTERSEN.   Sure. I slipped him a bottle of cognac.

MRS. SØRBY.   Oh, you could have found something better.

PETTERSEN.   Not at all, Mrs. Sørby. He knows nothing better than cognac.

THE FAT GUEST (*in the doorway, holding a score of music*). How about the two of us playing something, Mrs. Sørby?

MRS. SØRBY.   All right. Let's.

> (*The guests shout approval.* MRS. SØRBY *and the others exit right, through the inner room.* GREGERS *remains standing by the fireplace.* WERLE *looks for something on the writing table, seeming to wish that* GREGERS *would leave; when he fails to stir,* WERLE *crosses toward the door.*)

GREGERS.   Father, won't you wait a moment?

WERLE (*pausing*).   What is it?

GREGERS.   I must have a word with you.

WERLE.   Can't it wait till we're alone?

GREGERS.   No, it can't, because it just might occur that we never are alone.

WERLE (*coming closer*).   What does *that* mean?

> (*Distant piano music is heard from the music room during the following conversation.*)

GREGERS.   How could anyone here let that family decay so pitifully?

WERLE.   You're referring to the Ekdals, no doubt.

GREGERS.   Yes, I mean the Ekdals. Lieutenant Ekdal was once so close to you.

WERLE.   Yes, worse luck, he was all too close; and for that I've paid a price these many years. He's the one I can thank for putting something of a blot on my good name and reputation.

GREGERS (*quietly*).   Was *he* really the only guilty one?

WERLE.   Who else do you mean!

GREGERS.   You and he were both in on buying that big stand of timber—

WERLE.   But it was Ekdal, wasn't it, who made the survey of the sections—that incompetent survey? He was the one who carried out all the illegal logging on state property. In fact, he was in charge of the whole operation up there. I had no idea of what Lieutenant Ekdal was getting into.

GREGERS.   Lieutenant Ekdal himself had no idea of what he was getting into.

WERLE.   Very likely. But the fact remains that he was convicted and I was acquitted.

GREGERS.   Yes, I'm aware that no proof was found.

WERLE.   Acquittal is acquittal. Why do you rake up this ugly old story that's given me gray hair before my time? Is this what you've been brooding about all those years up there? I can assure you, Gregers—here in town the whole business has been forgotten long ago—as far as I'm concerned.

GREGERS.   But that miserable Ekdal family!

WERLE.   Seriously, what would you have me do for these people? When Ekdal was let out, he was a broken man, beyond any help. There are people in this world who plunge to the bottom when they've hardly been winged, and they never come up again. Take my word for it, Gregers; I've done everything I could, short of absolutely compromising myself and arousing all kinds of suspicion and gossip—

GREGERS.   Suspicion—? So that's it.

WERLE.   I've gotten Ekdal copying jobs from the office, and I pay him much, much more than his work is worth—

GREGERS (*without looking at him*).   Hm. No doubt.

WERLE.   You're laughing? Maybe you think what I'm saying isn't true? There's certainly nothing to show in my books; I don't record such payments.

GREGERS (*with a cold smile*).   No. I'm sure that certain payments are best left unrecorded.

WERLE (*surprised*).   What do you mean by *that*?

GREGERS (*plucking up his courage*).   Did you record what it cost you to have Hjalmar Ekdal study photography?

WERLE. I? Why should I?

GREGERS. I know now it was you who paid for that. And now I know, too, that it was you who set him up so comfortably in business.

WERLE. Well, and I suppose this still means that I've done nothing for the Ekdals! I can assure you, those people have already cost me enough expense.

GREGERS. Have you recorded any of the expenses?

WERLE. Why do you ask that?

GREGERS. Oh, there are reasons. Listen, tell me—the time when you developed such warmth for your old friend's son—wasn't that just when he was planning to marry?

WERLE. How the devil—how, after so many years, do you expect me—?

GREGERS. You wrote me a letter then—a business letter, naturally; and in a postscript it said, brief as could be, that Hjalmar Ekdal had gotten married to a Miss Hansen.

WERLE. Yes, that's right; that was her name.

GREGERS. But you never said that this Miss Hansen was Gina Hansen—our former housekeeper.

WERLE (*with a derisive, yet uneasy laugh*). No, it just never occurred to me that you'd be so very interested in our former housekeeper.

GREGERS. I wasn't. But—(*Dropping his voice.*) there were others in the house who were quite interested in her.

WERLE. What do you mean by that? (*Storming at him.*) You're not referring to me!

GREGERS (*quietly but firmly*). Yes, I'm referring to you.

WERLE. And you dare—! You have the insolence—! How could he, that ungrateful dog, that—photographer; how could he have the gall to make such insinuations?

GREGERS. Hjalmar hasn't breathed a word of it. I don't think he has the shadow of a doubt about all this.

WERLE. Then where did you get it from? Who could have said such a thing?

GREGERS. My poor, unhappy mother said it—the last time I saw her.

WERLE. Your mother! Yes, I might have guessed. She and you—you always stuck together. It was she who, right from the start, turned your mind against me.

GREGERS. No. It was everything she had to suffer and endure unti she broke down and died so miserably.

WERLE.   Oh, she had nothing to suffer and endure—no more, at least, than so many others. But you can't get anywhere with sick, high-strung people. I've certainly learned that. Now you're going around suspecting that sort of thing, digging up all manner of old rumors and slanders against your own father. Now listen, Gregers, I really think that at your age you could occupy yourself more usefully.

GREGERS.   Yes, all in due time.

WERLE.   Then your mind might be easier than it seems to be now. What can it lead to, you up there at the works, slaving away year in and year out like a common clerk, never taking a penny over your month's salary. It's pure stupidity.

GREGERS.   Yes, if only I were so sure of that.

WERLE.   I understand you well enough. You want to be independent, without obligation to me. But here's the very opportunity for you to become independent, your own man in every way.

GREGERS.   So? And by what means—?

WERLE.   When I wrote you that it was essential you come to town now, immediately—hmm—

GREGERS.   Yes. What is it you really want of me? I've been waiting all day to find out.

WERLE.   I'm suggesting that you come into the firm as a partner.

GREGERS.   I! In your firm? As a partner?

WERLE.   Yes. It wouldn't mean we'd need to be together much. You could take over the offices here in town, and then I'd move up to the mill.

GREGERS.   You *would*?

WERLE.   Yes. You see, I can't take on work now the way I once could. I have to spare my eyes, Gregers; they're beginning to fail.

GREGERS   They've always been weak.

WERLE.   Not like this. Besides—circumstances may make it desirable for me to live up there—at least for a while.

GREGERS.   I never dreamed of anything like this.

WERLE.   Listen, Gregers, there are so very many things that keep us apart, and yet, you know—we're father and son still. I think we should be able to reach some kind of understanding.

GREGERS. Just on the surface, is that what you mean?

WERLE. Well, at least that would be something. Think it over, Gregers. Don't you think it ought to be possible? Eh?

GREGERS (*looking at him coldly*). There's something behind all this.

WERLE. How so?

GREGERS. It might be that somehow you're using me.

WERLE. In a relationship as close as ours, one can always be of use to the other.

GREGERS. Yes, so they say.

WERLE. I'd like to have you home with me now for a while. I'm a lonely man, Gregers; I've always felt lonely—all my life through, but particularly now when the years are beginning to press me. I need to have someone around—

GREGERS. You have Mrs. Sørby.

WERLE. Yes, I do—and she's become, you might say, almost indispensable. She's witty, even-tempered; she livens up the house—and that's what I need so badly.

GREGERS. Well, then, you've got everything the way you want it.

WERLE. Yes, but I'm afraid it can't go on. The world is quick to make inferences about a woman in her position. Yes, I was going to say, a man doesn't gain by it either.

GREGERS. Oh, when a man gives dinner parties like yours, he can certainly take a few risks.

WERLE. Yes, Gregers, but what about her? I'm afraid she won't put up with it much longer. And even if she did—even if, out of her feeling for me, she ignored the gossip and the backbiting and so on—do you still think, Gregers, you with your sharp sense of justice—

GREGERS (*cutting him off*). Tell me short and sweet just one thing. Are you planning to marry her?

WERLE. And if I *were* planning such a thing—what then?

GREGERS. Yes, that's what I'm asking. What then?

WERLE. Would you be so irreconcilably set against it?

GREGERS. No, not at all. Not in any way.

WERLE. Well, I really didn't know whether, perhaps out of regard for your dead mother's memory—

GREGERS. I am not high-strung.

WERLE. Well, you may or may not be, but in any case

you've taken a great load off my mind. I'm really very happy that I can count on your support in this.

GREGERS (*staring intently at him*).   Now I see how you want to use me.

WERLE.   Use you! That's no way to talk!

GREGERS.   Oh, let's not be squeamish in our choice of words. At least, not when it's man to man. (*He laughs brusquely.*) So that's it! That's why I—damn it all!—had to make my personal appearance in town. On account of Mrs. Sørby, family life is in order in this house. Tableau of father with son! That's something new, all right!

WERLE.   How dare you speak in that tone!

GREGERS.   When has there ever been family life here? Never, as long as I can remember. But *now*, of course, there's need for a little of that. For who could deny what a fine impression it would make to hear that the son—on the wings of piety—came flying home to the aging father's wedding feast. What's left then of all the stories about what the poor dead woman suffered and endured? Not a scrap. Her own son ground them to dust.

WERLE.   Gregers—I don't think there's a man in this world you hate as much as me.

GREGERS (*quietly*).   I've seen you at too close quarters.

WERLE.   You've seen me with your mother's eyes. (*Dropping his voice.*) But you should remember that those eyes were—clouded at times.

GREGERS (*trembling*).   I know what you mean. But who bears the guilt for Mother's fatal weakness? You, and all those—! The last of them was that female that Hjalmar Ekdal was fixed up with when you had no more—ugh!

WERLE (*shrugs*).   Word for word, as if I were hearing your mother.

GREGERS (*paying no attention to him*).—and there he sits right now, he with his great, guileless, childlike mind plunged in deception—living under the same roof with that creature, not knowing that what he calls his home is built on a lie. (*Coming a step closer.*) When I look back on all you've done, it's as if I looked out over a battlefield with broken human beings on every side.

WERLE.   I almost think the gulf is too great between us.

GREGERS (*bows stiffly*).   So I've observed; therefore I'll take my hat and go.

WERLE.   You're going? Out of this house?

GREGERS.   Yes. Because now at last I can see a purpose to live for.

WERLE.   What purpose is that?

GREGERS.   You'd only laugh if you heard it.

WERLE.   A lonely man doesn't laugh so easily, Gregers.

GREGERS (*pointing toward the inner room*).   Look—your gentleman friends are playing blindman's buff with Mrs. Sørby. Good night and goodbye.

> (*He goes out at the right rear. Laughter and jok-*
> *ing from the company, which moves into view*
> *in the inner room.*)

WERLE (*muttering contemptuously after* GREGERS).   Huh! Poor fool—and he says he's not high-strung!

ACT TWO

HJALMAR EKDAL's *studio. The room, which is fairly spacious, appears to be a loft. To the right is a sloping roof with great panes of glass, half hidden by a blue curtain. In the far right corner is the entrance; nearer on the same side, a door to the living room. Similarly, at the left there are two doors, and between these an iron stove. At the back is a wide double door, designed to slide back to the sides. The studio is simply but comfortably furnished and decorated. Between the right-hand doors, slightly away from the wall, stands a sofa beside a table and some chairs; on the table is a lighted lamp with a shade; by the stove an old armchair. Photographic apparatus and equipment of various sorts are set up here and there in the room. At the left of the double doors stands a bookcase containing a few books, small boxes and flasks of chemicals, various tools, implements, and other objects. Photographs and such small articles as brushes, paper, and the like lie on the table.*

GINA EKDAL *sits on a chair by the table, sewing.* HEDVIG *sits on the sofa, hands shading her eyes, thumbs in her ears, reading a book.*

GINA (*having glanced over several times at* HEDVIG, *as if with anxiety*). Hedvig! (HEDVIG *does not hear.*)

GINA (*louder*). Hedvig!

HEDVIG (*removing her hands and looking up*). Yes, Mother?

GINA. Hedvig dear, you mustn't sit and read anymore.

HEDVIG. Oh, but Mother, can't I please read a little longer? Just a little!

GINA. No, no—you must set the book down. Your father doesn't like it; *he* never reads in the evening.

HEDVIG (*closing the book*). No, Daddy's no great one for reading.

GINA (*lays her sewing aside and takes a pencil and a small*

137

notebook from the table).   Do you remember how much we spent for butter today?

HEDVIG.   It was one sixty-five.

GINA.   That's right. (*Making a note.*) It's awful how much butter gets used in this house. And then so much for smoked sausage, and for cheese—let me see—(*Making more notes.*) and so much for ham—hmm. (*Adds.*) Yes, that adds right up to—

HEDVIG.   And then there's the beer.

GINA.   Yes, of course. (*Makes another note.*) It mounts up—but it can't be helped.

HEDVIG.   Oh, but you and I had no hot food for dinner, cause Daddy was out.

GINA.   No, and that's to the good. What's more, I also took in eight crowns fifty for photographs.

HEDVIG.   No! Was it that much?

GINA.   Exactly eight crowns fifty.

> (*Silence.* GINA *again picks up her sewing.* HED-
> VIG *takes paper and pencil and starts to draw,
> shading her eyes with her left hand.*)

HEDVIG.   Isn't it something to think that Daddy's at a big dinner party at old Mr. Werle's?

GINA.   You can't really say that he's at old Mr. Werle's. It was his son who sent him the invitation. (*After a pause.*) We have nothing to do with old Mr. Werle.

HEDVIG.   I can hardly wait for Daddy to come home. He promised he'd ask Mrs. Sørby about bringing me a treat.

GINA.   Yes, you can bet there are lots of treats to be had in *that* house.

HEDVIG (*again drawing*).   Besides, I'm a little hungry, too.

> (*Old* EKDAL, *with a bundle of papers under his
> arm and another bundle in his coat pocket,
> comes in through the hall door.*)

GINA.   My, but you're late today, Grandfather.

EKDAL.   They'd locked the office. Had to wait for Graaberg. And then I had to go through—uhh.

GINA.   Did they give you something new to copy, Grandfather?

EKDAL.   This whole pile. Just look.

GINA.   That's fine.

HEDVIG.   And you've got a bundle in your pocket, too.

EKDAL.   Oh? Nonsense; that's nothing. (*Puts his cane away in the corner.*) Here's work for a good spell, Gina, this here. (*Pulls one of the double doors slightly open.*) Shh! (*Peers into the room a moment, then carefully closes the door again.*) He, he! They're sound asleep, the lot of them. And she's bedded down in the basket all on her own. He, he!

HEDVIG.   Are you sure she won't be cold in the basket, Grandpa?

EKDAL.   What a thought! Cold? In all that straw? (*Goes toward the farther door on the left.*) I'll find some matches in here, eh?

GINA.   The matches are on the bureau.

(EKDAL *goes into his room.*)

HEDVIG.   It's wonderful that Grandpa got all that copying to do.

GINA.   Yes, poor old Father; he'll earn himself a little pocket money.

HEDVIG.   And he also won't be able to sit the whole morning down in that horrid Mrs. Eriksen's café.

GINA.   That too, yes. (*A short silence.*)

HEDVIG.   Do you think they're still at the dinner table?

GINA.   Lord only knows; it may well be.

HEDVIG.   Just think, all the lovely food Daddy's eaten! I'm sure he'll be happy and content when he comes. Don't you think so, Mother?

GINA.   Of course. Imagine if we could tell him now that we'd rented out the room.

HEDVIG.   But that's not necessary tonight.

GINA.   Oh, it could well come in handy, you know. It's no good to us as it is.

HEDVIG.   No, I mean it's not necessary because tonight Daddy's feeling good. It's better we have news about the room some other time.

GINA (*looking over at her*).   Are you glad when you have something nice to tell your father when he comes home at night?

HEDVIG.   Yes, for things here are pleasanter then.

GINA (*reflecting*).   Well, there's something to that.

(*Old* EKDAL *comes in again and starts out through the nearer door to the left.*)

GINA (*half turning in her chair*).   Does Grandfather want something from the kitchen?

EKDAL.   I do, yes. Don't stir. (*He goes out.*)

GINA.   He never fusses with the fire out there. (*After a moment.*) Hedvig, go see what he's doing.

(EKDAL *reenters with a small jug of steaming water.*)

HEDVIG.   Are you after hot water, Grandpa?

EKDAL.   Yes, I am. Need it for something. Have to write, and the ink is caked thick as porridge—hmm.

GINA.   But you ought to have supper first, Grandfather. It's all set and waiting in there.

EKDAL.   Never mind about the supper, Gina. Terribly busy, I tell you. I don't want anybody coming into my room—nobody. Hmm. (*He goes into his room.* GINA *and* HEDVIG *exchange glances.*)

GINA (*lowering her voice*).   Where do you figure he's gotten money?

HEDVIG.   He must have got it from Graaberg.

GINA.   Not a chance. Graaberg always sends the pay to me.

HEDVIG.   Maybe he got a bottle somewhere on credit.

GINA.   Poor Grandpa, no one'll give him credit.

(HJALMAR EKDAL, *wearing an overcoat and a gray felt hat, enters from the right.*)

GINA (*dropping her sewing and getting up*).   Ah, Hjalmar, here you are!

HEDVIG (*jumping up at the same time*).   At last you're home, Daddy!

HJALMAR (*putting his hat down*).   Yes, most of them were leaving.

HEDVIG.   So early?

HJALMAR.   Yes, it was only a dinner party. (*Starts to remove his overcoat.*)

GINA.   Let me help you.

HEDVIG.   Me too.

(*They take off his coat;* GINA *hangs it up on the rear wall.*)

HEDVIG.   Were there many there, Daddy?

HJALMAR.   Oh no, not many. We were some twelve, fourteen people at the table.

GINA.   And you got to talk with every one of them?

HJALMAR.   Oh yes, a little, though Gregers rather monopolized me.

GINA.   Is Gregers ugly as ever?

HJALMAR.   Well, he doesn't look any better. Isn't the old man home?

HEDVIG.   Yes, Grandpa's inside, writing.

HJALMAR.   Did he say anything?

GINA.   No, what should he say?

HJALMAR.   Didn't he mention anything of—I thought I heard that he'd been with Graaberg. I'll go in and have a word with him.

GINA.   No, no, don't bother.

HJALMAR.   Why not? Did he say he wouldn't see me?

GINA.   He doesn't want anyone in there this evening.

HEDVIG (*making signals*).   Uh—uh!

GINA (*not noticing*).   He's already been out here and gotten hot water.

HJALMAR.   Aha! Is he—?

GINA.   Yes, exactly.

HJALMAR.   Good Lord, my poor old white-haired father! Well, let him be, enjoying life's pleasures as he may.

(*Old* EKDAL *in a bathrobe, smoking a pipe, enters from his room.*)

EKDAL.   Home, eh? Thought it was your voice I heard.

HJALMAR.   I just arrived.

EKDAL.   You didn't see me at all, did you?

HJALMAR.   No, but they said you'd been through—so I thought I'd follow after.

EKDAL.   Hm, good of you, Hjalmar. Who were they, all those people?

HJALMAR.   Oh, different sorts. There was Flor—he's at the court—and Balle and Kaspersen and, uh—I forget his name, but people at court, all of them—

EKDAL (*nodding*). Listen to that, Gina! He travels only in the best circles.

GINA. Yes, it's real elegant in that house now.

HEDVIG. Did the court people sing, Daddy? Or give readings?

HJALMAR. No, they just babbled away. Of course they wanted *me* to recite for them, but I couldn't see that.

EKDAL. You couldn't see that, eh?

GINA. That you could easily have done.

HJALMAR. Never. One mustn't be a doormat for every passing foot. (*Walking about the room.*) At least, that's not my way.

EKDAL. No, no, that's not for Hjalmar.

HJALMAR. I don't know why I should always provide the entertainment, when I'm out in society so rarely. Let the others make an effort. There those fellows go from one banquet to the next, eating and drinking day in and day out. So let them do their tricks in return for all the good food they get.

GINA. But you didn't say that there?

HJALMAR (*humming*). Um—um—um—they were told a thing or two.

EKDAL. Right to the nobility!

HJALMAR. I don't see why not. (*Casually.*) Later we had a little quibble about Tokay.

EKDAL. Tokay, you mean? That's a fine wine, that.

HJALMAR (*coming to a halt*). On occasion. But I must tell you that not all years are equally good. Everything depends strictly on how much sun the grapes have had.

GINA. Really? Oh, Hjalmar, you know everything.

EKDAL. And they could argue about that?

HJALMAR. They tried to. But then they were informed that it's exactly the same with court officials. Among them as well, all years are not equally fine—it was said.

GINA. The things you think of!

EKDAL. He—he! So you served that up to them, eh?

HJALMAR. Smack between the eyes they got it.

EKDAL. Hear, Gina! He laid that one smack between the eyes of the nobility.

GINA. Just think, smack between the eyes.

HJALMAR. That's right. But I don't want a lot of talk about this. One doesn't speak of such things. Everything really went off in the most friendly spirit, naturally. They're all pleasant, genial people. How could I hurt their feelings? Never!

EKDAL.   But smack between the eyes—

HEDVIG (*ingratiatingly*).   How nice to see you in evening clothes, Daddy. You look so well in them.

HJALMAR.   Yes, don't you think so? And this one here really fits very well. It's almost as if it were made for me. A bit snug under the arms, maybe—help me, Hedvig. (*Takes off the coat.*) I'd rather wear my jacket. What did you do with my jacket, Gina?

GINA.   Here it is. (*Brings the jacket and helps him into it.*)

HJALMAR.   There! Now don't forget to give Molvik his coat back first thing in the morning.

GINA (*putting it away*).   I'll take care of it.

HJALMAR (*stretching*).   Ah, but this feels much more comfortable. This kind of free and easy dress suits my whole personality better. Don't you think so, Hedvig?

HEDVIG.   Yes, Daddy.

HJALMAR.   And when I pull my necktie out into a pair of flowing ends—so! Look! What then?

HEDVIG.   Yes, it goes so well with your mustache and your long, curly hair.

HJALMAR.   Curly? I wouldn't say it's that. I'd call it wavy.

HEDVIG.   Yes, but it *is* so curly.

HJALMAR.   No—wavy.

HEDVIG (*after a moment, tugs at his sleeve*).   Daddy!

HJALMAR.   What is it?

HEDVIG.   Oh, you know what.

HJALMAR.   No, I don't. Honestly.

HEDVIG (*laughing fretfully*).   Come on, Daddy, don't tease me any longer.

HJALMAR.   But what is it, then?

HEDVIG (*shaking him*).   Silly! Out with it, Daddy. You know—all the treats you promised me.

HJALMAR.   Oh—no! How did I ever forget that?

HEDVIG.   No, you can't fool me. Shame on you! Where have you hidden it?

HJALMAR.   So help me if I didn't forget. But wait a minute! I've got something else for you, Hedvig. (*Goes over and rummages in his coat pockets.*)

HEDVIG (*jumping and clapping her hands*).   Oh, Mother, Mother!

GINA.   You see, if you're only patient enough, then—

HJALMAR (*returning with a piece of paper*).   See, here we have it.

HEDVIG.   That? But that's just a piece of paper.

HJALMAR.   It's the bill of fare, the complete bill of fare. Here it says "menu"; that means "bill of fare."

HEDVIG.   Don't you have anything else?

HJALMAR.   I forgot to bring anything else, I tell you. But take my word for it: it's bad business, this doting on sugar candy. Now, if you'll sit down at the table and read the menu aloud, I'll describe for you just how each dish tasted. How's that, Hedvig?

HEDVIG (*swallowing her tears*).   Thanks. (*She sits, but does not read.* GINA *makes gestures at her, which* HJALMAR *notices.*)

HJALMAR (*pacing about the floor*).   What incredible things a family breadwinner is asked to remember; and if he forgets even the tiniest detail—immediately he's met with sour faces. Well, he has to get used to that, too. (*Pauses at the stove beside* EKDAL.) Have you looked inside this evening, Father?

EKDAL.   Oh, that you can be sure of. She's gone into the basket.

HJALMAR.   No! Into the basket? Then she's begun to get used to it.

EKDAL.   Yes. You see, it was just as I predicted. But now there are some little things to do—

HJALMAR.   Some improvements, eh?

EKDAL.   But they've got to be done, you know.

HJALMAR.   All right, let's talk a bit about the improvements, Father. Come, we'll sit here on the sofa.

EKDAL.   Very good. Umm—think I'll fill my pipe first. Needs cleaning, too. Hmm. (*He goes into his room.*)

GINA (*smiling at* HJALMAR).   Clean his pipe!

HJALMAR.   Ah, now, Gina, let him be. Poor old derelict. Yes, the improvements—it's best we get those off our hands tomorrow.

GINA.   Tomorrow you won't have time, Hjalmar—

HEDVIG (*interrupting*).   Oh yes, he will, Mother!

GINA.   Remember those prints that need retouching. They've been called for so many times already.

HJALMAR. Oh yes, those prints again. They'll be fin- ·
ished in no time. Did any new orders come in?

GINA. No such luck. For tomorrow, I have nothing except those two portrait sittings you know about.

HJALMAR. Nothing else? Ah, well, if people won't even
try, then naturally—

GINA. But what else can I do? I've put ads in the papers
time and again.

HJALMAR. Yes, ads, ads—you see what a help they are.
And of course nobody's been to look at the spare room
either?

GINA. No, not yet.

HJALMAR. That was to be expected. If one doesn't keep
wide awake— Gina, you've simply got to pull yourself
together.

HEDVIG (*going to him*). Let me bring you your flute,
Daddy.

HJALMAR. No, no flute. I want no pleasures in this
world. (*Pacing about.*) Ah, yes, work—I'll be deep in work
tomorrow; there'll be no lack of *that*. I'll sweat and slave
as long as my strength holds out—

GINA. But Hjalmar dear, I didn't mean it that way.

HEDVIG. Can't I get you a bottle of beer, then?

HJALMAR. Absolutely not. There's nothing I need.
(*Stopping.*) Beer? Did you say beer?

HEDVIG (*vivaciously*). Yes, Daddy, lovely cool beer.

HJALMAR. Well—if you really insist, I suppose you
could bring in a bottle.

GINA. Yes, do that. Then we'll have it cozy.

> (HEDVIG *runs toward the kitchen door.* HJALMAR
> *by the stove stops her, gazes at her, clasps her
> about the head and hugs her to him.*)

HJALMAR. Hedvig! Hedvig!

HEDVIG (*with tears of joy*). Oh, my dearest Daddy!

HJALMAR. No, don't call me that. There I sat, helping
myself at a rich man's table, gorging myself with all good
things—! I could at least have remembered—

GINA (*sitting at the table*). Oh, nonsense, Hjalmar.

HJALMAR. Yes, I could! But you mustn't be too hard
on me. You both know I love you anyway.

HEDVIG (*throwing her arms around him*). And we love you too, so much!

HJALMAR. And if I should seem unreasonable at times, then—good Lord—remember that I am a man assailed by a host of cares. Ah, yes! (*Drying his eyes.*) No beer at a time like this. Bring me my flute. (HEDVIG *runs to the bookcase and fetches it.*) Thank you. There—so. With flute in hand, and you two close by me—ahh!

> (HEDVIG *sits at the table by* GINA. HJALMAR *walks back and forth, then forcefully begins to play a Bohemian folk dance, but in a slow elegaic tempo with sentimental intonation. After a moment he breaks off the melody and extends his left hand to* GINA.)

HJALMAR (*with feeling*). So what if we skimp and scrape along under this roof, Gina—it's still our home. And I'll say this: it's good to be here. (*He starts playing again; immediately there comes a knock on the hall door.*)

GINA (*getting up*). Shh, Hjalmar. I think someone's there.

HJALMAR (*returning the flute to the bookcase*). What, again! (GINA *goes over and opens the door.*)

GREGERS WERLE (*out in the hallway*). Excuse me—

GINA (*drawing back slightly*). Oh!

GREGERS. But doesn't Mr. Ekdal, the photographer, live here?

GINA. Yes, that's right.

HJALMAR (*going toward the door*). Gregers! Is it really you? Well, come right in.

GREGERS (*entering*). I said I was going to drop in on you.

HJALMAR. But tonight? Have you left the party?

GREGERS. Left both party and family home. Good evening, Mrs. Ekdal. I don't know whether you recognize me?

GINA. Oh yes. Young Mr. Werle is not so hard to recognize.

GREGERS. No. I look like my mother, and you remember her, no doubt.

HJALMAR. Did you say you'd left your home?

GREGERS. Yes, I've moved into a hotel.

HJALMAR. I see. Well, now that you've come, take off your things and sit down.

GREGERS.   Thank you. (*Removes his overcoat. He is dressed now in a plain gray suit with a rustic look*.)

HJALMAR.   Here, on the sofa. Make yourself at home.

(GREGERS *sits on the sofa*, HJALMAR *on a chair at the table*.)

GREGERS (*looking around*).   So this is where you work, then, Hjalmar. And you live here as well.

HJALMAR.   This is the studio, as you can see—

GINA.   There's more room in here, so we like it better.

HJALMAR.   We had a better place before; but this apartment has one great advantage: it has such wonderful adjoining rooms—

GINA.   And so we have a room on the other side of the hall that we can rent out.

GREGERS (*to* HJALMAR).   Ah, then you have lodgers, too.

HJALMAR.   No, not yet. It's not that easy, you know. One has to keep wide awake. (*To* HEDVIG.) But how about that beer?

(HEDVIG *nods and goes into the kitchen*.)

GREGERS.   So that's your daughter, then?

HJALMAR.   Yes, that's Hedvig.

GREGERS.   An only child?

HJALMAR.   She's the only one, yes. She's the greatest joy of our lives, and—(*Lowering his voice*.) also our deepest sorrow, Gregers.

GREGERS.   What do you mean?

HJALMAR.   Yes. You see, there's the gravest imminent danger of her losing her sight.

GREGERS.   Going blind!

HJALMAR.   Yes. So far only the first signs are present, and things may go well for a while. All the same, the doctor has warned us. It will come inevitably.

GREGERS.   What a dreadful misfortune! How did this happen?

HJALMAR (*sighing*).   Heredity, most likely.

GREGERS (*startled*).   Heredity?

GINA.   Hjalmar's mother also had bad eyes.

HJALMAR.   Yes, so my father says. I don't remember her.

GREGERS.   Poor child. And how is she taking it?

HJALMAR.   Oh, you can well imagine, we haven't the

heart to tell her. She suspects nothing. She's carefree, gay, and singing like a tiny bird, she's fluttering into life's eternal night. (*Overcome.*) Oh, it's a brutal blow for me, Gregers.

> (HEDVIG *brings in beer and glasses on a tray, which she sets down on the table.*)

HJALMAR (*stroking her head*).   Thanks. Thanks, Hedvig.

> (HEDVIG *puts her arms around his neck and whispers in his ear.*)

HJALMAR.   No. No bread and butter now. (*Looking over.*) Or maybe Gregers will have a piece?

GREGERS (*making a gesture of refusal*).   No. No, thanks.

HJALMAR   (*his tone still mournful*).   Well, you can bring in a little anyway. If you have a crust, that would be fine. And please, put enough butter on, too.

> (HEDVIG *nods contentedly and returns to the kitchen.*)

GREGERS (*after following her with his eyes*).   In every other respect she looks so strong and healthy.

GINA.   Yes, thank God, she's got nothing else wrong with her.

GREGERS.   She'll certainly look like you when she grows up, Mrs. Ekdal. How old is she now?

GINA.   Hedvig is almost fourteen exactly; her birthday's the day after tomorrow.

GREGERS.   Rather tall for her age.

GINA.   Yes, she's shot right up this past year.

GREGERS.   Nothing like the growth of a child to show us how old we're getting. How long is it you've been married now?

GINA.   We've been married now for—yes, near fifteen years.

GREGERS.   No, truly! Has it been that long?

GINA (*looking at him, becoming wary*).   Yes, no doubt about it.

HJALMAR.   That's right. Fifteen years, short a few months. (*Changing the subject.*) They must have been long years for you, Gregers, up there at the works.

GREGERS.   They were long while I was living them—but now I scarcely know what became of the time.

(*Old* EKDAL *enters from his room, without his pipe, but with his old military cap on his head; his walk is a bit unsteady.*)

EKDAL.   There, now, Hjalmar. Now we can settle down and talk about that—umm. What was it again?

HJALMAR (*going toward him*).   Father, someone is here. Gregers Werle. I don't know if you remember him.

EKDAL (*regarding* GREGERS, *who has gotten up*). Werle? That's the son, isn't it? What does he want with me?

HJALMAR.   Nothing; it's me he's come to see.

EKDAL.   Well, then nothing's up, eh?

HJALMAR.   No, of course not.

EKDAL (*swinging his arms*).   It's not that I'm scared of anything, you know, but—

GREGERS (*going over to him*).   I just want to greet you from your old hunting grounds, Lieutenant Ekdal.

EKDAL.   Hunting grounds?

GREGERS.   Yes, up there around the Hoidal works.

EKDAL.   Oh, up there. Yes, I was well known there once.

GREGERS.   In those days you were a tremendous hunter.

EKDAL.   So I was. Still am, maybe. You're looking at my uniform. I ask nobody permission to wear it in here. As long as I don't walk in the streets with it— (HEDVIG *brings a plate of buttered bread, which she places on the table.*)

HJALMAR.   Sit down, Father, and have a glass of beer. Help yourself, Gregers.

(EKDAL *stumbles, muttering, over to the sofa.* GREGERS *sits on the chair nearest him,* HJALMAR *on the other side of* GREGERS. GINA *sits near the table and sews;* HEDVIG *stands beside her father.*)

GREGERS.   Do you remember, Lieutenant Ekdal, when Hjalmar and I would come up to visit you summers and at Christmas?

EKDAL.   Did you? No, no, no, I don't recall. But I'll tell you something: I've been a first-rate hunter. Bear—I've shot them, too. Shot nine in all.

GREGERS (*looking sympathetically at him*).   And now you hunt no more.

EKDAL.   Oh, I wouldn't say *that,* boy. Get some hunting

in now and then. Yes, but not that kind there. The woods, you see—the woods, the woods—(*Drinks.*) How do the woods look up there?

GREGERS.   Not so fine as in your time. They've been cut into heavily.

EKDAL.   Cut into? (*More quietly, as if in fear.*) It's a dangerous business, that. It catches up with you. The woods take revenge.

HJALMAR (*filling his glass*).   Here, a little more, Father.

GREGERS.   How can a man like you—such an out-doorsman—live in the middle of a stuffy city, cooped up in these four walls?

EKDAL (*half laughs and glances at* HJALMAR).   Oh, it's not so bad here. Not bad at all.

GREGERS.   But all those other things, the very roots of your soul—that cool, sweeping breeze, that free life of the moors and forests, among the animals and birds—?

EKDAL (*smiling*).   Hjalmar, should we show him?

HJALMAR (*quickly and a bit embarrassed*).   No, no, Father, not tonight.

GREGERS.   What's that he wants to show me?

HJALMAR.   Oh, it's only a sort of—you can see it some other time.

GREGERS (*speaking again to* EKDAL).   Yes, my point was this, Lieutenant Ekdal, that now you might as well return with me to the works, for I'm sure to be leaving very soon. Without a doubt, you could get some copying to do up there; and here you've nothing in the world to stir your blood and make you happy.

EKDAL (*staring at him, astonished*).   I have nothing, nothing at all—!

GREGERS.   Of course you have Hjalmar, but then again, he has his own. And a man like you, who's always felt himself so drawn to whatever is free and wild—

EKDAL (*striking the table*).   Hjalmar, now he's *got* to see it!

HJALMAR.   But Father, is it worth it now? It's dark, you know—

EKDAL.   Nonsense! There's moonlight. (*Getting up.*) I say he's got to see it. Let me by. Come and help me, Hjalmar!

HEDVIG.   Oh yes, do that, Father!

HJALMAR (*getting up*).   Well—all right.

GREGERS (*to* GINA).   What's this all about?

GINA.   Oh, you really mustn't expect anything special.

(EKDAL *and* HJALMAR *have gone to the back wall to push aside the two halves of the double door;* HEDVIG *helps her grandfather, while* GREGERS *remains standing by the sofa and* GINA *sits, imperturbably sewing. The doorway opens on an extensive, irregular loft room with many nooks and corners, and two separate chimney shafts ascending through it. Clear moonlight streams through skylights into certain parts of the large room; others lie in deep shadow.*)

EKDAL (*to* GREGERS).   All the way over here, please.

GREGERS (*going over to them*).   What *is* it, then?

EKDAL.   See for yourself—hmm.

HJALMAR (*somewhat self-conscious*).   All this belongs to Father, you understand.

GREGERS (*peering in at the doorway*).   So you keep poultry, Lieutenant Ekdal!

EKDAL.   I'll say we keep poultry! They're roosting now; but you just ought to see our poultry by daylight!

HEDVIG.   And then there's a—

EKDAL.   Shh, shh—don't say anything yet.

GREGERS.   And you've got pigeons too, I see.

EKDAL.   Oh yes, it might just be we've got some pigeons. They have their nesting boxes up there under the eaves; pigeons like to perch high, you know.

HJALMAR.   They're not ordinary pigeons, all of them.

EKDAL.   Ordinary! No, I should say not! We have tumblers, and we have a couple of pouters also. But look here! Can you see that hutch over there by the wall?

GREGERS.   Yes. What do you use that for?

EKDAL.   The rabbits sleep there at night, boy.

GREGERS.   Well, so you have rabbits too?

EKDAL.   Yes, what the devil do you think we have but rabbits! He asks if we have rabbits, Hjalmar! Hmm! But now listen, this is really something! This is it! Out of the way, Hedvig. Stand right here—that's it—and look straight down there. Do you see a basket there with straw in it?

GREGERS. Yes, and there's a bird nesting in the basket.

EKDAL. Hmm! "A bird"—

GREGERS. Isn't it a duck?

EKDAL (*hurt*). Yes, of course it's a duck.

HJALMAR. But what *kind* of duck?

HEDVIG. It's not just any old duck—

EKDAL. Shh!

GREGERS. And it's no exotic breed, either.

EKDAL. No, Mr.—Werle, it's not any exotic breed—because it's a wild duck.

GREGERS. No, is it really? A wild duck?

EKDAL. Oh yes, that's what it is. That "bird" as you said—that's a wild duck. That's our wild duck, boy.

HEDVIG. *My* wild duck—I own it.

GREGERS. And it can survive up here indoors? And do well?

EKDAL. You've got to understand, she's got a trough of water to splash around in.

HJALMAR. Fresh water every other day.

GINA (*turning to* HJALMAR). Hjalmar dear, it's freezing cold in here now.

EKDAL. Hmm, let's close up, then. Doesn't pay to disturb their rest either. Lend a hand, Hedvig dear. (HJALMAR *and* HEDVIG *push the double doors together.*) Another time you can get a proper look at her. (*Sits in the armchair by the stove.*) Oh, they're most curious, the wild ducks, you know.

GREGERS. But how did you capture it, Lieutenant Ekdal?

EKDAL. Didn't capture it myself. There's a certain man here in town we can thank for it.

GREGERS (*starts slightly*). That man—it wouldn't be my father?

EKDAL. Exactly right—your father. Hmm.

HJALMAR. It was odd you were able to guess that, Gregers.

GREGERS. Well, you said before that you owed Father for so many different things, so I thought here too—

GINA. But we didn't get the duck from Mr. Werle himself—

EKDAL. We might just as well thank Haakon Werle for her anyhow, Gina. (*To* GREGERS.) He was out in his boat—

follow me?—and he shot for her, but he sees so bad now, your father, that—hm—he only winged her.

GREGERS. I see. She took some shot in her body.

HJALMAR. Yes, some one, two—three pieces.

HEDVIG. She got it under the wing, and so she couldn't fly.

GREGERS. Ah, so she dived right for the bottom, eh?

EKDAL (*sleepily, with a thick voice*). You can bet on that. They always do, the wild ducks—streak for the bottom, deep as they can get, boy—bite right into the weeds and sea moss—and all that devil's beard that grows down there. And then they never come up again.

GREGERS. But Lieutenant Ekdal, *your* wild duck came up again.

EKDAL. He had such a remarkably clever dog, your father. And that dog—he dove down and brought her up.

GREGERS (*turning to* HJALMAR). And then you got her here.

HJALMAR. Not directly. First she went home to your father's, but there she didn't do well, so Pettersen got his orders to put an end to her—

EKDAL (*half asleep*). Hm—yes, Pettersen—that bonehead—

HJALMAR (*speaking more softly*). That's the way we got her, you see. Father knows Pettersen a bit and when he heard all this about the wild duck, he arranged to have her handed over to us.

GREGERS. And now she's absolutely thriving in that attic room.

HJALMAR. Yes, it's incredible. She's gotten fat. I think she's been in there so long, too, that she's forgotten her old wild life, and that's what it all comes down to.

GREGERS. You're certainly right there, Hjalmar. Just don't let her ever catch sight of the sea and the sky— But I mustn't stay any longer, for I think your father's asleep.

HJALMAR. Oh, don't bother about that.

GREGERS. But incidentally—you said you had a room for rent, a free room?

HJALMAR. Yes. Why? Do you know someone, perhaps—?

GREGERS. Could I take that room?

HJALMAR. You?

GINA. No, not *you*, Mr. Werle—

GREGERS.   Could I take the room? If so, I'll move in first thing in the morning.

HJALMAR.   By all means, with the greatest pleasure—

GINA.   No, but Mr. Werle, it's not at all the room for *you*.

HJALMAR.   But Gina, how can you say that?

GINA.   Oh, the room isn't large enough, or light enough, and—

GREGERS.   That really doesn't matter, Mrs. Ekdal.

HJALMAR.   I think it's a very pleasant room, and it's not badly furnished, either.

GINA.   But remember those two who live right below.

GREGERS.   What two are those?

GINA.   Oh, one of them's been a private tutor—

HJALMAR.   That's Molvik, from the university.

GINA.   And then there's a doctor named Relling.

GREGERS.   Relling? I know him somewhat. He practiced a while up in Hoidal.

GINA.   They're a pretty wild pair, those fellows. They go out on the town evenings and then come home in the dead of night, and they're not always so—

GREGERS.   One gets used to that soon enough. I'm hoping things will go for me the same as with the wild duck—

GINA.   Well, I think you ought to sleep on it first, anyway.

GREGERS.   You're not very anxious to have me in the house, Mrs. Ekdal.

GINA.   Goodness, what makes you think that?

HJALMAR.   Yes, Gina, this is really peculiar of you. (*To* GREGERS.) But tell me, do you expect to stay here in town for a while?

GREGERS (*putting on his overcoat*).   Yes, now I expect to stay on.

HJALMAR.   But not at home with your father? What do you plan to do with yourself?

GREGERS.   Yes, if I only knew that—then I'd be doing all right. But when one is cursed with being called Gregers—"Gregers"—and then "Werle" coming after—have you ever heard anything so disgusting?

HJALMAR.   Oh, I don't agree at all.

GREGERS.   Ugh! Phew! I feel I'd like to spit on any man

with a name like that. But when one has to *live* with that curse of being called Gregers, as I do—

HJALMAR (*laughing*). If you weren't Gregers Werle, who would you want to be?

GREGERS. If I could choose, above all else I'd like to be a clever dog.

GINA. A dog!

HEDVIG (*involuntarily*). Oh no!

GREGERS. Yes. A really fantastic, clever dog, the kind that goes to the bottom after wild ducks when they dive under and bite fast into the weeds down in the mire.

HJALMAR. You know, Gregers—I can't follow a word you're saying.

GREGERS. Never mind. There's really nothing very remarkable in it. But tomorrow morning, early, I'll be moving in. (*To* GINA.) I won't be any trouble to you; I do everything for myself. (*To* HJALMAR.) The rest we can talk over tomorrow. Good night, Mrs. Ekdal. (*Nods to* HEDVIG.) Good night.

GINA. Good night, Mr. Werle.

HEDVIG. Good night.

HJALMAR (*who has lit a lamp*). Just a minute. I'd better light your way; it's quite dark on the stairs.

(GREGERS *and* HJALMAR *go out through the hall.*)

GINA (*gazing into space, her sewing in her lap*). Wasn't that a queer business, his wanting to be a dog?

HEDVIG. I'll tell you something, Mother—it seemed to me he meant something else by that.

GINA. What else could he mean?

HEDVIG. I don't know—but it was just as if he meant something else from what he said, all the time.

GINA. Do you think so? It was strange, all right.

HJALMAR (*coming back*). The light was still lit. (*Putting out the lamp and setting it down.*) Ah, at last one can get a bite to eat. (*Beginning on the bread and butter.*) Well, now you see, Gina—if you simply keep wide awake, then—

GINA. What do you mean, wide awake?

HJALMAR. Well, it was lucky, then, that we got the room rented out for a while at last. And think—to a person like Gregers—a good old friend.

GINA. Yes. I don't know what to say. I don't.

HEDVIG.   Oh, Mother, you'll see. It'll be fun.

HJALMAR.   You really are peculiar. Before you were so eager to rent, and now you don't like it.

GINA.   Yes, Hjalmar, if it could only have been somebody else. What do you think the old man will say?

HJALMAR.   Old Werle? This doesn't concern him.

GINA.   But you can sure bet that something has come up between them, since the son is moving out. You know how those two get along together.

HJALMAR.   Yes, that may well be, but—

GINA.   And now maybe the old man thinks it's you that's behind—

HJALMAR.   He can think that as much as he likes! Old Werle has done a tremendous amount for me. God knows, I'm aware of that. But even so, I can't make myself eternally dependent on him.

GINA.   But Hjalmar dear, that can have its effect on Grandfather. He may now lose that miserable little income he gets from Graaberg.

HJALMAR.   I could almost say, so much the better! Isn't it rather humiliating for a man like me to see his gray-haired father go around like an outcast? But now time is gathering to a ripeness, I think. (*Takes another piece of bread and butter.*) Just as sure as I've got a mission in life, I'm going to carry it out!

HEDVIG.   Oh yes, Daddy! Do!

GINA.   Shh! Don't wake him up.

HJALMAR (*more quietly*).   I *will* carry it out, I tell you. There will come a day when— And that's why it's good we got the room rented out, for now I'm more independently fixed. Any man *must* be that, who's got a mission in life. (*Over by the armchair; emotionally.*) Poor old white-haired Father—lean on your Hjalmar. He has broad shoulders— powerful shoulders, in any case. One fine day you'll wake up and—(*To* GINA.) You do believe that, don't you?

GINA (*getting up*).   Yes, of course I do. But first let's see about getting him to bed.

HJALMAR.   Yes, let's do that.

(*Gently they lift up the old man.*)

ACT THREE

HJALMAR EKDAL's *studio. It is morning. Daylight streams through the large window in the sloping roof; the curtain is drawn back.*

HJALMAR *is sitting at the table, busy retouching a photograph; many other pictures lie in front of him. After a moment* GINA, *wearing a hat and coat, enters by the hall door; she has a covered basket on her arm.*

HJALMAR.   Back so soon, Gina?

GINA.   Oh yes. Got to keep moving. (*She sets the basket on a chair and takes her coat off.*)

HJALMAR.   Did you look in on Gregers?

GINA.   Um-hm, I certainly did. Looks real nice in there. The moment he came, he got his room in beautiful shape.

HJALMAR.   Oh?

GINA.   Yes. He wanted to do everything himself, he said. So he starts building a fire in the stove, and the next thing he's closed down the damper so the whole room is full of smoke. Phew! What a stink, enough to—

HJALMAR.   Oh no!

GINA.   But that's not the best part! So then he wants to put it out, so he empties his whole water pitcher into the stove and now the floor's swimming in the worst muck.

HJALMAR.   That's a nuisance.

GINA.   I got the janitor's wife to come and scrub up after him, the pig; but it'll be unfit to live in till afternoon.

HJALMAR.   What's he doing with himself in the meantime?

GINA.   Thought he'd take a little walk, he said.

HJALMAR.   I was in to see him for a moment too—after you left.

GINA.   I heard that. You asked him for lunch.

HJALMAR.   Just the tiniest little midday snack, you understand. It's the very first day—we could hardly avoid it. You always have something in the house.

GINA.   I'll see what I can find.

157

HJALMAR. But now don't make it too skimpy. Because Relling and Molvik are dropping in too, I think. I just met Relling on the stairs, you see, so of course I had to—

GINA. Oh? Must we have those two also?

HJALMAR. Good Lord, a couple of sandwiches more or less; what's the difference?

EKDAL (*opening his door and looking in*). Say, listen, Hjalmar—(*Noticing* GINA.) Oh, well.

GINA. Is there something Grandfather wants?

EKDAL. Oh no. Let it be. Hmm. (*Goes in again.*)

GINA (*picking up the basket*). Keep a sharp eye on him so he doesn't go out.

HJALMAR. Oh yes, I'll do that. Listen, Gina, a little herring salad would be awfully good—because Relling and Molvik were out on a binge last night.

GINA. Just so they don't come before I'm ready—

HJALMAR. Not a chance. Take your time.

GINA. That's fine, then—and meanwhile you can get a little work done.

HJALMAR. Can't you see how I'm working! I'm working for all I'm worth!

GINA. Because then you'll have *those* off your hands, you know. (*She carries the basket out to the kitchen.* HJALMAR *sits for a while, tinting the photograph in a glum and listless manner.*)

EKDAL (*peeks in, peers about the studio, and whispers*). Are you busy, boy?

HJALMAR. Of course. I'm sitting here struggling with these pictures—

EKDAL. Oh well, don't bother. If you're so busy, then— Hm! (*He reenters his room, leaving the door ajar.*)

HJALMAR (*continues a moment in silence, then puts down the brush and goes over to the door*). Father, are *you* busy?

EKDAL (*grumbling from within*). When you're busy— I'm busy too. Huh!

HJALMAR. Yes, of course. (*Returns to his work.*)

EKDAL (*a moment later, coming in again*). Hm. Well, now, Hjalmar, I'm really not *that* busy.

HJALMAR. I thought you had copying to do.

EKDAL. Oh, the devil! Can't he, Graaberg, wait a day or two? I'm sure it's no matter of life or death.

HJALMAR. No, and you're no slave, either.

EKDAL.   And then there was that other business inside—

HJALMAR.   Yes, that's just it. Maybe you want to go in? Shall I open it up for you?

EKDAL.   Wouldn't be a bad idea, really?

HJALMAR (*getting up*).   And then we'd have *that* off our hands.

EKDAL.   Yes, exactly. And it has to be ready first thing tomorrow. But it *is* tomorrow, isn't it?

HJALMAR.   It certainly is tomorrow.

> (HJALMAR *and* EKDAL *each push back one of the double doors. Within, morning sunlight shines through the skylights. A few doves fly back and forth; others perch, cooing, on the rafters. Chickens cackle now and then from back in the loft.*)

HJALMAR.   There, now you can get started, Father.

EKDAL (*going in*).   Aren't you coming along?

HJALMAR.   Well, you know what—I almost think—(*Sees* GINA *in the kitchen doorway.*) I? No, I haven't the time; I've got to work. But how about our new mechanism—

> (*He pulls a cord; inside a curtain descends, its lower portion composed of a strip of old sailcloth, the upper part being a piece of worn-out fishnetting. By this means, the floor of the loft is rendered invisible.*)

HJALMAR (*returning to the table*).   That's that. Now at last I can work in peace for a while.

GINA.   Is he in there, romping around again?

HJALMAR.   Isn't that better than having him run down to Mrs. Eriksen's? (*Sitting.*) Is there anything you want? You look so—

GINA.   I only wanted to ask, do you think we can set the lunch table in here?

HJALMAR.   Well, we haven't any portraits scheduled that early, have we?

GINA.   No. I don't expect anybody except that couple who want to be taken together.

HJALMAR.   Why the devil can't they be taken together some other day?

GINA. Now, Hjalmar dear, I've got them booked for during your midday nap.

HJALMAR. Well, that's fine, then. So we'll eat in here.

GINA. All right. But there's no hurry about setting the table; you can certainly use it a while longer.

HJALMAR. Oh, it's obvious I'm using the table as much as I can!

GINA. Because then you'll be free later on, you know. (*She goes back into the kitchen. A short pause.*)

EKDAL (*at the door to the loft, behind the net*). Hjalmar!

HJALMAR. Well?

EKDAL. 'Fraid we'll have to move the water trough after all.

HJALMAR. Yes, that's what I've been saying all along.

EKDAL. Hm—hm—hm. (*Disappears from the doorway.*)

(HJALMAR *works a bit, glances toward the loft, and half rises.* HEDVIG *enters from the kitchen.*)

HJALMAR (*hurriedly sitting again*). What do you want?

HEDVIG. I was just coming in to you, Daddy.

HJALMAR (*after a moment*). You seem to be kind of snooping around. Are you checking up, maybe?

HEDVIG. No, not at all.

HJALMAR. What's Mother doing out there now?

HEDVIG. Oh, she's half through the herring salad. (*Going over to the table.*) Don't you have some little thing I could help you with, Daddy?

HJALMAR. Oh no. It's better just to leave me alone with all this—so long as my strength holds out. Nothing to worry about, Hedvig—if only your father can keep his health—

HEDVIG. Oh, Daddy, no. That's horrid; you mustn't talk like that. (*She wanders about a little, stops by the loft doorway, and looks in.*)

HJALMAR. What's he trying to do now?

HEDVIG. It must be a new pathway up to the water trough.

HJALMAR. He can't possibly rig that up on his own! And I'm condemned to sit here—!

HEDVIG (*going to him*). Let *me* take the brush, Daddy. I know I can.

HJALMAR. Oh, nonsense, you'll only ruin your eyes.

HEDVIG.   No such thing. Give me the brush.

HJALMAR (*getting up*).   Well, it'll only be for a minute or two.

HEDVIG.   Pooh! How could that hurt me? (*Takes the brush.*) There now. (*Sitting.*) And here's one to go by.

HJALMAR.   But don't ruin your eyes! Hear me? I won't take the blame; you can take the blame yourself—you hear me?

HEDVIG (*at work retouching*).   Yes, yes, sure I will.

HJALMAR.   You're wonderfully clever, Hedvig. Just for a couple of minutes now.

> (*He slips around the edge of the curtain into the loft.* HEDVIG *sits at her work.* HJALMAR *and* EKDAL *are heard arguing inside.*)

HJALMAR (*appearing behind the net*).   Hedvig, just hand me the pliers from the shelf. And the chisel, please. (*Turning over his shoulder.*) Yes, now you'll see, Father. Will you give me a chance to show you the way I mean! (HEDVIG *fetches the desired tools from the bookcase and passes them in to him.*) Ah, thanks. See, dear, it was a good thing I came. (*He vanishes from the doorway; sounds of carpentry and bantering are heard.* HEDVIG *remains, looking in at them. A moment later, a knock at the hall door; she fails to notice it.*)

GREGERS (*bareheaded, and without his overcoat, enters, hesitating slightly at the door*).   Hm—

HEDVIG (*turning and going toward him*).   Good morning. Please come in.

GREGERS.   Thanks. (*Looking at the loft.*) You seem to have workmen in the house.

HEDVIG.   No, that's only Father and Grandfather. I'll go tell them.

GREGERS.   No, no, don't bother. I'd rather wait a bit. (*He sits on the sofa.*)

HEDVIG.   It's so messy here— (*Starts to remove the photographs.*)

GREGERS.   Oh, they can stay. Are those some pictures that have to be finished?

HEDVIG.   Yes, it's a little job I'm helping Daddy with.

GREGERS.   Please don't let me disturb you.

HEDVIG.   All right. (*She gathers her materials around her and sets to work again;* GREGERS *meanwhile regards her in silence.*)

GREGERS.   Did the wild duck sleep well last night?

HEDVIG.   Yes, I'm sure she did, thanks.

GREGERS (*turning toward the loft*).   It looks so very different by daylight than it did by moonlight.

HEDVIG.   Yes, it can change so completely. In the morning it looks different from in the afternoon; and when it rains it's different from when it's clear.

GREGERS.   Have you noticed that?

HEDVIG.   Sure. You can't help it.

GREGERS.   And do you like it in there with the wild duck, too?

HEDVIG.   Yes, whenever I can be there—

GREGERS.   But of course you don't have much free time; you do go to school, don't you?

HEDVIG.   No, not anymore. Daddy's afraid I'll hurt my eyes.

GREGERS.   Oh. Then he tutors you himself.

HEDVIG.   Daddy's promised to tutor me, but he hasn't found time for that yet.

GREGERS.   But isn't there anyone else to help you a little?

HEDVIG.   Sure, there's Mr. Molvik, but he isn't always exactly, really—well—

GREGERS.   He gets drunk, eh?

HEDVIG.   That's for sure.

GREGERS.   Well, then you do have time to yourself. And inside—I'll bet in there it's just like a world of its own—am I right?

HEDVIG.   Oh, completely! And then there are so many wonderful things.

GREGERS.   Really?

HEDVIG.   Yes, big cupboards with books in them; and lots of the books have pictures.

GREGERS.   Ah!

HEDVIG.   And then there's an old cabinet with drawers and compartments, and a huge clock with figures that are supposed to come out. But the clock doesn't go anymore.

GREGERS.   Even time doesn't exist in there—with the wild duck.

HEDVIG.   Yes. And then there are old watercolor sets and things like that. And then all the books.

GREGERS.   And of course you read the books?

HEDVIG.   Oh yes, whenever I can. But they're mostly in English, and I don't understand that. But then I look at the pictures. There's one just enormous book called *Harryson's History of London*; it must be a hundred years old, and it's got ever so many pictures in it. At the front there's a picture of Death with an hourglass and a girl. I think that's horrible. But then there are all the other pictures of churches and castles and streets and great ships sailing on the ocean.

GREGERS.   But tell me, where did all these rare things come from!

HEDVIG.   Oh, an old sea captain lived here once, and he brought them home. They called him "the flying Dutchman"— and that's the strangest thing, because he wasn't a Dutchman at all.

GREGERS.   No?

HEDVIG.   No. But then he didn't come back finally, and he left all these things behind.

GREGERS.   Listen, tell me—when you sit in there and look at pictures, don't you ever want to go out and see the real world all for yourself?

HEDVIG.   No, never! I'm going to stay at home always and help Daddy and Mother.

GREGERS.   You mean finishing photographs?

HEDVIG.   No, not just that. Most of all, I'd like to learn how to engrave pictures like those in the English books.

GREGERS.   Hm. What does your father say to that?

HEDVIG.   I don't think he likes it. Daddy's so funny about such things. Just think, he talks about me learning basketmaking and wickerwork! But I don't see anything in *that*.

GREGERS.   Oh no, I don't either.

HEDVIG.   But Daddy's right when he says that if I'd learned how to make baskets, I could have made the new basket for the wild duck.

GREGERS.   You could have, yes—and that really was up to you.

HEDVIG.   Yes, because it's *my* wild duck.

GREGERS.   Yes, of course it is.

HEDVIG.   Uh-huh, I own it. But Daddy and Grandpa can borrow it as much as they want.

GREGERS.   Oh? What do they do with it?

HEDVIG.   Oh, they look after it and build things for it and so on.

GREGERS.   I can well imagine. The wild duck rules supreme in there, doesn't she?

HEDVIG.   Yes, she does, and that's because she's a real wild bird. And then it's so sad for her; the poor thing has no one to turn to.

GREGERS.   No family, like the rabbits—

HEDVIG.   No. Even the chickens have all the others that they were baby chicks with, but she's so completely apart from any of her own. So you see, everything is so really mysterious about the wild duck. There's no one who knows her, and no one who knows where she's come from, either.

GREGERS.   And actually, she's been in the depths of the sea.

HEDVIG (*glances at him, suppresses a smile, and asks*).   Why did you say "depths of the sea"?

GREGERS.   What else should I say?

HEDVIG.   You could have said "bottom of the sea"—or "the sea's bottom"?

GREGERS.   But couldn't I just as well say "depths of the sea"?

HEDVIG.   Sure. But to me it sounds so strange when someone else says "depths of the sea."

GREGERS.   But why? Tell me why?

HEDVIG.   No, I won't. It's something so stupid.

GREGERS.   It couldn't be. Now tell me why you smiled.

HEDVIG.   That was because always, when all of a sudden—in a flash—I happen to think of that in there, it always seems to me that the whole room and everything in it is called "the depths of the sea"! But that's all so stupid.

GREGERS.   You musn't say that.

HEDVIG.   Oh yes, because it's only an attic.

GREGERS.   Are you so sure of that?

HEDVIG (*astonished*).   That it's an attic!

GREGERS.   Yes. Do you know that for certain?

> (HEDVIG, *speechless, stares at him open-mouthed.* GINA *enters from the kitchen with a tablecloth.*)

GREGERS (*getting up*).   I'm afraid I've come too early for you.

GINA.   Oh, I guess you have to be somewhere; and besides, it's almost ready now. Clear the table, Hedvig.

(HEDVIG *puts away the materials; during the following dialogue, she and* GINA *set the table.* GREGERS *settles in the armchair and pages through an album.*)

GREGERS.   I hear you can retouch photographs, Mrs. Ekdal.

GINA (*with a side-glance*).   Um-hm, so I can.

GREGERS.   That's really very lucky.

GINA.   Why "lucky"?

GREGERS.   With Hjalmar a photographer, I mean.

HEDVIG.   Mother can take pictures, too.

GINA.   Oh yes, I even got lessons in that.

GREGERS.   So we might say it's you who runs the business.

GINA.   Yes, when my husband hasn't the time himself—

GREGERS.   He finds himself so taken up with his old father, I suppose.

GINA.   Yes, and then a man like Hjalmar shouldn't have to go snapping pictures of every Tom, Dick and Harry.

GREGERS.   I agree; but once he's chosen this line of work, then—

GINA.   Mr. Werle, you must realize that my husband is not just any old photographer.

GREGERS.   Well, naturally; but even so—

(*A shot is fired in the loft.*)

GREGERS (*jumping up*).   What's that!

GINA.   Uff, now they're shooting again!

GREGERS.   They go shooting as well?

HEDVIG.   They go hunting.

GREGERS.   What! (*Going to the loft doorway.*) Have you gone hunting, Hjalmar?

HJALMAR (*behind the net*).   Are you here? I didn't realize; I was so occupied— (*To* HEDVIG.) And you, you didn't tell us. (*Comes into the studio.*)

GREGERS.   Do you go shooting in the loft?

HJALMAR (*producing a double-barreled pistol*).   Oh, only with this here.

GINA.   Yes, some day you and Grandfather'll have an accident with that there gun.

HJALMAR (*annoyed*).   I believe I've remarked that this type of firearm is called a pistol.

GINA.   I don't see that that makes it any better.

GREGERS.   So you've turned out a "hunter" as well, Hjalmar?

HJALMAR.   Just a little rabbit hunt, now and then. It's mainly for Father's sake, you understand.

GINA.   Men are so funny, really; they've always got to have their little diversities.

HJALMAR (*angrily*).   That's right, yes—they always have to have their little diversions.

GINA.   Yes, that's just what I was saying.

HJALMAR.   Oh, well! (*To* GREGERS.) So that's it, and then we're very lucky in the way the loft is placed—nobody can hear us when we're shooting. (*Puts the pistol on the highest bookshelf.*) Don't touch the pistol, Hedvig! One barrel's still loaded, don't forget.

GREGERS (*peering through the netting*).   You've got a hunting rifle too, I see.

HJALMAR.   Yes, that's Father's old rifle. It won't shoot anymore; something's gone wrong with the lock. But it's a lot of fun to have anyway, because we can take it all apart and clean it and grease it and put it together again— Of course, it's mostly Father who fools around with that sort of thing.

HEDVIG (*crossing to* GREGERS).   Now you can really see the wild duck.

GREGERS.   I was just now looking at her. She seems to drag one wing a little.

HJALMAR.   Well, no wonder; she took a bad wound.

GREGERS.   And then she limps a little. Isn't that so?

HJALMAR.   Maybe just a tiny bit.

HEDVIG.   Yes, that was the foot the dog bit her in.

HJALMAR.   But she hasn't a thing wrong with her otherwise; and that's simply remarkable when you think that she's had a charge of shot in her and been held by the teeth of a dog—

GREGERS (*with a glance at* HEDVIG). And been in the depths of the sea—so long.

HEDVIG (*smiling*). Yes.

GINA (*arranging the table*). Oh, that sacred duck— there's fuss enough made over her.

HJALMAR. Hm. Are you nearly ready?

GINA. Yes, right away. Hedvig, now you can come and help me.

(GINA *and* HEDVIG *exit into the kitchen.*)

HJALMAR (*in an undertone*). I don't think it's so good that you stand there, watching my father. He doesn't like it. (GREGERS *comes away from the loft doorway.*) And it's better, too, that I close up before the others come. (*Shooing away the menagerie with his hands.*) Hssh! Hssh! Go 'way now! (*With this he raises the curtain and draws the double doors together.*) I invented these contraptions myself. It's really great fun to have such things around to take care of and fix when they get out of whack. And besides, it's absolutely necessary, you know; Gina doesn't go for rabbits and chickens out here in the studio.

GREGERS. Of course not. And I suppose it *is* your wife who manages here?

HJALMAR. My general rule is to delegate the routine matters to her, and that leaves me free to retire to the living room to think over more important things.

GREGERS. And what sort of things are these, Hjalmar?

HJALMAR. I've been wondering why you haven't asked me that before. Or maybe you haven't heard about my invention.

GREGERS. Invention? No.

HJALMAR. Oh? Then you haven't? Well, no, up there in that waste and wilderness—

GREGERS. Then you've really invented something!

HJALMAR. Not completely invented it yet, but I'm getting very close. You must realize that when I decided to dedicate my life to photography, it wasn't my idea to spend time taking pictures of a lot of nobodies.

GREGERS. Yes, that's what your wife was just now saying.

HJALMAR. I swore that if I devoted my powers to the craft, I would then exalt it to such heights that it would become both an art and a science. That's when I decided on this amazing invention.

GREGERS.   And what does this invention consist of? What's its purpose?

HJALMAR.   Yes, Gregers, you mustn't ask for details like that yet. It takes time, you know. And you mustn't think it's vanity that's driving me, either. I'm certainly not working for myself. Oh no, it's my life's work that stands before me day and night.

GREGERS.   What life's work is that?

HJALMAR.   Are you forgetting the silver-haired old man?

GREGERS.   Your poor father. Yes, but actually what can you do for him?

HJALMAR.   I can raise his self-respect from the dead— by restoring the Ekdal name to dignity and honor.

GREGERS.   So that's your life's work.

HJALMAR.   Yes. I am going to rescue that shipwrecked man. That's just what he suffered—shipwreck—when the storm broke over him. When all those harrowing investigations took place, he wasn't himself anymore. That pistol, there—the one we use to shoot rabbits with—it's played a part in the tragedy of the Ekdals.

GREGERS.   Pistol! Oh?

HJALMAR.   When he was sentenced and facing prison, he had that pistol in his hand—

GREGERS.   You mean he—!

HJALMAR.   Yes. But he didn't dare. He was a coward. That shows how broken and degraded he'd become by then. Can you picture it? He, a soldier, a man who'd shot nine bears and was directly descended from two lieutenant colonels—I mean, one after the other, of course. Can you picture it, Gregers?

GREGERS.   Yes, I can picture it very well.

HJALMAR.   Well, I can't. And then that pistol intruded on our family history once again. When he was under lock and key, dressed like a common prisoner—oh, those were agonizing times for me, you can imagine. I kept the shades of both my windows drawn. When I looked out, I saw the sun shining the same as ever. I couldn't understand it. I saw the people going along the street, laughing and talking of trivial things. I couldn't understand it. I felt all creation should be standing still, like during an eclipse.

GREGERS.   I felt that way when my mother died.

HJALMAR.   During one of those times Hjalmar Ekdal put a pistol to his own breast.

GREGERS.   You were thinking of—

HJALMAR.   Yes.

GREGERS.   But you didn't shoot?

HJALMAR.   No. In that critical moment I won a victory over myself. I stayed alive. But you can bet it takes courage to choose life in those circumstances.

GREGERS.   Well, that depends on your point of view.

HJALMAR.   Oh, absolutely. But it was all for the best, because now I've nearly finished my invention; and then Dr. Relling thinks, just as I do, that they'll let Father wear his uniform again. That's the only reward I'm after.

GREGERS.   So it's really the uniform that he—?

HJALMAR.   Yes, that's what he really hungers and craves for. You've no idea how that makes my heart ache. Every time we throw a little family party—like Gina's and my wedding anniversary, or whatever—then the old man comes in, wearing that uniform from his happier days. But if there's even a knock at the door, he goes scuttering back in his room fast as the old legs will carry him. You see, he doesn't dare show himself to strangers. What a heartrending spectacle for a son!

GREGERS.   Approximately when do you think the invention will be finished?

HJALMAR.   Oh, good Lord, don't hold me to a timetable. An invention, that's something you can hardly dictate to. It depends a great deal on inspiration, on a sudden insight—and it's nearly impossible to say in advance when that will occur.

GREGERS.   But it *is* making progress?

HJALMAR.   Of course it's making progress. Every single day I think about my invention. I'm brimming with it. Every afternoon, right after lunch, I lock myself in the living room where I can meditate in peace. But it's no use driving me; it simply won't work. Relling says so too.

GREGERS.   And you don't think all those contraptions in the loft distract you and scatter your talents?

HJALMAR.   No, no, no, on the contrary. You mustn't say that. I can't always go around here, brooding over the same nerve-racking problems. I need some diversion to fill in the time. You see, inspiration, the moment of insight—when that comes, nothing can stop it.

GREGERS. My dear Hjalmar, I suspect you've got a bit of the wild duck in you.

HJALMAR. Of the wild duck? What do you mean?

GREGERS. You've plunged to the bottom and clamped hold of the seaweed.

HJALMAR. I suppose you mean that near-fatal shot that brought down Father—and me as well?

GREGERS. Not quite that. I wouldn't say you're wounded; but you're wandering in a poisonous swamp, Hjalmar. You've got an insidious disease in your system, and so you've gone to the bottom to die in the dark.

HJALMAR. Me? Die in the dark! You know what, Gregers—you'll really have to stop that talk.

GREGERS. But never mind. I'm going to raise you up again. You know, I've found my purpose in life, too. I found it yesterday.

HJALMAR. Yes, that may well be; but you can just leave me out of it. I can assure you that—apart from my quite understandable melancholy—I'm as well off as any man could wish to be.

GREGERS. And your thinking so is part of the sickness.

HJALMAR. Gregers, you're my old friend—please—don't talk any more about sickness and poison. I'm not used to that kind of conversation. In my house nobody talks to me about ugly things.

GREGERS. That's not hard to believe.

HJALMAR. Yes, because it isn't good for me. And there's no swamp air here, as you put it. In a poor photographer's house, life is cramped; I know that. My lot is a poor one—but, you know, I'm an inventor. And I'm the family breadwinner, too. *That's* what sustains me through all the pettiness. Ah, here they come with the lunch.

> (GINA *and* HEDVIG *bring in bottles of beer, a de-canter of brandy, glasses, and the like. At the same time,* RELLING *and* MOLVIK *enter from the hall. Neither wears a hat or overcoat;* MOL-VIK *is dressed in black.*)

GINA (*setting things down on the table*). Well, the two of them—right on time.

RELLING. Molvik was positive he could smell that herring salad, and there was just no holding him back. 'Morning for the second time, Ekdal.

HJALMAR. Gregers, I'd like you to meet Mr. Molvik. And Dr.—ah, but don't you know Relling?

GREGERS. Yes, slightly.

RELLING. Well, Mr. Werle junior. Yes, we've had a few run-ins together up at the Hoidal works. You've just moved in, haven't you?

GREGERS. I moved in this morning.

RELLING. And Molvik and I live downstairs; so you're not very far from a doctor and a priest, if you ever have need of such.

GREGERS. Thanks; that could happen. After all, we had thirteen at the table last night.

HJALMAR. Oh, don't start in on ugly subjects again!

RELLING. You don't have to worry, Hjalmar; Lord knows this doesn't involve you.

HJALMAR. I hope not, for my family's sake. But let's sit down and eat and drink and be merry.

GREGERS. Shouldn't we wait for your father?

HJALMAR. No, he'll have his lunch sent in to him later. Come now!

> (*The men sit at the table, eating and drinking.* GINA *and* HEDVIG *go in and out, serving the food.*)

RELLING. Last night Molvik was tight as a tick, Mrs. Ekdal.

GINA. Oh? Last night again?

RELLING. Didn't you hear him when I finally brought him home?

GINA. No, can't say I did.

RELLING. That's lucky—because Molvik was revolting last night.

GINA. Is that so, Molvik?

MOLVIK. Let's draw a veil over last night's activities. They have no bearing on my better self.

RELLING (*to* GREGERS). All of a sudden he's possessed by an impulse; and then I have to take him out on a bat. You see, Mr. Molvik is demonic.

GREGERS. Demonic?

RELLING.   Molvik is demonic, yes.

GREGERS.   Hm.

RELLING.   And demonic natures aren't made to go through life on the straight and narrow; they've got to take detours every so often. Well—and you're still sticking it out there at that dark, hideous mill.

GREGERS.   I've stuck it out till now.

RELLING.   And did you ever collect on that "summons" you were going around with?

GREGERS.   Summons? (*Understanding him.*) Oh, that.

HJALMAR.   Were you serving summonses, Gregers?

GREGERS.   Nonsense.

RELLING.   Oh, but he was, definitely. He was going around to all the farms and cabins with copies of something he called "Summons to the Ideal."

GREGERS.   I was young then.

RELLING.   You're right, there. You were very young. And that summons to the ideal—it wasn't ever honored during my time up there.

GREGERS.   Nor later, either.

RELLING.   Well, I guess you've learned enough to cut down your expectations a bit.

GREGERS.   Never with a man who really *is* a man.

HJALMAR.   Yes, that seems quite reasonable to me. A little butter, Gina.

RELLING.   And then a piece of pork for Molvik.

MOLVIK.   Ugh, no pork!

(*There is a knock at the loft door.*)

HJALMAR.   Open it, Hedvig; Father wants to get out.

(HEDVIG *goes to open the door a little; old* EKDAL *enters with a fresh rabbit skin. She closes the door after him.*)

EKDAL.   Good morning, gentlemen. Good hunting today. Shot a big one.

HJALMAR.   And you went ahead and skinned it without waiting for me!

EKDAL.   Salted it, too. It's nice tender meat, this rabbit meat. And it's so sweet. Tastes like sugar. Enjoy your food, gentlemen! (*He goes into his room.*)

MOLVIK (*getting up*). Pardon—I, I can't—got .o go downstairs right—

RELLING. Drink soda water, man!

MOLVIK (*rushing out the hall door*). Ugh—ugh!

RELLING (*to* HJALMAR). Let's empty a glass to the old hunter.

HJALMAR (*clinking glasses with him*). Yes, to the gallant sportsman on the brink of the grave.

RELLING. To the old, gray-haired—(*Drinks.*) Tell me something, is it gray hair he's got, or is it white?

HJALMAR. It's really a little of both. But as a matter of fact, he's scarcely got a hair on his head.

RELLING. Well, fake hair will take you through life, good as any. You know, Ekdal, you're really a very lucky man. You have your high mission in life to fight for—

HJALMAR. And I am fighting for it, too.

RELLING. And then you've got this clever wife of yours, padding around in her slippers and waggling her hips and keeping you neat and cozy.

HJALMAR. Yes. Gina—(*Nodding at her.*) you're a good companion for life's journey, you are.

GINA. Oh, don't sit there deprecating me.

RELLING. And what about your Hedvig, Ekdal?

HJALMAR (*stirred*). My child, yes! My child above all. Hedvig, come here to me. (*Caresses her head.*) What day is tomorrow, dear?

HEDVIG (*shaking him*). Oh, don't talk about it, Daddy!

HJALMAR. It's like a knife turning in my heart when I think how bare it's all going to be, just the tiniest celebration out in the loft—

HEDVIG. Oh, but that will be just wonderful!

RELLING. And wait till that marvelous invention comes to the world, Hedvig!

HJALMAR. Ah, yes—then you'll see! Hedvig, I've resolved to make your future secure. You'll be well taken care of as long as you live. I'll make sure you're provided with—something or other. That will be the poor inventor's sole reward.

HEDVIG (*whispering, with her arms around his neck*). Oh, you dear, dear Daddy!

RELLING (*to* GREGERS). Well, now, isn't it good for a

change to be sitting around a well-spread table in a happy family circle?

HJALMAR.   Yes, I really prize these hours around the table.

GREGERS.   I, for my part, don't thrive in marsh gas.

RELLING.   Marsh gas?

HJALMAR.   Oh, don't start that rubbish again!

GINA.   Lord knows there isn't any marsh gas here, Mr. Werle; every blessed day I air the place out.

GREGERS (*leaving the table*).   You can't air out the stench I mean.

HJALMAR.   Stench!

GINA.   What about that, Hjalmar!

RELLING.   Beg pardon—but it wouldn't be you who brought that stench in with you from the mines up there?

GREGERS.   It's just like you to call what I'm bringing into this house a stench.

RELLING (*crossing over to him*).   Listen, Mr. Werle junior, I've got a strong suspicion that you're still going around with the uncut version of that "Summons to the Ideal" in your back pocket.

GREGERS.   I've got it written in my heart.

RELLING.   I don't care where the devil you've got it; I wouldn't advise you to play process-server here as long as I'm around.

GREGERS.   And what if I do anyway?

RELLING.   Then you'll go head first down the stairs, that's what.

HJALMAR (*getting up*).   Come, now, Relling!

GREGERS.   Yes, just throw me out—

GINA (*coming between them*).   You can't do that, Relling. But I'll tell you this, Mr. Werle—that you, who made all that mess with your stove, have no right to come to me talking about smells.

(*A knock at the hall door.*)

HEDVIG.   Mother, somebody's knocking.

GINA.   I'll go—(*She crosses and opens the door, gives a start, shudders and shrinks back.*) Uff! Oh no!

(*Old* WERLE, *in a fur coat, steps into the room.*)

WERLE.   Excuse me, but I think my son is living in this house.

GINA (*catching her breath*).   Yes.

HJALMAR (*coming closer*).   If Mr. Werle will be so good as to—

WERLE.   Thanks, I'd just like to talk with my son.

GREGERS.   Yes, why not? Here I am.

WERLE.   I'd like to talk with you in your room.

GREGERS.   In my room—fine—(*Starts in.*)

GINA.   No. Good Lord, that's in no condition for—

WERLE.   Well, out in the hall, then. This is just between us.

HJALMAR.   You can talk here, Mr. Werle. Come into the living room, Relling.

> (HJALMAR *and* RELLING *go out to the right;* GINA *takes* HEDVIG *with her into the kitchen.*)

GREGERS (*after a brief interval*).   Well, now it's just the two of us.

WERLE.   You dropped a few remarks last night— And since you've now taken a room with the Ekdals, I must assume that you're planning something or other against me.

GREGERS.   I'm planning to open Hjalmar Ekdal's eyes. He's going to see his situation just as it is—that's all.

WERLE.   Is *that* the mission in life you talked about yesterday?

GREGERS.   Yes. You haven't left me any other.

WERLE.   Am I the one that spoiled your mind, Gregers?

GREGERS.   You've spoiled my entire life. I'm not thinking of all that with Mother. But you're the one I can thank for my going around, whipped and driven by this guilt-ridden conscience.

WERLE.   Ah, it's your conscience that's gone bad.

GREGERS.   I should have taken a stand against you when the trap was laid for Lieutenant Ekdal. I should have warned him, for I had a pretty good idea what was coming off.

WERLE.   Yes, you really should have spoken up then.

GREGERS.   I didn't dare; I was so cowed and frightened. I was unspeakably afraid of you—both then and for a long time after.

WERLE.   That fright seems to be over now.

GREGERS. It is, luckily. The harm done to old Ekdal, both by me and—others, can never be undone; but Hjalmar I can free from all the lies and evasions that are smothering him here.

WERLE. You believe you'd be doing him good by that?

GREGERS. I'm positive of that.

WERLE. Maybe you think Ekdal's the kind of man who'll thank you for that friendly service?

GREGERS. Yes! He *is* that kind of man.

WERLE. Hmm—we'll see.

GREGERS. And besides—if I'm ever to go on living, I'll have to find a cure for my sick conscience.

WERLE. It'll never be sound. Your conscience has been sickly from childhood. It's an inheritance from your mother, Gregers—the only inheritance she left you.

GREGERS (*with a wry half-smile*). You've never been able to accept the fact, have you, that you calculated wrong when you thought she'd bring you a fortune?

WERLE. Let's not get lost in irrelevancies. Then you're still intent on this goal of putting Ekdal on what you suppose is the right track?

GREGERS. Yes, I'm intent on that.

WERLE. Well, then I could have saved myself the walk up here. For there's no point in asking if you'll move back home with me?

GREGERS. No.

WERLE. And you won't come into the business either?

GREGERS. No.

WERLE. Very well. But since I'm now planning a second marriage, the estate, of course, will be divided between us.

GREGERS (*quickly*). No, I don't want that.

WERLE. You don't want it?

GREGERS. No, I wouldn't dare, for the sake of my conscience.

WERLE (*after a pause*). You going back to the works again?

GREGERS. No. I consider that I've retired from your service.

WERLE. But what are you going to do, then?

GREGERS. Simply carry out my life's mission; nothing else.

WERLE. Yes, but afterwards? What will you live on?

GREGERS.   I have some of my salary put aside.

WERLE.   Yes, that won't last long!

GREGERS.   I think it will last my time.

WERLE.   What do you mean by that?

GREGERS.   I'm not answering any more.

WERLE.   Good-bye then, Gregers.

GREGERS.   Good-bye.

(*Old* WERLE *goes out.*)

HJALMAR (*peering out*).   Has he gone?

GREGERS.   Yes.

(HJALMAR *and* RELLING *come in.* GINA *and* HED-VIG *also return from the kitchen.*)

RELLING.   There's one lunch gone to the dogs.

GREGERS.   Put your things on, Hjalmar; you've got to take a long walk with me.

HJALMAR.   Yes, gladly. What did your father want? Was it anything to do with me?

GREGERS.   Just come. We have some things to talk over. I'll go and get my coat. (*He leaves by the hall door.*)

GINA.   You mustn't go out with him, Hjalmar.

RELLING.   No, don't go. Stay where you are.

HJALMAR (*getting his hat and overcoat*).   But why? When a childhood friend feels a need to open his mind to me in private—

RELLING.   But damn it all! Can't you see the man's mad, crazy, out of his skull!

GINA.   Yes, that's the truth, if you'd listen. His mother, off and on, had those same conniption fits.

HJALMAR.   That's just why he needs a friend's watchful eye on him. (*To* GINA.) Be sure dinner's ready in plenty of time. See you later. (*Goes out the hall door.*)

RELLING.   It's really a shame that fellow didn't go straight to hell down one of the Hoidal mines.

GINA.   Mercy—why do you say that?

RELLING (*muttering*).   Oh, I've got my reasons.

GINA.   Do you think Gregers Werle is really crazy?

RELLING.   No, worse luck. He's no crazier than most people. But he's got a disease in his system all the same.

GINA.   What is it that's wrong with him?

RELLING.   All right, I'll tell you, Mrs. Ekdal. He's suffering from an acute case of moralistic fever.

GINA.   Moralistic fever?

HEDVIG.   Is that a kind of disease?

RELLING.   Oh yes, it's a national disease, but it only breaks out now and then. (*Nodding to* GINA.) Thanks for lunch. (*He goes out through the hall door.*)

GINA (*walking restlessly around the room*).   Ugh, that Gregers Werle—he was always a cold fish.

HEDVIG (*standing by the table, looking searchingly at her*).   This is all so strange to me.

ACT FOUR

HJALMAR EKDAL's *studio. A photograph has just been taken; a portrait camera covered with a cloth, a stand, a couple of chairs, a console table, among other things, stand well out in the room. Late afternoon light; it is near sunset; somewhat later it begins to grow dark.*

    GINA *is standing in the hall doorway with a plate-holder and a wet photographic plate in her hand, talking with someone outside.*

GINA.   Yes, that's definite. When I promise something, I keep my word. On Monday the first dozen will be ready. Good-bye. Good-bye. (*Footsteps are heard descending the stairs.* GINA *closes the door, puts the plate into the holder, and slips both back into the covered camera.*)

HEDVIG (*coming in from the kitchen*).   Are they gone?

GINA (*tidying up*).   Yes, thank goodness, at last I'm rid of them.

HEDVIG.   But why do you suppose Daddy isn't home yet?

GINA.   Are you sure he's not below with Relling?

HEDVIG.   No, he's not there. I ran down the back stairs just now and asked.

GINA.   And his dinner's standing and getting cold, too.

HEDVIG.   Just imagine—Daddy's always sure to be on time for dinner.

GINA.   Oh, he'll be right along, you'll see.

HEDVIG.   Oh, I wish he would come! Everything's so strange around here.

GINA (*calling out*).   There he is!

    (HJALMAR *comes in by the hall door.*)

HEDVIG (*running toward him*).   Daddy! Oh, we've waited ages for you!

GINA (*eyeing him*).   You've been out pretty long, Hjalmar.

HJALMAR (*without looking at her*).   I've been a while,

yes. *(He takes off his overcoat.* GINA *and* HEDVIG *start to help him; he waves them away.)*

GINA.   Did you eat with Werle, maybe?

HJALMAR *(hanging his coat up)*.   No.

GINA *(going toward the kitchen)*.   I'll bring your dinner in, then.

HJALMAR.   No, the dinner can wait. I don't want to eat now.

HEDVIG *(coming closer)*.   Don't you feel well, Daddy?

HJALMAR.   Well? Oh yes, well enough. We had an exhausting walk, Gregers and I.

GINA.   You shouldn't do that, Hjalmar; you're not used to it.

HJALMAR.   Hm. There are a lot of things a man's got to get used to in this world. *(Walking about the room a bit.)* Did anyone come while I was out?

GINA.   No one but that engaged couple.

HJALMAR.   No new orders?

GINA.   No, not today.

HEDVIG.   You'll see, there'll be some tomorrow, Daddy.

HJALMAR.   I certainly hope so, because tomorrow I'm going to throw myself into my work—completely.

HEDVIG.   Tomorrow! But don't you remember what day tomorrow is?

HJALMAR.   Oh yes, that's right. Well, the day after tomorrow, then. From now on, I'm doing everything myself; I just want to be left alone with all the work.

GINA.   But Hjalmar, what's the point of that? It'll only make your life miserable. Let me handle the photographing, and then you'll be free to work on the invention.

HEDVIG.   And free for the wild duck, Daddy—and for all the chickens and rabbits—

HJALMAR.   Don't talk to me about that rubbish! Starting tomorrow I shall never again set foot in that loft.

HEDVIG.   Yes, but Daddy, you promised me tomorrow there'd be a celebration.

HJALMAR.   Hm, that's true. Well, the day after, then. That infernal wild duck—I'd almost like to wring its neck!

HEDVIG *(crying out)*.   The wild duck!

GINA.   What an idea!

HEDVIG *(shaking him)*.   Yes, but Daddy—it's my wild duck!

HJALMAR.   That's why I won't do it. I haven't the heart—for your sake, Hedvig, I haven't the heart. But deep inside me I feel I ought to. I shouldn't tolerate under my roof a creature that's been in that man's hands.

GINA.   My goodness, just because Grandfather got her from that worthless Pettersen—

HJALMAR (*pacing the floor*).   There are certain standards—what should I call them—ideal standards, let's say—certain claims on us that a man can't put aside without damaging his soul.

HEDVIG (*following him*).   But think—the wild duck—the poor wild duck!

HJALMAR (*stopping*).   You heard me say I'd spare it—for your sake. It won't be hurt, not a hair on its—well, anyway, I'll spare it. There are more important matters to settle. But Hedvig, now you better get out for your afternoon walk; now's just the right shade of twilight for you.

HEDVIG.   No, I don't want to go out now.

HJALMAR.   Yes, go on. You seem to be blinking your eyes so. All these fumes in here aren't good for you; the air's not healthy under this roof.

HEDVIG.   All right, then, I'll run down the back stairs and take a little walk. My coat and hat? Oh, they're in my room. Daddy—promise you won't hurt the wild duck while I'm out.

HJALMAR.   There won't be a feather ruffled on its head. (*Drawing her to him.*) You and I, Hedvig—we two! Now run along, dear.

     (HEDVIG *nods to her parents and goes out through the kitchen.*)

HJALMAR (*walking around without looking up*).   Gina.

GINA.   Yes?

HJALMAR.   From tomorrow on—or let's say the day after tomorrow—I'd prefer to keep the household accounts myself.

GINA.   You want to keep the household accounts, too?

HJALMAR.   Yes, or keep track of the income, in any case.

GINA.   Lord love us, there's nothing to that.

HJALMAR.   One wouldn't think so. It seems to me you

can make our money stretch remarkably far. (*Stopping and looking at her.*) How *is* that?

GINA.   Hedvig and I, we don't need much.

HJALMAR.   Is it true that Father gets such good pay for the copying he does for Werle?

GINA.   I don't know how good it is. I don't know rates for such things.

HJALMAR.   Well, what does he get, just roughly? Tell me!

GINA.   It's never the same. I suppose it's roughly what he costs us, with a little pocket money thrown in.

HJALMAR.   What he costs us! That's something you've never told me before!

GINA.   No, I never could. You were always so happy thinking he got everything from you.

HJALMAR.   And instead it comes from Mr. Werle.

GINA.   Oh, but he's got plenty to spare, that one.

HJALMAR.   Let's have the lamp lit!

GINA (*lighting it*).   And then we can't know if it really is the old man; it could well be Graaberg—

HJALMAR.   Why try to put me off with Graaberg?

GINA.   No, I don't know. I just thought—

HJALMAR.   Hm!

GINA.   You know it wasn't me that got Grandfather the copying. It was Berta, that time she came here.

HJALMAR.   Your voice sounds so shaky.

GINA (*putting the shade on the lamp*).   It does?

HJALMAR.   And then your hands are trembling. Or aren't they?

GINA (*firmly*).   Say it straight out, Hjalmar. What is it he's gone and said about me?

HJALMAR.   Is it true—can it possibly be that—that there was some kind of involvement between you and Mr. Werle while you were in service there?

GINA.   That's not true. Not then, there wasn't. Werle was after me, all right. And his wife thought there was something to it, and she made a big fuss and bother, and she roasted me coming and going, she did—so I quit.

HJALMAR.   But then what!

GINA.   Yes, so then I went home. And Mother—well, she wasn't all you took her to be, Hjalmar; she ran on telling me one thing and another, because Werle was a widower by then.

HJALMAR.   Yes. And then!

GINA.   Well, you might as well know it all. He didn't give up till he had his way.

HJALMAR (*with a clap of his hands*).   And this is the mother of my child! How could you keep that hidden from me!

GINA.   Yes, I did the wrong thing; I really should have told you long ago.

HJALMAR.   Right at the start, you mean—so I could have known what sort you are.

GINA.   But would you have married me anyway?

HJALMAR.   How can you think that?

GINA.   No. But that's why I didn't dare say anything then. Because I'd come to be so terribly in love with you, as you know. And then how could I make myself utterly miserable—

HJALMAR (*walking about*).   And this is my Hedvig's mother! And then to know that everything I see around me—(*Kicking at a chair.*) my whole home—I owe to a favored predecessor. Ah, that charmer Werle!

GINA.   Do you regret the fourteen, fifteen years we've lived together?

HJALMAR (*stopping in front of her*).   Tell me—don't you every day, every hour, regret this spider web of deception you've spun around me? Answer me that! Don't you really go around in a torment of remorse?

GINA.   Hjalmar dear, I've got so much to think about just with the housework and the day's routine—

HJALMAR.   Then you never turn a critical eye on your past!

GINA.   No. Good Lord, I'd almost forgotten that old affair.

HJALMAR.   Oh, this dull, unfeeling content! To me there's something outrageous about it. Just think—not one regret!

GINA.   But Hjalmar, tell me now—what would have happened to you if you hadn't found a wife like me?

HJALMAR.   Like you—!

GINA.   Yes, because I've always been a bit more hard-headed and resourceful than you. Well, of course I'm a couple of years older.

HJALMAR.   What would have happened to me?

GINA.   You were pretty bad off at the time you met me; you can't deny that.

HJALMAR.   "Pretty bad off" you call it. Oh, you have no idea what a man goes through when he's deep in misery and despair—especially a man of my fiery temperament.

GINA.   No, that may be. And I shouldn't say nothing about it, either, because you turned out such a good-hearted husband as soon as you got a house and home—and now we've made it so snug and cozy here, and pretty soon both Hedvig and I could begin spending a little on food and clothes.

HJALMAR.   In the swamp of deception, yes.

GINA.   Ugh, that disgusting creature, tracking his way through our house!

HJALMAR.   I also thought this home was a good place to be. That was a pipe dream. Now where can I find the buoyancy I need to carry my invention into reality? Maybe it'll die with me; and then it'll be your past, Gina, that killed it.

GINA (close to tears).   No, you mustn't ever say such things, Hjalmar. All my days I've only wanted to do what's best for you!

HJALMAR.   I wonder—what happens now to the breadwinner's dream? When I lay in there on the sofa pondering my invention, I had a hunch it would drain my last bit of strength. I sensed that the day I took the patent in my hand—that would be the day of—departure. And it was my dream that then *you* would go on as the departed inventor's prosperous widow.

GINA (drying her eyes).   No, don't say that, Hjalmar. Lord knows I never want to see the day I'm a widow.

HJALMAR.   Oh, what does it matter? Everything's over and done with now. Everything!

(GREGERS *cautiously opens the hall door and looks in.*)

GREGERS.   May I come in?

HJALMAR.   Yes, do.

GREGERS (*advancing with a beaming countenance, hands*

outstretched as if to take theirs).   Now, you dear people—!
(*Looks from one to the other, then whispers to* HJALMAR.)
But isn't it done, then?

HJALMAR (*resoundingly*).   It's done.

GREGERS.   It is?

HJALMAR.   I've just known the bitterest hour of my life.

GREGERS.   But also the most exalted, I think.

HJALMAR.   Well, anyway, it's off our hands for the
moment.

GINA.   God forgive you, Mr. Werle.

GREGERS (*with great surprise*).   But I don't understand
this.

HJALMAR.   What don't you understand?

GREGERS.   With this great reckoning—the kind that
forges a whole new way of life—a life, a companionship in
truth with no more deception—

HJALMAR.   Yes, I know, I know all that.

GREGERS.   I was really positive that when I came
through that door I'd be met by a transfigured light in both
your faces. And what do I see instead but this gloomy,
heavy, dismal—

GINA.   Well, then. (*She removes the lampshade.*)

GREGERS.   You don't want to understand me, Mrs.
Ekdal. No, no, you'll need time— But you yourself,
Hjalmar? You must have gained a sense of high purpose
out of this great reckoning.

HJALMAR.   Yes, naturally. That is—more or less.

GREGERS.   Because there's nothing in the world that
compares with showing mercy to a sinner and lifting her up
in the arms of love.

HJALMAR.   Do you think a man can recover so easily
from the bitter cup I've just emptied!

GREGERS.   Not an ordinary man, no. But a man like
you—!

HJALMAR.   Good Lord, yes, I know that. But you
mustn't be driving me, Gregers. You see, these things take
time.

GREGERS.   You've *lots* of the wild duck in you, Hjalmar.

(RELLING *has entered through the hall door.*)

RELLING.   Aha! The wild duck's flying again, eh?

HJALMAR. Yes, the wounded trophy of old Werle's hunt.

RELLING. Old Werle? Is it him you're talking about?

HJALMAR. Him and—all of us.

RELLING (*under his breath to* GREGERS). The devil take you!

HJALMAR. What'd you say?

RELLING. I merely expressed my heartfelt desire that this quack would cut out for home. If he stays here, he's just the man to ruin you both.

GREGERS. They won't be ruined, Mr. Relling. Regarding Hjalmar, I'll say nothing. We know him. But she, too, surely, in the depths of her being, has something authentic, something sincere.

GINA (*near tears*). Well, if I *was* that, why didn't you leave me alone?

RELLING (*to* GREGERS). Would it be nosy to ask what you're really trying to do in this house?

GREGERS. I want to establish a true marriage.

RELLING. Then you don't think Ekdal's marriage is good enough as it is?

GREGERS. It's about as good a marriage as most, unfortunately. But it isn't yet a *true* marriage.

HJALMAR. You don't believe in ideals in life, Relling.

RELLING. Nonsense, sonny boy! Excuse me, Mr. Werle, but how many—in round numbers—how many "true marriages" have you seen in your time?

GREGERS. I believe I've hardly seen a single one.

RELLING. And I likewise.

GREGERS. But I've seen innumerable marriages of the opposite kind. And I've had a chance to see at close range what such a marriage can destroy in two people.

HJALMAR. A man's whole moral foundation can crumble under his feet; that's the dreadful thing.

RELLING. Well, I've never really exactly been married, so I'm no judge of these things. But I do know this, that the child is part of the marriage too. And you've got to leave the child in peace.

HJALMAR. Ah, Hedvig! My poor Hedvig!

RELLING. Yes, you'll please see that Hedvig's left out of it. You're both grown people; you're free, God knows, to slop up your private lives all you want. But I tell you,

you've got to be careful with Hedvig, or else you might do her some serious harm.

HJALMAR.   Harm!

RELLING.   Yes, or she could do harm to herself—and possibly others as well.

GINA.   But how can you know that, Relling?

HJALMAR.   There's no immediate threat to her eyes, is there?

RELLING.   This has nothing to do with her eyes. Hedvig's arrived at a difficult age. She's open to all kinds of erratic ideas.

GINA.   You know—she is at that! She's begun to fool around something awful with the fire in the kitchen stove. She calls it playing house afire. I'm often scared she *will* set the house on fire.

RELLING.   See what I mean? I knew it.

GREGERS (*to* RELLING).   But how do you explain something like that?

RELLING (*brusquely*).   Her voice is changing, junior.

HJALMAR.   As long as the child has *me*! As long as I'm above the sod.

(*A knock is heard at the door.*)

GINA.   Shh, Hjalmar, someone's in the hall. (*Calling out.*) Come on in!

(MRS. SØRBY, *wearing street clothes, enters.*)

MRS. SØRBY.   Good evening!

GINA (*going toward her*).   Is it you, Berta!

MRS. SØRBY.   Oh yes, it's me. But perhaps I came at an awkward time?

HJALMAR.   Oh, not at all; a messenger from *that* house—

MRS. SØRBY (*to* GINA).   As a matter of fact, I'd hoped that I wouldn't find your menfolk in at this hour, so I ran over just to have a word with you and say good-bye.

GINA.   Oh? Are you going away?

MRS. SØRBY.   Yes, tomorrow, early—up to Hoidal. Mr. Werle left this afternoon. (*Casually to* GREGERS.) He sends his regards.

GINA.   Just think!

HJALMAR.   So Mr. Werle has left? And you're following him?

MRS. SØRBY.   Yes, what do you say to that, Ekdal?

HJALMAR.   I say watch out.

GREGERS.   Let me explain. My father is marrying Mrs. Sørby.

HJALMAR.   He's marrying her!

GINA.   Oh, Berta, it's come at last!

RELLING (*his voice quavering slightly*).   This really can't be true.

MRS. SØRBY.   Yes, my dear Relling, it's completely true.

RELLING.   You want to marry again?

MRS. SØRBY.   Yes, so it seems. Werle has gotten a special license, and we're going to have a very quiet wedding up at the works.

GREGERS.   So I ought to wish you happiness, like a good stepson.

MRS. SØRBY.   Thank you, if you really mean it. I'm hoping it will bring us happiness, both Werle and me.

RELLING.   That's a reasonable hope. Mr. Werle never gets drunk—as far as *I* know; and he's certainly not given to beating up his wives the way the late horse doctor did.

MRS. SØRBY.   Oh, now let Sørby rest in peace. He did have some worthy traits, you know.

RELLING.   Old Werle's traits are worth rather more, I'll bet.

MRS. SØRBY.   At least he hasn't wasted the best that's in him. Any man who does *that* has to take the consequences.

RELLING.   Tonight I'm going out with Molvik.

MRS. SØRBY.   You shouldn't, Relling. Don't do it—for my sake.

RELLING.   What else is left? (*To* HJALMAR.) If you'd care to, you could come too.

GINA.   No, thanks. Hjalmar never goes dissipating.

HJALMAR (*in an angry undertone*).   Can't you keep quiet!

RELLING.   Good-bye, Mrs.—Werle. (*He goes out the hall door.*)

GREGERS (*to* MRS. SØRBY).   It would seem that you and Dr. Relling know each other quite intimately.

MRS. SØRBY.   Yes, we've known each other for many years. At one time something might have developed between us.

GREGERS.   It was certainly lucky for you that it didn't.

MRS. SØRBY.   Yes, that's true enough. But I've always been wary of following my impulses. After all, a woman can't just throw herself away.

GREGERS.   Aren't you even a little bit afraid that I'll drop my father a hint about this old friendship?

MRS. SØRBY.   You can be sure I've told him myself.

GREGERS.   Oh?

MRS. SØRBY.   Your father knows every last scrap of gossip that holds any grain of truth about me. I told him all of those things; it was the first thing I did when he made his intentions clear.

GREGERS.   Then I think you're more frank than most people.

MRS. SØRBY.   I've always been frank. In the long run, it's the best thing for us women to be.

HJALMAR.   What do you say to that, Gina?

GINA.   Oh, women are all so different. Some live one way and some live another.

MRS. SØRBY.   Well, Gina, I do think it's wisest to handle things as I have. And Werle, for his part, hasn't held back anything either. Really, it's this that's brought us so close together. Now he can sit and talk to me as freely as a child. He's never had that chance before. He, a healthy, vigorous man, had to spend his whole youth and all his best years hearing nothing but sermons on his sins. And generally those sermons were aimed at the most imaginary failings— at least from what *I* could see.

GINA.   Yes, that's just as true as you say.

GREGERS.   If you women are going to explore this subject, I'd better leave.

MRS. SØRBY.   You can just as well stay, for that matter; I won't say another word. But I did want you to understand that I haven't done anything sly or in any way underhanded. I suppose it looks like I've had quite a nice piece of luck, and that's true enough, up to a point. But, anyway, what I mean is that I'll not be taking any more than I give. One thing I'll never do is desert him. And I can be useful to him and care for him now better than anyone else after he's helpless.

HJALMAR.   After he's helpless?

GREGERS (*to* MRS. SØRBY).   All right, don't talk about that here.

MRS. SØRBY. No need to hide it any longer, much as he'd like to. He's going blind.

HJALMAR (*astounded*). He's going blind? But that's peculiar. Is he going blind too?

GINA. Lots of people do.

MRS. SØRBY. And you can imagine what that means for a businessman. Well, I'll try to make my eyes do for his as well as I can. But I mustn't stay any longer; I've so much to take care of now. Oh yes, I was supposed to tell you this, Ekdal—that if there's anything Werle can do for you, please just get in touch with Graaberg.

GREGERS. That offer Hjalmar Ekdal will certainly decline.

MRS. SØRBY. Come, now, I don't think that in the past he's—

GINA. No, Berta, Hjalmar doesn't need to take anything from Mr. Werle now.

HJALMAR (*slowly and ponderously*). Would you greet your future husband from me and say that I intend very shortly to call on his bookkeeper. Graaberg—

GREGERS. What! Is that what you want?

HJALMAR. To call on his bookkeeper Graaberg, as I said, to request an itemized account of what I owe his employer. I shall repay this debt of honor—(*Laughs.*) That's a good name for it, "debt of honor"! But never mind. I shall repay every penny of it, with five percent interest.

GINA. But Hjalmar dear, God knows we don't have the money for that.

HJALMAR. Will you tell your husband-to-be that I'm working away relentlessly at my invention. Would you tell him that what keeps my spirits up through this grueling ordeal is the desire to be quit of a painful burden of debt. That's why I'm making my invention. The entire proceeds will be devoted to shedding my monetary ties with your imminent partner.

MRS. SØRBY. Something has really happened in this house.

HJALMAR. Yes, it certainly has.

MRS. SØRBY. Well, good-bye, then. I still have a little more to talk about with you, Gina, but that can keep till another time. Good-bye.

(HJALMAR *and* GREGERS *silently nod;* GINA *accompanies* MRS. SØRBY *to the door.*)

HJALMAR.   Not across the threshold, Gina!

(MRS. SØRBY *leaves;* GINA *closes the door behind her.*)

HJALMAR.   There, now, Gregers—now I've got that pressing debt off my hands.

GREGERS.   You will soon, anyway.

HJALMAR.   I believe my attitude could be called correct.

GREGERS.   You're the man I always thought you were.

HJALMAR.   In certain circumstances it's impossible not to feel the summons of the ideal. As the family provider, you know, I've got to writhe and groan beneath it. Believe you me, it's really no joke for a man without means to try and pay off a long-standing debt over which the dust of oblivion, so to speak, had fallen. But it's got to be, all the same; my human self demands its rights.

GREGERS (*laying one hand on his shoulder*).   Ah, Hjalmar —wasn't it a good thing I came?

HJALMAR.   Yes.

GREGERS.   Getting a clear picture of the whole situation—wasn't that a good thing?

HJALMAR (*a bit impatiently*).   Of course it was good. But there's one thing that irks my sense of justice.

GREGERS.   What's that?

HJALMAR.   It's the fact that—oh, I don't know if I dare speak so freely about your father.

GREGERS.   Don't hold back on my account.

HJALMAR.   Well, uh—you see, I find something so irritating in the idea that I'm not the one, he's the one who's going to have the true marriage.

GREGERS.   How can you say such a thing!

HJALMAR.   But it's true. Your father and Mrs. Sørby are entering a marriage based on complete trust, one that's wholehearted and open on both sides. They haven't bottled up any secrets from each other; there isn't any reticence between them; they've declared—if you'll permit me—a mutual forgiveness of sins.

GREGERS.   All right. So what?

HJALMAR.   Yes, but that's the whole thing, then. You

said yourself that the reason for all these difficulties was the founding of a true marriage.

GREGERS. But that marriage is a very different sort, Hjalmar. You certainly wouldn't compare either you or her with those two—well, you know what I mean.

HJALMAR. Still, I can't get over the idea that there's something in all this that violates my sense of justice. It really seems as if there's no just order to the universe.

GINA. Good Lord, Hjalmar, you musn't say such things.

GREGERS. Hm, let's not start on that question.

HJALMAR. But then, on the other hand, I can definitely make out what seems to be the meticulous hand of fate. He's going blind.

GINA. Oh, that's not for sure.

HJALMAR. That is indisputable. Anyway, we oughtn't to doubt it, because it's precisely this fact that reveals the just retribution. Years back he abused the blind faith of a fellow human being—

GREGERS. I'm afraid he's done that to many others.

HJALMAR. And now a pitiless, mysterious something comes and claims the old man's eyes in return.

GINA. What a horrible thing to say! It really frightens me.

HJALMAR. It's useful sometimes to go down deep into the night side of existence.

(HEDVIG, *in her hat and coat, comes in, happy and breathless, through the hall door.*)

GINA. Back so soon?

HEDVIG. Yes, I got tired of walking, and it was just as well, 'cause then I met someone down at the door.

HJALMAR. That must have been Mrs. Sørby.

HEDVIG. Yes.

HJALMAR (*pacing back and forth*). I hope that's the last time you'll see her.

(*Silence.* HEDVIG *glances timidly from one to the other, as if trying to read their feelings.*)

HEDVIG (*coaxingly, as she approaches*). Daddy.

HJALMAR. Well—what is it, Hedvig?

HEDVIG. Mrs. Sørby brought along something for me.

HJALMAR (*stopping*). For you?

HEDVIG. Yes. It's something meant for tomorrow.

GINA. Berta's always brought some little gift for your birthday.

HJALMAR. What is it?

HEDVIG. No, you can't know that yet, because Mother has to bring it to me in bed first thing in the morning.

HJALMAR. Oh, all this conspiracy that I'm left out of!

HEDVIG (*hurriedly*). Oh, you can see it all right. It's a big letter. (*She takes the letter out of her coat pocket.*)

HJALMAR. A letter, too?

HEDVIG. Well, it's only the letter. I guess the rest will come later. But just think—a letter! I've never gotten a real letter before. And on the outside there, it says "Miss." (*She reads.*) "Miss Hedvig Ekdal." Just think—that's me.

HJALMAR. Let me see the letter.

HEDVIG (*handing it over*). See, there.

HJALMAR. That's old Werle's writing.

GINA. Are you positive, Hjalmar?

HJALMAR. See for yourself.

GINA. Oh, how would I know?

HJALMAR. Hedvig, mind if I open the letter—and read it?

HEDVIG. Sure. If you want to, go right ahead.

GINA. No, not tonight, Hjalmar. It's meant for tomorrow.

HEDVIG (*softly*). Oh, won't you let him read it! It's got to be something good, and then Daddy'll be happy and things will be pleasant again.

HJALMAR. May I open it, then?

HEDVIG. Yes, please do, Daddy. It'll be fun to find out what it is.

HJALMAR. Good. (*He opens the envelope, takes out a sheet of paper, and reads it through with growing bewilderment.*) Now what's this all about?

GINA. But what does it say?

HEDVIG. Oh yes, Daddy—tell us!

HJALMAR. Be quiet. (*He reads it through once more, turns pale, then speaks with evident restraint.*) This is a deed of gift, Hedvig.

HEDVIG. Honestly? What am I getting?

HJALMAR. Read for yourself.

(HEDVIG *goes over to the lamp and reads for a moment.*)

HJALMAR (*clenching his fists, in almost a whisper*). The eyes! The eyes—and now that letter!

HEDVIG (*interrupting her reading*). Yes, but I think the gift is for Grandfather.

HJALMAR (*taking the letter from her*). Gina—do you understand this?

GINA. I know nothing at all about it. Just tell me.

HJALMAR. Mr. Werle writes Hedvig to say that her old grandfather needn't trouble himself any longer with copying work, but that henceforth he can draw one hundred crowns a month from the office—

GREGERS. Aha!

HEDVIG. One hundred crowns, Mother! I read that.

GINA. That'll be nice for Grandfather.

HJALMAR. One hundred crowns, as long as he needs it. That means till death, of course.

GINA. Well, then he's provided for, poor dear.

HJALMAR. But there's more. You didn't read far enough, Hedvig. Afterwards this gift passes over to you.

HEDVIG. To me! All of it?

HJALMAR. You're assured the same income for the rest of your life, he writes. Hear that, Gina?

GINA. Yes, of course I heard.

HEDVIG. Imagine me getting all that money! (*Shaking* HJALMAR.) Daddy, Daddy, aren't you glad?

HJALMAR (*disengaging himself*). Glad! (*Walking about the room.*) Ah, what vistas—what perspectives it offers me. Hedvig is the one, she's the one he remembers so bountifully.

GINA. Of course, because it's Hedvig's birthday.

HEDVIG. And anyway, you'll have it, Daddy. You know that I'll give all the money to you and Mother.

HJALMAR. To Mother, yes! There we have it.

GREGERS. Hjalmar, this is a trap that's been set for you.

HJALMAR. You think it could be another trap?

GREGERS. When he was here this morning, he said, "Hjalmar Ekdal is not the man you think he is."

HJALMAR. Not the man—!

GREGERS. "You'll find that out," he said.

HJALMAR.   Find out if I could be bought off for a price, eh—!

HEDVIG.   But Mother, what's this all about?

GINA.   Go and take your things off.

(HEDVIG, *close to tears, goes out the kitchen door.*)

GREGERS.   Yes, Hjalmar—now we'll see who's right, he or I.

HJALMAR (*slowly tearing the paper in half and putting both pieces on the table*).   That is my answer.

GREGERS.   What I expected.

HJALMAR (*going over to* GINA, *who is standing by the stove, and speaking quietly*).   And now no more pretenses. If that thing between you and him was all over when you— came to be so terribly in love with me, as you put it—then why did he give us the means to get married?

GINA.   Maybe he thought he could come and go here.

HJALMAR.   Is that all? Wasn't he afraid of a certain possibility?

GINA.   I don't know what you mean.

HJALMAR.   I want to know if—your child has the right to live under my roof.

GINA (*draws herself up, her eyes flashing*).   And you can ask that?

HJALMAR.   Just answer me this: does Hedvig belong to me—or? Well!

GINA (*regarding him with chill defiance*).   I don't know.

HJALMAR (*with a slight quaver*).   You don't know!

GINA.   How would *I* know that? A woman of my sort—

HJALMAR (*softly, turning from her*).   Then I have nothing more to do in this house.

GREGERS.   You must think about this, Hjalmar.

HJALMAR (*putting on his overcoat*).   There's nothing to think about for a man like me.

GREGERS.   Oh, there's so very much to think about. You three have got to stay together if you're ever going to win through to a self-sacrificial, forgiving spirit.

HJALMAR.   I don't want that. Never, never! My hat! (*Takes his hat.*) My home is down in ruins around me. (*Breaks into tears.*) Gregers, I have no child!

HEDVIG (*who has opened the kitchen door*).   What are you saying! (*Running toward him.*) Daddy, Daddy!

GINA. Now look!

HJALMAR. Don't come near me, Hedvig! Keep away. I can't bear seeing you. Oh, the eyes! Goodbye. (*Starts for the door.*)

HEDVIG (*clinging fast to him and shrieking*). Oh no! Oh no! Don't leave me.

GINA (*crying out*). Look out for the child, Hjalmar! Look out for the child!

HJALMAR. I won't. I can't. I've got to get out—away from all this! (*He tears himself loose from* HEDVIG *and goes out through the hall door.*)

HEDVIG (*with desperate eyes*). He's left us, Mother! He's left us! He'll never come back again!

GINA. Now don't cry, Hedvig, Daddy's coming back.

HEDVIG (*throws herself, sobbing, on the sofa*). No, no, he'll never come home to us again.

GREGERS. Will you believe I've wanted everything for the best, Mrs. Ekdal?

GINA. Yes, I think I believe that—but God have mercy on you all the same.

HEDVIG (*lying on the sofa*). I think I'll die from all this. What did I do to him? Mother, you've got to make him come home!

GINA. Yes, yes, yes, just be calm, and I'll step out and look for him. (*Putting on her coat.*) Maybe he's gone down to Relling's. But now don't you lie there, wailing away. Will you promise?

HEDVIG (*sobbing convulsively*). Yes, I'll be all right—if only Daddy comes back.

GREGERS (*to* GINA, *about to leave*). Wouldn't it be better, though, to let him fight through his painful battle first?

GINA. Oh, he can do that later. First of all, we've got to comfort the child. (*She goes out the hall door.*)

HEDVIG (*sitting up and drying her tears*). Now you have to tell me what it's all about. Why does Daddy not want to see me anymore?

GREGERS. That's something you mustn't ask until you're big and grown-up.

HEDVIG (*catching her breath*). But I can't go on being so horribly unhappy till I'm big and grown-up. I bet I know what it is. Perhaps I'm really not Daddy's child.

GREGERS (*disturbed*). How could that ever be?

HEDVIG.   Mother could have found me. And now maybe Daddy's found out. I've read about these things.

GREGERS.   Well, but if that was the—

HEDVIG.   Yes, I think he could love me even so. Or maybe more. The wild duck was sent us as a present too, and I'm terribly fond of it, all the same.

GREGERS (*divertingly*).   Of course, the wild duck, that's true. Let's talk a bit about the wild duck, Hedvig.

HEDVIG.   The poor wild duck. He can't bear to see her again, either. Imagine, he wanted to wring her neck!

GREGERS.   Oh, he certainly wouldn't do that.

HEDVIG.   No, but that's what he said. And I think it was awful for Daddy to say, because each night I make a prayer for the wild duck and ask that she be delivered from death and everything evil.

GREGERS (*looking at her*).   Do you always say your prayers at night?

HEDVIG.   Uh-huh.

GREGERS.   Who taught you that?

HEDVIG.   I taught myself, and that was once when Daddy was so sick and had leeches on his neck, and then he said he was in the jaws of death.

GREGERS.   Oh yes?

HEDVIG.   So I said a prayer for him when I went to bed. And I've kept it up ever since.

GREGERS.   And now you pray for the wild duck, too?

HEDVIG.   I thought it was best to put the wild duck in, because she was ailing so at the start.

GREGERS.   Do you say morning prayers, too?

HEDVIG.   No, not at all.

GREGERS.   Why not morning prayers as well?

HEDVIG.   In the morning it's light, and so there's nothing much to be afraid of.

GREGERS.   And the wild duck you love so much—your father wants to wring her neck.

HEDVIG.   No. He said it would be the best thing for him if he did, but for my sake he would spare her; and that was good of Daddy.

GREGERS (*coming closer*).   But what if you now, of your own free will, sacrificed the wild duck for *his* sake.

HEDVIG (*rises*).   The wild duck!

GREGERS. What if you, in a sacrificing spirit, gave up the dearest thing you own and know in the whole world?

HEDVIG. Do you think that would help?

GREGERS. Try it, Hedvig.

HEDVIG (*softly, with shining eyes*). Yes, I'll try it.

GREGERS. And the strength of mind, do you think you have it?

HEDVIG. I'll ask Grandpa to shoot the wild duck for me.

GREGERS. Yes, do that. But not a word to your mother about all this!

HEDVIG. Why not?

GREGERS. She doesn't understand us.

HEDVIG. The wild duck? I'll try it tomorrow, early.

(GINA *comes in through the hall door.*)

HEDVIG (*going toward her*). Did you find him, Mother?

GINA. No. But I heard he'd looked in downstairs and gotten Relling along.

GREGERS. Are you sure of that?

GINA. Yes, I asked the janitor's wife. And Molvik was with them, she said.

GREGERS. And this, right when his mind needs nothing so much as to wrestle in solitude—!

GINA (*taking off her coat*). Oh, men are strange ones, they are. God knows where Relling has led him! I ran over to Mrs. Eriksen's café, but they weren't there.

HEDVIG (*struggling with her tears*). Oh, what if he never comes back again!

GREGERS. He *will* come back. I'll get a message to him tomorrow, and then you'll see—he'll be back. Believe that, Hedvig, and sleep well. Good night. (*He goes out the hall door.*)

HEDVIG (*throwing herself, sobbing, into* GINA'S *arms*). Mother, Mother!

GINA (*pats her on the back and sighs*). Ah, me, Relling was right. That's the way it goes when these crazy people come around, summoning up their ideals.

ACT FIVE

HJALMAR EKDAL's *studio. A cold, gray morning light filters in; wet snow lies on the huge panes of the skylight.* GINA, *wearing a pinafore, comes in from the kitchen, carrying a feather duster and a cleaning cloth, and makes for the living room door. At the same moment* HEDVIG *rushes in from the hallway.*

GINA (*stopping*). Well?

HEDVIG. You know, Mother, I'm pretty sure he's down at Relling's—

GINA. There, you see!

HEDVIG. 'Cause the janitor's wife said she heard Relling had two others with him when he came in last night.

GINA. That's about what I thought.

HEDVIG. But it's still no good if he won't come up to us.

GINA. At least I can go down there and talk with him.

(EKDAL, *in dressing gown and slippers, smoking a pipe, appears in the doorway to his room.*)

EKDAL. Say, Hjalmar— Isn't Hjalmar home?

GINA. No, he's gone out, I guess.

EKDAL. So early? In a raging blizzard like this? Oh, well, never mind; I'll take my morning walk alone, that's all.

(*He pulls the loft door ajar,* HEDVIG *helping him. He goes in; she closes up after him.*)

HEDVIG (*lowering her voice*). Just think, Mother, when Grandpa finds out that Daddy's leaving us.

GINA. Go on, Grandpa won't hear anything of the kind. It was a real stroke of providence he wasn't here yesterday in all that racket.

HEDVIG. Yes, but—

199

(GREGERS *comes in the hall entrance.*)

GREGERS. Well? Had any reports on him?

GINA. He should be down at Relling's, they tell me.

GREGERS. With Relling! Did he really go out with those fellows?

GINA. Apparently.

GREGERS. Yes, but he who needed so much to be alone to pull himself together—!

GINA. Yes, just as you say.

(RELLING *enters from the hall.*)

HEDVIG (*going toward him*). Is Daddy with you?

GINA (*simultaneously*). Is he there?

RELLING. Yes, of course he is.

HEDVIG. And you never told us!

RELLING. Oh, I'm a beast. But first of all, I had that other beast to manage—you know, the demonic one, him—and then, next, I fell so sound asleep that—

GINA. What's Hjalmar been saying today?

RELLING. He's said absolutely nothing.

HEDVIG. Hasn't he talked at all?

RELLING. Not a blessed word.

GREGERS. No, no, I can well understand that.

GINA. But what's he doing, then?

RELLING. He's laid out on the sofa, snoring.

GINA. Oh? Yes, Hjalmar's great at snoring.

HEDVIG. He's asleep? Can he sleep?

RELLING. Well, so it seems.

GREGERS. It's conceivable—when all that strife of spirit has torn him.

GINA. And then he's never been used to roaming around the streets at night.

HEDVIG. Maybe it's a good thing that he's getting some sleep, Mother.

GINA. I think so too. But then it's just as well we don't rouse him too soon. Thanks a lot, Relling. Now I've got to clean and straighten up here a bit, and then— Come and help me, Hedvig.

(GINA *and* HEDVIG *disappear into the living room.*)

GREGERS (*turning to* RELLING). Have you an explanation for the spiritual upheaval taking place within Hjalmar Ekdal?

RELLING.   For the life of me, I can't remember any spiritual upheaval in him.

GREGERS.   Wait! At a time of crisis like this, when his life has been recast? How can you believe that a rare personality like Hjalmar—?

RELLING.   Pah! Personality—him! If he's ever had a tendency toward anything so abnormal as what you call personality, it was ripped up, root and vine, by the time he was grown, and that's a fact.

GREGERS.   That's rather surprising—with all the loving care he had as a child.

RELLING.   From those two warped, hysterical maiden aunts, you mean?

GREGERS.   I want to tell you they were women who always summoned themselves to the highest ideals—yes, now of course you'll start mocking me again.

RELLING.   No, I'm hardly in a mood for that. Besides, I'm well informed here; he's regurgitated any amount of rhetoric about his "twin soul-mothers." I really don't believe he has much to thank them for. Ekdal's misfortune is that in his circle he's always been taken for a shining light—

GREGERS.   And isn't he, perhaps, exactly that? In his heart's core. I mean?

RELLING.   I've never noticed anything of the kind. His father thinks so—but that's nothing; the old lieutenant's been a fool all his life.

GREGERS.   He has, all his life, been a man with a childlike awareness; and that's something you just don't understand.

RELLING.   Oh, sure! But back when our dear, sweet Hjalmar became a student of sorts, right away he got taken up by his classmates as the great beacon of the future. Oh, he was good-looking, the lout—pink and white—just the way little moon-eyed girls like boys. And then he had that excitable manner and that heart-winning tremor in his voice, and he was so cute and clever at declaiming other people's poems and ideas—

GREGERS (*indignantly*).   Is it Hjalmar Ekdal you're speaking of that way?

RELLING. Yes, with your permission. That's an inside look at him, this idol you're groveling in front of.

GREGERS. I really didn't think I was utterly blind.

RELLING. Well, you're not far from it. Because you're a sick man too, you are.

GREGERS. There you're right.

RELLING. Oh yes. Your case has complications. First there's this virulent moralistic fever; and then something worse—you keep going off in deliriums of hero worship; you always have to have something to admire that's outside of yourself.

GREGERS. Yes, I certainly have to look for it outside myself.

RELLING. But you're so woefully wrong about these great miraculous beings you think you see and hear around you. You've simply come back to a cotter's cabin with your summons to the ideal; there's nobody solvent in this house.

GREGERS. If you've got no higher estimate of Hjalmar Ekdal than this, how can you ever enjoy seeing him day after day?

RELLING. Good Lord, I *am* supposed to be some kind of doctor, I'm ashamed to say. Well, then I ought to look after the poor sick people I live with.

GREGERS. Oh, come! Is Hjalmar Ekdal sick, too?

RELLING. Most of the world is sick, I'm afraid.

GREGERS. And what's your prescription for Hjalmar?

RELLING. My standard one. I try to keep up the life-lie in him.

GREGERS. The life-lie? I don't think I heard—

RELLING. Oh yes, I said the life-lie. The life-lie, don't you see—that's the animating principle of life.

GREGERS. May I ask what kind of lie has infected Hjalmar?

RELLING. No, thanks, I don't betray secrets like that to quacks. You'd just be able to damage him all the more for me. My method is tested, though. I've also used it on Molvik. I made him "demonic." That was my remedy for him.

GREGERS. Then he isn't demonic?

RELLING. What the devil does it mean to be demonic? That's just some hogwash I thought up to keep life going in him. If I hadn't done that, the poor innocent mutt would have given in years ago to self-contempt and despair. And then take the old lieutenant! But he really discovered his own cure himself.

GREGERS.   Lieutenant Ekdal? How so?

RELLING.   Well, what do you think of this bear hunter going into a dark loft to stalk rabbits? There isn't a happier sportsman in the world than the old man when he's prowling around in that junkyard. Those four or five dried-out Christmas trees he's got—to him they're like all the green forests of Hoidal; the hens and the rooster—they're the game birds up in the fir tops; and the rabbits hopping across the floor—they're the bears that call up his youth again, out in the mountain air.

GREGERS.   Poor, unhappy old Ekdal, yes. He certainly had to pare down his early ideals.

RELLING.   While I remember it, Mr. Werle junior— don't use that exotic word *ideals*. Not when we've got a fine native word—*lies*.

GREGERS.   You're implying the two have something in common?

RELLING.   Yes, about like typhus and typhoid fever.

GREGERS.   Dr. Relling, I won't rest till I've gotten Hjalmar out of your clutches.

RELLING.   So much the worse for him. Deprive the average man of his vital lie, and you've robbed him of happiness as well. (*To* HEDVIG, *entering from the living room.*) Well, little wild-duck mother, now I'll go down and see if Papa's still lying and pondering his marvelous invention. (*He goes out the hall door.*)

GREGERS (*approaching* HEDVIG).   I can see by your face that it isn't done.

HEDVIG.   What? Oh, about the wild duck. No.

GREGERS.   Your courage failed you when the time came to act, I suppose.

HEDVIG.   No, it's not exactly that. But when I woke up this morning early and thought of what we talked about, then it seemed so strange to me.

GREGERS.   Strange?

HEDVIG.   Yes, I don't know— Last night, right at the time, there was something so beautiful about it, but after I'd slept and then thought it over, it didn't seem like so much.

GREGERS. Ah, no, you couldn't grow up here without some taint in you.

HEDVIG. I don't care about that; if only Daddy would come up, then—

GREGERS. Oh, if only your eyes were really open to what makes life worth living—if only you had the true, joyful, courageous spirit of self-sacrifice, *then* you'd see him coming up to you. But I still have faith in you. (*He goes out the hall door.*)

> (HEDVIG *wanders across the room, then starts into the kitchen. At that moment a knock comes on the loft door,* HEDVIG *goes over and opens it a space;* EKDAL *slips out, and she slides it shut again.*)

EKDAL. Hm, a morning walk alone is no fun at all.

HEDVIG. Don't you want to go hunting. Grandpa?

EKDAL. The weather's no good for hunting. Awfully dark in there; you can hardly see ahead of you.

HEDVIG. Don't you ever want to shoot at anything but rabbits?

EKDAL. Aren't rabbits good enough, eh?

HEDVIG. Yes, but the wild duck, say?

EKDAL. Ha, ha! You're afraid I'll shoot the wild duck for you? Never in this world, dear. Never!

HEDVIG. No, you couldn't do that. It must be hard to shoot wild ducks.

EKDAL. Couldn't? I certainly could!

HEDVIG. How would you go about it, Grandpa?—I don't mean with *my* wild duck, but with others.

EKDAL. I'd be sure to shoot them in the breast, understand; that's the safest. And then they've got to be shot *against* the feathers, you see—not *with* the feathers.

HEDVIG. They die then, Grandpa?

EKDAL. Oh yes, they do indeed—if you shoot them right. Well, got to go in and clean up. Hm—you understand—hm. (*He goes into his room.*)

> (HEDVIG *waits a moment, glances at the living room door, goes to the bookcase, stands on tiptoe, takes down the double-barreled pistol from the shelf and looks at it.* GINA, *with duster*

and cloth, comes in from the living room. HED-
VIG *hastily sets down the pistol, unnoticed.*)

GINA.   Don't mess with your father's things, Hedvig.

HEDVIG (*leaving the bookcase*).   I was just straightening
up a little.

GINA.   Go out in the kitchen instead and make sure the
coffee's still hot; I'll take a tray along to him when I go
down.

> (HEDVIG *goes out;* GINA *begins to dust and clean
> up the studio. After a moment the hall door is
> cautiously opened, and* HJALMAR *peers in. He
> wears his overcoat, but no hat. He is un-
> washed, with tousled, unruly hair; his eyes are
> dull and inert.*)

GINA (*standing rooted with duster in hand, looking at
him*).   Don't tell me, Hjalmar—are you back after all?

HJALMAR (*steps in and answers in a thick voice*).   I'm
back—but only for one moment.

GINA.   Oh yes, I'm sure of that. But my goodness—what
a sight you are!

HJALMAR.   Sight?

GINA.   And then your good winter coat! Well, it's done
for.

HEDVIG (*at the kitchen door*).   Mother, should I—
(*Seeing* HJALMAR, *giving a squeal of delight, and running
toward him.*) Oh, Daddy, Daddy!

HJALMAR (*turning from her and waving her off*).   Get
away! Get away! (*To* GINA.) Make her get away from me,
will you!

GINA (*in an undertone*).   Go in the living room, Hedvig.

> (HEDVIG *silently goes out.*)

HJALMAR (*with a busy air, pulling out the table drawer*).   I must have my books along. Where are my books?

GINA.   What books?

HJALMAR.   My scientific works, of course—the technical
journals I use for my invention.

GINA (*looking over the bookshelves*).   Are these them,
the ones without covers?

HJALMAR.   Yes, exactly.

GINA (*putting a stack of booklets on the table*).   Could I get Hedvig to cut the pages for you?

HJALMAR.   Nobody has to cut pages for me. (*A short silence.*)

GINA.   Then it's definite that you're moving out, Hjalmar?

HJALMAR (*rummaging among the books*).   Yes, that would seem to me self-evident.

GINA.   I see.

HJALMAR.   How could I go on here and have my heart skewered every hour of the day!

GINA.   God forgive you for thinking so badly of me.

HJALMAR.   Show me proof—

GINA.   I think *you're* the one to show proof.

HJALMAR.   After your kind of past? There are certain standards—I'd like to call them ideal standards—

GINA.   But Grandfather? What'll happen to him, poor dear?

HJALMAR.   I know my duty; that helpless old soul leaves with me. I'm going downtown and make arrangements— hm—(*Hesitantly.*) Did anybody find my hat on the stairs?

GINA.   No. Have you lost your hat?

HJALMAR.   I had it on, naturally, when I came in last night; I'm positive of that. But today I couldn't find it.

GINA.   My Lord, where did you go with those two stumblebums?

HJALMAR.   Oh, don't bother me with petty questions. Do you think I'm in a mood to remember details?

GINA.   I just hope you didn't catch cold, Hjalmar. (*She goes out into the kitchen.*)

HJALMAR (*muttering to himself in exasperation, as he empties the table drawer*).   You're a sneak, Relling! A barbarian, that's what! Oh, snake in the grass! If I could just get someone to strangle you! (*He puts some old letters to one side, discovers the torn deed of the day before, picks it up and examines the pieces. He hurriedly puts them down as* GINA *enters.*)

GINA (*setting a breakfast tray on the table*).   Here's a drop of something hot, if you care for it. And there's some bread and butter and a few cold cuts.

HJALMAR (*glancing at the tray*).   Cold cuts? Never under this roof! It's true I've been starved of decent nourishment for nearly twenty-four hours; but that doesn't matter— My notes! My unfinished memoirs! Where can I find my journal and my important papers? (*Opens the living room door, then draws back.*) There she is again!

GINA. Well, goodness, the child has to be somewhere.

HJALMAR. Come out. (*He stands aside, and* HEDVIG, *terrified, comes into the studio.*)

HJALMAR (*with his hand on the doorknob, says to* GINA). These last moments I'm spending in my former home, I'd like to be free from intruders—(*Goes into the living room.*)

HEDVIG (*rushing to her mother, her voice hushed and trembling*). Does he mean me?

GINA. Stay in the kitchen, Hedvig. Or, no—go into your own room instead. (*Speaking to* HJALMAR *as she goes in to him.*) Just a minute, Hjalmar. Don't muss up the bureau like that; I know where everything is. (HEDVIG *stands for a moment as if frozen by fright and bewilderment, biting her lips to keep the tears back; then she clenches her fists convulsively.*)

HEDVIG (*softly*). The wild duck. (*She steals over and takes the pistol from the shelf, sets the loft door ajar, slips in and draws the door shut after her.* HJALMAR *and* GINA *start arguing in the living room.*)

HJALMAR (*reenters with some notebooks and old loose papers, which he lays on the table*). Oh, what good is that traveling bag! I've got a thousand things to take with me.

GINA (*following with the traveling bag*). So leave everything else for the time being, and just take a shirt and a pair of shorts with you.

HJALMAR. Phew! These agonizing preparations! (*Takes off his overcoat and throws it on the sofa.*)

GINA. And there's your coffee getting cold, too.

HJALMAR. Hm. (*Unthinkingly takes a sip and then another.*)

GINA. The hardest thing for you will be to find another room like that, big enough for all the rabbits.

HJALMAR. What! Do I have to take all the rabbits with me, too?

GINA. Yes, Grandfather couldn't live without the rabbits, I'm sure.

HJALMAR. He's simply got to get used to it. The joys of life *I* have to renounce are higher than rabbits.

GINA (*dusting the bookcase*). Should I put your flute in the traveling bag?

HJALMAR. No. No flute for me. But give me the pistol!

GINA. You want your pistol along?

HJALMAR. Yes. My loaded pistol.

GINA (*looking for it*). It's gone. He must have taken it inside.

HJALMAR. Is he in the loft?

GINA. Of course he's in the loft.

HJALMAR. Hm—lonely old man. (*He takes a piece of bread and butter, eats it, and finishes the cup of coffee.*)

GINA. Now if we only hadn't rented the room, you could have moved in there.

HJALMAR. I should stay on under the same roof as—! Never! Never!

GINA. But couldn't you put up in the living room just for a day or two? You've got everything you need in there.

HJALMAR. Never within these walls!

GINA. Well, how about down with Relling and Molvik?

HJALMAR. Don't mention those barbarians' names! I can almost lose my appetite just thinking about them. Oh no, I've got to go out in sleet and snow—tramp from house to house and seek shelter for Father and me.

GINA. But you haven't any hat, Hjalmar! You've lost your hat.

HJALMAR. Oh, those two vermin, wallowing in sin! The hat will have to be bought. (*Taking another piece of bread and butter.*) Someone's got to make arrangements. I certainly don't intend to risk my life. (*Looking for something on the tray.*)

GINA. What are you looking for?

HJALMAR. Butter.

GINA. Butter's coming right up. (*Goes into the kitchen.*)

HJALMAR (*calling after her*). Oh, never mind; I can just as easily eat dry bread.

GINA (*bringing in a butter dish*). Look. It's fresh today. (*She passes him another cup of coffee. He sits on the sofa, spreads more butter on the bread, eats and drinks a moment in silence.*)

HJALMAR. Could I—without being annoyed by any-

body—anybody at all—put up in the living room just for a
day or two?

GINA. Yes, of course you could, if you want to.

HJALMAR. Because I can't see any possibility of getting
all Father's things out in one trip.

GINA. And then there's this, too, that you've first got
to tell him you're not living with us any longer.

HJALMAR (*pushing the coffee cup away*). That too, yes.
All these intricate affairs to unravel. I've got to clear my
thinking; I need a breathing spell; I can't shoulder all these
burdens in one day.

GINA. No, and not when the weather's like it is out.

HJALMAR (*picking up* WERLE's *letter*). I see this letter's
still kicking around.

GINA. Yes, *I* haven't touched it.

HJALMAR. This trash is nothing to me—

GINA. Well, I'm not going to use it for anything.

HJALMAR. All the same, there's no point in throwing it
around helter-skelter. In all the confusion of my moving, it
could easily—

GINA. I'll take good care of it, Hjalmar.

HJALMAR. First and foremost, the deed of gift is Father's; it's really his affair whether or not he wants to use
it.

GINA (*sighing*). Yes, poor old Father—

HJALMAR. Just for safety's sake—where would I find
some paste?

GINA (*going to the bookcase*). Here's the pastepot.

HJALMAR. And then a brush.

GINA. Here's a brush, too. (*Bringing both.*)

HJALMAR (*taking a pair of scissors*). A strip of paper
down the back, that's all. (*Cutting and pasting.*) Far be it
from me to take liberties with another's property—least of
all, a penniless old man's. No, nor with—the other person's.
There, now. Let it lie a while. And when it's dry, then take
it away. I don't want to set eyes on that document again.
Ever!

(GREGERS *enters from the hall.*)

GREGERS (*somewhat surprised*). What? Are you lounging in here, Hjalmar?

HJALMAR (*springing up*). I was overcome by fatigue.

GREGERS. Still, you've had breakfast, I see.

HJALMAR. The body makes its claims now and then too.

GREGERS. What have you decided to do?

HJALMAR. For a man like me there's only one way open. I'm in the process of assembling my most important things. But that takes time, don't you know.

GINA (*a bit impatient*). Should I get the room ready for you, or should I pack your bag?

HJALMAR (*after a vexed glance at* GREGERS). Pack—and get the room ready!

GINA (*taking the traveling bag*). All right, then I'll put in the shirt and the rest. (*She goes into the living room, shutting the door behind her.*)

GREGERS (*after a short silence*). I never dreamed that things would end like this. Is it really necessary for you to leave house and home?

HJALMAR (*pacing restlessly about*). What would you have me do? I wasn't made to be unhappy, Gregers. I've got to have it snug and secure and peaceful around me.

GREGERS. But why can't you, then? Give it a try. Now I'd say you have solid ground to build on—so make a fresh start. And don't forget you have your invention to live for, too.

HJALMAR. Oh, don't talk about the invention. That seems such a long way off.

GREGERS. Oh?

HJALMAR. Good Lord, yes. What would you really have me invent? Other people have invented so much already. It gets more difficult every day—

GREGERS. And you've put so much work in it.

HJALMAR. It was that dissolute Relling who got me started.

GREGERS. Relling?

HJALMAR. Yes, he was the one who first made me aware that I had a real talent for inventing something in photography.

GREGERS. Aha—that was Relling!

HJALMAR. Oh, I was so blissfully happy as a result. Not so much from the invention itself, but because Hedvig believed in it—believed in it with all the power and force of a child's mind. Yes, in other words, fool that I am, I've gone around imagining that she believed in it.

GREGERS.   You can't really think that Hedvig could lie to you!

HJALMAR.   Now I can think anything. It's Hedvig that ruins it all. She's managed to blot the sun right out of my life.

GREGERS.   Hedvig! You mean Hedvig? How could she ever do that?

HJALMAR (*without answering*).   How inexpressibly I loved that child! How inexpressibly happy I was whenever I came home to my poor rooms and she came flying to meet me with those sweet, fluttering eyes. I was so unspeakably fond of her—and so I dreamed and deluded myself into thinking that she, too, was fond of me beyond words.

GREGERS.   Can you call *that* just a delusion?

HJALMAR.   How can I tell? I can't get anything out of Gina; and besides, she has no feeling at all for the ideal phase of these complications. But with you, Gregers, I feel impelled to open my mind. There's this horrible doubt— maybe Hedvig never really, truly has loved me.

GREGERS.   She may perhaps give you proof that she has. (*Listening.*) What's that? I thought I heard the wild duck cry.

HJALMAR.   The duck's quacking. Father's in the loft.

GREGERS.   Is he? (*His face radiates joy.*) I tell you, you may yet have proof that your poor, misjudged Hedvig loves you!

HJALMAR.   Oh, what proof could she give me? I don't dare hope to be reassured from that quarter.

GREGERS.   Hedvig's completely free of deceit.

HJALMAR.   Oh, Gregers, that's just what I can't be sure of. Who knows what Gina and this Mrs. Sørby have whispered and gossiped about in all the times they've sat here? And Hedvig uses her ears, you know. Maybe the deed of gift wasn't such a surprise, after all. In fact, I seemed to get that impression.

GREGERS.   What is this spirit that's gotten into you?

HJALMAR.   I've had my eyes opened. Just wait—you'll see; the deed of gift is only the beginning. Mrs. Sørby has always cared a lot for Hedvig, and now she has the power to do what she wants for the child. They can take her away from me any time they like.

GREGERS.   You're the last person in the world Hedvig would leave.

HJALMAR.   Don't be too sure of that. If they stand beckoning her with all they have—? Oh, I who've loved her so inexpressibly! I who'd find my highest joy in taking her tenderly by the hand and leading her as one leads a child terrified of the dark through a huge, empty room! I can feel it now with such gnawing certainty; the poor photographer up in this attic has never meant much to her. She's merely been clever to keep on a good footing with him till the right time came.

GREGERS.   You really don't believe that, Hjalmar.

HJALMAR.   The worst thing is precisely that I don't know what to believe—that I'll never know. But can you honestly doubt that it's just what I'm saying? (*With a bitter laugh.*) Ah, you're just too idealistic, my dear Gregers! Suppose the others come with their hands full of riches and call out to the child: Leave him. Life waits for you here with us—

GREGERS (*quickly*).   Yes, then what?

HJALMAR.   If I asked her then: Hedvig, are you willing to give up life for me? (*Laughs derisively.*) Yes, thanks—you'd hear all right what answer I'd get!

(*A pistol shot is heard in the loft.*)

GREGERS (*with a shout of joy*).   Hjalmar!

HJALMAR.   Hear that. He's got to go hunting as well.

GINA   (*coming in*).   Oh, Hjalmar, it sounds like Grandfather's shooting up the loft by himself.

HJALMAR.   I'll take a look—

GREGERS (*animated and exalted*).   Wait now! Do you know what that was?

HJALMAR.   Of course I know.

GREGERS.   No, you don't know. But *I* do. That was the proof!

HJALMAR.   What proof?

GREGERS.   That was a child's sacrifice. She's had your father shoot the wild duck.

HJALMAR.   Shoot the wild duck!

GINA.   No, really—!

HJALMAR.   What for?

GREGERS.   She wanted to sacrifice to you the best thing

she had in the world, because she thought then you'd have
to love her again.

HJALMAR (*stirred, gently*).   Ah, that child!

GINA.   Yes, the things she thinks of!

GREGERS.   She only wants your love again, Hjalmar; she
felt she couldn't live without it.

GINA (*struggling with tears*).   There you are, Hjalmar.

HJALMAR.   Gina, where's she gone?

GINA (*sniffling*).   Poor thing. I guess she's out in the
kitchen.

HJALMAR (*going over and flinging the kitchen door
open*).   Hedvig, come! Come here to me! (*Looking about.*)
No, she's not there.

GINA.   Then she's in her own little room.

HJALMAR (*out of sight*).   No, she's not there either.
(*Coming back in.*) She may have gone out.

GINA.   Yes, you didn't want her around anywhere in the
house.

HJALMAR.   Oh, if only she comes home soon—so I can
just let her know—! Things will work out now, Gregers—
for now I really believe we can start life over again.

GREGERS (*quietly*).   I knew it; through the child everything rights itself.

> (EKDAL *appears at the door to his room; he is in
> full uniform and is absorbed in buckling his
> sword.*)

HJALMAR (*astonished*).   Father! Are you there?

GINA.   Were you out gunning in your room?

EKDAL (*approaching angrily*).   So you've been hunting
alone, eh, Hjalmar?

HJALMAR (*baffled and anxious*).   Then it wasn't you who
fired a shot in the loft?

EKDAL.   Me, shoot? Hm!

GREGERS (*shouting to* HJALMAR).   She's shot the wild
duck herself!

HJALMAR.   What is all this! (*Rushes to the loft doors,
throws them open, looks in and cries:*) Hedvig!

GINA (*running to the door*).   Lord, what now!

HJALMAR (*going in*).   She's lying on the floor!

GINA (*simultaneously*).   Hedvig! (*Going into the loft.*)
No, no, no!

EKDAL.   Ha, ha! So she's a hunter, too.

> (HJALMAR, GINA, *and* GREGERS *carry* HEDVIG
> *into the studio; her right hand hangs down and
> her fingers curve tightly about the pistol.*)

HJALMAR (*distraught*).   The pistol's gone off. She's wounded herself. Call for help! Help!

GINA (*running into the hall and calling downstairs*).   Relling! Relling! Dr. Relling, come up as quick as you can!

EKDAL. (*hushed*).   The woods take revenge.

HJALMAR (*on his knees by her*).   She's just coming to now. She's coming to now—oh yes, yes.

GINA (*who has returned*).   Where is she wounded? I can't see anything—

> (RELLING *hurries in, and right after him,* MOL-
> VIK, *who is without vest or tie, his dress coat
> open.*)

RELLING.   What's up here?

GINA.   They say Hedvig shot herself.

HJALMAR.   Come here and help.

RELLING.   Shot herself! (*He shoves the table to one side and begins to examine her.*)

HJALMAR (*kneeling still, looking anxiously up at him*).   It can't be serious? Huh, Relling? She's hardly bleeding. It can't be serious?

RELLING.   How did this happen?

HJALMAR.   Oh, how do I know—

GINA.   She wanted to shoot the wild duck.

RELLING.   The wild duck?

HJALMAR.   The pistol must have gone off.

RELLING.   Hm. I see.

EKDAL.   The woods take revenge. But I'm not scared, even so. (*He goes into the loft, shutting the door after him.*)

HJALMAR.   But Relling—why don't you say something?

RELLING.   The bullet's entered the breast.

HJALMAR.   Yes, but she'll recover, won't she?

RELLING.   You can see for yourself that Hedvig is dead.

GINA (*breaking into tears*).   Oh, my child, my child!

GREGERS (*hoarsely*).   In the depths of the sea—

HJALMAR (*jumping up*).   No, no, she *must* live! Oh, in

God's name, Relling—just for a moment—just enough so I
can tell her how inexpressibly I loved her all the time!

RELLING.   It's reached the heart. Internal hemorrhage.
She died on the spot.

HJALMAR.   And I drove her from me like an animal!
And she crept terrified into the loft and died out of love
for me. (*Sobbing.*) Never to make it right again! Never to
let her know—! (*Clenching his fists and crying to heaven.*)
Oh, you up there—if you *do* exist. Why have you done this
to me!

GINA.   Hush, hush, you mustn't carry on like that. We
just didn't deserve to keep her, I guess.

MOLVIK.   The child isn't dead; she sleepeth.

RELLING.   Rubbish!

HJALMAR (*becoming calm, going over to the sofa to stand,
arms folded, looking at* HEDVIG).   There she lies, so stiff
and still.

RELLING (*trying to remove the pistol*).   She holds it so
tight, so tight.

GINA.   No, no, Relling, don't break her grip. Let the
gun be.

HJALMAR.   She should have it with her.

GINA.   Yes, let her. But the child shouldn't lie displayed
out here. She ought to go into her own little room, she
should. Give me a hand, Hjalmar.

(HJALMAR *and* GINA *lift* HEDVIG *between them.*)

HJALMAR (*as they carry her off*).   Oh, Gina, Gina, how
can you bear it!

GINA.   We must try to help each other. For now she
belongs to us both, you know.

MOLVIK (*outstretching his arms and mumbling*).   Praise
be to God. Dust to dust, dust to dust—

RELLING (*in a whisper*).   Shut up, you fool; you're
drunk.

(HJALMAR *and* GINA *carry the body out through
the kitchen door.* RELLING *closes it after them.*
MOLVIK *steals out the hall door.*)

RELLING (*going over to* GREGERS).   Nobody's ever going
to sell me the idea that this was an accident.

GREGERS (*who has stood in a convulsive fit of horror*). Who can say how this awful thing happened?

RELLING. There are powder burns on her blouse. She must have aimed the pistol point-blank at her breast and fired.

GREGERS. Hedvig did not die in vain. Did you notice how grief freed the greatness in him?

RELLING. The grief of death brings out greatness in almost everyone. But how long do you think this glory will last with *him*?

GREGERS. I should think it would last and grow all his life.

RELLING. In less than a year little Hedvig will be nothing more to him than a pretty theme for recitations.

GREGERS. You dare say that about Hjalmar Ekdal!

RELLING. We'll be lectured on this when the first grass shows on her grave. Then you can hear him spewing out phrases about "the child torn too soon from her father's heart," and you'll have your chance to watch him souse himself in conceit and self-pity. Wait and see.

GREGERS. If you're right, and I'm wrong, then life isn't worth living.

RELLING. Oh, life would be good in spite of all, if we only could have some peace from these damned shysters who come badgering us poor people with their "summons to the ideal."

GREGERS (*staring straight ahead*). In that case, I'm glad my destiny is what it is.

RELLING. Beg pardon—but what *is* your destiny?

GREGERS (*about to leave*). To be the thirteenth man at the table.

RELLING. Oh, the hell you say.

HEDDA GABLER

THE CHARACTERS

GEORGE TESMAN, research fellow in cultural history
HEDDA TESMAN, his wife
MISS JULIANA TESMAN, his aunt
MRS. ELVSTED
JUDGE BRACK
EILERT LØVBORG
BERTA, the TESMANS' maid

The action takes place in TESMAN's residence in the fashionable part of town.

ACT ONE

A large, attractively furnished drawing room, decorated in dark colors. In the rear wall, a wide doorway with curtains drawn back. The doorway opens into a smaller room in the same style as the drawing room. In the right wall of the front room, a folding door that leads to the hall. In the left wall opposite, a glass door, with curtains similarly drawn back. Through the panes one can see part of an overhanging veranda and trees in autumn colors. In the foreground is an oval table with tablecloth and chairs around it. By the right wall, a wide, dark porcelain stove, a high-backed armchair, a cushioned footstool, and two taborets. In the right-hand corner, a settee with a small round table in front. Nearer, on the left and slightly out from the wall, a piano. On either side of the doorway in back, étagères with terra-cotta and majolica ornaments. Against the back wall of the inner room, a sofa, a table, and a couple of chairs can be seen. Above this sofa hangs a portrait of a handsome, elderly man in a general's uniform. Over the table, a hanging lamp with an opalescent glass shade. A number of bouquets of flowers are placed about the drawing room in vases and glasses. Others lie on the tables. The floors in both rooms are covered with thick carpets. Morning light. The sun shines in through the glass door.

MISS JULIANA TESMAN, wearing a hat and carrying a parasol, comes in from the hall, followed by BERTA, *who holds a bouquet wrapped in paper.* MISS TESMAN *is a lady around sixty-five with a kind and good-natured look, nicely but simply dressed in a gray tailored suit.* BERTA *is a maid somewhat past middle age, with a plain and rather provincial appearance.*

MISS TESMAN (*stops close by the door, listens, and says softly*). Goodness, I don't think they're even up yet!

BERTA (*also softly*). That's just what I said, Miss Juliana. Remember how late the steamer got in last night. Yes,

221

and afterward! My gracious, how much the young bride had to unpack before she could get to bed.

MISS TESMAN.   Well, then—let them enjoy a good rest. But they must have some of this fresh morning air when they do come down. (*She goes to the glass door and opens it wide.*)

BERTA (*by the table, perplexed, with the bouquet in her hand*).   I swear there isn't a bit of space left. I think I'll have to put it here, miss. (*Places the bouquet on the piano.*)

MISS TESMAN.   So now you have a new mistress, Berta dear. Lord knows it was misery for me to give you up.

BERTA (*on the verge of tears*).   And for me, miss! What can I say? All those many blessed years I've been in your service, you and Miss Rina.

MISS TESMAN.   We must take it calmly, Berta. There's really nothing else to do. George needs you here in this house, you know that. You've looked after him since he was a little boy.

BERTA.   Yes, but miss, I'm all the time thinking of her, lying at home. Poor thing—completely helpless. And with that new maid! She'll never take proper care of an invalid, that one.

MISS TESMAN.   Oh, I'll manage to teach her. And most of it, you know, I'll do myself. So you mustn't be worrying over my poor sister.

BERTA.   Well, but there's something else too, miss. I'm really so afraid I won't please the young mistress.

MISS TESMAN.   Oh, well—there might be something or other at first—

BERTA.   Because she's so very particular.

MISS TESMAN.   Well, of course. General Gabler's daughter. What a life she had in the general's day! Remember seeing her out with her father—how she'd go galloping past in that long black riding outfit, with a feather in her hat?

BERTA.   Oh yes—I remember! But I never would have dreamed then that she and George Tesman would make a match of it.

MISS TESMAN.   Nor I either. But now, Berta—before I forget: from now on, you mustn't say George Tesman. You must call him Doctor Tesman.

BERTA.   Yes, the young mistress said the same thing—

last night, right after they came in the door. Is that true then, miss?

MISS TESMAN. Yes, absolutely. Think of it, Berta—they gave him his doctor's degree. Abroad, that is—on this trip, you know. I hadn't heard one word about it, till he told me down on the pier.

BERTA. Well, he's clever enough to be anything. But I never thought he'd go in for curing people.

MISS TESMAN. No, he wasn't made that kind of doctor. (*Nods significantly.*) But as a matter of fact, you may soon now have something still greater to call him.

BERTA. Oh, really! What's that, miss?

MISS TESMAN (*smiling*). Hm, wouldn't you like to know! (*Moved.*) Ah, dear God—if only my poor brother could look up from his grave and see what his little boy has become! (*Glancing about.*) But what's this, Berta? Why, you've taken all the slipcovers off the furniture—?

BERTA. Madam told me to. She doesn't like covers on chairs, she said.

MISS TESMAN. Are they going to make this their regular living room, then?

BERTA. It seems so—with her. For his part—the doctor—he said nothing.

(GEORGE TESMAN *enters the inner room from the right, singing to himself and carrying an empty, unstrapped suitcase. He is a youngish-looking man of thirty-three, medium sized, with an open, round, cheerful face, blond hair and beard. He wears glasses and is somewhat carelessly dressed in comfortable lounging clothes.*)

MISS TESMAN. Good morning, good morning, George!

TESMAN (*in the doorway*). Aunt Julie! Dear Aunt Julie! (*Goes over and warmly shakes her hand.*) Way out here—so early in the day—uh?

MISS TESMAN. Yes, you know I simply had to look in on you a moment.

TESMAN. And that without a decent night's sleep.

MISS TESMAN. Oh, that's nothing at all to me.

TESMAN. Well, then you did get home all right from the pier? Uh?

MISS TESMAN. Why, of course I did—thank goodness. Judge Brack was good enough to see me right to my door.

TESMAN. We were sorry we couldn't drive you up. But you saw for yourself—Hedda had all those boxes to bring along.

MISS TESMAN. Yes, that was quite something, the number of boxes she had.

BERTA (to TESMAN). Should I go in and ask Mrs. Tesman if there's anything I can help her with?

TESMAN. No, thanks, Berta—don't bother. She said she'd ring if she needed anything.

BERTA (going off toward the right). All right.

TESMAN. But wait now—you can take this suitcase with you.

BERTA (taking it). I'll put it away in the attic. (She goes out by the hall door.)

TESMAN. Just think, Aunt Julie—I had that whole suitcase stuffed full of notes. You just can't imagine all I've managed to find, rummaging through archives. Marvelous old documents that nobody knew existed—

MISS TESMAN. Yes, you've really not wasted any time on your wedding trip, George.

TESMAN. I certainly haven't. But do take your hat off, Auntie. Here—let me help you—uh?

MISS TESMAN (as he does so). Goodness—this is exactly as if you were still back at home with us.

TESMAN (turning the hat in his hand and studying it from all sides). My—what elegant hats you go in for!

MISS TESMAN. I bought that for Hedda's sake.

TESMAN. For Hedda's sake? Uh?

MISS TESMAN. Yes, so Hedda wouldn't feel ashamed of me if we walked down the street together.

TESMAN (patting her cheek). You think of everything, Aunt Julie! (Laying the hat on a chair by the table.) Sh— look, suppose we sit down on the sofa and have a little chat till Hedda comes. (They settle themselves. She puts her parasol on the corner of the sofa.)

MISS TESMAN (takes both of his hands and gazes at him). How wonderful it is having you here, right before my eyes again, George! You—dear Jochum's own boy!

TESMAN. And for me too, to see you again, Aunt Julie! You, who've been father and mother to me both.

MISS TESMAN. Yes, I'm sure you'll always keep a place in your heart for your old aunts.

TESMAN. But Auntie Rina—hm? Isn't she any better?

MISS TESMAN. Oh no—we can hardly expect that she'll ever be better, poor thing. She lies there, just as she has all these years. May God let me keep her a little while longer! Because otherwise, George, I don't know what I'd do with my life. The more so now, when I don't have you to look after.

TESMAN (*patting her on the back*). There, there, there—

MISS TESMAN (*suddenly changing her tone*). No, but to think of it, that now you're a married man! And that it was *you* who carried off Hedda Gabler. The beautiful Hedda Gabler! Imagine! She, who always had so many admirers!

TESMAN (*hums a little and smiles complacently*). Yes, I rather suspect I have several friends who'd like to trade places with me.

MISS TESMAN. And then to have such a wedding trip! Five—almost six months—

TESMAN. Well, remember, I used it for research, too. All those libraries I had to check—and so many books to read!

MISS TESMAN. Yes, no doubt. (*More confidentially; lowering her voice.*) But now listen, George—isn't there some-thing—something special you have to tell me?

TESMAN. From the trip?

MISS TESMAN. Yes.

TESMAN. No, I can't think of anything beyond what I wrote in my letters. I got my doctor's degree down there—but I told you that yesterday.

MISS TESMAN. Yes, of course. But I mean—whether you have any kind of—expectations—?

TESMAN. Expectations?

MISS TESMAN. My goodness, George—I'm your old aunt!

TESMAN. Why, naturally I have expectations.

MISS TESMAN. Ah!

TESMAN. I have every expectation in the world of be-coming a professor shortly.

MISS TESMAN. Oh, a professor, yes—

TESMAN. Or I might as well say, I'm sure of it. But, Aunt Julie—you know that perfectly well yourself.

MISS TESMAN *(with a little laugh)*. That's right, so I do. *(Changing the subject.)* But we were talking about your trip. It must have cost a terrible amount of money.

TESMAN. Well, that big fellowship, you know—it took us a good part of the way.

MISS TESMAN. But I don't see how you could stretch it enough for two.

TESMAN. No, that's not so easy to see—uh?

MISS TESMAN. And especially traveling with a lady. For I hear tell that's much more expensive.

TESMAN. Yes, of course—it's a bit more expensive. But Hedda just had to have that trip. She *had* to. There was nothing else to be done.

MISS TESMAN. No, no, I guess not. A honeymoon abroad seems to be the thing nowadays. But tell me—have you had a good look around your house?

TESMAN. You can bet I have! I've been up since daybreak.

MISS TESMAN. And how does it strike you, all in all?

TESMAN. First-rate! Absolutely first-rate! Only I don't know what we'll do with the two empty rooms between the back parlor and Hedda's bedroom.

MISS TESMAN *(laughing again)*. Oh, my dear George, I think you can use them—as time goes on.

TESMAN. Yes, you're quite right about that, Aunt Julie! In time, as I build up my library—uh?

MISS TESMAN. Of course, my dear boy. It was your library I meant.

TESMAN. I'm happiest now for Hedda's sake. Before we were engaged, she used to say so many times there was no place she'd rather live than here, in Secretary Falk's town house.

MISS TESMAN. Yes, and then to have it come on the market just after you'd sailed.

TESMAN. We really have had luck, haven't we?

MISS TESMAN. But expensive, George dear! You'll find it expensive, all this here.

TESMAN *(looks at her, somewhat crestfallen)*. Yes, I suppose I will.

MISS TESMAN. Oh, Lord, yes!

TESMAN. How much do you think? Approximately? Hm?

MISS TESMAN.   It's impossible to say till the bills are all in.

TESMAN.   Well, fortunately Judge Brack has gotten me quite easy terms. That's what he wrote Hedda.

MISS TESMAN.   Don't worry yourself about that, dear. I've also put up security to cover the carpets and furniture.

TESMAN.   Security? Aunt Julie, dear—you? What kind of security could *you* give?

MISS TESMAN.   I took out a mortgage on our pension.

TESMAN (*jumping up*).   What! On your—and Auntie Rina's pension!

MISS TESMAN.   I saw nothing else to do.

TESMAN (*standing in front of her*).   But you're out of your mind, Aunt Julie! That pension—it's all Aunt Rina and you have to live on.

MISS TESMAN.   Now, now—don't make so much of it. It's only a formality; Judge Brack said so. He was good enough to arrange the whole thing for me. Just a formality, he said.

TESMAN.   That's all well enough. But still—

MISS TESMAN.   You'll be drawing your own salary now. And, good gracious, if we have to lay out a bit, just now at the start—why, it's no more than a pleasure for us.

TESMAN.   Oh, Aunt Julie—you never get tired of making sacrifices for me!

MISS TESMAN (*rises and places her hands on his shoulders*).   What other joy do I have in this world than smoothing the path for you, my dear boy? You, without father or mother to turn to. And now we've come to the goal, George! Things may have looked black at times; but now, thank heaven, you've made it.

TESMAN.   Yes, it's remarkable, really, how everything's turned out for the best.

MISS TESMAN.   Yes—and those who stood against you— who wanted to bar your way—they've gone down. They've fallen, George. The one most dangerous to you—he fell farthest. And he's lying there now, in the bed he made— poor, misguided creature.

TESMAN.   Have you heard any news of Eilert? I mean, since I went away.

MISS TESMAN.   Only that he's supposed to have brought out a new book.

TESMAN.   What's that? Eilert Løvborg? Just recently, uh?

MISS TESMAN.   So they say. But considering everything, it can hardly amount to much. Ah, but when *your* new book comes out—it'll be a different story, George! What will it be about?

TESMAN.   It's going to treat the domestic handicrafts of Brabant in the Middle Ages.

MISS TESMAN.   Just imagine—that you can write about things like that!

TESMAN.   Actually, the book may take quite a while yet. I have this tremendous collection of material to put in order, you know.

MISS TESMAN.   Yes, collecting and ordering—you do that so well. You're not my brother's son for nothing.

TESMAN.   I look forward so much to getting started. Especially now, with a comfortable home of my own to work in.

MISS TESMAN.   And most of all, dear, now that you've won her, the wife of your heart.

TESMAN (*embracing her*).   Yes, yes, Aunt Julie! Hedda—that's the most beautiful part of it all! (*Glancing toward the doorway.*) But I think she's coming—uh?

(HEDDA *enters from the left through the inner room. She is a woman of twenty-nine. Her face and figure show breeding and distinction; her complexion is pallid and opaque. Her steel gray eyes express a cool, unruffled calm. Her hair is an attractive medium brown, but not particularly abundant. She wears a tasteful, rather loose-fitting gown.*)

MISS TESMAN (*going to meet* HEDDA).   Good morning, Hedda dear—how good to see you!

HEDDA (*holding out her hand*).   Good morning, my dear Miss Tesman! Calling so early? This *is* kind of you.

MISS TESMAN (*slightly embarrassed*).   Well—did the bride sleep well in her new home?

HEDDA.   Oh yes, thanks. Quite adequately.

TESMAN.   Adequately! Oh, I like that, Hedda! You were sleeping like a stone when I got up.

HEDDA.   Fortunately. But of course one has to grow accustomed to anything new, Miss Tesman—little by little. *(Looking toward the left.)* Oh! That maid has left the door open—and the sunlight's just flooding in.

MISS TESMAN *(going toward the door).* Well, we can close it.

HEDDA. No, no—don't! *(To Tesman.)* There, dear, draw the curtains. It gives a softer light.

TESMAN *(by the glass door).* All right—all right. Look, Hedda—now you have shade and fresh air both.

HEDDA. Yes, we really need some fresh air here, with all these piles of flowers— But—won't you sit down, Miss Tesman?

MISS TESMAN. Oh no, thank you. Now that I know that everything's fine—thank goodness—I will have to run along home. My sister's lying there waiting, poor thing.

TESMAN. Give her my very, very best, won't you? And say I'll be looking in on her later today.

MISS TESMAN. Oh, you can be sure I will. But what do you know, George—*(Searching in her bag.)*—I nearly forgot. I have something here for you.

TESMAN. What's that, Aunt Julie? Hm?

MISS TESMAN *(brings out a flat package wrapped in newspaper and hands it to him).* There, dear. Look.

TESMAN *(opening it).* Oh, my—you kept them for me, Aunt Julie! Hedda! That's really touching! Uh!

HEDDA *(by the étagère on the right).* Yes, dear, what is it?

TESMAN. My old bedroom slippers! My slippers!

HEDDA. Oh yes. I remember how often you spoke of them during the trip.

TESMAN. Yes, I missed them terribly! *(Going over to her.)* Now you can see them, Hedda!

HEDDA *(moves toward the stove).* Thanks, but I really don't care to.

TESMAN *(following her).* Imagine—Auntie Rina lay and embroidered them, sick as she was. Oh, you couldn't believe how many memories are bound up in them.

HEDDA *(at the table).* But not for me.

MISS TESMAN. I think Hedda is right, George.

TESMAN. Yes, but I only thought, now that she's part of the family—

HEDDA (*interrupting*). We're never going to manage with this maid, Tesman.

MISS TESMAN. Not manage with Berta?

TESMAN. But dear—why do you say that? Uh?

HEDDA (*pointing*). See there! She's left her old hat lying out on a chair.

TESMAN (*shocked; dropping the slippers*). But Hedda—!

HEDDA. Suppose someone came in and saw it.

TESMAN. Hedda—that's Aunt Julie's hat!

HEDDA. Really?

MISS TESMAN (*picking it up*). That's right, it's mine. And what's more, it certainly is not old—Mrs. Tesman.

HEDDA. I really hadn't looked closely at it, Miss Tesman.

MISS TESMAN (*putting on the hat*). It's actually the first time I've had it on. The very first time.

TESMAN. And it's lovely, too. Most attractive!

MISS TESMAN. Oh, it's hardly all that, George. (*Looks about.*) My parasol—? Ah, here. (*Takes it.*) For that's mine too. (*Murmurs.*) Not Berta's.

TESMAN. New hat and new parasol! Just imagine, Hedda!

HEDDA. Quite charming, really.

TESMAN. Yes, aren't they, uh? But Auntie, take a good look at Hedda before you leave. See how charming *she* is!

MISS TESMAN. But George dear, there's nothing new in that. Hedda's been lovely all her life. (*She nods and starts out, right.*)

TESMAN (*following her*). But have you noticed how plump and buxom she's grown? How much she's filled out on the trip?

HEDDA (*crossing the room*). Oh, do be quiet—!

MISS TESMAN (*who has stopped and turned*). Filled out?

TESMAN. Of course, you can't see it so well when she has that dressing gown on. But I, who have the opportunity to—

HEDDA (*by the glass door, impatiently*). Oh, you have no opportunity for anything!

TESMAN. It must have been the mountain air, down in the Tyrol—

HEDDA (*brusquely interrupting*). I'm exactly as I was when I left.

TESMAN. Yes, that's your claim. But you certainly are not. Auntie, don't you agree?

MISS TESMAN (*gazing at her with folded hands*). Hedda is lovely—lovely—lovely. (*Goes up to her, takes her head in both hands, bends it down and kisses her hair.*) God bless and keep Hedda Tesman—for George's sake.

HEDDA (*gently freeing herself*). Oh—! Let me go.

MISS TESMAN (*with quiet feeling*). I won't let a day go by without looking in on you two.

TESMAN. Yes, please do that, Aunt Julie! Uh?

MISS TESMAN. Good-bye—good-bye!

(*She goes out by the hall door.* TESMAN *accompanies her, leaving the door half open. He can be heard reiterating his greetings to Aunt Rina and his thanks for the slippers. At the same time,* HEDDA *moves about the room, raising her arms and clenching her fists as if in a frenzy. Then she flings back the curtains from the glass door and stands there, looking out. A moment later* TESMAN *comes back, closing the door after him.*)

TESMAN (*retrieving the slippers from the floor*). What are you standing and looking at, Hedda?

HEDDA (*again calm and controlled*). I'm just looking at the leaves—they're so yellow—and so withered.

TESMAN (*wraps up the slippers and puts them on the table*). Yes, well, we're into September now.

HEDDA (*once more restless*). Yes, to think—that already we're in—in September.

TESMAN. Didn't Aunt Julie seem a bit strange? A little—almost formal? What do you suppose was bothering her? Hm?

HEDDA. I hardly know her at all. Isn't that how she usually is?

TESMAN. No, not like this, today.

HEDDA (*leaving the glass door*). Do you think this thing with the hat upset her?

TESMAN. Oh, not very much. A little, just at the moment, perhaps—

HEDDA. But really, what kind of manners has she—to

go throwing her hat about in a drawing room! It's just not proper.

TESMAN. Well, you can be sure Aunt Julie won't do it again.

HEDDA. Anyhow, I'll manage to smooth it over with her.

TESMAN. Yes, Hedda dear, I wish you would!

HEDDA. When you go in to see them later on, you might ask her out for the evening.

TESMAN. Yes, I'll do that. And there's something else you could do that would make her terribly happy.

HEDDA. Oh?

TESMAN. If only you could bring yourself to speak to her warmly, by her first name. For my sake, Hedda? Uh?

HEDDA. No, no—don't ask me to do that. I told you this once before. I'll try to call her "Aunt." That should be enough.

TESMAN. Oh, all right. I was only thinking, now that you belong to the family—

HEDDA. Hm—I really don't know— (*She crosses the room to the doorway.*)

TESMAN (*after a pause*). Is something the matter, Hedda? Uh?

HEDDA. I'm just looking at my old piano. It doesn't really fit in with all these other things.

TESMAN. With the first salary I draw, we can see about trading it in on a new one.

HEDDA. No, not traded in. I don't want to part with it. We can put it there, in the inner room, and get another here in its place. When there's a chance, I mean.

TESMAN (*slightly cast down*). Yes, we could do that, of course.

HEDDA (*picks up the bouquet from the piano*). These flowers weren't here when we got in last night.

TESMAN. Aunt Julie must have brought them for you.

HEDDA (*examining the bouquet*). A visiting card. (*Takes it out and reads it.*) "Will stop back later today." Can you guess who this is from?

TESMAN. No. Who? Hm?

HEDDA. It says "Mrs. Elvsted."

TESMAN. No, really? Sheriff Elvsted's wife. Miss Rysing, she used to be.

HEDDA. Exactly. The one with the irritating hair that she was always showing off. An old flame of yours, I've heard.

TESMAN (*laughing*). Oh, that wasn't for long. And it was before I knew you, Hedda. But imagine—that she's here in town.

HEDDA. It's odd that she calls on us. I've hardly seen her since we were in school.

TESMAN. Yes, I haven't seen her either—since God knows when. I wonder how she can stand living in such an out-of-the-way place. Hm?

HEDDA (*thinks a moment, then bursts out*). But wait—isn't it somewhere up in those parts that he—that Eilert Løvborg lives?

TESMAN. Yes, it's someplace right around there. (BERTA *enters by the hall door.*)

BERTA. She's back again, ma'am—that lady who stopped by and left the flowers an hour ago. (*Pointing*) The ones you have in your hand, ma'am.

HEDDA. Oh, is she? Good. Would you ask her to come in.

(BERTA *opens the door for* MRS. ELVSTED *and goes out.* MRS. ELVSTED *is a slender woman with soft, pretty features. Her eyes are light blue, large, round, and somewhat prominent, with a startled, questioning look. Her hair is remarkably light, almost a white-gold, and un-usually abundant and wavy. She is a couple of years younger than* HEDDA. *She wears a dark visiting dress, tasteful, but not quite in the latest fashion.*)

HEDDA (*going to greet her warmly*). Good morning, my dear Mrs. Elvsted. How delightful to see you again!

MRS. ELVSTED (*nervously; struggling to control her-self*). Yes, it's a very long time since we last met.

TESMAN (*gives her his hand*). Or since *we* met, uh?

HEDDA. Thank you for your beautiful flowers—

MRS. ELVSTED. Oh, that's nothing—I would have come straight out here yesterday afternoon, but then I heard you weren't at home—

TESMAN. Have you just now come to town? Uh?

MRS. ELVSTED.   I got in yesterday toward noon. Oh, I was in desperation when I heard that you weren't at home.

HEDDA.   Desperation! Why?

TESMAN.   But my dear Mrs. Rysing—Mrs. Elvsted, I mean—

HEDDA.   You're not in some kind of trouble?

MRS. ELVSTED.   Yes, I am. And I don't know another living soul down here I can turn to.

HEDDA (*putting the bouquet down on the table*).   Come, then—let's sit here on the sofa—

MRS. ELVSTED.   Oh, I can't sit down. I'm really too much on edge!

HEDDA.   Why, of course you can. Come here.

(*She draws* MRS. ELVSTED *down on the sofa and sits beside her.*)

TESMAN.   Well? What is it, Mrs. Elvsted?

HEDDA.   Has anything particular happened at home?

MRS. ELVSTED.   Yes, that's both it—and not it. Oh, I do want so much that you don't misunderstand me—

HEDDA.   But then the best thing, Mrs. Elvsted, is simply to speak your mind.

TESMAN.   Because I suppose that's why you've come. Hm?

MRS. ELVSTED.   Oh yes, that's why. Well, then, I have to tell you—if you don't already know—that Eilert Løvborg's also in town.

HEDDA.   Løvborg—!

TESMAN.   What! Is Eilert Løvborg back! Just think, Hedda!

HEDDA.   Good Lord, I can hear.

MRS. ELVSTED.   He's been back all of a week's time now. A whole week—in this dangerous town! Alone! With all the bad company that's around.

HEDDA.   But my dear Mrs. Elvsted, what does *he* have to do with you?

MRS. ELVSTED (*glances anxiously at her and says quickly*).   He was the children's tutor.

HEDDA.   Your children's?

MRS. ELVSTED.   My husband's. I have none.

HEDDA.   Your stepchildren's, then.

MRS. ELVSTED. Yes.

TESMAN (*somewhat hesitantly*). But was he—I don't know quite how to put it—was he sufficiently—responsible in his habits for such a job? Uh?

MRS. ELVSTED. In these last two years, there wasn't a word to be said against him.

TESMAN. Not a word? Just think of that, Hedda!

HEDDA. I heard it.

MRS. ELVSTED. Not even a murmur, I can assure you! Nothing. But anyway—now that I know he's here—in this big city—and with so much money in his hands—then I'm just frightened to death for him.

TESMAN. But why didn't he stay up there where he was? With you and your husband? Uh?

MRS. ELVSTED. After the book came out, he just couldn't rest content with us.

TESMAN. Yes, that's right—Aunt Julie was saying he'd published a new book.

MRS. ELVSTED. Yes, a great new book, on the course of civilization—in all its stages. It's been out two weeks. And now it's been bought and read so much—and it's made a tremendous stir—

TESMAN. Has it really? It must be something he's had lying around from his better days.

MRS. ELVSTED. Years back, you mean?

TESMAN. I suppose.

MRS. ELVSTED. No, he's written it all up there with us. Now—in this last year.

TESMAN. That's marvelous to hear. Hedda! Just imagine!

MRS. ELVSTED. Yes, if only it can go on like this!

HEDDA. Have you seen him here in town?

MRS. ELVSTED. No, not yet. I had such trouble finding out his address. But this morning I got it at last.

HEDDA (*looks searchingly at her*). I must say it seems rather odd of your husband—

MRS. ELVSTED (*with a nervous start*). Of my husband—! What?

HEDDA. To send you to town on this sort of errand. Not to come and look after his friend himself.

MRS. ELVSTED. No, no, my husband hasn't the time for that. And then I had—some shopping to do.

HEDDA (*with a slight smile*). Oh, that's different.

MRS. ELVSTED (*getting up quickly and uneasily*). I beg you, please, Mr. Tesman—be good to Eilert Løvborg if he comes to you. And he will, I'm sure. You know—you were such good friends in the old days. And you're both doing the same kind of work. The same type of research—from what I can gather.

TESMAN. We were once, at any rate.

MRS. ELVSTED. Yes, and that's why I'm asking you, please—you too—to keep an eye on him. Oh, you will do that, Mr. Tesman—promise me that?

TESMAN. I'll be only too glad to, Mrs. Rysing—

HEDDA. Elvsted.

TESMAN. I'll certainly do everything in my power for Eilert. You can depend on that.

MRS. ELVSTED. Oh, how terribly kind of you! (*Pressing his hands.*) Many, many thanks! (*Frightened.*) He means so much to my husband, you know.

HEDDA (*rising*). You ought to write him, dear. He might not come by on his own.

TESMAN. Yes, that probably would be the best, Hedda? Hm?

HEDDA. And the sooner the better. Right now, I'd say.

MRS. ELVSTED (*imploringly*). Oh yes, if you could!

TESMAN. I'll write him this very moment. Have you got his address, Mrs.—Mrs. Elvsted?

MRS. ELVSTED. Yes. (*Takes a slip of paper from her pocket and hands it to him.*) Here it is.

TESMAN. Good, good. Then I'll go in— (*Looking about.*) But wait—my slippers? Ah! Here. (*Takes the package and starts to leave.*)

HEDDA. Write him a really warm, friendly letter. Nice and long, too.

TESMAN. Don't worry, I will.

MRS. ELVSTED. But please, not a word that I asked you to!

TESMAN. No, that goes without saying. Uh? (*Leaves by the inner room, to the right.*)

HEDDA (*goes over to* MRS. ELVSTED, *smiles, and speaks softly*). How's that! Now we've killed two birds with one stone.

MRS. ELVSTED. What do you mean?

HEDDA. Didn't you see that I wanted him out of the room?

MRS. ELVSTED. Yes, to write the letter—

HEDDA. But also to talk with you alone.

MRS. ELVSTED (*confused*). About this same thing?

HEDDA. Precisely.

MRS. ELVSTED (*upset*). But Mrs. Tesman, there's nothing more to say! Nothing!

HEDDA. Oh yes, but there is. There's a great deal more—I can see that. Come, sit here—and let's speak openly now, the two of us. (*She forces* MRS. ELVSTED *down into the armchair by the stove and sits on one of the taborets.*)

MRS. ELVSTED (*anxiously glancing at her watch*). But Mrs. Tesman, dear—I was just planning to leave.

HEDDA. Oh, you can't be in such a rush— Now! Tell me a little about how things are going at home.

MRS. ELVSTED. Oh, that's the last thing I'd ever want to discuss.

HEDDA. But with me, dear—? After all, we were in school together.

MRS. ELVSTED. Yes, but you were a class ahead of me. Oh, I was terribly afraid of you then!

HEDDA. Afraid of me?

MRS. ELVSTED. Yes, terribly. Because whenever we met on the stairs, you'd always pull my hair.

HEDDA. Did I really?

MRS. ELVSTED. Yes, and once you said you would burn it off.

HEDDA. Oh, that was just foolish talk, you know.

MRS. ELVSTED. Yes, but I was so stupid then. And, anyway, since then—we've drifted so far—far apart from each other. We've moved in such different circles.

HEDDA. Well, let's try now to come closer again. Listen, at school we were quite good friends, and we called each other by our first names—

MRS. ELVSTED. No, I'm sure you're mistaken.

HEDDA. Oh, I couldn't be! I remember it clearly. And that's why we have to be perfectly open, just as we were. (*Moves the stool nearer* MRS. ELVSTED.) There now! (*Kissing her cheek.*) You have to call me Hedda.

MRS. ELVSTED (*pressing and patting her hands*). Oh, you're so good and kind—! It's not at all what I'm used to.

HEDDA. There, there! And I'm going to call you my own dear Thora.

MRS. ELVSTED. My name is Thea.

HEDDA. Oh yes, of course. I meant Thea. (*Looks at her compassionately.*) So you're not much used to goodness or kindness, Thea? In your own home?

MRS. ELVSTED. If only I had a home! But I don't. I never have.

HEDDA (*glances quickly at her*). I thought it had to be something like that.

MRS. ELVSTED (*gazing helplessly into space*). Yes—yes—yes.

HEDDA. I can't quite remember now—but wasn't it as a housekeeper that you first came up to the Elvsteds?

MRS. ELVSTED. Actually as a governess. But his wife—his first wife—she was an invalid and mostly kept to her bed. So I had to take care of the house too.

HEDDA. But finally you became mistress of the house yourself.

MRS. ELVSTED (*heavily*). Yes, I did.

HEDDA. Let me see—about how long ago was that?

MRS. ELVSTED. That I was married?

HEDDA. Yes.

MRS. ELVSTED. It's five years now.

HEDDA. That's right. It must be.

MRS. ELVSTED. Oh, these five years—! Or the last two or three, anyway. Oh, if you only knew, Mrs. Tesman—

HEDDA (*gives her hand a little slap*). Mrs. Tesman! Now, Thea!

MRS. ELVSTED. I'm sorry; I'll try— Yes, if you could only understand—Hedda—

HEDDA (*casually*). Eilert Løvborg has lived up there about three years too, hasn't he?

MRS. ELVSTED (*looks at her doubtfully*). Eilert Løvborg? Yes—he has.

HEDDA. Had you already known him here in town?

MRS. ELVSTED. Hardly at all. Well, I mean—by name, of course.

HEDDA. But up there—I suppose he'd visit you both?

MRS. ELVSTED. Yes, he came to see us every day. He

was tutoring the children, you know. Because, in the long run, I couldn't do it all myself.

HEDDA. No, that's obvious. And your husband—? I suppose he often has to be away?

MRS. ELVSTED. Yes, you can imagine, as sheriff, how much traveling he does around in the district.

HEDDA (leaning against the chair arm). Thea—my poor, sweet Thea—now you must tell me everything—just as it is.

MRS. ELVSTED. Well, then you have to ask the questions.

HEDDA. What sort of man is your husband, Thea? I mean—you know—to be with. Is he good to you?

MRS. ELVSTED (evasively). He believes he does everything for the best.

HEDDA. I only think he must be much too old for you. More than twenty years older, isn't he?

MRS. ELVSTED (irritated). That's true. Along with everything else. I just can't stand him! We haven't a single thought in common. Nothing at all—he and I.

HEDDA. But doesn't he care for you all the same—in his own way?

MRS. ELVSTED. Oh, I don't know what he feels. I'm no more than useful to him. And then it doesn't cost much to keep me. I'm inexpensive.

HEDDA. That's stupid of you.

MRS. ELVSTED (shaking her head). It can't be otherwise. Not with him. He really doesn't care for anyone but himself—and maybe a little for the children.

HEDDA. And for Eilert Løvborg, Thea.

MRS. ELVSTED (looking at her). Eilert Løvborg! Why do you think so?

HEDDA. But my dear—it seems to me, when he sends you all the way into town to look after him—(Smiles almost imperceptibly.) Besides, it's what you told my husband.

MRS. ELVSTED (with a little nervous shudder). Really? Yes, I suppose I did. (In a quiet outburst.) No—I might as well tell you here and now! It's bound to come out in time.

HEDDA. But my dear Thea—?

MRS. ELVSTED. All right, then! My husband never knew I was coming here.

HEDDA. What! Your husband never knew—

MRS. ELVSTED. Of course not. Anyway, he wasn't at

home. Off traveling somewhere. Oh, I couldn't bear it any longer, Hedda. It was impossible! I would have been so alone up there now.

HEDDA. Well? What then?

MRS. ELVSTED. So I packed a few of my things together—the barest necessities—without saying a word. And I slipped away from the house.

HEDDA. Right then and there?

MRS. ELVSTED. Yes, and took the train straight into town.

HEDDA. But my dearest girl—that you could dare to do such a thing!

MRS. ELVSTED (*rising and walking about the room*). What else could I possibly do!

HEDDA. But what do you think your husband will say when you go back home?

MRS. ELVSTED (*by the table, looking at her*). Back to him?

HEDDA. Yes, of course.

MRS. ELVSTED. I'll never go back to him.

HEDDA (*rising and approaching her*). You mean you've left, in dead earnest, for good?

MRS. ELVSTED. Yes. There didn't seem anything else to do.

HEDDA. But—to go away so openly.

MRS. ELVSTED. Oh, you can't keep a thing like that secret.

HEDDA. But what do you think people will say about you, Thea?

MRS. ELVSTED. God knows they'll say what they please. (*Sitting wearily and sadly on the sofa.*) I only did what I had to do.

HEDDA (*after a short silence*). What do you plan on now? What kind of work?

MRS. ELVSTED. I don't know yet. I only know I have to live here, where Eilert Løvborg is—if I'm going to live at all.

HEDDA (*moves a chair over from the table, sits beside her, and strokes her hands*). Thea dear—how did this—this friendship—between you and Eilert Løvborg come about?

MRS. ELVSTED. Oh, it happened little by little. I got some kind of power, almost, over him.

HEDDA. Really?

MRS. ELVSTED. He gave up his old habits. Not because I'd asked him to. I never dared do that. But he could tell they upset me, and so he dropped them.

HEDDA (*hiding an involuntary, scornful smile*). My dear little Thea—just as they say—you rehabilitated him.

MRS. ELVSTED. Well, he says so, at any rate. And he— on his part—he's made a real human being out of me. Taught me to think—and understand so many things.

HEDDA. You mean he tutored you also?

MRS. ELVSTED. No, not exactly. But he'd talk to me— talk endlessly on about one thing after another. And then came the wonderful, happy time when I could share in his work! When I could help him!

HEDDA. Could you really?

MRS. ELVSTED. Yes! Whenever he wrote anything, we'd always work on it together.

HEDDA. Like two true companions.

MRS. ELVSTED (*eagerly*). Companions! You know, Hedda—that's what he said too! Oh, I ought to feel so happy—but I can't. I just don't know if it's going to last.

HEDDA. You're no more sure of him than that?

MRS. ELVSTED (*despondently*). There's a woman's shadow between Eilert Løvborg and me.

HEDDA (*looks at her intently*). Who could that be?

MRS. ELVSTED. I don't know. Someone out of his—his past. Someone he's really never forgotten.

HEDDA. What has he said—about this!

MRS. ELVSTED. It's only once—and just vaguely—that he touched on it.

HEDDA. Well! And what did he say!

MRS. ELVSTED. He said that when they broke off she was going to shoot him with a pistol.

HEDDA (*with cold constraint*). That's nonsense! Nobody behaves that way around here.

MRS. ELVSTED. No. And that's why I think it must have been that redheaded singer that at one time he—

HEDDA. Yes, quite likely.

MRS. ELVSTED. I remember they used to say about her that she carried loaded weapons.

HEDDA. Ah—then of course it must have been her.

MRS. ELVSTED (*wringing her hands*). But you know

what, Hedda—I've heard that this singer—that she's in town
again! Oh, it has me out of my mind—

HEDDA (*glancing toward the inner room*).   Shh! Tesman's
coming. (*Gets up and whispers.*) Thea—keep all this just
between us.

MRS. ELVSTED (*jumping up*).   Oh yes! In heaven's
name—!

(GEORGE TESMAN, *with a letter in his hand, enters from the right through the inner room.*)

TESMAN.   There, now—the letter's signed and sealed.

HEDDA.   That's fine. I think Mrs. Elvsted was just leaving. Wait a minute. I'll go with you to the garden gate.

TESMAN.   Hedda, dear—could Berta maybe look after
this?

HEDDA (*taking the letter*.)   I'll tell her to.

(BERTA *enters from the hall.*)

BERTA.   Judge Brack is here and says he'd like to greet
you and the Doctor, ma'am.

HEDDA.   Yes, ask Judge Brack to come in. And, here—
put this letter in the mail.

BERTA (*takes the letter*).   Yes, ma'am.

> (*She opens the door for* JUDGE BRACK *and goes
> out.* BRACK *is a man of forty-five, thickset, yet
> well-built, with supple movements. His face is
> roundish, with a distinguished profile. His hair
> is short, still mostly black, and carefully
> groomed. His eyes are bright and lively. Thick
> eyebrows; a mustache to match, with neatly
> clipped ends. He wears a trimly tailored walk-
> ing suit, a bit too youthful for his age. Uses a
> monocle, which he now and then lets fall.*)

JUDGE BRACK (*hat in hand, bowing*).   May one dare to
call so early?

HEDDA.   Of course one may.

TESMAN (*shakes his hand*).   You're always welcome
here. (*Introducing him.*) Judge Brack—Miss Rysing—

HEDDA.   Ah—!

BRACK (*bowing*).   I'm delighted.

HEDDA (*looks at him and laughs*).   It's really a treat to see you by daylight, Judge!

BRACK.   You find me—changed?

HEDDA.   Yes. A bit younger, I think.

BRACK.   Thank you, most kindly.

TESMAN.   But what do you say for Hedda, uh? Doesn't she look flourishing? She's actually—

HEDDA.   Oh, leave me out of it! You might thank Judge Brack for all the trouble he's gone to—

BRACK.   Nonsense—it was a pleasure—

HEDDA.   Yes, you're a true friend. But here's Thea, standing here, aching to get away. Excuse me, Judge; I'll be right back.

(*Mutual good-byes.* MRS. ELVSTED *and* HEDDA *go out by the hall door.*)

BRACK.   So—is your wife fairly well satisfied, then—?

TESMAN.   Yes, we can't thank you enough. Of course— I gather there's some rearrangement called for here and there. And one or two things are lacking. We still have to buy a few minor items.

BRACK.   Really?

TESMAN.   But that's nothing for you to worry about. Hedda said she'd pick up those things herself. Why don't we sit down, hm?

BRACK.   Thanks. Just for a moment. (*Sits by the table.*) There's something I'd like to discuss with you, Tesman.

TESMAN.   What? Oh, I understand! (*Sitting.*) It's the serious part of the banquet we're coming to, uh?

BRACK.   Oh, as far as money matters go, there's no great rush—though I must say I wish we'd managed things a bit more economically.

TESMAN.   But that was completely impossible! Think about Hedda, Judge! You, who know her so well— I simply couldn't have her live like a grocer's wife.

BRACK.   No, no—that's the trouble, exactly.

TESMAN.   And then—fortunately—it can't be long before I get my appointment.

BRACK.   Well, you know—these things can often hang fire.

TESMAN.   Have you heard something further? Hm?

BRACK. Nothing really definite— (*Changing the subject.*) But incidentally—I do have one piece of news for you.

TESMAN. Well?

BRACK. Your old friend Eilert Løvborg is back in town.

TESMAN. I already know.

BRACK. Oh? How did you hear?

TESMAN. She told me. The lady that left with Hedda.

BRACK. I see. What was her name again? I didn't quite catch it—

TESMAN. Mrs. Elvsted.

BRACK. Aha—Sheriff Elvsted's wife. Yes—it's up near them he's been staying.

TESMAN. And, just think—what a pleasure to hear that he's completely stable again!

BRACK. Yes, that's what they claim.

TESMAN. And that he's published a new book, uh?

BRACK. Oh yes!

TESMAN. And it's created quite a sensation.

BRACK. An extraordinary sensation.

TESMAN. Just imagine—isn't that marvelous? He, with his remarkable talents—I was so very afraid that he'd really gone down for good.

BRACK. That's what everyone thought.

TESMAN. But I've no idea what he'll find to do now. How on earth can he ever make a living? Hm?

(*During the last words,* HEDDA *comes in by the hall door.*)

HEDDA (*to* BRACK, *laughing, with a touch of scorn*). Tesman always goes around worrying about how people are going to make a living.

TESMAN. My Lord—it's poor Eilert Løvborg we're talking of, dear.

HEDDA (*glancing quickly at him*). Oh, really? (*Sits in the armchair by the stove and asks casually.*) What's the matter with him?

TESMAN. Well—he must have run through his inheritance long ago. And he can't write a new book every year. Uh? So I was asking, really, what's going to become of him.

BRACK. Perhaps I can shed some light on that.

TESMAN. Oh?

BRACK. You must remember that he does have relatives with a great deal of influence.

TESMAN. Yes, but they've washed their hands of him altogether.

BRACK. They used to call him the family's white hope.

TESMAN. They used to, yes! But he spoiled all that himself.

HEDDA. Who knows? (*With a slight smile.*) He's been rehabilitated up at the Elvsteds—

BRACK. And then this book that he's published—

TESMAN. Oh, well, let's hope they really help him some way or other. I just now wrote to him. Hedda dear, I asked him out here this evening.

BRACK. But my dear fellow, you're coming to my stag party this evening. You promised down on the pier last night.

HEDDA. Had you forgotten, Tesman?

TESMAN. Yes, I absolutely had.

BRACK. For that matter, you can rest assured that he'd never come.

TESMAN. What makes you say that, hm?

BRACK (*hesitating, rising and leaning on the back of the chair*). My dear Tesman—and you too, Mrs. Tesman—I can't, in all conscience, let you go on without knowing something that—that—

TESMAN. Something involving Eilert—?

BRACK. Both you and him.

TESMAN. But my dear Judge, then tell us!

BRACK. You must be prepared that your appointment may not come through as quickly as you've wished or expected.

TESMAN (*jumping up nervously*). Has something gone wrong? Uh?

BRACK. It may turn out that there'll have to be a competition for the post—

TESMAN. A competition! Imagine, Hedda!

HEDDA (*leaning further back in the chair*). Ah, there— you see!

TESMAN. But with whom! You can't mean—?

BRACK. Yes, exactly. With Eilert Løvborg.

TESMAN (*striking his hands together*). No, no—that's completely unthinkable! It's impossible! Uh?

BRACK. Hm—but it may come about, all the same.

TESMAN. No, but, Judge Brack—that would just be incredibly inconsiderate toward me! (*Waving his arms.*) Yes, because—you know—I'm a married man! We married on my prospects, Hedda and I. We went into debt. And even borrowed money from Aunt Julie. Because that job—my Lord, it was as good as promised to me, uh?

BRACK. Easy now—I'm sure you'll get the appointment. But you will have to compete for it.

HEDDA (*motionless in the armchair*). Just think, Tesman—it will be like a kind of championship match.

TESMAN. But Hedda dearest, how can you take it so calmly!

HEDDA (*as before*). I'm not the least bit calm. I can't wait to see how it turns out.

BRACK. In any case, Mrs. Tesman, it's well that you know now how things stand. I mean—with respect to those little purchases I hear you've been threatening to make.

HEDDA. This business can't change anything.

BRACK. I see! Well, that's another matter. Good-bye. (*To* TESMAN.) When I take my afternoon walk, I'll stop by and fetch you.

TESMAN. Oh yes, please do—I don't know where I'm at.

HEDDA (*leaning back and reaching out her hand*). Good-bye, Judge. And come again soon.

BRACK. Many thanks. Good-bye now.

TESMAN (*accompanying him to the door*). Good-bye, Judge! You really must excuse me—

(BRACK *goes out by the hall door.*)

TESMAN (*pacing about the room*). Oh, Hedda—one should never go off and lose oneself in dreams, uh?

HEDDA (*looks at him and smiles*). Do *you* do *that?*

TESMAN. No use denying it. It was living in dreams to go and get married and set up house on nothing but expectations.

HEDDA. Perhaps you're right about that.

TESMAN. Well, at least we have our comfortable home, Hedda! The home that we always wanted. That we both fell in love with, I could almost say. Hm?

HEDDA (*rising slowly and wearily*). It was part of our

bargain that we'd live in society—that we'd keep a great house—

TESMAN. Yes of course—how I'd looked forward to that! Imagine—seeing you as a hostess—in our own select circle of friends! Yes, yes—well, for a while, we two will just have to get on by ourselves, Hedda. Perhaps have Aunt Julie here now and then. Oh, you—for you I wanted to have things so—so utterly different—!

HEDDA. Naturally this means I can't have a butler now.

TESMAN. Oh no—I'm sorry, a butler—we can't even talk about that, you know.

HEDDA. And the riding horse I was going to have—

TESMAN (*appalled*). Riding horse!

HEDDA. I suppose I can't think of that anymore.

TESMAN. Good Lord, no—that's obvious!

HEDDA (*crossing the room*). Well, at least I have one thing left to amuse myself with.

TESMAN (*beaming*). Ah, thank heaven for that! What is it, Hedda? Uh?

HEDDA (*in the center doorway, looking at him with veiled scorn*). My pistols, George.

TESMAN (*in fright*). Your pistols!

HEDDA (*her eyes cold*). General Gabler's pistols. (*She goes through the inner room and out to the left.*)

TESMAN (*runs to the center doorway and calls after her*). No, for heaven's sake, Hedda darling—don't touch those dangerous things! For my sake, Hedda! Uh?

ACT TWO

The rooms at the TESMANS', *same as in the first act, except that the piano has been moved out, and an elegant little writing table with a bookcase put in its place. A smaller table stands by the sofa to the left. Most of the flowers have been removed.* MRS. ELVSTED'*s bouquet stands on the large table in the foreground. It is afternoon.*

HEDDA, *dressed to receive callers, is alone in the room. She stands by the open glass door, loading a revolver. The match to it lies in an open pistol case on the writing table.*

HEDDA (*looking down into the garden and calling*). Good to see you again, Judge!

BRACK (*heard from below, at a distance*). Likewise, Mrs. Tesman!

HEDDA (*raises the pistol and aims*). And now, Judge, I'm going to shoot you!

BRACK (*shouting from below*). No-no-no! Don't point that thing at me!

HEDDA. That's what comes of sneaking in the back way. (*She fires.*)

BRACK (*nearer*). Are you out of your mind—!

HEDDA. Oh, dear—I didn't hit you, did I?

BRACK (*still outside*). Just stop this nonsense!

HEDDA. All right, you can come in, Judge.

> (JUDGE BRACK, *dressed for a stag party, enters through the glass door. He carries a light overcoat on his arm.*)

BRACK. Good God! Are you still playing such games? W at are you shooting at?

HEDDA. Oh, I was just shooting into the sky.

BRACK (*gently taking the pistol out of her hand*). Permit me (*Looks at it.*) Ah, this one—I know it well. (*Glancing around.*) Where's the case? Ah, here. (*Puts the pistol away and shuts the case.*) We'll have no more of that kind of fun today.

HEDDA.   Well, what in heaven's name do you want me to do with myself?

BRACK.   You haven't had any visitors?

HEDDA (*closing the glass door*).   Not a single one. All of our set are still in the country, I guess.

BRACK.   And Tesman isn't home either?

HEDDA (*at the writing table, putting the pistol case away in a drawer*).   No. Right after lunch he ran over to his aunts. He didn't expect you so soon.

BRACK.   Hm— I should have realized. That was stupid of me.

HEDDA (*turning her head and looking at him*).   Why stupid?

BRACK.   Because in that case I would have stopped by a little bit—earlier.

HEDDA (*crossing the room*).   Well, you'd have found no one here then at all. I've been up in my room dressing since lunch.

BRACK.   And there's not the least little crack in the door we could have conferred through.

HEDDA.   You forgot to arrange it.

BRACK.   Also stupid of me.

HEDDA.   Well, we'll just have to settle down here—and wait. Tesman won't be back for a while.

BRACK.   Don't worry, I can be patient.

> (HEDDA *sits in the corner of the sofa.* BRACK *lays his coat over the back of the nearest chair and sits down, keeping his hat in his hand. A short pause. They look at each other.*)

HEDDA.   Well?

BRACK (*in the same tone*).   Well?

HEDDA.   I spoke first.

BRACK (*leaning slightly forward*).   Then let's have a nice little cozy chat, Mrs. Hedda.

HEDDA (*leaning further back on the sofa*).   Doesn't it seem like a whole eternity since the last time we talked together? Oh, a few words last night and this morning—but they don't count.

BRACK. You mean, like this—between ourselves? Just the two of us?

HEDDA. Well, more or less.

BRACK. There wasn't a day that I didn't wish you were home again.

HEDDA. And I was wishing exactly the same.

BRACK. You? Really, Mrs. Hedda? And I thought you were having such a marvelous time on this trip.

HEDDA. Oh, you can imagine!

BRACK. But that's what Tesman always wrote.

HEDDA. Oh, him! There's nothing he likes better than grubbing around in libraries and copying out old parchments, or whatever you call them.

BRACK (*with a touch of malice*). But after all, it's his calling in life. In good part, anyway.

HEDDA. Yes, that's true. So there's nothing wrong with it— But what about *me*! Oh, Judge, you don't know—I've been so dreadfully bored.

BRACK (*sympathetically*). You really mean that? In all seriousness?

HEDDA. Well, you can understand—! To go for a whole six months without meeting a soul who knew the least bit about our circle. No one that one could talk to about our kind of things.

BRACK. Ah, yes—I think that would bother me too.

HEDDA. But then the most unbearable thing of all—

BRACK. What?

HEDDA. To be everlastingly together with—with one and the same person—

BRACK (*nodding in agreement*). Morning, noon, and night—yes. At every conceivable hour.

HEDDA. I said "everlastingly."

BRACK. All right. But with our good friend Tesman, I really should have thought—

HEDDA. My dear Judge, Tesman is—a specialist.

BRACK. Undeniably.

HEDDA. And specialists aren't at all amusing to travel with. Not in the long run, anyway.

BRACK. Not even—the specialist that one *loves*.

HEDDA. Ugh—don't use that syrupy word!

BRACK (*startled*). What's that, Mrs. Hedda!

HEDDA (*half laughing, half annoyed*). Well, just try it

yourself! Try listening to the history of civilization morning, noon, and—

BRACK. Everlastingly.

HEDDA. Yes! Yes! And then all this business about domestic crafts in the Middle Ages—! That really is just too revolting!

BRACK (*looks searchingly at her*). But tell me—I can't see how it ever came about that—? Hm—

HEDDA. That George Tesman and I could make a match?

BRACK. All right, let's put it that way.

HEDDA. Good Lord, does it seem so remarkable?

BRACK. Well, yes—and no, Mrs. Hedda.

HEDDA. I really had danced myself out, Judge. My time was up. (*With a slight shudder.*) Ugh! No, I don't want to say that. Or think it, either.

BRACK. You certainly have no reason to.

HEDDA. Oh—reasons— (*Watching him carefully.*) And George Tesman—he is, after all, a thoroughly acceptable choice.

BRACK. Acceptable and dependable, beyond a doubt.

HEDDA. And I don't find anything especially ridiculous about him. Do you?

BRACK. Ridiculous? No-o-o, I wouldn't say that.

HEDDA. Hm. Anyway, he works incredibly hard on his research! There's every chance that, in time, he could still make a name for himself.

BRACK (*looking at her with some uncertainty*). I thought you believed, like everyone else, that he was going to be quite famous some day.

HEDDA (*wearily*). Yes, so I did. And then when he kept pressing and pleading to be allowed to take care of me—I didn't see why I ought to resist.

BRACK. No. From that point of view, of course not—

HEDDA. It was certainly more than my other admirers were willing to do for me, Judge.

BRACK (*laughing*). Well, I can't exactly answer for all the others. But as far as I'm concerned, you know that I've always cherished a—a certain respect for the marriage bond. Generally speaking, that is.

HEDDA (*bantering*). Oh, I never really held out any hopes for *you*.

BRACK. All I want is to have a warm circle of intimate friends, where I can be of use one way or another, with the freedom to come and go as—as a trusted friend—

HEDDA. Of the man of the house, you mean?

BRACK (*with a bow*). Frankly—I prefer the lady. But the man, too, of course, in his place. That kind of—let's say, triangular arrangement—you can't imagine how satisfying it can be all around.

HEDDA. Yes, I must say I longed for some third person so many times on that trip. Oh—those endless tête-à-têtes in railway compartments—!

BRACK. Fortunately the wedding trip's over now.

HEDDA (*shaking her head*). The trip will go on—and on. I've only come to one stop on the line.

BRACK. Well, then what you do is jump out—and stretch yourself a little, Mrs. Hedda.

HEDDA. I'll never jump out.

BRACK. Never?

HEDDA. No. Because there's always someone on the platform who—

BRACK (*with a laugh*). Who looks at your legs, is that it?

HEDDA. Precisely.

BRACK. Yes, but after all—

HEDDA (*with a disdainful gesture*). I'm not interested. I'd rather keep my seat—right here, where I am. Tête-à-tête.

BRACK. Well, but suppose a third person came on board and joined the couple.

HEDDA. Ah! That's entirely different.

BRACK. A trusted friend, who understands—

HEDDA. And can talk about all kinds of lively things—

BRACK. Who's not in the least a specialist.

HEDDA (*with an audible sigh*). Yes, that would be a relief.

BRACK (*hearing the front door open and glancing toward it*). The triangle is complete.

HEDDA (*lowering her voice*). And the train goes on.

(GEORGE TESMAN, *in a gray walking suit and a soft felt hat, enters from the hall. He has a good number of unbound books under his arm and in his pockets.*)

TESMAN (*going up to the table by the corner settee*). Phew! Let me tell you, that's hot work—carrying all these. (*Setting the books down.*) I'm actually sweating, Hedda. And what's this—you're already here, Judge? Hm? Berta didn't tell me.

BRACK (*rising*). I came in through the garden.

HEDDA. What are all these books you've gotten?

TESMAN (*stands leafing through them*). They're new publications in my special field. I absolutely need them.

HEDDA. Your special field?

BRACK. Of course. Books in his special field, Mrs. Tesman.

(BRACK *and* HEDDA *exchange a knowing smile.*)

HEDDA. You need still more books in your special field?

TESMAN. Hedda, my dear, it's impossible ever to have too many. You have to keep up with what's written and published.

HEDDA. Oh, I suppose so.

TESMAN (*searching among the books*). And look—I picked up Eilert Løvborg's new book too. (*Offering it to her.*) Maybe you'd like to have a look at it? Uh?

HEDDA. No, thank you. Or—well, perhaps later.

TESMAN. I skimmed through some of it on the way home.

BRACK. Well, what do you think of it—as a specialist?

TESMAN. I think it's amazing how well it holds up. He's never written like this before. (*Gathers up the books.*) But I'll take these into the study now. I can't wait to cut the pages—! And then I better dress up a bit. (*To* BRACK.) We don't have to rush right off, do we? Hm?

BRACK. No, not at all. There's ample time.

TESMAN. Ah, then I'll be at my leisure. (*Starts out with the books, but pauses and turns in the doorway.*) Oh, incidentally, Hedda—Aunt Julie won't be by to see you this evening.

HEDDA. She won't? I suppose it's that business with the hat?

TESMAN. Not at all. How can you think that of Aunt Julie? Imagine—! No, it's Auntie Rina—she's very ill.

HEDDA. She always is.

TESMAN.   Yes, but today she really took a turn for the worse.

HEDDA.   Well, then it's only sensible for her sister to stay with her. I'll have to bear with it.

TESMAN.   But you can't imagine how delighted Aunt Julie was all the same—because you'd filled out so nicely on the trip!

HEDDA (*under her breath; rising*).   Oh, these eternal aunts!

TESMAN.   What?

HEDDA (*going over to the glass door*).   Nothing.

TESMAN.   All right, then. (*He goes through the inner room and out, right.*)

BRACK.   What were you saying about a hat?

HEDDA.   Oh, it's something that happened with Miss Tesman this morning. She'd put her hat down over there on the chair. (*Looks at him and smiles.*) And I pretended I thought it was the maid's.

BRACK (*shaking his head*).   But my dear Mrs. Hedda, how could you do that! Hurt that nice old lady!

HEDDA (*nervously, pacing the room*).   Well, it's—these things come over me, just like that, suddenly. And I can't hold back. (*Throws herself down in the armchair by the stove.*) Oh, I don't know myself how to explain it.

BRACK (*behind the armchair*).   You're not really happy— that's the heart of it.

HEDDA (*gazing straight ahead*).   And I don't know why I ought to be—happy. Or maybe you can tell me why?

BRACK.   Yes—among other things, because you've gotten just the home you've always wanted.

HEDDA (*looks up at him and laughs*).   You believe that story too?

BRACK.   You mean there's nothing to it?

HEDDA.   Oh yes—there's something to it.

BRACK.   Well?

HEDDA.   There's this much to it, that I used Tesman as my escort home from parties last summer—

BRACK.   Unfortunately—I was headed quite a different way.

HEDDA.   How true. Yes, you went several different ways last summer.

BRACK (*laughing*). For shame, Mrs. Hedda! Well—so you and Tesman—?

HEDDA. Yes, so one evening we walked by this place. And Tesman, poor thing, was writhing in torment, because he couldn't find anything to say. And I felt sorry for a man of such learning—

BRACK (*smiling skeptically*). Did you? Hm—

HEDDA. No, I honestly did. And so—just to help him off the hook—I came out with some rash remark about this lovely house being where I'd always wanted to live.

BRACK. No more than that?

HEDDA. No more that evening.

BRACK. But afterward?

HEDDA. Yes, my rashness had its consequences, Judge.

BRACK. I'm afraid our rashness all too often does, Mrs. Hedda.

HEDDA. Thanks! But don't you see, it was this passion for the old Falk mansion that drew George Tesman and me together! It was nothing more than that, that brought on our engagement and the marriage and the wedding trip and everything else. Oh yes, Judge—I was going to say, you make your bed and then you lie in it.

BRACK. But that's priceless! So actually you couldn't care less about all this?

HEDDA. God knows, not in the least.

BRACK. But even now? Now that we've got it furnished a bit cosier for you here?

HEDDA. Ugh—all the rooms seem to smell of lavender and dried roses. But maybe that scent was brought in by Aunt Julie.

BRACK (*laughing*). No, I think it's a bequest from the late Mrs. Falk.

HEDDA. Yes, there's something in it of the odor of death. It's like a corsage—the day after the dance. (*Folds her hands behind her neck, leans back in her chair, and looks at him.*) Oh, my dear Judge—you can't imagine how horribly I'm going to bore myself here.

BRACK. But couldn't you find some goal in life to work toward? Others do, Mrs. Hedda.

HEDDA. A goal—that would really absorb me?

BRACK. Yes, preferably.

HEDDA.   God only knows what that could be. I often wonder if— (*Breaks off.*) But that's impossible too.

BRACK.   Who knows? Tell me.

HEDDA.   I was thinking—if I could get Tesman to go into politics.

BRACK (*laughing*).   Tesman! No, I can promise you— politics is absolutely out of his line.

HEDDA.   No, I can believe you. But even so, I wonder if I could get him into it?

BRACK.   Well, what satisfaction would you have in that, if he can't succeed? Why push him in that direction?

HEDDA.   Because, I've told you, I'm bored! (*After a pause.*) Then you think it's really out of the question that he could ever be a cabinet minister?

BRACK.   Hm—you see, Mrs. Hedda—to be anything like that, he'd have to be fairly wealthy to start with.

HEDDA (*rising impatiently*).   Yes, there it is! It's this tight little world I've stumbled into— (*Crossing the room.*) That's what makes life so miserable! So utterly ludicrous! Because that's what it *is*.

BRACK.   I'd say the fault lies elsewhere.

HEDDA.   Where?

BRACK.   You've never experienced anything that's really stirred you.

HEDDA.   Anything serious, you mean.

BRACK.   Well, you can call it that, if you like. But now perhaps it's on the way.

HEDDA (*tossing her head*).   Oh, you mean all the fuss over that wretched professorship! But that's Tesman's problem. I'm not going to give it a single thought.

BRACK.   No, that isn't—ah, never mind. But suppose you were to be confronted now by what—in rather elegant language—is called your most solemn responsibility. (*Smiling.*) A new responsibility, Mrs. Hedda.

HEDDA (*angrily*).   Be quiet! You'll never see me like that!

BRACK (*delicately*).   We'll discuss it again in a year's time—at the latest.

HEDDA (*curtly*).   I have no talent for such things, Judge. I won't have responsibilities!

BRACK.   Don't you think you've a talent for what almost every woman finds the most meaningful—

HEDDA (*over by the glass door*). Oh, I told you, be quiet! I often think I have talent for only one thing in life.

BRACK (*moving closer*). And what, may I ask, is that?

HEDDA (*stands looking out*). Boring myself to death. And that's the truth. (*Turns, looks toward the inner room, and laughs.*) See what I mean! Here comes the professor.

BRACK (*in a low tone of warning*). Ah-ah-ah, Mrs. Hedda!

> (GEORGE TESMAN, *dressed for the party, with hat and gloves in hand, enters from the right through the inner room.*)

TESMAN. Hedda—there's been no word from Eilert Løvborg, has there? Hm?

HEDDA. No.

TESMAN. Well, he's bound to be here soon then. You'll see.

BRACK. You really believe he'll come?

TESMAN. Yes, I'm almost positive of it. Because I'm sure they're nothing but rumors, what you told us this morning.

BRACK. Oh?

TESMAN. Yes. At least Aunt Julie said she couldn't for the world believe that he'd stand in my way again. Can you imagine that!

BRACK. So, then everything's well and good.

TESMAN (*putting his hat with the gloves inside on a chair to the right*). Yes, but I really would like to wait for him as long as possible.

BRACK. We have plenty of time for that. There's no one due at my place till seven or half past.

TESMAN. Why, then we can keep Hedda company for a while. And see what turns up. Uh?

HEDDA (*taking* BRACK's *hat and coat over to the settee*). And if worst comes to worst, Mr. Løvborg can sit and talk with me.

BRACK (*trying to take his things himself*). Ah, please, Mrs. Tesman—! What do you mean by "worst," in this case?

HEDDA. If he won't go with you and Tesman.

TESMAN (*looks doubtfully at her*). But Hedda dear—is

it quite right that he stays with you here? Uh? Remember
that Aunt Julie isn't coming.

HEDDA.   No, but Mrs. Elvsted is. The three of us can
have tea together.

TESMAN.   Oh, well, that's all right.

BRACK (*smiling*).   And that might be the soundest plan
for him too.

HEDDA.   Why?

BRACK.   Well, really, Mrs. Tesman, you've made enough
pointed remarks about my little bachelor parties. You've
always said they're only fit for men of the strictest
principles.

HEDDA.   But Mr. Løvborg is surely a man of principle
now. After all, a reformed sinner—

(BERTA *appears at the hall door.*)

BERTA.   Ma'am, there's a gentleman here who'd like to
see you—

HEDDA.   Yes, show him in.

TESMAN (*softly*).   I'm sure it's him! Just think!

(EILERT LØVBORG *enters from the hall. He is lean
and gaunt, the same age as* TESMAN, *but looks
older and somewhat run-down. His hair and
beard are dark brown, his face long and pale,
but with reddish patches over the cheekbones.
He is dressed in a trim black suit, quite new,
and holds dark gloves and a top hat in his
hand. He hesitates by the door and bows
abruptly. He seems somewhat embarrassed.*)

TESMAN (*crosses over and shakes his hand*).   Ah, my
dear Eilert—so at last we meet again!

EILERT LØVBORG (*speaking in a hushed voice*).   Thanks
for your letter, George! (*Approaching* HEDDA.) May I
shake hands with you too, Mrs. Tesman?

HEDDA (*taking his hand*).   So glad to see you, Mr.
Løvborg. (*Gesturing with her hand.*) I don't know if you two
gentlemen—?

LØVBORG (*bowing slightly*).   Judge Brack, I believe.

BRACK (*reciprocating*).   Of course. It's been some
years—

TESMAN (*to* LØVBORG, *with his hands on his shoul-*

ders). And now, Eilert, make yourself at home, completely! Right, Hedda? I hear you'll be settling down here in town again? Uh?

LØVBORG.   I plan to.

TESMAN.   Well, that makes sense. Listen—I just got hold of your new book. But I really haven't had time to read it yet.

LØVBORG.   You can save yourself the bother.

TESMAN.   Why? What do you mean?

LØVBORG.   There's very little to it.

TESMAN.   Imagine—you can say that!

BRACK.   But it's won such high praise, I hear.

LØVBORG.   That's exactly what I wanted. So I wrote a book that everyone could agree with.

BRACK.   Very sound.

TESMAN.   Yes, but my dear Eilert—!

LØVBORG.   Because now I want to build up my position again—and try to make a fresh start.

TESMAN (*somewhat distressed*).   Yes, that is what you want, I suppose. Uh?

LØVBORG (*smiling, puts down his hat and takes a packet wrapped in brown paper out of his coat pocket*).   But when this comes out—George Tesman—you'll have to read it. Because this is the real book—the one that speaks for my true self.

TESMAN.   Oh, really? What sort of book is that?

LØVBORG.   It's the sequel.

TESMAN.   Sequel? To what?

LØVBORG.   To the book.

TESMAN.   The one just out?

LØVBORG.   Of course.

TESMAN.   Yes, but my dear Eilert—that comes right down to our own time!

LØVBORG.   Yes, it does. And this one deals with the future.

TESMAN.   The future! But good Lord, there's nothing we know about that!

LØVBORG.   True. But there are one or two things worth saying about it all the same. (*Opens the packet.*) Here, take a look—

TESMAN.   But that's not your handwriting.

LØVBORG.   I dictated it. (*Paging through the manu-*

script.) It's divided into two sections. The first is about the forces shaping the civilization of the future. And the second part, here—(*Paging further on.*) suggests what lines of development it's likely to take.

TESMAN.   How extraordinary! It never would have occurred to me to write about anything like that.

HEDDA (*at the glass door, drumming on the pane*).   Hm—no, of course not.

LØVBORG (*puts the manuscript back in its wrapping and lays it on the table*).   I brought it along because I thought I might read you a bit of it this evening.

TESMAN.   Ah, that's very good of you, Eilert; but this evening— (*Glancing at* BRACK.) I'm really not sure that it's possible—

LØVBORG.   Well, some other time, then. There's no hurry.

BRACK.   I should explain, Mr. Løvborg—there's a little party at my place tonight. Mostly for Tesman, you understand.

LØVBORG (*looking for his hat*).   Ah—then I won't stay—

BRACK.   No, listen—won't you give me the pleasure of having you join us?

LØVBORG (*sharply and decisively*).   No, I can't. Thanks very much.

BRACK.   Oh, nonsense! Do that. We'll be a small, select group. And you can bet we'll have it "lively," as Mrs. Hed—Mrs. Tesman says.

LØVBORG.   I don't doubt it. But nevertheless—

BRACK.   You could bring your manuscript with you and read it to Tesman there, at my place. I have plenty of rooms.

TESMAN.   Why, of course, Eilert—you could do that, couldn't you? Uh?

HEDDA (*intervening*).   But dear, if Mr. Løvborg simply doesn't want to! I'm sure Mr. Løvborg would much prefer to settle down here and have supper with me.

LØVBORG (*looking at her*).   With you, Mrs. Tesman!

HEDDA.   And with Mrs. Elvsted.

LØVBORG.   Ah. (*Casually.*) I saw her a moment this afternoon.

HEDDA.   Oh, did you? Well, she'll be here soon. So it's

almost essential for you to stay, Mr. Løvborg. Otherwise, she'll have no one to see her home.

LØVBORG.   That's true. Yes, thank you, Mrs. Tesman— I'll be staying, then.

HEDDA.   Then let me just tell the maid—

(*She goes to the hall door and rings.* BERTA *enters.* HEDDA *talks to her quietly and points toward the inner room.* BERTA *nods and goes out again.*)

TESMAN (*at the same time, to* LØVBORG). Tell me, Eilert—is it this new material—about the future—that you're going to be lecturing on?

LØVBORG.   Yes.

TESMAN.   Because I heard at the bookstore that you'll be giving a lecture series here this autumn.

LØVBORG.   I intend to. I hope you won't be offended, Tesman.

TESMAN.   Why, of course not! But—?

LØVBORG.   I can easily understand that it makes things rather difficult for you.

TESMAN (*dispiritedly*).   Oh, I could hardly expect that for my sake you'd—

LØVBORG.   But I'm going to wait till you have your appointment.

TESMAN.   You'll wait! Yes, but—but—you're not competing for it, then? Uh?

LØVBORG.   No. I only want to win in the eyes of the world.

TESMAN.   But, my Lord—then Aunt Julie was right after all! Oh yes—I knew it all along! Hedda! Can you imagine— Eilert Løvborg won't stand in our way!

HEDDA (*brusquely*).   Our way? Leave me out of it.

(*She goes up toward the inner room where* BERTA *is putting a tray with decanters and glasses on the table.* HEDDA *nods her approval and comes back again.* BERTA *goes out.*)

TESMAN (*at the same time*).   But you, Judge—what do you say to all this? Uh?

BRACK.   Well, I'd say that victory and honor—hm—after all, they're very sweet—

TESMAN.   Yes, of course. But still—

HEDDA (*regarding* TESMAN *with a cold smile*).   You look as if you'd been struck by lightning.

TESMAN.   Yes—something like it—I guess—

BRACK.   That's because a thunderstorm just passed over us, Mrs. Tesman.

HEDDA (*pointing toward the inner room*).   Won't you gentlemen please help yourselves to a glass of cold punch?

BRACK (*looking at his watch*).   A parting cup? That's not such a bad idea.

TESMAN.   Marvelous, Hedda! Simply marvelous! The way I feel now, with this weight off my mind—

HEDDA.   Please, Mr. Løvborg, you too,

LØVBORG (*with a gesture of refusal*).   No, thank you. Not for me.

BRACK.   Good Lord, cold punch—it isn't poison, you know.

LØVBORG.   Perhaps not for everyone.

HEDDA.   I'll keep Mr. Løvborg company a while.

TESMAN.   All right, Hedda dear, you do that.

> (*He and* BRACK *go into the inner room, sit down, drink punch, smoke cigarettes, and talk animatedly during the following.* LØVBORG *remains standing by the stove.* HEDDA *goes to the writing table.*)

HEDDA (*slightly raising her voice*).   I can show you some photographs, if you like. Tesman and I traveled through the Tyrol on our way home.

> (*She brings over an album and lays it on the table by the sofa, seating herself in the farthest corner.* EILERT LØVBORG *comes closer, stops and looks at her. Then he takes a chair and sits down on her left, his back toward the inner room.*)

HEDDA (*opening the album*).   You see this view of the mountains, Mr. Løvborg. That's the Ortler group. Tesman's labeled them underneath. Here it is: "The Ortler group, near Meran."

LØVBORG (*whose eyes have never left her, speaking in a low, soft voice*).   Hedda—Gabler!

HEDDA (*with a quick glance at him*).   Ah! Shh!

LØVBORG (*repeating softly*).   Hedda Gabler!

HEDDA (*looks at the album*).   Yes, I used to be called that. In those days—when we two knew each other.

LØVBORG.   And from now on—for the rest of my life—I have to teach myself not to say Hedda Gabler.

HEDDA (*turning the pages*).   Yes, you have to. And I think you ought to start practicing it. The sooner the better, I'd say.

LØVBORG (*resentment in his voice*).   Hedda Gabler married? And to George Tesman!

HEDDA.   Yes—that's how it goes.

LØVBORG.   Oh, Hedda, Hedda—how could you throw yourself away like that!

HEDDA (*looks at him sharply*).   All right—no more of that!

LØVBORG.   What do you mean?

(TESMAN *comes in and over to the sofa.*)

HEDDA (*hears him coming and says casually*).   And this one, Mr. Løvborg, was taken from the Val d'Ampezzo. Just look at the peaks of those mountains. (*Looks warmly up at* TESMAN.) Now what were those marvelous mountains called, dear?

TESMAN.   Let me see. Oh, those are the Dolomites.

HEDDA.   Why, of course! Those are the Dolomites, Mr. Løvborg.

TESMAN.   Hedda dear—I only wanted to ask if we shouldn't bring in some punch anyway. At least for you, hm?

HEDDA.   Yes, thank you. And a couple of *petits fours*, please.

TESMAN.   No cigarettes?

HEDDA.   No.

TESMAN.   Right.

(*He goes through the inner room and out to the right.* BRACK *remains sitting inside, keeping his eye from time to time on* HEDDA *and* LØVBORG.)

LØVBORG (*softly, as before*).   Answer me, Hedda—how could you go and do such a thing?

HEDDA (*apparently immersed in the album*).   If you keep on saying Hedda like that to me, I won't talk to you.

LØVBORG.   Can't I say Hedda even when we're alone?

HEDDA.   No. You can think it, but you mustn't say it like that.

LØVBORG.   Ah, I understand. It offends your—love for George Tesman.

HEDDA (*glances at him and smiles*).   Love? You *are* absurd!

LØVBORG.   Then you don't love him!

HEDDA.   I don't expect to be unfaithful, either. I'm not having any of that!

LØVBORG.   Hedda, just answer me one thing—

HEDDA.   Shh!

(TESMAN, *carrying a tray, enters from the inner room.*)

TESMAN.   Look out! Here come the goodies. (*He sets the tray on the table.*)

HEDDA.   Why do you do the serving?

TESMAN (*filling the glasses*).   Because I think it's such fun to wait on you, Hedda.

HEDDA.   But now you've poured out two glasses. And you know Mr. Løvborg doesn't want—

TESMAN.   Well, but Mrs. Elvsted will be along soon.

HEDDA.   Yes, that's right—Mrs. Elvsted—

TESMAN.   Had you forgotten her? Uh?

HEDDA.   We've been so caught up in these. (*Showing him a picture.*) Do you remember this little village?

TESMAN.   Oh, that's the one just below the Brenner Pass! It was there that we stayed overnight—

HEDDA.   And met all those lively summer people.

TESMAN.   Yes, that's the place. Just think—if we could have had *you* with us, Eilert! My! (*He goes back and sits beside* BRACK.)

LØVBORG.   Answer me just one thing, Hedda—

HEDDA.   Yes?

LØVBORG.   Was there no love with respect to me, either? Not a spark—not one glimmer of love at all?

HEDDA.   I wonder, really, was there? To me it was as if we were two true companions—two very close friends. (*Smiling.*) You, especially, were so open with me.

LØVBORG.   You wanted it that way.

HEDDA.   When I look back on it now, there was really something beautiful and fascinating—and daring, it seems to me, about—about our secret closeness—our companionship that no one, not a soul, suspected.

LØVBORG.   Yes, Hedda, that's true! Wasn't there? When I'd come over to your father's in the afternoon—and the general sat by the window reading his papers—with his back to us—

HEDDA.   And we'd sit on the corner sofa—

LØVBORG.   Always with the same illustrated magazine in front of us—

HEDDA.   Yes, for the lack of an album.

LØVBORG.   Yes, Hedda—and the confessions I used to make—telling you things about myself that no one else knew of then. About the way I'd go out, the drinking, the madness that went on day and night, for days at a time. Ah, what power was it in you, Hedda, that made me tell you such things?

HEDDA.   You think it was some kind of power in me?

LØVBORG.   How else can I explain it? And all those—those devious questions you asked me—

HEDDA.   That you understood so remarkably well—

LØVBORG.   To think you could sit there and ask such questions! So boldly.

HEDDA.   Deviously, please.

LØVBORG.   Yes, but boldly, all the same. Interrogating me about—all that kind of thing!

HEDDA.   And to think you could answer, Mr. Løvborg.

LØVBORG.   Yes, that's exactly what I don't understand—now, looking back. But tell me, Hedda—the root of that bond between us, wasn't it love? Didn't you feel, on your part, as if you wanted to cleanse and absolve me—when I brought those confessions to you? Wasn't that it?

HEDDA.   No, not quite.

LØVBORG.   What made you do it, then?

HEDDA.   Do you find it so very surprising that a young girl—if there's no chance of anyone knowing—

LØVBORG.   Yes?

HEDDA.   That she'd like some glimpse of a world that—

LØVBORG.   That—?

HEDDA.   That she's forbidden to know anything about.

LØVBORG. So that was it?

HEDDA. Partly. Partly that, I guess.

LØVBORG. Companionship in a thirst for life. But why, then, couldn't it have gone on?

HEDDA. But that was your fault.

LØVBORG. You broke it off.

HEDDA. Yes, when that closeness of ours threatened to grow more serious. Shame on you, Eilert Løvborg! How could you violate my trust when I'd been so—so bold with my friendship?

LØVBORG (*clenching his fists*). Oh, why didn't you do what you said! Why didn't you shoot me down!

HEDDA. I'm—much too afraid of scandal.

LØVBORG. Yes, Hedda, you're a coward at heart.

HEDDA. A terrible coward. (*Changing her tone.*) But that was lucky for you. And now you're so nicely consoled at the Elvsteds'.

LØVBORG. I know what Thea's been telling you.

HEDDA. And perhaps you've been telling her all about us?

LØVBORG. Not a word. She's too stupid for that sort of thing.

HEDDA. Stupid?

LØVBORG. When it comes to those things, she's stupid.

HEDDA. And I'm a coward. (*Leans closer, without looking him in the eyes, and speaks softly.*) But there *is* something now that I can tell you.

LØVBORG (*intently*). What?

HEDDA. When I didn't dare shoot you—

LØVBORG. Yes?

HEDDA. That wasn't my worst cowardice—that night.

LØVBORG (*looks at her a moment, understands, and whispers passionately*). Oh, Hedda! Hedda Gabler! Now I begin to see it, the hidden reason why we've been so close! You and I—! It was the hunger for *life* in you—

HEDDA (*quietly, with a sharp glance*). Careful! That's no way to think!

(*It has begun to grow dark. The hall door is opened from without by* BERTA.)

HEDDA (*clapping the album shut and calling out with a smile*). Well, at last! Thea dear—please come in!

(MRS. ELVSTED *enters from the hall. She is in evening dress. The door is closed behind her.*)

HEDDA (*on the sofa, stretching her arms out toward her*).   Thea, my sweet—I thought you were never coming!

(*In passing,* MRS. ELVSTED *exchanges light greetings with the gentlemen in the inner room, then comes over to the table and extends her hand to* HEDDA. LØVBORG *has gotten up. He and* MRS. ELVSTED *greet each other with a silent nod.*)

MRS. ELVSTED.   Perhaps I ought to go in and talk a bit with your husband?

HEDDA.   Oh, nonsense. Let them be. They're leaving soon.

MRS. ELVSTED.   They're leaving?

HEDDA.   Yes, for a drinking party.

MRS. ELVSTED (*quickly, to* LØVBORG).   But you're not?

LØVBORG.   No.

HEDDA.   Mr. Løvborg—is staying with us.

MRS. ELVSTED (*taking a chair, about to sit down beside him*).   Oh, it's so good to be here!

HEDDA.   No, no, Thea dear! Not there! You have to come over here by me. I want to be in the middle.

MRS. ELVSTED.   Any way you please.

(*She goes around the table and sits on the sofa to* HEDDA'S *right.* LØVBORG *resumes his seat.*)

LØVBORG (*after a brief pause, to* HEDDA).   Isn't she lovely to look at?

HEDDA (*lightly stroking her hair*).   Only to look at?

LØVBORG.   Yes. Because we two—she and I—we really *are* true companions. We trust each other completely. We can talk things out together without any reservations—

HEDDA.   Never anything devious, Mr. Løvborg?

LØVBORG.   Well—

MRS. ELVSTED (*quietly, leaning close to* HEDDA).   Oh, Hedda, you don't know how happy I am! Just think—he says that I've inspired him.

HEDDA (*regarding her with a smile*).   Really, dear; did he say that?

LØVBORG. And then the courage she has, Mrs. Tesman, when it's put to the test.

MRS. ELVSTED. Good heavens, me! Courage!

LØVBORG. Enormous courage—where I'm concerned.

HEDDA. Yes, courage—yes! If one only had that.

LØVBORG. Then what?

HEDDA. Then life might still be bearable. (*Suddenly changing her tone.*) But now, Thea dearest—you really must have a nice glass of cold punch.

MRS. ELVSTED. No, thank you. I never drink that sort of thing.

HEDDA. Well, then you, Mr. Løvborg.

LØVBORG. Thanks, not for me either.

MRS. ELVSTED. No, not for him either!

HEDDA (*looking intently at him*). But if I insist?

LØVBORG. Makes no difference.

HEDDA (*with a laugh*). Poor me, then I have no power over you at all?

LØVBORG. Not in that area.

HEDDA. But seriously, I think you ought to, all the same. For your own sake.

MRS. ELVSTED. But Hedda—!

LØVBORG. Why do you think so?

HEDDA. Or, to be more exact, for others' sakes.

LØVBORG. Oh?

HEDDA. Otherwise, people might get the idea that you're not very bold at heart. That you're not really sure of yourself at all.

MRS. ELVSTED (*softly*). Oh, Hedda, don't—!

LØVBORG. People can think whatever they like, for all I care.

MRS. ELVSTED (*happily*). Yes, that's right!

HEDDA. I saw it so clearly in Judge Brack a moment ago.

LØVBORG. What did you see?

HEDDA. The contempt in his smile when you didn't dare join them for a drink.

LØVBORG. Didn't dare! Obviously I'd rather stay here and talk with you.

MRS. ELVSTED. That's only reasonable, Hedda.

HEDDA. But how could the judge know that? And besides, I noticed him smile and glance at Tesman when you couldn't bring yourself to go to their wretched little party.

LØVBORG.   Couldn't! Are you saying I couldn't?

HEDDA.   I'm not. But that's the way Judge Brack sees it.

LØVBORG.   All right, let him.

HEDDA.   Then you won't go along?

LØVBORG.   I'm staying here with you and Thea.

MRS. ELVSTED.   Yes, Hedda—you can be sure he is!

HEDDA (*smiles and nods approvingly at* LØVBORG). I see. Firm as a rock. True to principle, to the end of time. There, that's what a man ought to be! (*Turning to* MRS. ELVSTED *and patting her.*) Well, now, didn't I tell you that, when you came here so distraught this morning—

LØVBORG (*surprised*).   Distraught?

MRS. ELVSTED (*terrified*).   Hedda—! But Hedda—!

HEDDA.   Can't you see for yourself? There's no need at all for your going around so deathly afraid that— (*Changing her tone.*) There! Now we can all enjoy ourselves!

LØVBORG (*shaken*).   What is all this, Mrs. Tesman?

MRS. ELVSTED.   Oh, God, oh, God, Hedda! What are you saying! What are you doing!

HEDDA.   Not so loud. That disgusting judge is watching you.

LØVBORG.   So deathly afraid? For my sake?

MRS. ELVSTED (*in a low moan*).   Oh, Hedda, you've made me so miserable!

LØVBORG (*looks intently at her a moment, his face drawn*).   So that's how completely you trusted me.

MRS. ELVSTED (*imploringly*).   Oh, my dearest—if you'll only listen—!

LØVBORG (*takes one of the glasses of punch, raises it, and says in a low, hoarse voice*).   Your health, Thea! (*He empties the glass, puts it down, and takes the other.*)

MRS. ELVSTED (*softly*).   Oh, Hedda, Hedda—how could you want such a thing!

HEDDA.   Want it? I? Are you crazy?

LØVBORG.   And your health too, Mrs. Tesman. Thanks for the truth. Long live truth! (*Drains the glass and starts to refill it.*)

HEDDA (*laying her hand on his arm*).   All right—no more for now. Remember, you're going to a party.

MRS. ELVSTED.   No, no, no!

HEDDA.   Shh! They're watching you.

LØVBORG (*putting down his glass*).   Now, Thea—tell me honestly—

MRS. ELVSTED.   Yes!

LØVBORG.   Did your husband know that you followed me?

MRS. ELVSTED (*wringing her hands*).   Oh, Hedda—listen to him!

LØVBORG.   Did you have it arranged, you and he, that you should come down into town and spy on me? Or maybe he got you to do it himself? Ah, yes—I'm sure he needed me back in the office! Or maybe he missed my hand at cards?

MRS. ELVSTED (*softly, in anguish*).   Oh, Eilert, Eilert—!

LØVBORG (*seizing his glass to fill it*).   Skoal to the old sheriff, too!

HEDDA (*stopping him*).   That's enough. Don't forget, you're giving a reading for Tesman.

LØVBORG (*calmly, setting down his glass*).   That was stupid of me, Thea. I mean, taking it like this. Don't be angry at me, my dearest. You'll see—you and all the others—that if I stumbled and fell—I'm back on my feet again now! With your help, Thea.

MRS. ELVSTED (*radiant with joy*).   Oh, thank God—!

>   (BRACK, *in the meantime, has looked at his watch. He and* TESMAN *stand up and enter the drawing room.*)

BRACK (*takes his hat and overcoat*).   Well, Mrs. Tesman, our time is up.

HEDDA.   I suppose it is.

LØVBORG (*rising*).   Mine too, Judge.

MRS. ELVSTED (*softly pleading*).   Oh, Eilert—don't!

HEDDA (*pinching her arm*).   They can hear you!

MRS. ELVSTED (*with a small cry*).   Ow!

LØVBORG> (*to* BRACK).   You were kind enough to ask me along.

BRACK.   Oh, then you *are* coming, after all?

LØVBORG.   Yes, thank you.

BRACK.   I'm delighted—

LØVBORG (*putting the packet back in his pocket, to*

TESMAN). I'd like to show you one or two things before I turn this in.

TESMAN. Just think—how exciting! But Hedda dear, how will Mrs. Elvsted get home? Uh?

HEDDA. Oh, we'll hit on something.

LØVBORG (*glancing toward the ladies*). Mrs. Elvsted? Don't worry, I'll stop back and fetch her. (*Coming nearer.*) Say about ten o'clock, Mrs. Tesman? Will that do?

HEDDA. Yes. That will do very nicely.

TESMAN. Well, then everything's all set. But you mustn't expect *me* that early, Hedda.

HEDDA. Dear, you stay as long—just as long as you like.

MRS. ELVSTED (*with suppressed anxiety*). Mr. Løvborg— I'll be waiting here till you come.

LØVBORG (*his hat in his hand*). Yes, I understand.

BRACK. So, gentlemen—the excursion train is leaving! I hope it's going to be lively, as a certain fair lady puts it.

HEDDA. Ah, if only that fair lady could be there, invisible—

BRACK. Why invisible?

HEDDA. To hear a little of your unadulterated liveliness, Judge.

BRACK (*laughs*). I wouldn't advise the fair lady to try.

TESMAN (*also laughing*). Oh, Hedda, that's a good one! Just imagine!

BRACK. Well, good night. Good night, ladies.

LØVBORG (*bowing*). About ten o'clock, then.

> (BRACK, LØVBORG, and TESMAN *go out the hall door. At the same time,* BERTA *enters from the inner room with a lighted lamp, which she sets on the drawing room table, then goes out the same way.*)

MRS. ELVSTED (*having risen, moving restlessly about the room*). Hedda—Hedda—what's going to come of all this?

HEDDA. At ten o'clock—he'll be here. I can see him now—with vine leaves in his hair—fiery and bold—

MRS. ELVSTED. Oh, how good that would be!

HEDDA. And then, you'll see—he'll be back in control of himself. He'll be a free man, then, for the rest of his days.

MRS. ELVSTED.   Oh, God—if only he comes as you see him now!

HEDDA.   He'll come back like that, and no other way! (*Gets up and goes closer.*) Go on and doubt him as much as you like. *I* believe in him. And now we'll find out—

MRS. ELVSTED.   There's something behind what you're doing, Hedda.

HEDDA.   Yes, there is. For once in my life, I want to have power over a human being.

MRS. ELVSTED.   But don't you have that?

HEDDA.   I don't have it. I've never had it.

MRS. ELVSTED.   Not with your husband?

HEDDA.   Yes, what a bargain *that* was! Oh, if you only could understand how poor I am. And you're allowed to be so rich! (*Passionately throws her arms about her.*) I think I'll burn your hair off, after all!

MRS. ELVSTED.   Let go! Let me go! I'm afraid of you, Hedda!

BERTA (*in the doorway to the inner room*).   Supper's waiting in the dining room, ma'am.

HEDDA.   All right, we're coming.

MRS. ELVSTED.   No, no, no! I'd rather go home alone! Right away—now!

HEDDA.   Nonsense! First you're going to have tea, you little fool. And then—ten o'clock—Eilert Løvborg comes—with vine leaves in his hair.

(*She drags* MRS. ELVSTED, *almost by force, toward the doorway.*)

ACT THREE

The same rooms at the TESMANS'. *The curtains are down across the doorway to the inner room, and also across the glass door. The lamp, shaded and turned down low, is burning on the table. The door to the stove stands open; the fire has nearly gone out.*

MRS. ELVSTED, *wrapped in a large shawl, with her feet up on a footstool, lies back in the armchair close by the stove.* HEDDA, *fully dressed, is asleep on the sofa, with a blanket over her. After a pause,* MRS. ELVSTED *suddenly sits straight up in the chair, listening tensely. Then she sinks wearily back again.*

MRS. ELVSTED (*in a low moan*). Not yet—oh, God—oh, God—not yet!

> (BERTA *slips in cautiously by the hall door. She holds a letter in her hand.*)

MRS. ELVSTED (*turns and whispers anxiously*). Yes? Has anyone come?

BERTA (*softly*). Yes, a girl just now stopped by with this letter.

MRS. ELVSTED (*quickly, reaching out her hand*). A letter! Give it to me!

BERTA. No, it's for the Doctor, ma'am.

MRS. ELVSTED. Oh.

BERTA. It was Miss Tesman's maid that brought it. I'll leave it here on the table.

MRS. ELVSTED. Yes, do.

BERTA (*putting the letter down*). I think I'd best put out the lamp. It's smoking.

MRS. ELVSTED. Yes, put it out. It'll be daylight soon.

BERTA (*does so*). It's broad daylight already, ma'am.

MRS. ELVSTED. It's daylight! And still no one's come—!

BERTA. Oh, mercy—I knew it would go like this.

MRS. ELVSTED. You knew?

BERTA. Yes, when I saw that a certain gentleman was

273

back here in town—and that he went off with them. We've heard plenty about that gentleman over the years.

MRS. ELVSTED. Don't talk so loud. You'll wake Mrs. Tesman.

BERTA (*looks toward the sofa and sighs*). Goodness me—yes, let her sleep, poor thing. Should I put a bit more on the fire?

MRS. ELVSTED. Thanks, not for me.

BERTA. All right. (*She goes quietly out the hall door.*)

HEDDA (*wakes as the door shuts and looks up*). What's that?

MRS. ELVSTED. It was just the maid—

HEDDA (*glancing about*). In here—? Oh yes, I remember now. (*Sits up on the sofa, stretches, and rubs her eyes.*) What time is it, Thea?

MRS. ELVSTED (*looking at her watch*). It's after seven.

HEDDA. When did Tesman get in?

MRS. ELVSTED. He isn't back.

HEDDA. Not back yet?

MRS. ELVSTED (*getting up*). No one's come in.

HEDDA. And we sat here and waited up for them till four o'clock—

MRS. ELVSTED (*wringing her hands*). And *how* I've waited for him!

HEDDA (*yawns, and speaks with her hand in front of her mouth*). Oh, dear—we could have saved ourselves the trouble.

MRS. ELVSTED. Did you get any sleep?

HEDDA. Oh yes. I slept quite well, I think. Didn't you?

MRS. ELVSTED. No, not at all. I couldn't, Hedda! It was just impossible.

HEDDA (*rising and going toward her*). There, there, now! There's nothing to worry about. It's not hard to guess what happened.

MRS. ELVSTED. Oh, what? Tell me!

HEDDA. Well, it's clear that the party must have gone on till all hours—

MRS. ELVSTED. Oh, Lord, yes—it must have. But even so—

HEDDA. And then, of course, Tesman didn't want to come home and make a commotion in the middle of the night. (*Laughs.*) Probably didn't care to show himself, either—so full of his party spirits.

MRS. ELVSTED. But where else could he have gone?

HEDDA. He must have gone up to his aunts' to sleep. They keep his old room ready.

MRS. ELVSTED. No, he can't be with them. Because he just now got a letter from Miss Tesman. It's over there.

HEDDA. Oh? (*Looking at the address.*) Yes, that's Aunt Julie's handwriting, all right. Well, then he must have stayed over at Judge Brack's. And Eilert Løvborg—he's sitting with vine leaves in his hair, reading away.

MRS. ELVSTED. Oh, Hedda, you say these things, and you really don't believe them at all.

HEDDA. You're such a little fool, Thea.

MRS. ELVSTED. That's true; I guess I am.

HEDDA. And you really look dead tired.

MRS. ELVSTED. Yes, I feel dead tired.

HEDDA. Well, you just do as I say, then. Go in my room and stretch out on the bed for a while.

MRS. ELVSTED. No, no—I still wouldn't get any sleep.

HEDDA. Why, of course you would.

MRS. ELVSTED. Well, but your husband's sure to be home now soon. And I've got to know right away—

HEDDA. I'll call you the moment he comes.

MRS. ELVSTED. Yes? Promise me, Hedda?

HEDDA. You can count on it. Just go and get some sleep.

MRS. ELVSTED. Thanks. I'll try. (*She goes out through the inner room.*)

> (HEDDA *goes over to the glass door and draws the curtains back. Bright daylight streams into the room. She goes over to the writing table, takes out a small hand mirror, regards herself and arranges her hair. She then goes to the hall door and presses the bell. After a moment,* BERTA *enters.*)

BERTA. Did you want something, ma'am?

HEDDA. Yes, you can build up the fire. I'm freezing in here.

BERTA. Why, my goodness—we'll have it warm in no

time. (*She rakes the embers together and puts some wood on, then stops and listens.*) There's the front doorbell, ma'am.

HEDDA.   Go see who it is. I'll take care of the stove.

BERTA.   It'll be burning soon. (*She goes out the hall door.*)

> (HEDDA *kneels on the footstool and lays more wood on the fire. After a moment,* GEORGE TESMAN *comes in from the hall. He looks tired and rather serious. He tiptoes toward the doorway to the inner room and is about to slip through the curtains.*)

HEDDA (*at the stove, without looking up*).   Good morning.

TESMAN (*turns*).   Hedda! (*Approaching her.*) But what on earth—! You're up so early? Uh?

HEDDA.   Yes, I'm up quite early today.

TESMAN.   And I was so sure you were still in bed sleeping. Isn't that something, Hedda!

HEDDA.   Not so loud. Mrs. Elvsted's resting in my room.

TESMAN.   Was Mrs. Elvsted here all night?

HEDDA.   Well, no one returned to take her home.

TESMAN.   No, I guess that's right.

HEDDA (*shuts the door to the stove and gets up*).   So—did you enjoy your party?

TESMAN.   Were you worried about me? Hm?

HEDDA.   No, that never occurred to me. I just asked if you'd had a good time.

TESMAN.   Oh yes, I really did, for once. But more at the beginning, I'd say—when Eilert read to me out of his book. We got there more than an hour too soon—imagine! And Brack had so much to get ready. But then Eilert read to me.

HEDDA (*sitting at the right-hand side of the table*).   Well? Tell me about it—

TESMAN (*sitting on a footstool by the stove*).   Really, Hedda—you can't imagine what a book that's going to be! I do believe it's one of the most remarkable things ever written. Just think!

HEDDA.   Yes, yes, I don't care about that—

TESMAN.   But I have to make a confession, Hedda. When he'd finished reading—I had such a nasty feeling—

HEDDA. Nasty?

TESMAN. I found myself envying Eilert, that he was able to write such a book. Can you imagine, Hedda!

HEDDA. Oh yes, I can imagine!

TESMAN. And then how sad to see—that with all his gifts—he's still quite irreclaimable.

HEDDA. Don't you mean that he has more courage to live than the others?

TESMAN. Good Lord, no—I mean, he simply can't take his pleasures in moderation.

HEDDA. Well, what happened then—at the end?

TESMAN. I suppose I'd have to say it turned into an orgy, Hedda.

HEDDA. Were there vine leaves in his hair?

TESMAN. Vine leaves? Not that I noticed. But he gave a long, muddled speech in honor of the woman who'd inspired his work. Yes, that was his phrase for it.

HEDDA. Did he give her name?

TESMAN. No, he didn't. But it seems to me it has to be Mrs. Elvsted. Wait and see!

HEDDA. Oh? Where did you leave him?

TESMAN. On the way here. We broke up—the last of us—all together. And Brack came along with us too, to get a little fresh air. And then we did want to make sure that Eilert got home safe. Because he really had a load on, you know.

HEDDA. He must have.

TESMAN. But here's the curious part of it, Hedda. Or perhaps I should say, the distressing part. Oh, I'm almost ashamed to speak of it—for Eilert's sake—

HEDDA. Yes, go on—

TESMAN. Well, as we were walking toward town, you see, I happened to drop back a little behind the others. Only for a minute or two—you follow me?

HEDDA. Yes, yes, so—?

TESMAN. And then when I was catching up with the rest of them, what do you think I found on the sidewalk? Uh?

HEDDA. Oh, how should I know!

TESMAN. You mustn't breathe a word to anyone, Hedda—you hear me? Promise me that, for Eilert's sake. (*Takes a manila envelope out of his coat pocket.*) Just think—I found this.

HEDDA.   Isn't that what he had with him yesterday?

TESMAN.   That's right. It's the whole of his precious, ir-replaceable manuscript. And he went and lost it—without even noticing. Can you imagine, Hedda! How distressing—

HEDDA.   But why didn't you give it right back to him?

TESMAN.   No, I didn't dare do that—in the state he was in—

HEDDA.   And you didn't tell any of the others you'd found it?

TESMAN.   Of course not. I'd never do that, you know—for Eilert's sake.

HEDDA.   Then there's no one who knows you have Eilert Løvborg's manuscript?

TESMAN.   No. And no one must ever know, either.

HEDDA.   What did you say to him afterwards?

TESMAN.   I had no chance at all to speak with him. As soon as we reached the edge of town, he and a couple of others got away from us and disappeared. Imagine!

HEDDA.   Oh? I expect they saw him home.

TESMAN.   Yes, they probably did, I suppose. And also Brack went home.

HEDDA.   And where've you been carrying on since then?

TESMAM.   Well, I and some of the others—we were in-vited up by one of the fellows and had morning coffee at his place. Or a post-midnight snack, maybe—uh? But as soon as I've had a little rest—and given poor Eilert time to sleep it off, then I've got to take this back to him.

HEDDA (*reaching out for the envelope*).   No—don't give it back! Not yet, I mean. Let me read it first.

TESMAN.   Hedda dearest, no. My Lord, I can't do that.

HEDDA.   You can't?

TESMAN.   No. Why, you can just imagine the anguish he'll feel when he wakes up and misses the manuscript. He hasn't any copy of it, you know. He told me that himself.

HEDDA (*looks searchingly at him*).   Can't such a work be rewritten? I mean, over again?

TESMAN.   Oh, I don't see how it could. Because the in-spiration, you know—

HEDDA.   Yes, yes—that's the thing, I suppose. (*Casu-ally.*) Oh, by the way—there's a letter for you.

TESMAN.   No, really—?

HEDDA (*handing it to him*).   It came early this morning.

TESMAN. Dear, from Aunt Julie! What could that be? (*Sets the envelope on the other taboret, opens the letter, skims through it, and springs to his feet.*) Oh, Hedda—she says poor Auntie Rina's dying!

HEDDA. It's no more than we've been expecting.

TESMAN. And if I want to see her one last time, I've got to hurry. I'll have to hop right over.

HEDDA (*suppressing a smile*). Hop?

TESMAN. Oh, Hedda dearest, if you could only bring yourself to come with me! Think of it!

HEDDA (*rises and dismisses the thought wearily*). No, no, don't ask me to do such things. I don't want to look on sickness and death. I want to be free of everything ugly.

TESMAN. Yes, all right, then— (*Dashing about.*) My hat—? My overcoat—? Oh, in the hall—I do hope I'm not there too late, Hedda! Hm?

HEDDA. Oh, if you just hop to it—

(BERTA *appears at the hall door.*)

BERTA. Judge Brack's outside, asking if he might stop in.

TESMAN. At a time like this! No, I can't possibly see him now.

HEDDA. But I can. (*To* BERTA.) Ask the judge to come in.

(BERTA *goes out.*)

HEDDA (*quickly, in a whisper*). Tesman, the manuscript! (*She snatches it from the taboret.*)

TESMAN. Yes, give it here!

HEDDA. No, no, I'll keep it till you're back.

(*She moves over to the writing table and slips it in the bookcase.* TESMAN *stands flustered, unable to get his gloves on.* BRACK *enters from the hall.*)

HEDDA. Well, aren't you the early bird.

BRACK. Yes, wouldn't you say so? (*To* TESMAN.) Are you off and away too?

TESMAN. Yes, I absolutely have to get over to my aunts'. Just think—the invalid one, she's dying.

BRACK.   Good Lord, she is? But then you mustn't let me detain you. Not at a moment like this—

TESMAN.   Yes, I really must run— Good-bye! Good-bye! (*He goes hurriedly out the hall door.*)

HEDDA.   It would seem you had quite a time of it last night, Judge.

BRACK.   I've not been out of my clothes yet, Mrs. Hedda.

HEDDA.   Not you, either?

BRACK.   No, as you can see. But what's Tesman been telling you about our night's adventures?

HEDDA.   Oh, some tedious tale. Something about stopping up somewhere for coffee.

BRACK.   Yes, I know all about the coffee party. Eilert Løvborg wasn't with them, I expect?

HEDDA.   No, they'd already taken him home.

BRACK.   Tesman, as well.

HEDDA.   No, but he said some others had.

BRACK (*smiles*).   George Tesman is really a simple soul, Mrs. Hedda.

HEDDA.   God knows he's that. But was there something else that went on?

BRACK.   Oh, you might say so.

HEDDA.   Well, now! Let's sit down, Judge; you'll talk more easily then.

(*She sits at the left-hand side of the table, with* BRACK *at the long side, near her.*)

HEDDA.   So?

BRACK.   I had particular reasons for keeping track of my guests—or, I should say, certain of my guests, last night.

HEDDA.   And among them Eilert Løvborg, perhaps?

BRACK.   To be frank—yes.

HEDDA.   Now you really have me curious—

BRACK.   You know where he and a couple of the others spent the rest of the night, Mrs. Hedda?

HEDDA.   Tell me—if it's fit to be told.

BRACK.   Oh, it's very much fit to be told. Well, it seems they showed up at a quite animated soirée.

HEDDA.   Of the lively sort.

BRACK.   Of the liveliest.

HEDDA.   Do go on, Judge—

BRACK.   Løvborg, and the others also, had advance invitations. I knew all about it. But Løvborg had begged off, because now, of course, he was supposed to have become a new man, as you know.

HEDDA.   Up at the Elvsteds', yes. But he went anyway?

BRACK.   Well, you see, Mrs. Hedda—unfortunately the spirit moved him up at my place last evening—

HEDDA.   Yes, I hear that he *was* inspired there.

BRACK.   To a very powerful degree, I'd say. Well, so his mind turned to other things, that's clear. We males, sad to say—we're not always so true to principle as we ought to be.

HEDDA.   Oh, I'm sure you're an exception, Judge. But what about Løvborg—?

BRACK.   Well, to cut it short—the result was that he wound up in Mademoiselle Diana's parlors.

HEDDA.   Mademoiselle Diana's?

BRACK.   It was Mademoiselle Diana who was holding the soirée. For a select circle of lady friends and admirers.

HEDDA.   Is she a redhaired woman?

BRACK.   Precisely.

HEDDA.   Sort of a—singer?

BRACK.   Oh yes—she's that too. And also a mighty huntress—of men, Mrs. Hedda. You've undoubtedly heard about her. Løvborg was one of her ruling favorites—back there in his palmy days.

HEDDA.   And how did all this end?

BRACK.   Less amicably, it seems. She gave him a most tender welcoming, with open arms, but before long she'd taken to fists.

HEDDA.   Against Løvborg?

BRACK.   That's right. He accused her or her friends of having robbed him. He claimed that his wallet was missing—along with some other things. In short, he must have made a frightful scene.

HEDDA.   And what did it come to?

BRACK.   It came to a regular free-for-all, the men and the women both. Luckily the police finally got there.

HEDDA.   The police too?

BRACK.   Yes. But it's likely to prove an expensive little romp for Eilert Løvborg. That crazy fool.

HEDDA.   So?

BRACK. He apparently made violent resistance. Struck one of the officers on the side of the head and ripped his coat. So they took him along to the station house.

HEDDA. Where did you hear all this?

BRACK. From the police themselves.

HEDDA (*gazing straight ahead*). So that's how it went. Then he had no vine leaves in his hair.

BRACK. Vine leaves, Mrs. Hedda?

HEDDA (*changing her tone*). But tell me, Judge—just why do you go around like this, spying on Eilert Løvborg?

BRACK. In the first place, it's hardly a matter of no concern to me, if it's brought out during the investigation that he'd come direct from my house.

HEDDA. There'll be an investigation—?

BRACK. Naturally. Anyway, that takes care of itself. But I felt that as a friend of the family I owed you and Tesman a full account of his nocturnal exploits.

HEDDA. Why, exactly?

BRACK. Well, because I have a strong suspicion that he'll try to use you as a kind of screen.

HEDDA. Oh, how could you ever think such a thing!

BRACK. Good Lord—we're really not blind, Mrs. Hedda. You'll see! This Mrs. Elvsted, she won't be going home now so quickly.

HEDDA. Well, even supposing there were something between them, there are plenty of other places where they could meet.

BRACK. Not one single home. From now on, every decent house will be closed to Eilert Løvborg.

HEDDA. So mine ought to be too, is that what you mean?

BRACK. Yes. I'll admit I'd find it more than annoying if that gentleman were to have free access here. If he came like an intruder, an irrelevancy, forcing his way into—

HEDDA. Into the triangle?

BRACK. Precisely. It would almost be like turning me out of my home.

HEDDA (*looks at him with a smile*). I see. The one cock of the walk—that's what you want to be.

BRACK (*nodding slowly and lowering his voice*). Yes, that's what I want to be. And that's what I'll fight for— with every means at my disposal.

HEDDA (*her smile vanishing*).   You can be a dangerous person, can't you—in a tight corner.

BRACK.   Do you think so?

HEDDA.   Yes, now I'm beginning to think so. And I'm thoroughly grateful—that you have no kind of hold over me.

BRACK (*with an ambiguous laugh*).   Ah, yes, Mrs. Hedda—perhaps you're right about that. If I had, then who knows just what I might do?

HEDDA.   Now you listen here, Judge! That sounds too much like a threat.

BRACK (*rising*).   Oh, nothing of the kind! A triangle, after all—is best fortified and defended by volunteers.

HEDDA.   There we're agreed.

BRACK.   Well, now that I've said all I have to say, I'd better get back to town. Good-bye, Mrs. Hedda. (*He goes toward the glass door.*)

HEDDA (*rising*).   Are you going through the garden?

BRACK.   Yes, I find it's shorter.

HEDDA.   Yes, and then it's the back way, too.

BRACK.   How true. I have nothing against back ways. At certain times they can be rather piquant.

HEDDA.   You mean, when somebody's sharpshooting?

BRACK (*in the doorway, laughing*).   Oh, people don't shoot their tame roosters!

HEDDA (*also laughing*).   I guess not. Not when there's only one—

> (*Still laughing, they nod good-bye to each other. He goes. She shuts the door after him, then stands for a moment, quite serious, looking out. She then goes over and glances through the curtains to the inner room. Moves to the writing table, takes* LØVBORG's *envelope from the bookcase, and is about to page through it, when* BERTA's *voice is heard loudly in the hall.* HEDDA *turns and listens. She hurriedly locks the envelope in the drawer and lays the key on the desk.* EILERT LØVBORG, *with his overcoat on and his hat in his hand, throws open the hall door. He looks confused and excited.*)

LØVBORG (*turned toward the hall*).   And I'm telling you, I have to go in! I will, you hear me! (*He shuts the door, turns, sees* HEDDA, *immediately gains control of himself and bows.*)

HEDDA (*at the writing table*).   Well, Mr. Løvborg, it's late to call for Thea.

LØVBORG.   Or rather early to call on you. You must forgive me.

HEDDA.   How did you know she was still with me?

LØVBORG.   They said at her lodgings that she'd been out all night. .

HEDDA (*goes to the center table*).   Did you notice anything in their faces when they said that?

LØVBORG (*looking at her inquiringly*).   Notice anything?

HEDDA.   I mean, did it look like they had their own thoughts on the matter?

LØVBORG (*suddenly understanding*).   Oh yes, that's true! I'm dragging her down with me! Actually, I didn't notice anything. Tesman—I don't suppose he's up yet?

HEDDA.   No, I don't think so.

LØVBORG.   When did he get in? •

HEDDA.   Very late.

LØVBORG.   Did he tell you anything?

HEDDA.   Well, I heard you'd had a high time of it out at Judge Brack's.

LØVBORG.   Anything else?

HEDDA.   No, I don't think so. As a matter of fact, I was terribly sleepy—

(MRS. ELVSTED *comes in through the curtains to the inner room.*)

MRS. ELVSTED (*running toward him*).   Oh, Eilert! At last—!

LØVBORG.   Yes, at last. And too late.

MRS. ELVSTED (*looking anxiously at him*).   What's too late?

LØVBORG.   Everything's too late now. It's over with me.

MRS. ELVSTED.   Oh no, no—don't say that!

LØVBORG.   You'll say the same thing when you've heard—

MRS. ELVSTED.   I won't hear anything!

HEDDA.   Maybe you'd prefer to talk with her alone. I can leave.

LØVBORG.   No, stay—you too. Please.

MRS. ELVSTED. But I tell you, I don't want to hear anything!

LØVBORG. It's nothing about last night.

MRS. ELVSTED. What is it, then—?

LØVBORG. It's simply this, that from now on, we separate.

MRS. ELVSTED. Separate!

HEDDA (*involuntarily*). I knew it!

LØVBORG. Because I have no more use for you, Thea.

MRS. ELVSTED. And you can stand there and say that! No more use for me! Then I'm not going to help you now, as I have? We're not going to go on working together?

LØVBORG. I have no plans for any more work.

MRS. ELVSTED (*in desperation*). Then what will I do with my life?

LØVBORG. You must try to go on living as if you'd never known me.

MRS. ELVSTED. But I can't do that!

LØVBORG. You must try to, Thea. You'll have to go home again—

MRS. ELVSTED (*in a fury of protest*). Never! No! Where you are, that's where I want to be! I won't be driven away like this! I'm going to stay right here—and be together with you when the book comes out.

HEDDA (*in a tense whisper*). Ah, yes—the book!

LØVBORG (*looks at her*). My book and Thea's—for that's what it is.

MRS. ELVSTED. Yes, that's what I feel it is. And that's why I have the right, as well, to be with you when it comes out. I want to see you covered with honor and respect again. And the joy—I want to share the joy of it with you too.

LØVBORG. Thea—our book's never coming out.

HEDDA. Ah!

MRS. ELVSTED. Never coming out!

LØVBORG. *Can* never come out.

MRS. ELVSTED (*with anguished foreboding*). Eilert— what have you done with the manuscript?

HEDDA (*watching him intently*). Yes, the manuscript—?

MRS. ELVSTED. Where is it!

LØVBORG. Oh, Thea—don't ask me that.

MRS. ELVSTED. Yes, yes, I have to know. I've got a right to know, this minute!

LØVBORG. The manuscript—well, you see—I tore the manuscript into a thousand pieces.

MRS. ELVSTED (*screams*). Oh no, no—!

HEDDA (*involuntarily*). But that just isn't—!

LØVBORG (*looks at her*). Isn't so, you think?

HEDDA (*composing herself*). All right. Of course; if you say it yourself. But it sounds so incredible—

LØVBORG. It's true, all the same.

MRS. ELVSTED (*wringing her hands*). Oh, God—oh, God, Hedda—to tear his own work to bits!

LØVBORG. I've torn my own life to bits. So why not tear up my life's work as well—

MRS. ELVSTED. And you did this thing last night!

LØVBORG. Yes, you heard me. In a thousand pieces. And scattered them into the fjord. Far out. At least there, there's clean salt water. Let them drift out to sea—drift with the tide and the wind. And after a while, they'll sink. Deeper and deeper. As I will, Thea.

MRS. ELVSTED. Do you know, Eilert, this thing you've done with the book—for the rest of my life it will seem to me as if you'd killed a little child.

LØVBORG. You're right. It was like murdering a child.

MRS. ELVSTED. But how could you do it—! It was my child too.

HEDDA (*almost inaudible*). Ah, the child—

MRS. ELVSTED (*breathes heavily*). Then it *is* all over. Yes, yes, I'm going now, Hedda.

HEDDA. But you're not leaving town, are you?

MRS. ELVSTED. Oh, I don't know myself what I'll do. Everything's dark for me now. (*She goes out the hall door.*)

HEDDA (*stands waiting a moment*). You're not going to take her home, then, Mr. Løvborg?

LØVBORG. I? Through the streets? So people could see that she'd been with me?

HEDDA. I don't know what else may have happened last night. But is it so completely irredeemable?

LØVBORG. It won't just end with last night—I know that well enough. But the thing is, I've lost all desire for that kind of life. I don't want to start it again, not now. It's the courage and daring for life—that's what she's broken in me.

HEDDA (*staring straight ahead*). To think that pretty little fool could have a man's fate in her hands. (*Looks at him.*) But still, how could you treat her so heartlessly?

LØVBORG. Oh, don't say it was heartless!

HEDDA. To go ahead and destroy what's filled her whole being for months and years! That's not heartless?

LØVBORG. To you, Hedda—I can tell the truth.

HEDDA. The truth?

LØVBORG. Promise me first—give me your word that what I tell you now, you'll never let Thea know.

HEDDA. You have my word.

LØVBORG. Good. I can tell you, then, that what I said here just now isn't true.

HEDDA. About the manuscript?

LØVBORG. Yes. I didn't tear it up—or throw it in the fjord.

HEDDA. No, but—where is it, then?

LØVBORG. I've destroyed it all the same, Hedda. Utterly destroyed it.

HEDDA. I don't understand.

LØVBORG. Thea said that what I've done, for her was like killing a child.

HEDDA. Yes—that's what she said.

LØVBORG. But killing his child—that's not the worst thing a father can do.

HEDDA. *That's* not the worst?

LØVBORG. No. I wanted to spare Thea the worst.

HEDDA. And what's that—the worst?

LØVBORG. Suppose now, Hedda, that a man—in the early morning hours, say—after a wild, drunken night, comes home to his child's mother and says: "Listen—I've been out to this place and that—here and there. And I had our child with me. In this place and that. And I lost the child. Just lost it. God only knows what hands it's come into. Or who's got hold of it."

HEDDA. Well—but when all's said and done—it was only a book—

LØVBORG. Thea's pure soul was in that book.

HEDDA. Yes, I understand.

LØVBORG. Well, then you can understand that for her and me there's no future possible any more.

HEDDA. What do you intend to do?

LØVBORG.   Nothing. Just put an end to it all. The sooner the better.

HEDDA (*coming a step closer*).   Eilert Løvborg—listen to me. Couldn't you arrange that—that it's done beautifully?

LØVBORG.   Beautifully? (*Smiles.*) With vine leaves in my hair, as you used to dream in the old days—

HEDDA.   No. I don't believe in vine leaves any more. But beautifully, all the same. For this once—! Good-bye! You must go now—and never come here again.

LØVBORG.   Good-bye, then. And give my best to George Tesman. (*He turns to leave.*)

HEDDA.   No, wait. I want you to have a souvenir from me.

(*She goes to the writing desk and opens the drawer and the pistol case, then comes back to* LØVBORG *with one of the pistols.*)

LØVBORG (*looks at her*).   That? Is that the souvenir?

HEDDA (*nods slowly*).   Do you recognize it? It was aimed at you once.

LØVBORG.   You should have used it then.

HEDDA.   Here! Use it now.

LØVBORG (*puts the pistol in his breast pocket*).   Thanks.

HEDDA.   And beautifully, Eilert Løvborg. Promise me that!

LØVBORG.   Good-bye, Hedda Gabler.

(*He goes out the hall door.* HEDDA *listens a moment at the door. Then she goes over to the writing table, takes out the envelope with the manuscript, glances inside, pulls some of the sheets half out and looks at them. She then goes over to the armchair by the stove and sits, with the envelope in her lap. After a moment, she opens the stove door, then brings out the manuscript.*)

HEDDA (*throwing some of the sheets into the fire and whispering to herself*).   Now I'm burning your child, Thea! You, with your curly hair! (*Throwing another sheaf in the stove.*) Your child and Eilert Løvborg's. (*Throwing in the rest.*) Now I'm burning—I'm burning the child.

ACT FOUR

The same rooms at the TESMANS'. *It is evening. The draw-ing room is in darkness. The inner room is lit by the hanging lamp over the table. The curtains are drawn across the glass door.* HEDDA, *dressed in black, is pacing back and forth in the dark room. She then enters the inner room, moving out of sight toward the left. Several chords are heard on the piano. She comes in view again, returning into the drawing room.* BERTA *enters from the right through the inner room with a lighted lamp, which she puts on the table in front of the settee in the drawing room. Her eyes are red from crying, and she has black ribbons on her cap. She goes quietly and discreetly out to the right.* HEDDA *moves to the glass door, lifts the curtains aside slightly, and gazes out into the darkness.*

Shortly after, MISS TESMAN, *in mourning, with a hat and veil, comes in from the hall.* HEDDA *goes toward her, extending her hand.*

MISS TESMAN. Well, Hedda, here I am, all dressed in mourning. My poor sister's ordeal is finally over.

HEDDA. As you see, I've already heard. Tesman sent me a note.

MISS TESMAN. Yes, he promised he would. But all the same I thought that, to Hedda—here in the house of life— I ought to bear the news of death myself.

HEDDA. That was very kind of you.

MISS TESMAN. Ah, Rina ought not to have passed on just now. This is no time for grief in Hedda's house.

HEDDA (*changing the subject*). She had a peaceful death, then, Miss Tesman?

MISS TESMAN. Oh, she went so calmly, so beautifully. And so inexpressibly happy that she could see George once again. And say good-bye to him properly. Is it possible that he's still not home?

HEDDA. No, he wrote that I shouldn't expect him too early. But won't you sit down?

289

MISS TESMAN.   No, thank you, my dear—blessed Hedda. I'd love to, but I have so little time. I want to see her dressed and made ready as best as I can. She should go to her grave looking her finest.

HEDDA.   Can't I help you with something?

MISS TESMAN.   Oh, you mustn't think of it. This is nothing for Hedda Tesman to put her hands to. Or let her thoughts dwell on, either. Not at a time like this, no.

HEDDA.   Ah, thoughts—they're not so easy to control—

MISS TESMAN (*continuing*).   Well, there's life for you. At my house now we'll be sewing a shroud for Rina. And here, too, there'll be sewing soon, I imagine. But a far different kind, praise God!

(GEORGE TESMAN *enters from the hall.*)

HEDDA.   Well, at last! It's about time.

TESMAN.   Are you here, Aunt Julie? With Hedda? Think of that!

MISS TESMAN.   I was just this minute leaving, dear boy. Well, did you get done all you promised you would?

TESMAN.   No, I'm really afraid I've forgotten half. I'll have to run over and see you tomorrow. My brain's completely in a whirl today. I can't keep my thoughts together.

MISS TESMAN.   But George dear, you mustn't take it that way.

TESMAN.   Oh? Well, how should I, then?

MISS TESMAN.   You should rejoice in your grief. Rejoice in everything that's happened, as I do.

TESMAN.   Oh yes, of course. You're thinking of Auntie Rina.

HEDDA.   It's going to be lonely for you, Miss Tesman.

MISS TESMAN.   For the first few days, yes. But it won't be for long, I hope. I won't let dear Rina's little room stand empty.

TESMAN.   No? Who would you want to have in it? Hm?

MISS TESMAN.   Oh, there's always some poor invalid in need of care and attention.

HEDDA.   Would you really take another burden like that on yourself?

MISS TESMAN.   Burden! Mercy on you, child—it's been no burden for me.

HEDDA.   But now, with a stranger—

MISS TESMAN.   Oh, you soon make friends with an invalid. And I do so much need someone to live for—I, too. Well, thank God, in this house as well, there soon ought to be work that an old aunt can turn her hand to.

HEDDA.   Oh, forget about us—

TESMAN.   Yes, think how pleasant it could be for the three of us if—

HEDDA.   If—?

TESMAN (*uneasily*).   Oh, nothing. It'll all take care of itself. Let's hope so. Uh?

MISS TESMAN.   Ah, yes. Well, I expect you two have things to talk about. (*Smiles.*) And perhaps Hedda has something to tell you, George. Good-bye. I'll have to get home now to Rina. (*Turning at the door.*) Goodness me, how strange! Now Rina's both with me and with poor dear Jochum as well.

TESMAN.   Yes, imagine that, Aunt Julie! Hm?

(MISS TESMAN *goes out the hall door.*)

HEDDA (*follows* TESMAN *with a cold, probing look*).   I almost think you feel this death more than she.

TESMAN.   Oh, it's not just Auntie Rina's death. It's Eilert who has me worried.

HEDDA (*quickly*).   Any news about him?

TESMAN.   I stopped up at his place this afternoon, thinking to tell him that the manuscript was safe.

HEDDA.   Well? Didn't you see him then?

TESMAN.   No, he wasn't home. But afterward I met Mrs. Elvsted, and she said he'd been here early this morning.

HEDDA.   Yes, right after you left.

TESMAN.   And apparently he said he'd torn his manuscript up. Uh?

HEDDA.   Yes, he claimed that he had.

TESMAN.   But good Lord, then he must have been completely demented! Well, then I guess you didn't dare give it back to him, Hedda, did you?

HEDDA.   No, he didn't get it.

TESMAN.   But you did tell him we had it, I suppose?

HEDDA.   No. (*Quickly.*) Did you tell Mrs. Elvsted anything?

TESMAN.   No, I thought I'd better not. But you should have said something to him. Just think, if he goes off in desperation and does himself some harm! Give me the manuscript, Hedda! I'm taking it back to him right away. Where do you have it?

HEDDA (*cold and impassive, leaning against the arm-chair*). I don't have it anymore.

TESMAN. You don't have it! What on earth do you mean by that?

HEDDA. I burned it—the whole thing.

TESMAN (*with a start of terror*). Burned it! Burned Eilert Løvborg's manuscript!

HEDDA. Stop shouting. The maid could hear you.

TESMAN. Burned it! But my God in heaven—! No, no, no—that's impossible!

HEDDA. Yes, but it's true, all the same.

TESMAN. But do you realize what you've done, Hedda! It's illegal disposition of lost property. Just think! Yes, you can ask Judge Brack; he'll tell you.

HEDDA. It would be wiser not mentioning this—either to the judge or to anyone else.

TESMAN. But how could you go and do such an incredible thing! Whatever put it into your head? What got into you, anyway? Answer me! Well?

HEDDA (*suppressing an almost imperceptible smile*). I did it for your sake, George.

TESMAN. For my sake!

HEDDA. When you came home this morning and told about how he'd read to you—

TESMAN. Yes, yes, then what?

HEDDA. Then you confessed that you envied him this book.

TESMAN. Good Lord, I didn't mean it literally.

HEDDA. Never mind. I still couldn't bear the thought that anyone should eclipse you.

TESMAN (*in an outburst of mingled doubt and joy*). Hedda—is this true, what you say! Yes, but—but—I never dreamed you could show your love like this. Imagine!

HEDDA. Well, then it's best you know that—that I'm going to— (*Impatiently, breaking off.*) No, no—you ask your Aunt Julie. She's the one who can tell you.

TESMAN. Oh, I'm beginning to understand you, Hedda! (*Claps his hands together.*) Good heavens, no! Is it actually *that*! Can it be? Uh?

HEDDA.   Don't shout so. The maid can hear you.

TESMAN.   The maid! Oh, Hedda, you're priceless, really! The maid—but that's Berta! Why, I'll go out and tell her myself.

HEDDA (*clenching her fists in despair*).   Oh, I'll die—I'll die of all this!

TESMAN.   Of what, Hedda? Uh?

HEDDA.   Of all these—absurdities—George.

TESMAN.   Absurdities? What's absurd about my being so happy? Well, all right—I guess there's no point in my saying anything to Berta.

HEDDA.   Oh, go ahead—why not that, too?

TESMAN.   No, no, not yet. But Aunt Julie will have to hear. And then, that you've started to call me George, too! Imagine! Oh, Aunt Julie will be so glad—so glad!

HEDDA.   When she hears that I burned Eilert Løvborg's book—for your sake?

TESMAN.   Well, as far as that goes—this thing with the book—of course, no one's to know about that. But that you have a love that burns for me, Hedda—Aunt Julie can certainly share in that! You know, I wonder, really, if things such as this are common among young wives? Hm?

HEDDA.   I think you should ask Aunt Julie about that, too.

TESMAN.   Yes, I'll do it definitely, when I have the chance. (*Again looks distressed and preoccupied.*) No, but—but the manuscript! My Lord, it's just terrible to think about poor Eilert.

(MRS. ELVSTED, *dressed as on her first visit, with hat and coat, comes in the hall door.*)

MRS. ELVSTED (*greets them hurriedly and speaks in agitation*).   Oh, Hedda dear, don't be annoyed that I'm back again.

HEDDA.   Has something happened, Thea?

TESMAN.   Something with Eilert Løvborg? Uh?

MRS. ELVSTED.   Yes, I'm so terribly afraid he's met with an accident.

HEDDA (*seizing her arm*).   Ah—you think so!

TESMAN.   But, Mrs. Elvsted, where did you get that idea?

MRS. ELVSTED.   Well, because I heard them speaking of

him at the boardinghouse, just as I came in. Oh, there are the most incredible rumors about him in town today.

TESMAN.   Yes, you know, I heard them too! And yet I could swear that he went right home to bed last night. Imagine!

HEDDA.   Well—what did they say at the boardinghouse?

MRS. ELVSTED.   Oh, I couldn't get anything clearly. They either didn't know much themselves, or else—They stopped talking when they saw me. And I didn't dare to ask.

TESMAN (*restlessly moving about*).   Let's hope—let's hope you misunderstood them, Mrs. Elvsted!

MRS. ELVSTED.   No, no, I'm sure they were talking of him. And then I heard them say something or other about the hospital, or—

TESMAN.   The hospital!

HEDDA.   No—but that's impossible!

MRS. ELVSTED.   Oh, I'm so deathly afraid for him now. And later I went up to his lodging to ask about him.

HEDDA.   But was that very wise to do, Thea?

MRS. ELVSTED.   What else could I do? I couldn't bear the uncertainty any longer.

TESMAN.   But didn't you find him there either? Hm?

MRS. ELVSTED.   No. And no one had any word of him. He hadn't been in since yesterday afternoon, they said.

TESMAN.   Yesterday! Imagine them saying that!

MRS. ELVSTED.   I think there can only be one reason—something terrible must have happened to him!

TESMAN.   Hedda dear—suppose I went over and made a few inquiries—?

HEDDA.   No, no—don't you get mixed up in this business.

(JUDGE BRACK, *with hat in hand, enters from the hall,* BERTA *letting him in and shutting the door after him. He looks grave and bows silently.*)

TESMAN.   Oh, is that you, Judge? Uh?

BRACK.   Yes, it's imperative that I see you this evening.

TESMAN.   I can see that you've heard the news from Aunt Julie.

BRACK.   Among other things, yes.

TESMAN.   It's sad, isn't it? Uh?

BRACK. Well, my dear Tesman, that depends on how you look at it.

TESMAN (*eyes him doubtfully*). Has anything else happened?

BRACK. Yes, as a matter of fact.

HEDDA (*intently*). Something distressing, Judge?

BRACK. Again, that depends on how you look at it, Mrs. Tesman.

MRS. ELVSTED (*in an uncontrollable outburst*). Oh, it's something about Eilert Løvborg!

BRACK (*glancing at her*). Now how did you hit upon that, Mrs. Elvsted? Have you, perhaps, heard something already—?

MRS. ELVSTED (*in confusion*). No, no, nothing like that—but—

TESMAN. Oh, for heaven's sake, tell us!

BRACK (*with a shrug*). Well—I'm sorry, but—Eilert Løvborg's been taken to the hospital. He's dying.

MRS. ELVSTED (*crying out*). Oh, God, oh, God—!

TESMAN. To the hospital! And dying!

HEDDA (*involuntarily*). All so soon—!

MRS. ELVSTED (*wailing*). And we parted in anger, Hedda!

HEDDA (*in a whisper*). Thea—be careful, Thea!

MRS. ELVSTED (*ignoring her*). I have to see him! I have to see him alive!

BRACK. No use, Mrs. Elvsted. No one's allowed in to see him.

MRS. ELVSTED. Oh, but tell me, at least, what happened to him! What is it?

TESMAN. Don't tell me he tried to—! Uh?

HEDDA. Yes, he did, I'm sure of it.

TESMAN. Hedda—how can you say—!

BRACK (*his eyes steadily on her*). Unhappily, you've guessed exactly right, Mrs. Tesman.

MRS. ELVSTED. Oh, how horrible!

TESMAN. Did it himself! Imagine!

HEDDA. Shot himself!

BRACK. Again, exactly right, Mrs. Tesman.

MRS. ELVSTED (*trying to control herself*). When did it happen, Mr. Brack?

BRACK. This afternoon. Between three and four.

TESMAN. But good Lord—where did he do it, then? Hm?

BRACK (*hesitating slightly*). Where? Why—in his room, I suppose.

MRS. ELVSTED. No, that can't be right. I was there between six and seven.

BRACK. Well, somewhere else, then. I don't know exactly. I only know he was found like that. Shot—in the chest.

MRS. ELVSTED. What a horrible thought! That he should end that way!

HEDDA (*to* BRACK). In the chest, you say.

BRACK. Yes—I told you.

HEDDA. Not the temple?

BRACK. In the chest, Mrs. Tesman.

HEDDA. Well—well, the chest is just as good.

BRACK. Why, Mrs. Tesman?

HEDDA (*evasively*). Oh, nothing—never mind.

TESMAN. And the wound is critical, you say? Uh?

BRACK. The wound is absolutely fatal. Most likely, it's over already.

MRS. ELVSTED. Yes, yes, I can feel that it is! It's over! All over! Oh, Hedda—!

TESMAN. But tell me now—how did you learn about this?

BRACK (*brusquely*). One of the police. Someone I had to talk to.

HEDDA (*in a clear, bold voice.*) At last, something truly done!

TESMAN (*shocked*). My God, what are you saying, Hedda!

HEDDA. I'm saying there's beauty in all this.

BRACK. Hm, Mrs. Tesman—

TESMAN. Beauty! What an idea!

MRS. ELVSTED. Oh, Hedda, how can you talk about beauty in such a thing?

HEDDA. Eilert Løvborg's settled accounts with himself. He's had the courage to do what—what had to be done.

MRS. ELVSTED. Don't you believe it! It never happened like that. When he did this, he was in a delirium!

TESMAN. In despair, you mean.

HEDDA. No, he wasn't. I'm certain of that.

MRS. ELVSTED. But he was! In delirium! The way he was when he tore up our book.

BRACK (*startled*). The book? His manuscript, you mean? He tore it up?

MRS. ELVSTED. Yes. Last night.

TESMAN (*in a low whisper*). Oh, Hedda, we'll never come clear of all this.

BRACK. Hm, that's very strange.

TESMAN (*walking about the room*). To think Eilert could be gone like that! And then not to have left behind the one thing that could have made his name live on.

MRS. ELVSTED. Oh, if it could only be put together again!

TESMAN. Yes, imagine if that were possible! I don't know what I wouldn't give—

MRS. ELVSTED. Perhaps it can, Mr. Tesman.

TESMAN. What do you mean?

MRS. ELVSTED (*searching in the pockets of her dress*). Look here. I've kept all these notes that he used to dictate from.

HEDDA (*coming a step closer*). Ah—!

TESMAN. You've kept them, Mrs. Elvsted! Uh?

MRS. ELVSTED. Yes, here they are. I took them along when I left home. And they've stayed right here in my pocket—

TESMAN. Oh, let me look!

MRS. ELVSTED (*hands him a sheaf of small papers*). But they're in such a mess. All mixed up.

TESMAN. But just think, if we could decipher them, even so! Maybe the two of us could help each other—

MRS. ELVSTED. Oh yes! At least, we could try—

TESMAN. We can do it! We *must*! I'll give my whole life to this!

HEDDA. You, George. Your life?

TESMAN. Yes. Or, let's say, all the time I can spare. My own research will have to wait. You can understand, Hedda. Hm! It's something I owe to Eilert's memory.

HEDDA. Perhaps.

TESMAN. And so, my dear Mrs. Elvsted, let's pull ourselves together. Good Lord, there's no use brooding over what's gone by. Uh? We must try to compose our thoughts as much as we can, in order that—

MRS. ELVSTED.   Yes, yes, Mr. Tesman, I'll do the best I can.

TESMAN.   Come on, then. Let's look over these notes right away. Where shall we sit? Here? No, in there, in the back room. Excuse us, Judge. You come with me, Mrs. Elvsted.

MRS. ELVSTED.   Dear God—if only we can do this!

(TESMAN *and* MRS. ELVSTED *go into the inner room. She takes off her hat and coat. They both sit at the table under the hanging lamp and become totally immersed in examining the papers.* HEDDA *goes toward the stove and sits in the armchair. After a moment,* BRACK *goes over by her.*)

HEDDA (*her voice lowered*).   Ah, Judge—what a liberation it is, this act of Eilert Løvborg's.

BRACK.   Liberation, Mrs. Hedda? Well, yes, for him; you could certainly say he's been liberated—

HEDDA.   I mean for me. It's liberating to know that there can still actually be a free and courageous action in this world. Something that shimmers with spontaneous beauty.

BRACK (*smiling*).   Hm—my dear Mrs. Hedda—

HEDDA.   Oh, I already know what you're going to say. Because you're a kind of specialist too, you know, just like— Oh, well!

BRACK (*looking fixedly at her*).   Eilert Løvborg meant more to you than you're willing to admit, perhaps even to yourself. Or am I wrong about that?

HEDDA.   I won't answer that sort of question. I simply know that Eilert Løvborg's had the courage to live life after his own mind. And now—this last great act, filled with beauty! That he had the strength and the will to break away from the banquet of life—so young.

BRACK.   It grieves me, Mrs. Hedda—but I'm afraid I have to disburden you of this beautiful illusion.

HEDDA.   Illusion?

BRACK.   One that, in any case, you'd soon be deprived of.

HEDDA.   And what's that?

BRACK.   He didn't shoot himself—of his own free will.

HEDDA. He didn't—!

BRACK. No. This whole affair didn't go off quite the way I described it.

HEDDA (*in suspense*). You've hidden something? What is it?

BRACK. For poor Mrs. Elvsted's sake, I did a little editing here and there.

HEDDA. Where?

BRACK. First, the fact that he's already dead.

HEDDA. In the hospital?

BRACK. Yes. Without regaining consciousness.

HEDDA. What else did you hide?

BRACK. That the incident didn't occur in his room.

HEDDA. Well, that's rather unimportant.

BRACK. Not entirely. Suppose I were to tell you that Eilert Løvborg was found shot in—in Mademoiselle Diana's boudoir.

HEDDA (*half rises, then sinks back again*). That's impossible, Judge! He wouldn't have gone there again today!

BRACK. He was there this afternoon. He went there, demanding something he said they'd stolen from him. Kept raving about a lost child—

HEDDA. Ah—so that was it—

BRACK. I thought perhaps that might be his manuscript. But, I hear now, he destroyed that himself. So it must have been his wallet.

HEDDA. I suppose so. Then, there—that's where they found him.

BRACK. Yes, there. With a discharged pistol in his breast pocket. The bullet had wounded him fatally.

HEDDA. In the chest—yes.

BRACK. No—in the stomach—more or less.

HEDDA (*stares up at him with a look of revulsion*). That too! What is it, this—this curse—that everything I touch turns ridiculous and vile?

BRACK. There's something else, Mrs. Hedda. Another ugly aspect to the case.

HEDDA. What's that?

BRACK. The pistol he was carrying—

HEDDA (*breathlessly*). Well! What about it!

BRACK. He must have stolen it.

HEDDA (*springs up*). Stolen! That's not true! He didn't!

BRACK.   It seems impossible otherwise. He must have
stolen it—shh!

> (TESMAN *and* MRS. ELVSTED *have gotten up from
> the table in the inner room and come into the
> drawing room.*)

TESMAN (*with both hands full of papers*).   Hedda dear—
it's nearly impossible to see in there under that overhead
lamp. You know?

HEDDA.   Yes, I know.

TESMAN.   Do you think it would be all right if we used
your table for a while? Hm?

HEDDA.   Yes, I don't mind. (*Quickly.*) Wait! No, let me
clear it off first.

TESMAN.   Oh, don't bother, Hedda. There's plenty of
room.

HEDDA.   No, no, let me just clear it off, can't you? I'll
put all this in by the piano. There!

> (*She has pulled out an object covered with sheet
> music from under the bookcase, adds more
> music to it, and carries the whole thing into the
> inner room and off left.* TESMAN *puts the
> scraps of paper on the writing table and moves
> the lamp over from the corner table. He and*
> MRS. ELVSTED *sit down and go on with their
> work.* HEDDA *comes back.*)

HEDDA (*behind* MRS. ELVSTED'S *chair, gently ruffling her
hair*).   Well, my sweet little Thea—how is it going with
Eilert Løvborg's monument?

MRS. ELVSTED (*looking despondently up at her*).   Oh,
dear—it's going to be terribly hard to set these in order.

TESMAN.   It's got to be done. There's just no alternative.
Besides, setting other people's papers in order—it's exactly
what I can do best.

> (HEDDA *goes over by the stove and sits on one
> of the taborets.* BRACK *stands over her, leaning
> on the armchair.*)

HEDDA (*whispering*).   What did you say about the pistol?

BRACK (*softly*).   That he must have stolen it.

HEDDA.   Why, necessarily, that?

BRACK.   Because every other explanation would seem impossible, Mrs. Hedda.

HEDDA.   I see.

BRACK (*glancing at her*).   Of course, Eilert Løvborg was here this morning. Wasn't he?

HEDDA.   Yes.

BRACK.   Were you alone with him?

HEDDA.   Yes, briefly.

BRACK.   Did you leave the room while he was here?

HEDDA.   No.

BRACK.   Consider. You didn't leave, even for a moment.

HEDDA.   Well, yes, perhaps, just for a moment—into the hall.

BRACK.   And where did you have your pistol case?

HEDDA.   I had it put away in—

BRACK.   Yes, Mrs. Hedda?

HEDDA.   It was lying over there, on the writing table.

BRACK.   Have you looked since to see if both pistols are there?

HEDDA.   No.

BRACK.   No need to. I saw the pistol. Løvborg had it on him. I knew it immediately, from yesterday. And other days too.

HEDDA.   Do you have it, maybe?

BRACK.   No, the police have it.

HEDDA.   What will they do with it?

BRACK.   Try to trace it to the owner.

HEDDA.   Do you think they'll succeed?

BRACK (*bending over her and whispering*).   No, Hedda Gabler—as long as I keep quiet.

HEDDA (*looking at him anxiously*).   And if you don't keep quiet—then what?

BRACK (*with a shrug*).   Counsel could always claim that the pistol was stolen.

HEDDA (*decisively*).   I'd rather die!

BRACK (*smiling*).   People *say* such things. But they don't *do* them.

HEDDA (*without answering*).   And what, then, if the pistol wasn't stolen. And they found the owner. What would happen?

BRACK.   Well, Hedda—there'd be a scandal.

HEDDA.   A scandal!

BRACK. A scandal, yes—the kind you're so deathly afraid of. Naturally, you'd appear in court—you and Mademoiselle Diana. She'd have to explain how the whole thing occurred. Whether it was an accident or homicide. Was he trying to pull the pistol out of his pocket to threaten her? Is that why it went off? Or had she torn the pistol out of his hand, shot him, and slipped it back in his pocket again? It's rather like her to do that, you know. She's a solid piece of work, this Mademoiselle Diana.

HEDDA. But all that sordid business is no concern of mine.

BRACK. No. But you'll have to answer the question: why did you give Eilert Løvborg the pistol? And what conclusions will people draw from the fact that you did give it to him?

HEDDA (*her head sinking*). That's true. I hadn't thought of that.

BRACK. Well, luckily there's no danger, as long as I keep quiet.

HEDDA. So I'm in your power, Judge. You have your hold over me from now on.

BRACK (*whispers more softly*). My dearest Hedda—believe me—I won't abuse my position.

HEDDA. All the same, I'm in your power. Tied to your will and desire. Not free. Not free, then! (*Rises angrily*). No—I can't bear the thought of it. Never!

BRACK (*looks at her half mockingly*). One usually manages to adjust to the inevitable.

HEDDA (*returning his look*). Yes, perhaps so. (*She goes over to the writing table. Suppressing an involuntary smile, she imitates* TESMAN's *intonation*.) Well? Getting on with it, George? Uh?

TESMAN. Goodness knows, dear. It's going to mean months and months of work, in any case.

HEDDA (*as before*). Imagine that! (*Runs her hand lightly through* MRS. ELVSTED'S *hair.*). Don't you find it strange, Thea? Here you are, sitting now beside Tesman—just as you used to sit with Eilert Løvborg.

MRS. ELVSTED. Oh, if I could only inspire your husband in the same way.

HEDDA. Oh, that will surely come—in time.

TESMAN. Yes, you know what, Hedda—I really think

I'm beginning to feel something of the kind. But you go back and sit with Judge Brack.

HEDDA.   Is there nothing the two of you can use me for here?

TESMAN.   No, nothing in the world. (*Turning his head.*) From now on, Judge, you'll have to be good enough to keep Hedda company.

BRACK (*with a glance at* HEDDA). I'll take the greatest pleasure in that.

HEDDA.   Thanks. But I'm tired this evening. I want to rest a while in there on the sofa.

TESMAN.   Yes, do that, dear. Uh?

(HEDDA *goes into the inner room, pulling the curtains closed after her. Short pause. Suddenly she is heard playing a wild dance melody on the piano.*)

MRS. ELVSTED (*starting up from her chair*).   Oh—what's that?

TESMAN (*running to the center doorway*).   But Hedda dearest—don't go playing dance music tonight! Think of Auntie Rina! And Eilert, too!

HEDDA (*putting her head out between the curtains*).   And Auntie Julie. And all the rest of them. From now on I'll be quiet. (*She closes the curtains again.*)

TESMAN (*at the writing table*).   She can't feel very happy seeing us do this melancholy work. You know what, Mrs. Elvsted—you must move in with Aunt Julie. Then I can come over evenings. And then we can sit and work *there*. Uh?

MRS. ELVSTED.   Yes, perhaps that would be best—

HEDDA (*from the inner room*) I can hear everything you say, Tesman. But what will I do evenings over here?

TESMAN (*leafing through the notes*).   Oh, I'm sure Judge Brack will be good enough to stop by and see you.

BRACK (*in the armchair, calling out gaily*).   Gladly, every blessed evening, Mrs. Tesman! We'll have great times here together, the two of us!

HEDDA (*in a clear, ringing voice*).   Yes, don't you hope so, Judge? You, the one cock of the walk—

(*A shot is heard within.* TESMAN, MRS. ELVSTED, *and* BRACK *start from their chairs.*)

TESMAN. Oh, now she's fooling with those pistols again.

(*He throws the curtains back and runs in.*
MRS. ELVSTED *follows.* HEDDA *lies, lifeless,
stretched out on the sofa. Confusion and cries.*
BERTA *comes in, bewildered, from the right.*)

TESMAN (*shrieking to* BRACK). Shot herself! Shot herself
in the temple! Can you imagine!

BRACK (*in the armchair, prostrated*). But good God!
People don't *do* such things!

THE MASTER BUILDER

THE CHARACTERS

HALVARD SOLNESS, Master Builder
ALINE SOLNESS, his wife
DR. HERDAL, the family doctor
KNUT BROVIK, former architect, now assistant to SOLNESS
RAGNAR BROVIK, his son, a draftsman
KAJA FOSLI, his niece, a bookkeeper
MISS HILDA WANGEL
SOME LADIES
A CROWD IN THE STREET

The action takes place in and around SOLNESS's *house.*

ACT ONE

A plainly furnished workroom in SOLNESS's *house. Folding doors in the wall to the left lead to the entryway. To the right is a door to the inner rooms. In the rear wall a door stands open on the drafting room. Downstage left, a desk with books, papers, and writing materials. Upstage, beyond the folding doors, a stove. In the right-hand corner, a sofa with a table and a couple of chairs. On the table, a carafe of water and a glass. A smaller table with a rocker and an armchair in the right foreground. Lights for working lit over the drafting room table, on the table in the corner, and on the desk.*

In the drafting room KNUT BROVIK *and his son* RAGNAR *are sitting, busy with blueprints and calculations. At the desk in the workroom* KAJA FOSLI *stands, writing in a ledger.* KNUT BROVIK *is a gaunt old man with white hair and beard. He wears a rather threadbare but well-preserved black coat, glasses, and a white muffler somewhat yellowed by age.* RAGNAR BROVIK *is in his thirties, well-dressed, blond, with a slight stoop.* KAJA FOSLI *is a delicate young girl of twenty some years, trimly dressed, but rather sickly in appearance. She is wearing a green eyeshade. All three work on for a time in silence.*

KNUT BROVIK (*suddenly stands up from the drafting table, as if in fright, his breathing heavy and labored as he comes forward into the doorway*). No, I can't go on much longer!

KAJA (*moves over to him*). Are you feeling quite bad tonight, Uncle?

BROVIK. Oh, I think it gets worse every day.

RAGNAR (*having risen and approached them*). Father, you'd better go home. Try to get some sleep—

BROVIK (*impatiently*). Take to my bed, hm? You want to have me suffocate for good!

KAJA. Go out for a little walk, then.

RAGNAR. Yes, go on. I'll walk with you.

BROVIK (*vehemently*).   I won't go till he's back! Tonight I'm putting it straight up to— (*With suppressed resentment.*) to him—to the chief.

KAJA (*upset*).   Oh no, Uncle—please, let it wait!

RAGNAR.   Yes, Father, wait a while!

BROVIK (*struggling for breath*).   Uhh—uhh! I haven't much time to wait.

KAJA (*listening*).   Shh! I hear him down on the stairs. (*All three return to work. Short silence.*)

> (HALVARD SOLNESS *comes in from the entry hall. He is a middle-aged man, strong and forceful, with close-cropped, curly hair, a dark mustache and thick, dark eyebrows. His jacket, gray-green with wide lapels, is buttoned, with the collar turned up. On his head is a soft gray felt hat, and under his arm a couple of portfolios.*)

SOLNESS (*by the door, pointing at the drafting room and whispering*).   Are they gone?

KAJA (*softly, shaking her head*).   No. (*She removes the eyeshade.* SOLNESS *crosses the room, tosses his hat on a chair, sets the folios on the sofa table and then comes back toward the desk.* KAJA *steadily continues writing, but seems nervous and ill at ease.*)

SOLNESS (*aloud*).   What's that you're putting down there, Miss Fosli?

KAJA (*with a start*).   Oh, it's just something that—

SOLNESS.   Here, let me see. (*Bends over her, pretending to examine the ledger, and whispers.*) Kaja?

KAJA (*softly, as she writes*).   Yes.

SOLNESS.   Why do you always take off that shade when I'm around?

KAJA (*as before*).   You know it makes me look so ugly.

SOLNESS (*smiling*).   And you don't want that, do you, Kaja?

KAJA (*half glancing up at him*).   Not for all the world. Not for *you* to see.

SOLNESS (*lightly stroking her hair*).   Poor, poor little Kaja—

KAJA (*ducking her head*).   Shh—they can hear you!

(SOLNESS *strolls across the room to the right, turns, and pauses at the drafting room door.*)

SOLNESS.   Has anyone been in to see me?

RAGNAR (*getting up*).   Yes, the young couple that want to build out at Løvstrand.

SOLNESS (*growling*).   Oh, them. Well, they can wait. I'm not quite clear on the plans yet.

RAGNAR (*coming forward and rather hesitantly*).   They did want so badly to have those drawings soon.

SOLNESS (*as before*).   Good God—they all want that!

BROVIK (*looking up*).   They said they had such a longing to move into their own place.

SOLNESS.   All right, all right—we know that! So they'll make do with anything—any kind of a—a roost. Just a peg to hang their hats. But not a home. No—no, thanks! They can go find somebody else. Tell them that when they come again.

BROVIK (*pushing his glasses up on his forehead and staring at him in amazement*).   Find somebody else? You'd turn that commission down?

SOLNESS (*impatiently*).   Yes, damn it all, yes! If that's how it's going to be— It's better than slapping a shack together. (*Exploding.*) What do I know about these people!

BROVIK.   They're good solid people. Ragnar knows them. He's like one of the family. Very solid people.

SOLNESS.   Ahh, solid—solid! That's not what I mean. Lord—don't *you* understand me either? (*Sharply.*) I'll have nothing to do with strangers. They can find anyone they please, for all I care!

BROVIK (*rising*).   Seriously, you mean that?

SOLNESS (*sullenly*).   Yes—for once. (*He paces across the room.*)

(BROVIK *exchanges a look with* RAGNAR, *who makes a warning gesture. He then comes into the workroom.*)

BROVIK.   May I have a word or two with you?

SOLNESS.   Gladly.

BROVIK (*to* KAJA).   Kaja, go inside a while.

KAJA (*uneasily*).   Oh, but Uncle—

BROVIK.   Do as I say, child. And close the door after you.

(KAJA *goes reluctantly into the drafting room and, with a fearful and imploring look at* SOL-NESS, *shuts the door.*)

BROVIK (*dropping his voice*).   I don't want the poor children knowing how sick I am.

SOLNESS.   Yes, you're looking quite done in these days.

BROVIK.   It's almost over with me. My strength—it's less every day.

SOLNESS.   Sit down, rest a bit.

BROVIK.   Thanks—may I?

SOLNESS (*adjusting the armchair*).   Here, please. Well?

BROVIK (*having seated himself with difficulty*).   Yes, well, it's Ragnar; he's on my mind. What's going to happen with him?

SOLNESS.   Your son, he can stay on here with me, naturally, as long as he wants.

BROVIK.   But that's just the thing: it's not what he wants. He thinks he can't—now, any longer.

SOLNESS.   Well, I'd say he's got a very nice salary. But if he's out for a little more, I wouldn't be averse to—

BROVIK.   No, no, it isn't that! (*Impatiently.*) But he needs a chance to work on his own.

SOLNESS (*not looking at him*).   Do you think Ragnar has really enough talent for that?

BROVIK.   Don't you see, *that's* the worst of it. That I'm beginning to have my doubts about the boy. For you've never said so much as—as one word of encouragement about him. But then I think it can't be any other way—he *must* have the talent.

SOLNESS.   Well, but he hasn't learned anything yet—nothing basic. Nothing but drafting.

BROVIK (*looking at him with veiled hatred, his voice hoarse*).   You hadn't learned anything either, back when you worked for me. But you got along all right. (*Breathing heavily.*) Pushed your way up. Cut the ground out from under me—and so many others.

SOLNESS.   Well—I had luck on my side.

BROVIK.   True enough. Everything was on your side. But you can't have the heart, then, to let me die—without seeing what Ragnar can do. And then, I'd like so much to see them married—before I'm gone.

SOLNESS (*sharply*).   Is she the one who wants that?

BROVIK.   Not so much Kaja. But Ragnar talks of it every day. (*Beseeching him.*) You must—you *must* help him get some independent work now! I've got to see something the boy has done. You hear me!

SOLNESS (*angrily*).   What the hell—you think I can pull down commissions out of the moon for him!

BROVIK.   He could have a fine commission right now. A big piece of work.

SOLNESS (*surprised and disconcerted*).   He could?

BROVIK.   If you'd give permission.

SOLNESS.   What work is that?

BROVIK (*hesitating a bit*).   He could build that house at Løvstrand.

SOLNESS.   That! But I'm building that!

BROVIK.   Oh, but you have no more interest in it.

SOLNESS (*flaring up*).   No interest! Me! Who says so?

BROVIK.   You said it yourself just now.

SOLNESS.   Oh, don't listen to what I—say. Would they give Ragnar that job?

BROVIK.   Yes. He knows the family. And then, just for fun, he's worked out the plans and the estimate, the whole thing—

SOLNESS.   And they like the plans? Those people—?

BROVIK.   Yes. So if you'd just go over them and give your approval, then—

SOLNESS.   Then they'd invite Ragnar to build their home.

BROVIK.   They really liked what he wants to do. They thought it was completely new and different—that's what they said.

SOLNESS.   Aha! New! Modern! None of the old-fashioned stuff I build!

BROVIK.   They thought it was something—different.

SOLNESS (*with suppressed bitterness*).   And they came here to Ragnar—while I was out!

BROVIK.   They came to see you—and also to ask if you'd be willing to give up—

SOLNESS (*erupting*).   Give up! I!

BROVIK.   That is, if you found Ragnar's plans—

SOLNESS.   I—give up for your son!

BROVIK.   Give up the commission, they meant.

SOLNESS.   Oh, it's one and the same. (*With a wry laugh.*) So that's it! Halvard Solness—he ought to start giving up now! Make room for youth. For even the youngest. Just make room! Room! Room!

BROVIK.   Good Lord, there's room enough here for more than one man—

SOLNESS.   There's not that much room here anymore. But, never mind—I'm not giving up! I never give ground. Not voluntarily. Never in this world, never!

BROVIK (*rising with effort*).   And I—must I give up life without hope? Without joy? Without faith and trust in Ragnar? Without seeing a single one of his works? Is that it?

SOLNESS (*half turning away, in a whisper*).   Don't ask any more now.

BROVIK.   Yes, answer me. Shall I go into death so poor?

SOLNESS (*after an inner struggle, he speaks at last in a low but firm voice*).   You have to face death the best you can.

BROVIK.   Then that's it. (*He walks away.*)

SOLNESS (*following him, half in desperation*).   Don't you see—what else can I do! I'm made the way I am! I can't change myself over!

BROVIK.   No, no, I guess you can't. (*Stumbles and halts by the sofa table.*) May I have a glass of water?

SOLNESS.   Please. (*Pours and hands him the glass.*)

BROVIK.   Thanks. (*Drinks and sets the glass down.*)

SOLNESS (*going over and opening the door to the drafting room*).   Ragnar—come take your father home.

(RAGNAR *quickly gets up. He and* KAJA *come into the workroom.*)

RAGNAR.   Father, what is it?

BROVIK.   Give me your arm. Then we'll go.

RAGNAR.   All right. You get your things too, Kaja.

SOLNESS.   Miss Fosli will have to stay on a moment— I've a letter to be written.

BROVIK (*looking at* SOLNESS).   Good night. Sleep well— if you can.

SOLNESS.   Good night.

(BROVIK *and* RAGNAR *leave by way of the entry hall.* KAJA *goes over to the desk.* SOLNESS *stands, head bent, to the right by the armchair.*)

KAJA (*hesitating*). Is there a letter—?

SOLNESS (*brusquely*). Of course not. (*With a fierce look at her.*) Kaja!

KAJA (*frightened, softly*). Yes?

SOLNESS (*decisively, beckoning her*). Over here! Quick!

KAJA (*reluctantly*). Yes.

SOLNESS (*as before*). Closer!

KAJA (*obeying*). What do you want of me?

SOLNESS (*looking at her a moment*). Are you at the root of all this?

KAJA. No, no, don't believe that!

SOLNESS. But marriage—that's what you want now.

KAJA (*quietly*). Ragnar and I have been engaged four or five years, and so—

SOLNESS. So you think it just can't go on forever—isn't that it?

KAJA. Ragnar and Uncle tell me I must—so I think I'll have to give in.

SOLNESS (*more gently*). Kaja, don't you really care a little for Ragnar too?

KAJA. I cared very much for Ragnar once—before I came here to you.

SOLNESS. But no more? Not at all?

KAJA (*passionately, extending her clasped hands out toward him*). Oh, you know I care now for one, only one! Nobody else in this whole world. I'll never care for anyone else!

SOLNESS. Yes, you say that. And then you desert me all the same. Leave me to struggle with everything alone.

KAJA. But couldn't I stay on with you even if Ragnar—?

SOLNESS. No, no, that's out of the question. If Ragnar goes out on his own, he'll be needing you himself.

KAJA (*wringing her hands*). Oh, I don't see how I *can* ever part from you! It's just so completely impossible.

SOLNESS. Then try to rid Ragnar of these stupid ideas. Marry him as much as you like—(*Changing his tone.*) Well, I mean—don't let him throw over a good job here with me. Because—then I can keep *you* too, Kaja dear.

KAJA. Oh yes, how lovely that would be, if only we could manage it!

SOLNESS (*caressing her head with both hands and whispering*). Because I can't be without you. You understand? I've got to have you close to me every day.

KAJA (*shivering with excitement*). Oh, God! God!

SOLNESS (*kissing her hair*). Kaja—Kaja!

KAJA (*sinks down before him*). Oh, how good you are to me! How incredibly good you are!

SOLNESS (*intensely*). Get up! Get up now, I—I hear someone coming!

> (*He helps her up. She falters over to the desk.
> MRS. SOLNESS enters by the door on the right.
> She looks thin and careworn, but traces of former beauty still show. Blonde ringlets. Dressed stylishly, entirely in black. Speaks rather slowly in a plaintive voice.*)

MRS. SOLNESS (*in the doorway*). Halvard!

SOLNESS (*turning*). Oh, is it you, dear—?

MRS. SOLNESS (*with a glance at* KAJA). I'm afraid I'm intruding.

SOLNESS. Not a bit. Miss Fosli has one short letter to write.

MRS. SOLNESS. Yes—I see that.

SOLNESS. What did you want me for, Aline?

MRS. SOLNESS. I just wanted to say that Dr. Herdal's in the living room. Maybe you could join us, Halvard?

SOLNESS (*looks suspiciously at her*). Hm—is the doctor so anxious to talk with me?

MRS. SOLNESS. No, not exactly anxious. He stopped by to see me, but he'd like to say hello to you too.

SOLNESS (*laughing to himself*). Yes, I can imagine. Well, then you'd better ask him to wait a while.

MRS. SOLNESS. And you'll look in on him later?

SOLNESS. Possibly. Later—later, dear. In a while.

MRS. SOLNESS (*glancing again at* KAJA). Don't forget now, Halvard. (*She leaves, closing the door after her.*)

KAJA (*softly*). Oh, my Lord—she must think the worst of me!

SOLNESS. Oh, certainly not. No more than usual, anyway. Still, it's best if you go now, Kaja.

KAJA.   Yes, I've *got* to go now.

SOLNESS (*sternly*).   And then you'll settle up that business for me—you hear!

KAJA.   Oh, if only it were just up to *me*, then—

SOLNESS.   Listen, I want it settled! Tomorrow the latest!

KAJA (*apprehensively*).   If it doesn't work out, then I'd rather break off with him.

SOLNESS (*explosively*).   Break off with him! Are you crazy, completely! You'd break it off?

KAJA (*in desperation*).   Yes. I have to—have to stay here with you! I can't ever leave you! Ever! That's impossible!

SOLNESS (*in an outburst*).   But damn it—Ragnar! Ragnar's the one that I—

KAJA (*looking at him with terrified eyes*).   Is it more for Ragnar's sake that—that you—?

SOLNESS (*checking himself*).   Of course not! Oh, you don't see what I mean either. (*Gently and softly.*) Obviously, it's you that I need here. You above all, Kaja. But that's precisely why you have to make Ragnar hang onto his job. There, there—run along home now.

KAJA.   All right—good night, then.

SOLNESS.   Good night. (*As she starts out.*) Oh, wait—are Ragnar's drawings in there?

KAJA.   Yes, I don't think he took them along.

SOLNESS.   See if you can locate them for me. I could give them a look maybe, after all.

KAJA (*in delight*).   Oh yes, please do!

SOLNESS.   For your sake, Kaja, my sweet. Now let's have them in a hurry, you hear?

> (KAJA *runs into the drafting room, rummages anxiously in the table drawer, pulls out a portfolio and brings it.*)

KAJA.   All the drawings are here.

SOLNESS.   Fine. Lay them over there on the table.

KAJA (*does so*).   Good night. (*Imploringly.*) And please—think well of me.

SOLNESS.   Oh, you know I do, always. Good night, my dear little Kaja. (*Glancing to the right.*) Go on now—go!

> (MRS. SOLNESS *and* DR. HERDAL *enter through the door on the right. He is a plump, elderly man*

*with a round, complacent face, smooth shaven;
he has light, thinning hair, and gold
spectacles.*)

MRS. SOLNESS (*standing in the doorway*). Halvard, I
can't keep the doctor any longer.

SOLNESS. Well, come in, then.

MRS. SOLNESS (*to* KAJA, *who is dimming the desk lamp*).
All finished with the letter, Miss Fosli?

KAJA (*confused*). The letter—?

SOLNESS. Yes, it was very short.

MRS. SOLNESS. I'm sure it was terribly short.

SOLNESS. You may as well leave, Miss Fosli. And be
here on time in the morning.

KAJA. I certainly will. Good night, Mrs. Solness. (*She
goes out by the hall door.*)

MRS. SOLNESS. You've certainly been in luck, Halvard,
to have gotten hold of that girl.

SOLNESS. Oh yes. She's useful in all kinds of ways.

MRS. SOLNESS. She looks it.

HERDAL. A clever bookkeeper, too?

SOLNESS. Well—she's had a lot of experience these past
two years. And then she's willing and eager to take on
anything.

MRS. SOLNESS. Yes, that must be such a great comfort—

SOLNESS. It it—especially when one's so used to doing
without.

MRS. SOLNESS (*in a tone of mild reproach*). Can *you*
really say *that*, Halvard?

SOLNESS. Ah, my dear Aline, no, no. I beg your
pardon.

MRS. SOLNESS. Don't trouble yourself. Well, Doctor, so
you'll stop in again later and have some tea with us?

HERDAL. As soon as I've made that house call, I'll be
back.

MRS. SOLNESS. Thank you. (*She goes out the door right.*)

SOLNESS. Are you pressed for time, Doctor?

HERDAL. No, not a bit.

SOLNESS. May I have a few words with you?

HERDAL. Yes, by all means.

SOLNESS. Then let's sit down. (*He motions the doctor
toward the rocker, and after seating himself in the armchair,*

looks at him sharply.) Tell me—did you notice anything about Aline?

HERDAL.   Just now, you mean, when she was here?

SOLNESS.   Yes. With respect to me. Did you notice anything?

HERDAL (*smiling*).   Well, really—one could hardly help noticing that your wife—hm—

SOLNESS.   Go on.

HERDAL.   That your wife doesn't think very much of this Miss Fosli.

SOLNESS.   Nothing else? I could tell that myself.

HERDAL.   And, after all, it's not so very surprising.

SOLNESS.   What?

HERDAL.   That she isn't exactly pleased that you enjoy another woman's company every day.

SOLNESS.   That's true, you're right—and so is Aline. But it can't be changed.

HERDAL.   Couldn't you hire a man instead?

SOLNESS.   Just anyone off the street? No, thanks—that isn't the way I work.

HERDAL.   But what if your wife—? When she *is* so delicate, what if she can't endure this thing?

SOLNESS.   Even so—I'm tempted to say it can't make a bit of difference. I've got to keep Kaja Fosli. Nobody else will do.

HERDAL.   Nobody else?

SOLNESS (*curtly*).   No, nobody else.

HERDAL (*draws his chair in closer*).   If I may, Mr. Solness, I'd like to ask you something, just between us.

SOLNESS.   Yes, go ahead.

HERDAL.   Women, you know—in certain areas they do have a painfully keen intuition—

SOLNESS.   That they do. So—?

HERDAL.   Well. All right, then. If your wife simply can't bear this Kaja Fosli—

SOLNESS.   Yes, what then?

HERDAL.   Hasn't she perhaps some tiny grounds for this instinctive dislike?

SOLNESS (*looks at him and rises*).   Aha!

HERDAL.   Now don't get excited. But really—hasn't she?

SOLNESS (*his voice clipped and decisive*).   No.

HERDAL.   Not the slightest grounds?

SOLNESS.   Nothing, except her own suspicious mind.

HERDAL.   I realize you've known a good many women in your life.

SOLNESS.   I have, yes.

HERDAL.   And thought very well of some of them, too.

SOLNESS.   Oh yes, that also.

HERDAL.   But in this case—there's nothing of that kind involved?

SOLNESS.   No. Nothing whatever—on my side.

HERDAL.   But on hers?

SOLNESS.   I don't think you've any right to ask about that, Doctor.

HERDAL.   We were discussing your wife's intuition.

SOLNESS.   We were, yes. And for that matter—(*Dropping his voice.*) Aline's intuition, as you call it—you know, to a certain extent it's proved itself.

HERDAL.   There—see!

SOLNESS.   Dr. Herdal—let me tell you a strange story. That is, if you don't mind listening.

HERDAL.   I like listening to strange stories.

SOLNESS.   Ah, that's good. I guess you remember how I took on Knut Brovik and his son here—that time when the old man nearly went under.

HERDAL.   I vaguely remember, yes.

SOLNESS.   Because, you know, they're really a clever pair, those two. They've got ability, each in his own way. But then the son went out and got engaged. And then, of course, he was all for getting married—and launching his own career as a builder. Because the young people today, that's all they ever think about.

HERDAL (*laughing*).   Yes, they have this bad habit of pairing off.

SOLNESS.   Well, but *I* can't be bothered by that. You see, I need Ragnar—and the old man as well. He has a real knack for calculating stresses, cubic content—all that damned detail work.

HERDAL.   Of course, that's important too.

SOLNESS.   Yes, it is. But Ragnar, he felt he wanted and he had to be out on his own. There just wasn't any reasoning with him.

HERDAL.   Even so, he stayed on with you.

SOLNESS.   Yes, but now listen to what happened. One

day she came in, this Kaja Fosli, on some errand for them. First time she'd ever been here. And when I saw those two, how completely wrapped up in each other they were, then the thought struck me: suppose I could get her here in the office, then maybe Ragnar would stay put too.

HERDAL.   That was reasonable enough.

SOLNESS.   But I didn't breathe a word of any of this then—just stood looking at her—every ounce of me wishing that I had her here. I made a little friendly conversation about one thing or another. And then she went away.

HERDAL.   So?

SOLNESS.   But the next day, in the late evening, after old Brovik and Ragnar had gone, she came by to see me again, acting as if we'd already struck a bargain.

HERDAL.   Bargain? What about?

SOLNESS.   About precisely what I'd been standing there wishing before—even though I hadn't uttered a word of it.

HERDAL.   That *is* strange.

SOLNESS.   Yes, isn't it? So she wanted to know what her job would be—and whether she'd be starting the very next morning. Things like that.

HERDAL.   Don't you think she did that to be with her fiancé?

SOLNESS.   I thought so too, at first. But no, that wasn't it. From the moment she came here to work, she started drifting away from him.

HERDAL.   And over to you?

SOLNESS.   Yes, completely. If I look at her when her back is turned, I can tell she feels it. She trembles and quivers if I even come near her. What do you make of it?

HERDAL.   Hm—it's easy enough to explain.

SOLNESS.   Well, but the rest of it, then? The fact that she thought I'd told her what I had only wished and willed— all in silence, inwardly. To myself. What do you say about that? Can you explain such a thing, Dr. Herdal?

HERDAL.   No, I wouldn't attempt to.

SOLNESS.   I thought as much. That's why I've never cared to discuss it till now. But you see, as time goes on, I'm finding it such a damned nuisance. Here, day after day, I have to keep on pretending that I'm— And then, poor girl, it's not fair to her. (*Furiously.*) But I can't help it! If she runs off—then Ragnar will follow, out on his own.

HERDAL. And you haven't told your wife this whole story.

SOLNESS. No.

HERDAL. Why in the world haven't you?

SOLNESS (*looking intently at him, his voice constrained*). Because I feel that there's almost a kind of beneficial self-torment in letting Aline do me an injustice.

HERDAL (*shaking his head*). I don't understand one blessed word of this.

SOLNESS. Yes, don't you see—it's rather like making a small payment on a boundless, incalculable debt—

HERDAL. To your wife?

SOLNESS. Yes. And it always eases the mind a bit. Then you can breathe more freely for a while, you know.

HERDAL. God help me if I understand a word—

SOLNESS (*breaking in, and again getting up*). Yes, all right—so we won't speak of it anymore, then. (*He meanders across the room, comes back, and stops by the table. Looks at the doctor with a quiet smile.*) Now you really think you've done a neat job of drawing me out, hm, Doctor?

HERDAL (*somewhat upset*). Drawing you out? Mr. Solness, I'm still very much in the dark.

SOLNESS. Oh, come now—confess. Because really, you know, it's been so obvious to me!

HERDAL. *What's* so obvious to you?

SOLNESS (*slowly, in an undertone*). That behind this genial manner, you're keeping your eye on me.

HERDAL. Am I! Why on earth should I do that?

SOLNESS. Because you think I'm— (*Explosively.*) Oh, dammit! You think the same as Aline about me.

HERDAL. But what does she think of you, then?

SOLNESS. She's begun to think that I'm—I'm somewhat ill.

HERDAL. Ill! You! She's never breathed a word of it to me. What is it that's wrong with you, then?

SOLNESS (*leans over the back of the chair and whispers*). Aline's got the idea that I'm mad. *That's* what she thinks.

HERDAL (*rising*). But my dear Mr. Solness—!

SOLNESS. Yes, on my soul she does! And she has you thinking the same. Oh, I tell you, Doctor—I can see it in you so clear, so clear. Because I'm not so easily fooled, I'm not, I can tell you that.

HERDAL (*stares at him, amazed*). I've never, Mr. Solness—never had the least inkling of anything like this.

SOLNESS (*with a skeptical smile*). Really? Not at all?

HERDAL. No, never! And your wife certainly hasn't either—I'd almost swear to that.

SOLNESS. Well, you'd better not. Because, you know, maybe, in a way—maybe she's not so far off.

HERDAL. Look, I'm telling you now, really—!

SOLNESS (*breaking in, with a sweep of his hand*). All right there, Doctor—then let's not go on with this. Each to his own, that's the best. (*His tone changes to quiet amusement.*) But now listen, Doctor—hm—

HERDAL. Yes?

SOLNESS. If you don't think, then, that I'm, somehow—ill—or crazy or mad and that sort of thing—

HERDAL. Then what, hm?

SOLNESS. Then I guess you must imagine that I'm a very happy man.

HERDAL. Is *that* no more than imagination?

SOLNESS (*with a laugh*). Oh no, not a chance! God forbid! Just think—to be Solness, the master builder! Halvard Solness! Oh, thanks a lot!

HERDAL. Yes, I must say, to *me* it seems that you've had luck with you to an incredible degree.

SOLNESS (*masking a wan smile*). So I have. Can't complain of that.

HERDAL. First, that hideous old robbers' den burned down for you. And that was really a stroke of luck.

SOLNESS (*seriously*). It was Aline's family home that burned—don't forget.

HERDAL. Yes, for *her* it must have been a heavy loss.

SOLNESS. She hasn't recovered right to this day. Not in all these twelve–thirteen years.

HERDAL. What followed after, that must have been the worst blow for her.

SOLNESS. The two together.

HERDAL. But you yourself—*you* rose from those ashes. You began as a poor boy from the country—and now you stand the top man in your field. Ah, yes, Mr. Solness, you've surely had luck on your side.

SOLNESS (*glancing nervously at him*).   Yes, but that's exactly why I've got this horrible fear.

HERDAL.   Fear? For having luck on your side?

SOLNESS.   It racks me, this fear—it racks me, morning and night. Because someday things have to change, you'll see.

HERDAL.   Oh, rot! Where's this change coming from?

SOLNESS (*with firm conviction*).   From the young.

HERDAL.   Hah! The young! I'd hardly say that you're obsolete. No, you've probably never been better established than you are now.

SOLNESS.   The change is coming. I can sense it. And I feel that it's coming closer. Someone or other will set up the cry: Step back for *me*! And all the others will storm in after, shaking their fists and shouting: Make room—make room—make room! Yes, Doctor, you better look out. Someday youth will come here, knocking at the door—

HERDAL (*laughing*).   Well, good Lord, what if they do?

SOLNESS.   What if they do? Well, then it's the end of Solness, the master builder.

(*A knock at the door to the left.*)

SOLNESS (*with a start*).   What's that? Did you hear it?

HERDAL.   Somebody's knocking.

SOLNESS (*loudly*).   Come in!

> (HILDA WANGEL *enters from the hall. She is of medium height, supple and well-formed. Slight sunburn. Dressed in hiking clothes, with shortened skirt, sailor blouse open at the throat, and a little sailor hat. She has a knapsack on her back, a plaid in a strap, and a long alpenstock.*)

HILDA (*goes directly to* SOLNESS, *her eyes shining with happiness*).   Good evening!

SOLNESS (*looking hesitantly at her*).   Good evening—

HILDA (*laughing*).   I almost think you don't recognize me!

SOLNESS.   No—really—I must say, just at the moment—

HERDAL (*coming over*).   But I recognize you, young lady—

HILDA (*delighted*).   Oh no! It's you, that—?

HERDAL.   That's right, it's me. (*To* SOLNESS.) We met up at one of the mountain lodges last summer. (*To* HILDA.) What happened to all those other ladies?

HILDA.   Oh, they went off down the west slope.

HERDAL.   They didn't quite like all our fun in the evenings.

HILDA.   No, they certainly didn't.

HERDAL (*shaking his finger at her*).   Of course, we can't quite say you didn't flirt with us a bit.

HILDA.   I'd a lot rather do that than sit knitting knee socks with all the old hens.

HERDAL (*laughing*).   I couldn't agree with you more!

SOLNESS.   Did you just get in town this evening?

HILDA.   Yes, just now.

HERDAL.   All by yourself, Miss Wangel?

HILDA.   Of course!

SOLNESS.   Wangel? Is your name Wangel?

HILDA (*looks at him with amused surprise*).   Well, I should hope so.

SOLNESS.   Then aren't you the daughter of the public health officer up at Lysanger?

HILDA (*still amused*).   Sure. Whose daughter did you think I was?

SOLNESS.   Ah, so that's where we met, up *there*. The summer I went up and built a tower on the old church.

HILDA (*more serious*).   Yes, it was then.

SOLNESS.   Well, that's a long time back.

HILDA (*her eyes fixed on him*).   It's exactly ten years to the day.

SOLNESS.   I'd swear you weren't any more than a child then.

HILDA (*carelessly*).   Around twelve—thirteen, maybe.

HERDAL.   Is this the first time you've been here in town, Miss Wangel?

HILDA.   Yes, that's right.

SOLNESS.   And you probably don't know anyone, hm?

HILDA.   No one but you. Yes, and of course your wife.

SOLNESS.   Then you know *her* too?

HILDA.   Just slightly. We were together a few days at that health resort.

SOLNESS.   Ah, up *there*.

HILDA.   She told me please to visit her if I ever came

down into town. (*Smiles.*) Even though she really didn't
have to.

SOLNESS.   Funny she never spoke of it—

> (HILDA *puts her stick down by the stove, slips off
> the knapsack, and sets it and the plaid on the
> sofa.* DR. HERDAL *tries to assist.* SOLNESS
> *stands, gazing at her.*)

HILDA (*going up to him*).   So now, if I may, I'd like to
stay here overnight.

SOLNESS.   I'm sure that can be arranged.

HILDA.   'Cause I haven't any other clothes, except what
I've got on. Oh, and a set of underthings in my knapsack.
But they better be washed. They're real grimy.

SOLNESS.   Oh, well, that's easy to manage. Just let me
speak to my wife—

HERDAL.   Then I'll go on to my house call.

SOLNESS.   Yes, do that. And stop back again later.

HERDAL (*playfully, with a glance at* HILDA).   Oh, you
can bet I will! (*Laughing.*) You read the future all right,
Mr. Solness!

SOLNESS.   How so?

HERDAL.   Youth *did* come along, knocking at your door.

SOLNESS (*buoyantly*).   Yes, but that was something else
completely.

HERDAL.   Oh yes, yes. Definitely!

> (*He goes out the hall door.* SOLNESS *opens the
> door on the right and calls into the room
> beyond.*)

SOLNESS.   Aline! Would you come in here, please. A
Miss Wangel is here, whom you know.

MRS. SOLNESS (*appearing at the door*).   Who did you say?
(*Sees* HILDA.) Oh, is it you, then? (*Goes over and takes her
hand.*) So you've come to town after all.

SOLNESS.   Miss Wangel's just arrived. And she's wondering if she might stay here overnight.

MRS. SOLNESS.   Here with us? Why, of course.

SOLNESS.   To get her clothes fixed up a bit, you know.

MRS. SOLNESS.   I'll do what I can for you. It's no more
than my duty. Is your trunk on the way?

HILDA.   I haven't any trunk.

MRS. SOLNESS.   Well, it'll all work out, I guess. Now if you'll just make yourself at home here with my husband a while, I'll see about getting a room comfortable for you.

SOLNESS.   Can't we give up one of the nurseries? They're all ready and waiting.

MRS. SOLNESS.   Oh yes. We've more than enough room there. (*To* HILDA.) Just sit down and rest a bit. (*She goes out, right.*)

> (HILDA, *her hands behind her back, wanders around the room, looking at one thing and another.* SOLNESS *stands in front of the table, his hands also behind his back, following her with his eyes.*)

HILDA (*stops and looks at him*).   You have several nurseries?

SOLNESS.   There are three nurseries in the house.

HILDA.   That's plenty. You must have an awful lot of children.

SOLNESS.   No. We have no children. But now you can be the child here for a while.

HILDA.   Yes, for tonight. There won't be a peep out of me. I'm going to try to sleep like a stone.

SOLNESS.   Yes, you're pretty tired, I'll bet.

HILDA.   Oh no! But, after all— You know it is so ravishing just to lie and dream.

SOLNESS.   Do you often dream at night?

HILDA.   Oh yes! Nearly always.

SOLNESS.   What do you dream about most?

HILDA.   I won't tell you, not tonight. Some other time— maybe. (*She starts wandering about the room again, stops at the desk, and fingers the books and papers a little.*)

SOLNESS (*approaching her*).   Something you're looking for?

HILDA.   No, it's only to see all this here. (*Turning.*) But I shouldn't, maybe?

SOLNESS.   Yes, go ahead.

HILDA.   Is it you that writes in this big ledger?

SOLNESS.   No, that's the bookkeeper.

HILDA.   A woman?

SOLNESS (*smiles*).   Of course.

HILDA.   Someone you have working here?

SOLNESS. Yes.

HILDA. Is she married?

SOLNESS. No, she's single.

HILDA. I see.

SOLNESS. But I understand she's getting married now quite soon.

HILDA. That's very nice—for her.

SOLNESS. But not so nice for me. Because then I'll have no one to help me.

HILDA. Can't you find somebody else who's just as good?

SOLNESS. Maybe you'd like to stay here and—and write in the ledger?

HILDA (*giving him a dark look*). Yes, wouldn't that suit you! No, thanks—we're not having any of that. (*She strolls across the room again and settles into the rocker.* SOLNESS *follows her over to the table.* HILDA *goes on in the same tone.*) Because there are plenty of other things to be done around here. (*Looks up at him, smiling.*) Don't you think so too?

SOLNESS. Why, of course. First of all, I expect you'll want to tour the shops and do yourself up in style.

HILDA (*amused*). No, somehow I think I'll pass that up.

SOLNESS. Oh?

HILDA. Yes—since, you see, I'm completely broke.

SOLNESS (*laughing*). No trunk, or money either!

HILDA. Nothing of both. But shoot! What's the difference, anyway?

SOLNESS. Ah, I really like you for that!

HILDA. Only for that?

SOLNESS. Among other things. (*Sits in the armchair.*) Is your father still living?

HILDA. Yes, still living.

SOLNESS. And are you thinking of studying here now?

HILDA. No, that's not what I'd thought.

SOLNESS. But you *are* staying here for some time, I suppose?

HILDA. Depends how things go. (*A pause, while she sits rocking and looking at him half seriously, half with a suppressed smile. She then takes off her hat and places it on the table before her.*) Mr. Solness?

SOLNESS. Yes?

HILDA.   Are you very forgetful?

SOLNESS.   Forgetful? No, not as far as *I* know.

HILDA.   But do you absolutely not want to talk to me about what happened up there?

SOLNESS (*with a momentary start*).   Up at Lysanger? (*Carelessly.*) Well, there's not much to talk about, I'd say.

HILDA (*gazing reproachfully at him*).   How can you sit there and say that!

SOLNESS.   All right, *you* tell me about it then.

HILDA.   When the tower was finished, we had a big function in town.

SOLNESS.   Yes, that's one day I won't soon forget.

HILDA (*smiling*).   Won't you? So good of you!

SOLNESS.   Good?

HILDA.   They had music in the churchyard. And there were hundreds and hundreds of people. We schoolgirls were all dressed in white, and we had flags, all of us.

SOLNESS.   Oh yes, the flags—I remember them, all right.

HILDA.   Then you climbed straight up the scaffolding, straight to the very top—and you had a great wreath with you—and you hung it up high on the weather vane.

SOLNESS (*interrupting brusquely*).   I did that back in those days. It's an old custom.

HILDA.   It was so wonderfully thrilling to stand below, looking up at you. What if he slipped and fell—he, the master builder himself!

SOLNESS (*as if thrusting the subject aside*).   Yes, all right, that could have happened too. Because one of those little devils in white—how she carried on, screaming up at me—

HILDA (*eyes sparkling in delight*).   "Hurray for Mr. Solness, the master builder!" Yes!

SOLNESS.   Waving her flag and flourishing it till my—my head nearly spun at the sight of it.

HILDA (*growing more quiet and serious*).   That little devil —that was *me*.

SOLNESS (*peering fixedly at her*).   I'm sure of that now.

HILDA (*vivacious again*).   It was so terribly thrilling and lovely. I'd never dreamt that anywhere in the world there was a builder who could build a tower so high. And then, that you could stand there right at the top, large as life! And that you weren't the least bit dizzy! That's what made me so—almost dizzy to realize.

SOLNESS.   What makes you so sure I wasn't—?

HILDA (*deprecatingly*).   Oh, honestly—come on! I felt it within me. How else could you stand up there singing?

SOLNESS (*stares astonished at her*).   Singing? I sang?

HILDA.   Yes, really you did.

SOLNESS (*shaking his head*).   I've never sung a note in my life.

HILDA.   Yes, you were singing then. It sounded like harps in the air.

SOLNESS (*thoughtfully*).   It's something very peculiar—this.

HILDA (*silent a moment, then looking at him and speaking softly*).   But then—afterwards—came the *real* thing.

SOLNESS.   The real thing?

HILDA (*her vivacity kindling again*).   Oh, now I don't have to remind you of that!

SOLNESS.   Better give me a little reminder there, too.

HILDA.   Don't you remember a big banquet for you at the club?

SOLNESS.   Of course. That must have been the same afternoon—because I left the next morning.

HILDA.   And after the club, you were asked home to our place for the evening.

SOLNESS.   You're right, Miss Wangel. Amazing how you can keep all these details clear in your mind.

HILDA.   Details! Oh, you! I suppose it was just another detail that I was alone in the room when you came in?

SOLNESS.   Were you?

HILDA (*not answering him*).   You didn't call me any little devil then.

SOLNESS.   No, I guess not.

HILDA.   You said I was lovely in my white dress—and that I looked like a little princess.

SOLNESS.   I'm sure you did, Miss Wangel. And then, feeling the way I did that day, so light and free—

HILDA.   And then you said that when I grew up, I could be *your* princess.

SOLNESS (*with a short laugh*).   Really—I said that too?

HILDA.   Yes, you did. And when I asked how long I should wait, then you said you'd come back in ten years, like a troll, and carry me off—to Spain or someplace. And there you promised to buy me a kingdom.

SOLNESS (*as before*).   Well, after a good meal one's not in a mood to count pennies. But did I really *say* all that?

HILDA (*laughing softly*).   Yes, and you also said what the kingdom would be called.

SOLNESS.   Oh? What?

HILDA.   It was going to be the Kingdom of Orangia, you said.

SOLNESS.   Ah, that's a delectable name.

HILDA.   No, I didn't like it at all. It was as if you were out to make fun of me.

SOLNESS.   But I hadn't the slightest intention to.

HILDA.   No, it wouldn't seem so—not after what you did next—

SOLNESS.   What on earth did I do next?

HILDA.   Well, this is really the limit if you've even forgotten *that!* A thing like that I think anybody ought to remember.

SOLNESS.   All right, just give me a tiny hint, then, maybe—hm?

HILDA (*looking intently at him*).   You caught me up and kissed me, Mr. Solness.

SOLNESS (*open-mouthed, getting up*).   I *did!*

HILDA.   Oh yes, that you did. You held me in both your arms and bent me back and kissed me—many times.

SOLNESS.   But, my dear Miss Wangel—!

HILDA (*rising*).   You can't deny it, can you?

SOLNESS.   Yes, I most emphatically do deny it!

HILDA (*looking scornfully at him*).   I see. (*She turns and walks slowly over close by the stove and remains standing motionless, face averted from him, hands behind her back. A short pause.*)

SOLNESS (*going cautiously over behind her*).   Miss Wangel—? (HILDA *stays silent, not moving.*) Don't stand there like a statue. These things you've been saying—you must have dreamed them. (*Putting his hand on her arm.*) Now listen—(HILDA *moves her arm impatiently.* SOLNESS *appears struck by a sudden thought.*) Or else—wait a minute! There's something strange in back of all this, you'll see! (*In a hushed but emphatic voice.*) This all must have been in my thoughts. I must have willed it. Wished it. Desired it. And so—Doesn't that make sense? (HILDA *remains still.*

SOLNESS *speaks impatiently*.) Oh, all right, for God's sake—
so I *did* the thing too!

HILDA (*turning her head a bit, but without looking at
him*).   Then you confess?

SOLNESS.   Yes. Whatever you please.

HILDA.   That you threw your arms around me?

SOLNESS.   All right!

HILDA.   And bent me back.

SOLNESS.   Way over back.

HILDA.   And kissed me.

SOLNESS.   Yes, I did it.

HILDA.   Many times?

SOLNESS.   As many as you ever could want.

HILDA (*whirling about to face him, the sparkle once again
in her delighted eyes*).   There, you see—I did get it out of
you in the end!

SOLNESS (*with a thin smile*).   Yes—imagine my forgetting
something like that.

HILDA (*sulking a little once more, moving away from
him*).   Oh, you've kissed a good many in your time, I
think.

SOLNESS.   No, you mustn't believe that of me.

(HILDA *sits in the armchair.* SOLNESS *stands leaning on the rocking chair, watching her closely.*)

SOLNESS.   Miss Wangel?

HILDA.   Yes.

SOLNESS.   How was it, now? What went on next—with
us?

HILDA.   Nothing else went on. You know that well
enough. Because then all the others came in, and—ffft!

SOLNESS.   That's right. The others came. And I could
forget that too.

HILDA.   Oh, you haven't forgotten a thing. You're just
a little ashamed. Nobody forgets this kind of thing.

SOLNESS.   No, it wouldn't seem likely.

HILDA (*looking at him, vivacious again*).   Or maybe
you've even forgotten what day it was?

SOLNESS.   What day—?

HILDA.   Yes, what day you hung the wreath on the
tower? Well? Quick, say it!

SOLNESS.　Hm—I guess I've forgotten the actual date. I only know it was ten years ago. Sometime in the fall.

HILDA (*nodding her head slowly several times*).　It was ten years ago. The nineteenth of September.

SOLNESS.　Ah, yes, it must have been about then. So you've remembered that too! (*Hesitates.*) But wait a minute—! Yes—today it's also the nineteenth of September.

HILDA.　Yes, it is. And the ten years are up. And you didn't come—as you promised me.

SOLNESS.　Promised you? Threatened, don't you mean?

HILDA.　It never struck me as some kind of threat.

SOLNESS.　Well, teased that I would, then.

HILDA.　Is that all you wanted? To tease me?

SOLNESS.　Well, or to joke a bit with you. then! Lord knows I don't remember. But it must have been something like that—for you were only a child at the time.

HILDA.　Oh, maybe I wasn't so much of a child either. Not quite the little kitten you thought.

SOLNESS (*looks searchingly at her*).　Did you really in all seriousness get the idea I'd be coming back?

HILDA (*hiding a rather roguish smile*).　Of course! That's what I expected.

SOLNESS.　That I'd come to your home and carry you off with me?

HILDA.　Just like a troll, yes.

SOLNESS.　And make you a princess?

HILDA.　It's what you promised.

SOLNESS.　And give you a kingdom, too?

HILDA (*gazing at the ceiling*).　Why not? After all, it didn't have to be the everyday, garden-variety kingdom.

SOLNESS.　But something else that was just as good.

HILDA.　Oh, at least just as good. (*Glancing at him.*) If you could build the highest church tower in the world, it seemed to me you certainly should be able to come up with some kind of kingdom, too.

SOLNESS. (*shaking his head*).　I just can't figure you out, Miss Wangel.

HILDA.　You can't? I think it's so simple.

SOLNESS.　No, I can't make out whether you mean all you say—or whether you're just having some fun—

HILDA (*smiles*).　Fooling around—and teasing, maybe. I too?

SOLNESS.   Exactly. Making fools—of both of us. (*Looking at her.*) How long have you known I was married?

HILDA.   Right from the start. Why do you ask about *that*?

SOLNESS (*casually*).   Oh, nothing—just wondered. (*Lowering his voice, with a straight look at her.*) Why have you come?

HILDA.   I want my kingdom. Time's up.

SOLNESS (*laughing in spite of himself*).   You are the limit!

HILDA (*gaily*).   Give us the kingdom, come on! (*Drumming with her fingers.*) One kingdom, on the line!

SOLNESS (*pushing the rocking chair closer and sitting*).   Seriously now—why have you come? What do you really want to do here?

HILDA.   Oh, to begin with, I want to go around and look at everything you've built.

SOLNESS.   That'll keep you going a while.

HILDA.   Yes, you've built such an awful lot.

SOLNESS.   I have, yes. Mainly these later years.

HILDA.   Many more church towers? Enormously high ones?

SOLNESS.   No, I don't build any church towers now. Nor churches either.

HILDA.   What *do* you build then?

SOLNESS.   Homes for human beings.

HILDA (*reflectively*).   Couldn't you put a small—a small church tower up over the homes as well?

SOLNESS (*with a start*).   What do you mean by that?

HILDA.   I mean—something pointing—free, sort of, into the sky. With a weather vane way up in the reeling heights.

SOLNESS (*musing*).   How odd that you should say that. It's exactly what, most of all, I've wanted.

HILDA (*impatiently*).   But why don't you do it, then!

SOLNESS (*shaking his head*).   Because people won't have it.

HILDA.   Imagine—not to want that!

SOLNESS (*more lightly*).   But I'm building a new home now—right opposite this.

HILDA.   For yourself?

SOLNESS.   Yes. It's almost ready. And it has a tower.

HILDA.   A high one?

SOLNESS. Yes.

HILDA. Very high?

SOLNESS. People are bound to say, too high. At least for a home.

HILDA. I'll be out looking at that tower first thing in the morning.

SOLNESS (*sitting with his hand propping his cheek, gazing at her*). Miss Wangel, tell me—what's your name? Your first name, I mean?

HILDA. You know—it's Hilda.

SOLNESS (*as before*). Hilda? So?

HILDA. You don't remember *that*? You called me Hilda yourself—the day when you acted up.

SOLNESS. I did that, too?

HILDA. But then you said "little Hilda," and I didn't care for that.

SOLNESS. So, Miss Hilda, you didn't care for that.

HILDA. Not at such a time, no. But—Princess Hilda— that's going to sound quite nice, I think.

SOLNESS. No doubt. Princess Hilda of—of that kingdom, what was it called?

HILDA. Ish! I'm through with that stupid kingdom! I want a different one, completely.

SOLNESS (*who has leaned back in his chair, goes on studying her*). Isn't it strange—? The more I think about it, the more it seems to me that all these years I've been going around tormented by—hm—

HILDA. By what?

SOLNESS. By a search for something—some old experience I thought I'd forgotten. But I've never had an inkling of what it could be.

HILDA. You should have tied a knot in your handkerchief, Mr. Solness.

SOLNESS. Then I'd only wind up puzzling over what the knot might mean.

HILDA. Yes, there's even that kind of troll in the world too.

SOLNESS (*slowly gets up*). It's really so good that you've come to me now.

HILDA (*with a probing look*). Is it?

SOLNESS. I've been so alone here—and felt so utterly helpless watching it all. (*Dropping his voice.*) I should tell you—I've begun to grow afraid—so awfully afraid of the young.

HILDA (*sniffing scornfully*).   Pooh! Are the young anything to fear!

SOLNESS.   Decidedly. That's why I've locked and bolted myself in. (*Mysteriously.*) Wait and see, the young will come here, thundering at the door! Breaking in on me!

HILDA.   Then I think you should go out and open your door to the young.

SOLNESS.   Open the door?

HILDA.   Yes. Let them come in to you—as friends.

SOLNESS.   No, no, no! The young—don't you see, they're retribution—the spearhead of change—as if they came marching under some new flag.

HILDA (*rises, looks at him, her lips trembling as she speaks*).   Can you find a use for *me*, Mr. Solness?

SOLNESS.   Oh, of course I can! Because I feel that you've come, too, almost—under some new flag. And then it's youth against youth—!

(DR. HERDAL *comes in by the hall door.*)

HERDAL.   So? You and Miss Wangel still here?

SOLNESS.   Yes. We've had a great many things to talk about.

HILDA.   Both old and new.

HERDAL.   Oh, have you?

HILDA.   Really, it's been such fun. Because Mr. Solness—he's got just a fantastic memory. He remembers the tiniest little details in a flash.

(MRS. SOLNESS *enters by the door to the right.*)

MRS. SOLNESS.   All right, Miss Wangel, your room's all ready for you now.

HILDA.   Oh, how kind of you.

SOLNESS (*to his wife*).   Nursery?

MRS. SOLNESS.   Yes, the middle one. But first we ought to have a bite to eat, don't you think?

SOLNESS (*nodding to* HILDA).   So Hilda sleeps in the nursery, then.

MRS. SOLNESS (*looking at him*).   Hilda?

SOLNESS.   Yes, Miss Wangel's name is Hilda. I knew her when she was small.

MRS. SOLNESS. No, did you really, Halvard? Well—shall we? Supper's waiting.

> (*She takes* DR. HERDAL's *arm and they go out, right.* HILDA *meanwhile gathers up her hiking gear.*)

HILDA (*softly and quickly to* SOLNESS).   Is that true, what you said? *Can* you find a use for me?

SOLNESS (*taking her things away from her*).   You're the one person I've needed the most.

HILDA (*clasping her hands and looking at him with wondering eyes full of joy*).   Oh, you beautiful, big world—!

SOLNESS (*tensely*).   What—?

HILDA.   Then I have my kingdom!

SOLNESS (*involuntarily*).   Hilda—!

HILDA (*her lips suddenly trembling again*). Almost—that's what I meant.

> (*She goes out to the right, with* SOLNESS *following.*)

ACT TWO

An attractively furnished small living room in SOLNESS's *house. A glass door in the back wall opens on the veranda and garden. Diagonally cutting the right-hand corner is a broad bow window with flower stands before it. The left-hand corner is similarly cut by a wall containing a door papered to match. In each of the side walls, an ordinary door. In the right foreground, a console table and a large mirror. Flowers and plants richly displayed. In the left foreground, a sofa, along with table and chairs. Further back, a bookcase. Out in the room in front of the bow window, a little table and a couple of chairs. It is early in the morning.*

  SOLNESS is sitting at the little table with RAGNAR BROV-IK's *portfolio open before him. He is leafing through the drawings and now and then looks sharply at one.* MRS. SOLNESS *moves silently about with a small watering can, freshening the flowers. She wears black, as before. Her hat, coat, and parasol lie on a chair by the mirror. Unnoticed by her,* SOLNESS *follows her several times with his eyes. Neither of them speaks.*

  KAJA FOSLI *comes quietly in by the door on the left.*

SOLNESS (*turns his head and speaks with careless indifference*).   Oh, is that you?

KAJA.   I just wanted to tell you I'm here.

SOLNESS.   Yes, that's fine. Isn't Ragnar there too?

KAJA.   No, not yet. He had to wait a bit for the doctor. But he'll be along soon to find out—

SOLNESS.   How's the old man getting on?

KAJA.   Poorly. He's so very sorry, but he can't leave his bed today.

SOLNESS.   Of course not. He mustn't stir. But you go on to your work.

KAJA.   Yes. (*Pauses at the door.*) Will you want to speak to Ragnar when he gets in?

SOLNESS.   No—I've nothing special to say.

338

(KAJA *goes out again to the left.* SOLNESS *continues to sit and leaf through the drawings.*)

MRS. SOLNESS (*over by the plants*).   I wonder if he won't die now, he too.

SOLNESS (*looking at her*).   He—and who else?

MRS. SOLNESS (*not answering*).   Yes, old Brovik—he's going to die now too, Halvard. You wait and see.

SOLNESS.   Aline dear, couldn't you do with a little walk?

MRS. SOLNESS.   Yes, I really suppose I could. (*She goes on tending the flowers.*)

SOLNESS (*bent over the drawings*).   Is she still sleeping?

MRS. SOLNESS (*looking at him*).   Is it Miss Wangel you're sitting there thinking about?

SOLNESS (*casually*).   I just happened to remember her.

MRS. SOLNESS.   Miss Wangel's been up for hours.

SOLNESS.   Oh, she has?

MRS. SOLNESS.   When I looked in, she was busy arranging her things. (*She goes to the mirror and begins slowly putting her hat on.*)

SOLNESS (*after a short silence*).   So we did find use for one of the nurseries after all, Aline.

MRS. SOLNESS.   Yes, we did.

SOLNESS.   And I think that's better, really, than all of them standing empty.

MRS. SOLNESS.   You're right—that emptiness, it's horrible.

SOLNESS (*closes the portfolio, rises, and approaches her*).   You're only going to see *this*, Aline—that from now on things'll go better for us. Much pleasanter. Life will be easier—especially for you.

MRS. SOLNESS (*looking at him*).   From now on?

SOLNESS.   Yes, believe me, Aline—

MRS. SOLNESS.   You mean—because *she's* come?

SOLNESS (*restraining himself*).   I mean, of course, once we're in the new house.

MRS. SOLNESS (*taking her coat*).   Yes, do you think so, Halvard? That things will go better there?

SOLNESS.   I'm sure of it. And you, don't you have the same feeling?

MRS. SOLNESS.   I feel absolutely nothing about the new house.

SOLNESS (*dejected*).   Well, that's certainly hard for me to hear. It's mostly for your sake that I built it. (*He makes a motion toward helping her on with her coat.*)

MRS. SOLNESS (*evading him*).   As it is, you do all too much for my sake.

SOLNESS (*rather heatedly*).   No, no, Aline, don't talk like that! I can't stand hearing you say such things.

MRS. SOLNESS.   All right, then I won't say them, Halvard.

SOLNESS.   But I swear I'm right. You'll see, it'll go so well for you over there.

MRS. SOLNESS.   Oh, Lord—so well for me—!

SOLNESS (*eagerly*).   Oh yes, it will! Just trust that it will. Because over there—you'll see, there'll be so very much to remind you of your own old home—

MRS. SOLNESS.   Of what was Mother and Father's—that burned to the ground.

SOLNESS (*gently*).   Yes, my poor Aline. That was a terrible blow for you.

MRS. SOLNESS (*breaking out in lamentation*).   You can build as much as you ever want, Halvard—but for *me* you can never build up a real home again.

SOLNESS (*pacing across the room*).   Then, for God's sake, let's not discuss it anymore.

MRS. SOLNESS.   We don't ordinarily discuss it at all. Because you only push it aside—

SOLNESS (*stops short and looks at her*).   Do I? And why should I do that? Push it aside?

MRS. SOLNESS.   Oh, don't you think I know you, Halvard? You want so much to spare me—to find excuses for me, all that you can.

SOLNESS (*eyes wide in amazement*).   For *you*! Is it you—yourself you're talking of, Aline?

MRS. SOLNESS.   Yes, it has to be me, of course.

SOLNESS (*involuntarily, to himself*).   That, too!

MRS. SOLNESS.   After all, with the old house—it couldn't have happened otherwise. Once disaster's on the wind, then—

SOLNESS.   Yes, you're right. There's no running away from trouble—they say.

MRS. SOLNESS.   But it's the horror after the fire—*that's* the thing! That, that, that!

SOLNESS (*vehemently*). Don't think about it, Aline!

MRS. SOLNESS. Oh, but it's what I have to think about, exactly that. And finally talk about for once, too. Because I don't see how I can bear it any longer. And then, never the least chance to forgive myself—!

SOLNESS (*exclaiming*). Yourself!

MRS. SOLNESS. Yes, you know I had my duties on both sides—both to you and to the babies. I should have made myself strong. Not let fear take hold of me so. Or grief either, because my old home had burned. (*Wringing her hands.*) Oh, if I'd only been strong enough, Halvard!

SOLNESS (*softly, moved, coming closer*). Aline—you must promise me never to think these thoughts again. Promise me now.

MRS. SOLNESS. Good heavens—promise! Promise! Anyone can promise—

SOLNESS (*clenching his fists and crossing the room*). Oh, how hopeless it is! Never a touch of sun! Not the least glimmer of light in this home!

MRS. SOLNESS. This is no home, Halvard.

SOLNESS. No, that's true enough. (*Heavily.*) And God knows if you're not right that it'll be no better for us in the new place.

MRS. SOLNESS. It can never be different. Just as empty—just as barren—there as here.

SOLNESS (*fiercely*). But why in the world did we build it, then? Tell me that?

MRS. SOLNESS. No, that answer you'll have to find in yourself.

SOLNESS (*glancing at her suspiciously*). What do you mean by *that*, Aline?

MRS. SOLNESS. What do I mean?

SOLNESS. Yes, damn it—! You said it so strangely—as if you were holding something back.

MRS. SOLNESS. No, I can assure you—

SOLNESS (*coming closer*). Ah, thanks a lot! I know what I know. I've got eyes and ears, Aline, don't forget.

MRS. SOLNESS. But what's this about? What is it?

SOLNESS (*planting himself in front of her*). Aren't you out to discover some sly, hidden meaning in the most innocent thing I say?

MRS. SOLNESS. *I*, you say? *I* do that?

SOLNESS (*laughing*). Of course that's only natural, Aline—when you've got a sick man around to deal with—

MRS. SOLNESS (*anxiously*). Sick? Are you ill, Halvard?

SOLNESS (*in an outburst*). Half mad, then. A crazy man. Anything you want to call me.

MRS. SOLNESS (*groping for a chair and sitting*). Halvard—for God's sake—!

SOLNESS. But you're wrong, both of you. Both you and the doctor. It's no such thing with me. (*He paces back and forth,* MRS. SOLNESS *following him anxiously with her eyes, until he goes over and speaks quietly to her.*) In fact, there's nothing the matter with me at all.

MRS. SOLNESS. No, of course not. But what is it, then, that's upsetting you?

SOLNESS. It's this, that I often feel that I'm going to sink under this awful burden of debt—

MRS. SOLNESS. Debt? But you're not in debt to anyone, Halvard.

SOLNESS (*softly, with emotion*). Infinitely in debt to you—to you, Aline—to you.

MRS. SOLNESS (*rising slowly*). What's back of all this? Might as well tell me right now.

SOLNESS. But nothing's back of it. I've never done anything against you—not that I've ever known. And yet—there's this sense of some enormous guilt hanging over me, crushing me down.

MRS. SOLNESS. A guilt toward *me*?

SOLNESS. Toward you most of all.

MRS. SOLNESS. Then you are—ill, after all, Halvard.

SOLNESS (*wearily*). I suppose so—something like that. (*Looks toward the door to the right, as it opens.*) Ah! But it's brightening up.

> (HILDA WANGEL *comes in. She has made some changes in her clothes and let down her skirt.*)

HILDA. Good morning, Mr. Solness!

SOLNESS (*nodding*). Sleep well?

HILDA. Beautifully! Like a child in a cradle. Oh—I lay and stretched myself like—like a princess.

SOLNESS (*smiling a little*). Just the thing for you.

HILDA. I expect so.

SOLNESS. And I suppose you dreamed?

HILDA.   Oh yes. But that was awful.

SOLNESS.   So?

HILDA.   Yes, 'cause I dreamed I was falling over a terribly high, steep cliff. *You* ever dream such things?

SOLNESS.   Oh yes—now and then—

HILDA.   It's wonderfully thrilling—just to fall and fall.

SOLNESS.   It makes my blood run cold.

HILDA.   You pull your legs up under you while you fall?

SOLNESS.   Of course, as high as possible.

HILDA.   Me too.

MRS. SOLNESS (*taking her parasol*).   I've got to go down into town now, Halvard. (*To* HILDA.) And I'll try to pick up a few of the things you need.

HILDA (*about to throw her arms around her*).   Oh, Mrs. Solness, you're a dear! You're really too kind—terribly kind—

MRS. SOLNESS (*deprecatingly, freeing herself*).   Oh, not at all. It's simply my duty, so I'm quite happy to do it.

HILDA (*piqued and pouting*).   Actually, I don't see any reason why I can't go out myself—with my clothes all neat again. Why can't I?

MRS. SOLNESS.   To tell the truth, I rather think people would be staring at you a bit.

HILDA (*sniffing*).   Pooh! Is that all? But that's fun.

SOLNESS (*with suppressed bad temper*).   Yes, but you see people might get the idea that *you* were mad too.

HILDA.   Mad? Are there so many mad people in town here?

SOLNESS (*points at his forehead*).   Here's one, at least.

HILDA.   You—Mr. Solness!

MRS. SOLNESS.   Oh, Halvard, really!

SOLNESS.   You mean you haven't noticed *that*?

HILDA.   No, I certainly have not. (*Reflects a moment and laughs a little.*) Well, maybe in just one thing.

SOLNESS.   Ah, hear that, Aline?

MRS. SOLNESS.   What sort of thing, Miss Wangel?

HILDA.   I'm not saying.

SOLNESS.   Oh yes, come on!

HILDA.   No thanks—I'm not *that* crazy.

MRS. SOLNESS.   When Miss Wangel and you are alone, I'm sure she'll tell you, Halvard.

SOLNESS.   Oh—you think so?

MRS. SOLNESS. Why, of course. After all, you've known her so well in the past. Ever since she was a child—you tell me. (*She goes out by the door on the left.*)

HILDA (*after a brief pause*).   Does your wife not like me at all?

SOLNESS.   Does it seem so to you?

HILDA.   Couldn't you see it yourself?

SOLNESS (*evasively*).   These last years Aline's become very shy around people.

HILDA.   Has she really?

SOLNESS.   But if only you got to know her well— Because underneath, she's so kind—so good—such a fine person—

HILDA (*impatiently*).   But if she *is* all that—why does she run on so about duty!

SOLNESS.   Duty?

HILDA.   Yes. She said she'd go out and buy me some things because that was her *duty*. Oh, I can't stand that mean, ugly word!

SOLNESS.   Why not?

HILDA.   No, it sounds so cold and sharp and cutting. Duty, duty, duty! Don't you feel it too? As if it's made to cut.

SOLNESS.   Hm—never thought of it, really.

HILDA.   But it's true! And if she's so kind—the way you say—why would she put it like that?

SOLNESS.   But, my Lord, what would you want her to say?

HILDA.   She could have said she'd do it because she liked me a lot. Something like that she could have said. Something really warm and straight from the heart—you know?

SOLNESS (*looking at her*).   Is *that* what you'd want?

HILDA.   Yes, just that. (*She strolls around the room, stopping at the bookcase and examining the books.*)

HILDA.   You have an awful lot of books.

SOLNESS.   Oh, I've picked up a fair number.

HILDA.   Do you read them all, too?

SOLNESS.   I used to try, in the old days. Do *you* do much reading?

HILDA.   No, never! At least, not now. I can't connect with them anymore.

SOLNESS.   It's exactly the same for me.

(HILDA *wanders about a little, stops by the small
table, opens the portfolio and turns over some
sketches.*)

HILDA.   Did you do all these designs?

SOLNESS.   No, they're done by a young man I've had
helping me.

HILDA.   Someone you've been teaching?

SOLNESS.   Oh yes, I guess he's learned something from
me, all right.

HILDA (*sitting*).   Then he must be quite clever, hm?
(*Studies one of the sketches a moment.*) Isn't he?

SOLNESS.   Oh, could be worse. For *my* work, though—

HILDA.   Oh yes! He must be dreadfully clever.

SOLNESS.   You think you can see it in the drawings?

HILDA.   Ffft! These scribbles! But if he's been studying
with *you,* then—

SOLNESS.   Oh, for that matter, there've been plenty of
others who've studied with me, and none of them have ever
come to much.

HILDA (*looks at him, shaking her head*).   For the life of
me, I don't understand how you can be so stupid.

SOLNESS.   Stupid? You really think I'm so stupid?

HILDA.   Yes, really I do. When you can take time to go
on teaching these fellows—

SOLNESS (*with a start*).   Well, why not?

HILDA (*rising, half serious, half laughing*).   Oh, come on,
Mr. Solness! What's the point of it? Nobody but you should
have a right to build. You should be all alone in that. Have
the field to yourself. Now you know.

SOLNESS (*involuntarily*).   Hilda—!

HILDA.   Well?

SOLNESS.   What on earth gave you that idea?

HILDA.   Am I so very wrong, then?

SOLNESS.   No, that's not it. But let me tell you something.

HILDA.   What?

SOLNESS.   Here, in my solitude and silence—endlessly—
I've been brooding on that same idea.

HILDA.   Well, it seems only natural to me.

SOLNESS (*looks rather sharply at her*).   And I'm sure
you've already noticed it.

HILDA. No, not a bit.

SOLNESS. But before—when you said you thought I was—unbalanced, there was one thing—

HILDA. Oh, I was thinking of something quite different.

SOLNESS. What do you mean, different?

HILDA. Never you mind, Mr. Solness.

SOLNESS (*crossing the room*). All right—have it your way. (*Stops at the bow window.*) Come over here, and I'll show you something.

HILDA (*approaching*). What's that?

SOLNESS. You see—out there in the garden—?

HILDA. Yes?

SOLNESS (*pointing*). Right above that big quarry?

HILDA. The new house, you mean?

SOLNESS. The one under construction, yes. Nearly finished.

HILDA. I think it's got a very high tower.

SOLNESS. The scaffolding's still up.

HILDA. That's your new house?

SOLNESS. Yes.

HILDA. The one you're about to move into?

SOLNESS. Yes.

HILDA (*looking at him*). Are there nurseries in that house too?

SOLNESS. Three, same as here.

HILDA. And no children.

SOLNESS. Not now—nor ever.

HILDA (*half smiling*). So, isn't that just what I said—?

SOLNESS. Namely—?

HILDA. Namely, that you are a little—sort of mad, after all.

SOLNESS. Was that what you were thinking of?

HILDA. Yes, of all those empty nurseries I slept in.

SOLNESS (*dropping his voice*). We did have children— Aline and I.

HILDA (*looking intently at him*). You did—?

SOLNESS. Two little boys. Both the same age.

HILDA. Twins.

SOLNESS. Yes, twins. That's some eleven, twelve years ago now.

HILDA (*cautiously*). And both of them are—? The twins—they're not with you anymore?

SOLNESS (*with quiet feeling*).   We had them only about three weeks. Not even that. (*In an outburst.*) Oh, Hilda, how amazingly lucky for me that you've come! Now at last I've got someone I can talk to.

HILDA.   You can't talk with—*her?*

SOLNESS.   Not about this. Not the way I want to and need to. (*Heavily.*) And there's so much else I can never talk out.

HILDA (*her voice subdued*).   Was that all you meant when you said you needed me?

SOLNESS.   Mostly that, I guess. Yesterday, anyhow. Today I'm not so sure—(*Breaking off.*) Come here, Hilda, and let's get settled. Sit there on the sofa—then you can look out in the garden. (HILDA *sits in the corner of the sofa.* SOLNESS *draws over a chair.*) Would you care to hear about it?

HILDA.   Yes, I like listening to you.

SOLNESS (*sitting*).   Then I'll give you the whole story.

HILDA.   Now I'm looking at both the garden and you, Mr. Solness. So tell me. Now!

SOLNESS (*pointing out the bow window*).   Over on that ridge there—where you see the new house—

HILDA.   Yes.

SOLNESS.   That's where Aline and I lived in those early years. There was an old house up there then, one that had belonged to her mother—and then passed on to us. And this whole enormous garden came with it.

HILDA.   Did that house have a tower too?

SOLNESS.   No, not at all. From the outside it was an ugly, dark, overgrown packing case. And yet, for all that, it was snug and cozy enough inside.

HILDA.   Did you tear the old crate down, then?

SOLNESS.   No, it burned.

HILDA.   To the ground?

SOLNESS.   Yes.

HILDA.   Was it a terrible loss for you?

SOLNESS.   Depends how you look at it. As a builder, the fire put me in business—

HILDA.   Well, but—?

SOLNESS.   We'd just had the two little boys at the time—

HILDA.   The poor little twins, yes.

SOLNESS.   They'd come so plump and healthy into life. And every day you could see them growing.

HILDA.   Babies grow fast at the start.

SOLNESS.   There was nothing finer in the world to see than Aline, lying there, holding those two— But then it came, the night of the fire—

HILDA (*excitedly*).   What happened? Go on! Was anyone burned?

SOLNESS.   No, not that. They were all rescued out of the house—

HILDA.   Well, but then what—?

SOLNESS.   The fright shook Aline to the core. The alarms—getting out of the house—and all the confusion— the whole thing at night, in the freezing cold to boot. They had to be carried out just as they lay—both she and the babies.

HILDA.   And they didn't survive?

SOLNESS.   Oh, *they* pulled through it all right. But Aline came down with fever—and it affected her milk. Nurse them herself, she insisted on that. It was her duty, she said. And both of our little boys, they— (*Knotting his hands.*) they—oh!

HILDA.   They couldn't survive that.

SOLNESS.   No, that they couldn't survive. It's how we lost them.

HILDA.   It must have been terribly hard for you.

SOLNESS.   Hard enough for me—but ten times harder for Aline. (*Clenching his fists in suppressed fury.*) Oh, why are such things allowed to happen in life! (*Brusquely and firmly.*) From the day I lost them, I never wanted to build another church.

HILDA.   And the church tower in our town—you disliked doing that?

SOLNESS.   Very much. I remember when it was finished how relieved I felt.

HILDA.   *I* remember too.

SOLNESS.   And now I'll never build those things any-more—never! No church towers, or churches.

HILDA (*nodding slowly*).   Only houses for people to live in.

SOLNESS.   Homes for human beings, Hilda.

HILDA.   But homes with high towers and spires on them.

SOLNESS. If possible. (*In a lighter tone.*) Anyhow—as I said before—the fire put me in business. As a builder, I mean.

HILDA. Why don't you call yourself an architect like the others?

SOLNESS. Never went through the training. Almost all I know I've had to find out for myself.

HILDA. But still you've made a success.

SOLNESS. Out of the fire, yes. I subdivided nearly the whole garden into small lots, where I could build exactly the way I wanted. And after that, things really began to move for me.

HILDA (*looking at him searchingly*). How happy you must be—with the life you've made.

SOLNESS (*darkly*). Happy? You say it too? Same as all the others.

HILDA. Yes, you have to be, I really think so. If you just could stop thinking about the little twins—

SOLNESS (*slowly*). The little twins—they're not so easy to forget, Hilda.

HILDA (*with some uncertainty*). They really still bother you? After so many years?

SOLNESS (*regarding her steadily, without answering*). A happy man, you said—

HILDA. Yes, but aren't you—I mean, otherwise?

SOLNESS (*continues to look at her*). When I told you all that about the fire—

HILDA. Yes?

SOLNESS. Did nothing strike you then—nothing special?

HILDA (*puzzling a moment*). No. Was there something special?

SOLNESS (*quietly stressing his words*). By means of that fire, and that alone, I won my chance to build homes for human beings. Snug, cozy, sunlit homes, where a father and mother and a whole drove of children could live safe and happy, feeling what a sweet thing it is to be alive in this world. And mostly, knowing they belonged to each other—in the big things and the small.

HILDA (*animated*). Yes, but isn't it really a joy for you then, to create these beautiful homes?

SOLNESS. The price, Hilda. The awful price I've had to pay for that chance.

HILDA. But can you never get over that?

SOLNESS. No. For this chance to build homes for others, I've had to give up—give up forever any home of my own—I mean a home for many children. And for their father and mother, too.

HILDA (*delicately*). But did you have to? Absolutely, that is?

SOLNESS (*slowly nodding*). That was the price for my famous luck. Luck—hm. This good luck, Hilda—it couldn't be bought for less.

HILDA (*as before*). But still, mightn't it all work out?

SOLNESS. Never in this world. Never. That also comes out of the fire. And Aline's sickness after.

HILDA (*looks at him with an enigmatic expression*). And so you go and build all these nurseries.

SOLNESS (*seriously*). Have you ever noticed, Hilda, how the impossible—how it seems to whisper and call to you?

HILDA (*reflecting*). The impossible? (*Vivaciously.*) Oh yes! *You* know it too?

SOLNESS. Yes.

HILDA. Then I guess there's—something of a troll in you as well?

SOLNESS. Why a troll?

HILDA. Well, what would *you* call it, then?

SOLNESS (*getting up*). Hm, yes, could be. (*Furiously.*) But why shouldn't the troll be in me—the way things go for me all the time, in everything! In everything!

HILDA. What do you mean?

SOLNESS (*hushed and inwardly stirred*). Pay attention to what I tell you, Hilda. All I've been given to do, to build and shape into beauty, security, a good life—into even a kind of splendor— (*Knotting his fists.*) Oh, how awful just to think of it—!

HILDA. What's so awful?

SOLNESS. That I've got to make up for it all. Pay up. Not with money, but with human happiness. And not just my own happiness. With others', too. You understand, Hilda! That's the price my name as an artist has cost me—and others. And every single day I've got to look on here and see that price being paid for me again and again—over and over and over, endlessly!

HILDA (*rises, looking intently at him*).   Now you're think-ing of—of her.

SOLNESS.   Yes, mostly of Aline. Because Aline—she had her lifework too—just as I had mine. (*His voice trembles.*) But *her* lifework had to be cut down, crushed, broken to bits, so that mine could win through to—to some kind of great victory. Aline, you know—she had a talent for build-ing too.

HILDA.   She! For building?

SOLNESS (*shaking his head*).   Not houses and towers and spires—the kind of thing I do—

HILDA.   What, then?

SOLNESS (*gently, with feeling*).   For building up the small souls of children, Hilda. Building those souls up to stand on their own, poised, in beautiful, noble forms—till they'd grown into the upright human spirit. *That's* what Aline had a talent for. And now, there it lies, all of it—unused and useless forever. And for what earthly reason. Just like charred ruins after a fire.

HILDA.   Yes, but even if this were so—?

SOLNESS.   It *is* so! It *is!* I know.

HILDA.   Well, but in any case it's not *your* fault.

SOLNESS (*fixing his eyes on her and nodding slowly*).   Ah, you see—that's the enormous, ugly riddle—the doubt that gnaws at me day and night.

HILDA.   That?

SOLNESS.   Put it this way. Suppose it *was* my fault, in some sense.

HILDA.   You! For the fire?

SOLNESS.   For everything, the whole business. And yet, perhaps—completely innocent all the same.

HILDA (*looks at him anxiously*).   Mr. Solness—when you can talk like that, then it sounds like you are—ill, after all.

SOLNESS.   Hm—I don't think I'll ever be quite sound in that department.

(RAGNAR BROVIK *cautiously opens the small cor-ner door at the left.* HILDA *crosses the room.*)

RAGNAR (*on seeing* HILDA).   Oh—excuse me, Mr. Sol-ness. *(He starts to leave.)*

SOLNESS.   No, no, don't go. Let's be done with it.

RAGNAR.   Yes, if we only could!

SOLNESS. Your father's no better, I hear.

RAGNAR. He's going downhill fast now. And that's why I'm begging you, please—give me a good word or two, just something on one of the drawings for Father to read before he—

SOLNESS (*explosively*). Stop talking to me about those drawings of yours!

RAGNAR. Have you looked them over?

SOLNESS. Yes—I have.

RAGNAR. And they're worthless? And no doubt I'm worthless too?

SOLNESS (*evasively*). You stay on here with me, Ragnar. You'll get everything the way you want it. You can marry Kaja then and have it easy—happy even. Just don't think about doing your own building.

RAGNAR. Oh, sure, I should go home and tell that to my father. Because I promised to. *Shall* I tell him that— before he dies?

SOLNESS (*with a groan*). Oh, tell him—tell him—don't ask me what to say! Anything. Better still to say nothing. (*In an outburst.*) I can't do any more than I'm doing, Ragnar.

RAGNAR. May I take along my drawings, then?

SOLNESS. Yes, take them—help yourself! They're on the table.

RAGNAR (*going to the table*). Thanks.

HILDA (*putting her hand on the portfolio*). No, no, leave them.

SOLNESS. Why?

HILDA. Because *I* want to see them too.

SOLNESS. But you've already— (*To* RAGNAR.) All right, then, just leave them.

RAGNAR. Gladly.

SOLNESS. And go right home to your father.

RAGNAR. Yes, I guess I'll have to.

SOLNESS (*with an air of desperation*). Ragnar—don't ask me for what I can't give! You hear, Ragnar? You mustn't!

RAGNAR. No, no. Excuse me— (*He bows and goes out through the corner door.* HILDA *goes over and sits on a chair by the mirror.*)

HILDA (*looking angrily at* SOLNESS). That was really mean of you.

SOLNESS.   You think so too?

HILDA.   Yes, it was terribly mean. And hard and wicked and cruel.

SOLNESS.   You don't know my side of it.

HILDA.   All the same. No, you shouldn't be like that.

SOLNESS.   You were only just now saying that no one but me should be allowed to build.

HILDA.   *I* can say that—but *you* mustn't.

SOLNESS.   But I can, most of all—when I've paid such a price for my recognition.

HILDA.   That's right—with what you think of as the comfortable life—that sort of thing.

SOLNESS.   And my inner peace in the bargain.

HILDA (*rising*).   Inner peace! (*Intensely.*) Yes, yes, you're right! Poor Mr. Solness—you imagine that—

SOLNESS (*with a quiet laugh*).   Sit down again, Hilda—if you want to hear something funny.

HILDA (*expectantly, sitting down*).   Well?

SOLNESS.   It sounds like such a ridiculous little thing. You see, the whole business revolves about no more than a crack in a chimney.

HILDA.   Nothing else?

SOLNESS.   No; at least, not at the start. (*He moves a chair closer to* HILDA *and sits.*)

HILDA (*impatiently, tapping her knee*).   So—the crack in the chimney!

SOLNESS.   I'd noticed that tiny opening in the flue long, long before the fire. Every time I was up in the attic, I checked to see that it was still there.

HILDA.   And was it?

SOLNESS.   Yes. Because no one else knew.

HILDA.   And you said nothing?

SOLNESS.   No. Nothing.

HILDA.   Never thought of fixing the flue, either?

SOLNESS.   I thought, yes—but never got to it. Every time I wanted to start repairing it, it was exactly as if a hand were there, holding me back. Not today, I'd think. Tomorrow. So nothing came of it.

HILDA.   But why did you keep on postponing?

SOLNESS.   Because I went on thinking. (*Slowly, in an undertone.*) Through that little black opening in the chimney I could force my way to success—as a builder.

HILDA (*looking straight ahead of her*).   That must have been thrilling.

SOLNESS.   Irresistible, almost. Completely irresistible. Because the whole thing, then, seemed so easy and obvious to me. I wanted it to happen on some winter's day, a little before noon. I'd be out with Aline for a drive in the sleigh. The people at home would have fires blazing in the stoves—

HILDA.   Yes, because the day should be bitterly cold—

SOLNESS.   Yes, quite raw. And they'd want it snug and warm for Aline when she got in.

HILDA.   Because I'm sure her temperature's normally low.

SOLNESS.   It is, you know. So then, driving home it was, that we were supposed to see the smoke.

HILDA.   Only the smoke?

SOLNESS.   The smoke first. But when we'd pull in at the garden gate, there the old packing case would stand, a roaring inferno. At least, that's how I wanted it.

HILDA.   Oh, but if it only could have gone that way!

SOLNESS.   Yes, you can say that well enough, Hilda.

HILDA.   But wait a minute, Mr. Solness—how can you be so sure the fire started from that little crack in the chimney?

SOLNESS.   I can't, not at all. In fact, I'm absolutely certain it had nothing whatever to do with the fire.

HILDA.   What!

SOLNESS.   It's been proved without a shadow of a doubt that the fire broke out in a clothes closet, in quite another part of the house.

HILDA.   Then what's the point in all this sitting and mooning around about a cracked chimney!

SOLNESS.   You mind if I go on talking a bit, Hilda?

HILDA.   No, if only you'll talk sense—

SOLNESS.   I'll try. (*He moves his chair in closer.*)

HILDA.   So—go on then, Mr. Solness.

SOLNESS (*confidingly*).   Don't you believe with me, Hilda, that there are certain special, chosen people who have a gift and power and capacity to *wish* something, *desire* something, *will* something—so insistently and so—so inevitably—that at last it *has* to be theirs? Don't you believe that?

HILDA (*with an inscrutable look in her eyes*). If that's true, then we'll see someday—if *I'm* one of the chosen.

SOLNESS. It's not one's self alone that makes great things. Oh no—the helpers and servers—they've got to be with you if you're going to succeed. But they never come by themselves. One has to call on them, incessantly—within oneself, I mean.

HILDA. What are these helpers and servers?

SOLNESS. Oh, we can talk about that some other time. Let's stay with the fire now.

HILDA. Don't you think the fire still would have come— even if you hadn't wished it?

SOLNESS. If old Knut Brovik had owned the house, it never would have burned down so conveniently for him— I'm positive of that. Because he doesn't know how to call on the helpers, or the servers either. (*Gets up restlessly.*) So you see, Hilda—it *is* my fault that the twins had to die. And isn't it my fault, too, that Aline's never become the woman she could have and should have been? And wanted to be, more than anything?

HILDA. Yes, but if it's really these helpers and servers, then—?

SOLNESS. Who called for the helpers and servers? I did! And they came and did what I willed. (*In rising agitation.*) That's what all the nice people call "having the luck." But I can tell you what this luck feels like. It feels as if a big piece of skin had been stripped, right here, from my chest. And the helpers and servers go on flaying the skin off other people to patch *my* wound. But the wound never heals— never! Oh, if you knew how sometimes it leeches and burns.

HILDA (*looking at him attentively*). You *are* ill, Mr. Solness. Very ill, I almost think.

SOLNESS. Insane. You can say it. It's what you mean.

HILDA. No, I don't think you've lost your reason.

SOLNESS. *What,* then? Out with it!

HILDA. I'm wondering if maybe you didn't enter life with a frail conscience.

SOLNESS. A frail conscience? What in hell's name does that mean?

HILDA. I mean your conscience is very fragile. Overrefined, sort of. It isn't made to struggle with things—to pick up what's heavy and bear it.

SOLNESS (*growling*).   Hm! And what kind of conscience do you recommend?

HILDA.   I could wish that your conscience was—well, quite robust.

SOLNESS.   Oh? Robust? And I suppose *you* have a robust conscience?

HILDA.   Yes, I think so. I've never noticed it wasn't.

SOLNESS.   I'd say you've never had a real test to face up to, either.

HILDA (*with tremulous lips*).   Oh, it wasn't so easy to leave Father, when I'm so terribly fond of him.

SOLNESS.   Come on! Just for a month or two—

HILDA.   I'm never going home again.

SOLNESS.   Never? Why did you leave home, then?

HILDA (*half serious, half teasing*).   You still keep forgetting that the ten years are up?

SOLNESS.   Nonsense. Was something wrong there at home? Hm?

HILDA (*fully serious*).   It was inside me, something goading and driving me here. Coaxing and luring me, too.

SOLNESS (*eagerly*).   That's it! That's it, Hilda! There's a troll in you—same as in me. It's that troll in us, don't you see—that's what calls on the powers out there. And then we *have* to give in—whether we want to or not.

HILDA.   I almost believe you're right, Mr. Solness.

SOLNESS (*walking about the room*).   Oh, Hilda, there are so many devils one can't see loose in the world!

HILDA.   Devils, too?

SOLNESS (*stops*).   Good devils and bad devils. Blond devils and black-haired ones. And if only you always knew if the light or the dark ones had you! (*Pacing about; with a laugh.*) Wouldn't it be simple then!

HILDA (*her eyes following him*).   Or if you had a really strong conscience, brimming with health—so you could dare what you most wanted.

SOLNESS (*stopping by the console table*).   Still, I think most people, in this respect, are just as weak as I am.

HILDA.   Probably.

SOLNESS (*leaning against the table*).   In the sagas— Ever done any reading in the old sagas?

HILDA.   Oh yes! In the days when I used to read books—

SOLNESS.   In the sagas it tells about Vikings that sailed

to foreign countries and plundered and burned and killed the men—

HILDA.   And captured the women—

SOLNESS.   And carried them off—

HILDA.   Took them home in their ships—

SOLNESS.   And treated them like—like the worst of trolls.

HILDA (*looking straight ahead with half-veiled eyes*). I think that must have been thrilling.

SOLNESS (*with a short, deep laugh*).   Capturing women, hm?

HILDA.   *Being* captured.

SOLNESS (*studying her a moment*).   I see.

HILDA (*as if breaking the train of thought*).   But what are you getting at with all these Vikings, Mr. Solness?

SOLNESS.   Just that there's your robust conscience—in *those* boys! When they got back home, they went on eating and drinking and living lighthearted as children. And the women as well! They soon had no urge, most of them, ever to give up their men. Does that make sense to you, Hilda?

HILDA.   Those women make perfect sense to me.

SOLNESS.   Aha! Perhaps you could go and do likewise?

HILDA.   Why not?

SOLNESS.   Live, of your own free will, with a barbarian like that?

HILDA.   If it was a barbarian that I really loved—

SOLNESS.   But *could* you ever love one?

HILDA.   My Lord, you don't just plan whom you're going to love.

SOLNESS (*gazing thoughtfully at her*).   No—I suppose it's the troll within that decides.

HILDA (*half laughing*).   Yes, and all those enchanting little devils—your friends. The blond and the black-haired both.

SOLNESS (*with quiet warmth*).   Then I'll ask that the devils choose tenderly for you, Hilda.

HILDA.   For me they've already chosen. Now and forever.

SOLNESS (*looks at her probingly*).   Hilda—you're like some wild bird of the woods.

HILDA.   Hardly. I don't go hiding away under bushes.

SOLNESS.   No. No, there's more in you of the bird of prey.

HILDA.   More that—perhaps. (*With great vehemence.*) And why not a bird of prey? Why shouldn't I go hunting as well? Take the spoil I'm after? If I can once set my claws in it and have my own way.

SOLNESS.   Hilda—you know what you are?

HILDA.   Yes, I'm some strange kind of bird.

SOLNESS.   No. You're like a dawning day. When I look at you—then it's as if I looked into the sunrise.

HILDA.   Tell me, Mr. Solness—are you quite sure that you've never called for me? Within yourself, I mean?

SOLNESS (*slowly and softly*).   I almost think I must have.

HILDA.   What did you want with me?

SOLNESS.   You, Hilda, are youth.

HILDA (*smiles*).   Youth that you're so afraid of?

SOLNESS (*nodding slowly*).   And that, deep within me, I'm so much hungering for.

(HILDA *rises, goes over to the small table, and takes up* RAGNAR BROVIK's *portfolio.*)

HILDA (*holding the portfolio out toward him*).   Then, about these drawings—

SOLNESS (*sharply, waving them aside*).   Put those things away! I've seen enough of them.

HILDA.   Yes, but you've got to write your comment on them.

SOLNESS.   Write a comment! Never!

HILDA.   But now, with that poor old man near death! Can't you do him and his son a kindness before they're parted? And maybe later he could build from these drawings.

SOLNESS.   Yes, that's exactly what he would do. The young pup's made sure of that.

HILDA.   But, my Lord, if that's all—then can't you tell a little white lie?

SOLNESS.   A lie? (*Furious.*) Hilda—get away with those damned drawings!

HILDA (*pulls back the portfolio a bit*).   Now, now, now— don't bite me. You talk about trolls. I think you're acting like a troll yourself. (*Glancing about.*) Where's your pen and ink?

SOLNESS.   Haven't got any.

HILDA (*going toward the door*).   But out there where that girl works—

SOLNESS.   Hilda, stay here—! You said I could lie a little. Well, I guess, for the old man's sake, I could manage it. I did beat him down in his time—and broke him—

HILDA.   Him too?

SOLNESS.   I had to have room for myself. But this Ragnar—he mustn't be given the least chance to rise.

HILDA.   Poor boy, his chances are slim enough—if he simply hasn't got it in him—

SOLNSSS (*comes closer, looks at her and whispers*).   If Ragnar Brovik gets his chance, he'll hammer me to the ground. Break me—same as I broke his father.

HILDA.   Break you? Can he do that?

SOLNESS.   You bet he can! He's all the youth that's waiting to come thundering at my door—to do away with master builder Solness.

HILDA (*with a quietly reproachful look*).   And so you'll still try to lock him out. For shame, Mr. Solness!

SOLNESS.   It's cost me heart's blood enough to fight my battle. And then—the helpers and servers, I'm afraid they won't obey me anymore.

HILDA.   Then you'll have to get along on your own, that's all.

SOLNESS.   Hopeless, Hilda. The change, it's coming. Maybe a little sooner, maybe later. But the retribution—it's inescapable.

HILDA (*pressing her hands to her ears in fright*).   Don't say those things! You want to kill me? You want to take what's even more than my life?

SOLNESS.   And what's that?

HILDA.   I want to see you great. See you with a wreath in your hand—high, high up on a church tower! (*Calm again.*) So—out with your pencil. You do have a pencil on you?

SOLNESS (*brings one out with his pocket sketchbook*).   Here's one.

HILDA (*puts the portfolio down on the table*).   Good. Now let's get settled here, Mr. Solness, the two of us.

(SOLNESS *sits at the table.* HILDA, *behind him, leans over the back of his chair.*)

HILDA. And now let's write on these drawings—something really warm and nice—for this nasty Roar—or whoever he is.

SOLNESS (*writes a few lines, then turns his head and looks up at her*). Tell me one thing, Hilda.

HILDA. Yes?

SOLNESS. If you've really been waiting for me all these ten years—

HILDA. Then what?

SOLNESS. Why didn't you write to me? I could have answered you then.

HILDA (*hurriedly*). No, no, no! That's just what I didn't want.

SOLNESS. Why not?

HILDA. I was afraid then the whole thing'd be ruined— But we should be writing on the drawings, Mr. Solness.

SOLNESS. Yes, of course.

HILDA (*bends forward, watching as he writes*). Something heartfelt and kind. Oh, how I hate—how I hate this Roald—

SOLNESS (*writing*). Have you never really loved anyone, Hilda?

HILDA (*harshly*). What did you say?

SOLNESS. Have you never loved anyone?

HILDA. Anyone else. Is that what you mean?

SOLNESS (*glancing up at her*). Anyone else, yes. You never have—in ten whole years? Never?

HILDA. Oh yes, now and then. When I was really furious at you for not coming.

SOLNESS. So you did care for others too?

HILDA. A little bit—for a week or so. Oh, honestly, Mr. Solness, you ought to know that kind of thing.

SOLNESS. Hilda—what are you here for?

HILDA. Don't waste time talking. That poor old man could easily be dying on us.

SOLNESS. Answer me, Hilda. What do you want from me?

HILDA. I want my kingdom.

SOLNESS. Hm—

> (*He gives a quick glance toward the door on the left and resumes writing on the drawings. At*

the same moment MRS. SOLNESS *enters; she has several packages with her.*)

MRS. SOLNESS.   I brought along a little something here for you, Miss Wangel. They'll send the big parcels out later.

HILDA.   Oh, how wonderfully kind of you!

MRS. SOLNESS.   No more than my duty, that's all.

SOLNESS (*reading over his comments*).   Aline.

MRS. SOLNESS.   Yes?

SOLNESS.   Did you notice if she—if the bookkeeper's out there?

MRS. SOLNESS.   Oh *she's* there, don't worry.

SOLNESS (*sliding the drawings back in the portfolio*). Hm—

MRS. SOLNESS.   She's right at her desk, as she always is—whenever *I* go through the room.

SOLNESS (*getting up*).   Then I'll give her this, and tell her that—

HILDA (*taking the portfolio from him*).   Oh no, let me have the pleasure. (*Goes toward the door, then turns.*) What's her name?

SOLNESS.   Miss Fosli.

HILDA.   Ah, that's much too cold! I mean her first name.

SOLNESS.   Kaja—I think.

HILDA (*opens the door and calls*).   Kaja, come in here! Hurry up! The master builder wants to speak to you.

(KAJA FOSLI *appears at the door.*)

KAJA (*looking fearfully at him*).   Here I am—?

HILDA (*handing her the portfolio*).   See here, Kaja—you can have this now. The master builder's written his opinion.

KAJA.   Oh, at last!

SOLNESS.   Get it to old Brovik soon as you can.

KAJA.   I'll go right over with it.

SOLNESS.   Yes, go on. Now Ragnar can do some building.

KAJA.   Oh, can he stop by and thank you for all—?

SOLNESS (*sharply*).   I want no thanks! Tell him that, with my respects.

KAJA.   Yes, I'll—

SOLNESS.   And tell him as well that hereafter I won't be needing his services. Nor yours, either.

KAJA (*her voice low and quavering*). Nor mine, either?

SOLNESS. You'll have other things to think about now. A lot to do. And that's only right. So run along home with the drawings, Miss Fosli. Quick! Hear me?

KAJA (*as before*). Yes, Mr. Solness. (*She goes out.*)

MRS. SOLNESS. My, what scheming eyes she has.

SOLNESS. She? That poor little fool.

MRS. SOLNESS. Oh—I see just what I see, Halvard. Are you really letting them go?

SOLNESS. Yes.

MRS. SOLNESS. Her too?

SOLNESS. Isn't that the way you wanted it?

MRS. SOLNESS. But to get rid of *her*—? Oh, well, Halvard, I'm sure you have one in reserve.

HILDA (*playfully*). As for me, I just can't function behind a desk.

SOLNESS. There, there, now—it'll all work out, Aline. Don't think of anything now except moving into the new home—as soon as you can. We'll be hanging the wreath up this evening—(*Turning to* HILDA.) way up high at the top of the tower. What do you say to that, Miss Hilda?

HILDA (*gazing at him with sparkling eyes*). It'll be so marvelous seeing you high up there again!

SOLNESS. Me!

MRS. SOLNESS. For heaven's sake, Miss Wangel, what are you thinking of! My husband—who gets so dizzy!

HILDA. He dizzy? Impossible!

MRS. SOLNESS. Oh yes, it's true, though.

HILDA. But I've seen him myself, right at the top of a high church tower!

MRS. SOLNESS. Yes, I've heard people talk about that. But it's so completely impossible—

SOLNESS (*forcefully*). Impossible—yes, impossible! But all the same I stood there!

MRS. SOLNESS. Oh, Halvard, how can you say that? You can't even bear going out on the second-story balcony here. You've always been like that.

SOLNESS. Maybe this evening you'll see something new.

MRS. SOLNESS (*terrified*). No, no, no, I hope to God I never see that! I'm getting in touch with the doctor right away. He'll know how to stop you from this.

SOLNESS. But Aline—!

MRS. SOLNESS.   Yes, because you know you're sick, Halvard. This only proves it! God—oh, God! (*She goes hurriedly out to the right.*)

HILDA (*looking intently at him*).   *Is* it true, or isn't it?

SOLNESS.   That I get dizzy?

HILDA.   That my master builder dares not—and *can* not climb as high as he builds?

SOLNESS.   Is that the way you see it?

HILDA.   Yes.

SOLNESS.   I think soon I won't have a corner in me safe from you.

HILDA (*looking toward the bow window*).   So then, up. Right up there.

SOLNESS (*coming closer*).   In the topmost room of the tower—that's where you could live, Hilda—live like a princess.

HILDA (*ambiguously; half playing, half serious*).   Sure, it's what you promised.

SOLNESS.   Did I really?

HILDA.   Oh, come on, Mr. Solness! You said I'd be a princess—and you'd give me a kingdom. So you went and—well?

SOLNESS (*warily*).   Are you quite positive this isn't some kind of dream—some fantasy that's taken hold of you?

HILDA (*caustically*).   Meaning you didn't do it, hm?

SOLNESS.   I hardly know myself. (*Dropping his voice.*) But one thing I know for certain—that I—

HILDA.   That you—? Go on!

SOLNESS.   That I *ought* to have done it.

HILDA (*exclaiming spiritedly*).   *You* could never be dizzy!

SOLNESS.   So we'll hang the wreath this evening—Princess Hilda.

HILDA (*with a wry face*).   Over your new home, yes.

SOLNESS.   Over the new house—that'll never be home for me. (*He goes out by the garden door.*)

HILDA (*looks straight ahead with a veiled look, whispering to herself. The only words heard are:*) Terribly thrilling—

ACT THREE

A large, broad veranda, part of SOLNESS's *house. A portion of the house, with a door leading onto the veranda, is visible left. A railing running along it to the right. Far back at the end of the veranda, steps lead down to the garden below. Huge old trees in the garden spread their branches over the veranda and toward the house. Through the trees at the far right, a glimpse of the lower structure of the new house, scaffolding rising around the base of the tower. In the background, the garden is bordered by an old wooden fence. Beyond the fence, a street with small, low, dilapidated houses. The evening sky is streaked with sunlit clouds.*

On the veranda a garden bench stands along the wall of the house, and in front of the bench a long table. On the other side of the table are an armchair and some stools. All the furniture is wickerwork.

MRS. SOLNESS, *wrapped in a large white crepe shawl, sits resting in the armchair and gazing off to the right. After a moment* HILDA WANGEL *comes up the steps from the garden. She is dressed the same as before and is wearing her hat. On her blouse she has a little bouquet of small common flowers.*

MRS. SOLNESS (*turning her head slightly*).   Have you had a walk in the garden, Miss Wangel?

HILDA.   Yes, I've been having a look around.

MRS. SOLNESS.   And found some flowers too, I see.

HILDA.   Oh yes! They're just growing thick in through the bushes.

MRS. SOLNESS.   Oh, are they really? Still? I hardly ever get down there, you know.

HILDA (*approaching*).   Honestly? You don't run down to the garden every day?

MRS. SOLNESS (*with a faint smile*).   I don't "run" any place, not anymore.

364

HILDA.   Well, but don't you go down even once in a while and visit all those lovely things?

MRS. SOLNESS.   It's grown so strange to me, all of it. I'm almost frightened of seeing it again.

HILDA.   Your own garden!

MRS. SOLNESS.   I don't feel it's mine anymore.

HILDA.   What's *that* mean—?

MRS. SOLNESS.   No, no, it isn't. Not what it used to be, in Mother and Father's time. They've taken so much of the garden away, it's painful, Miss Wangel. Can you imagine—they've cut it up and built houses for strangers. People I don't know. And they can sit at their windows and look in on me.

HILDA (*her face lighting up*).   Mrs. Solness?

MRS. SOLNESS.   Yes?

HILDA.   May I stay here a while with you?

MRS. SOLNESS.   Yes, of course, if you want to.

HILDA (*moving a stool over to the armchair and sitting*).   Ah—you can sit and really sun yourself here, like a cat.

MRS. SOLNESS (*laying her hand gently on* HILDA'S *neck*).   It's kind of you to want to sit with me. I thought you'd be going in to my husband.

HILDA.   What would I want with him?

MRS. SOLNESS.   To help him, I thought.

HILDA.   No, thanks. Besides, he's not in. He's over there with the workmen. But he looked so ferocious I didn't dare speak to him.

MRS. SOLNESS.   Oh, underneath he's so mild and softhearted.

HILDA.   *Him!*

MRS. SOLNESS.   You hardly know him yet, Miss Wangel.

HILDA (*looking at her warmly*).   Are you happy to be moving into the new place?

MRS. SOLNESS.   I *should* be happy. It's what Halvard wants—

HILDA.   Oh, but not just for that reason.

MRS. SOLNESS.   Oh yes, Miss Wangel. For that's no more than my duty, giving in to him. But it isn't always so easy forcing your thoughts to obey.

HILDA.   I'm sure it can't be.

MRS. SOLNESS. Believe me, it's not, When one's no better a person than I am, then—

HILDA. You mean, when one's gone through all the sorrow you have—

MRS. SOLNESS. How did you hear of that?

HILDA. Your husband told me.

MRS. SOLNESS. With me he hardly ever mentions those things. Yes, I've been through more than my share in life, Miss Wangel.

HILDA (*regarding her sympathetically and slowly nodding*). Poor Mrs. Solness. First you had the fire—

MRS. SOLNESS (*with a sigh*). Yes. Everything of mine burned.

HILDA. And then what was worse followed.

MRS. SOLNESS (*looks questioningly at her*). Worse?

HILDA. The worst of all.

MRS. SOLNESS. What do you mean?

HILDA (*softly*). You lost your two little boys.

MRS. SOLNESS. Oh, *them*, yes. Yes, you see, that's something quite different, that. That was an act of Providence, you know. And there one can only bow one's head and submit. And be grateful.

HILDA. And are you?

MRS. SOLNESS. Not always, I'm afraid. I know very well it's my duty. But all the same, I *can't*.

HILDA. Of course not. That's only natural.

MRS. SOLNESS. And time and again I have to remind myself that it was a just punishment for me—

HILDA. Why?

MRS. SOLNESS. Because I wasn't staunch enough under misfortune.

HILDA. But I don't see that—

MRS. SOLNESS. Oh no, no, Miss Wangel. Don't talk anymore to me about the two little boys. We can only be happy for them. Because they're well off—so well off now. No, it's the small losses in life that strike at your heart. Losing all of those things that other people value at next to nothing.

HILDA (*laying her arms on* MRS. SOLNESS's *knee and looking up at her fondly*). Dear Mrs. Solness—what sort of things? Tell me.

MRS. SOLNESS. As I say—just little things. There were

all the old portraits on the walls that burned. And all the old silk dresses. They'd been in the family for ever so long, generations—they burned. And all Mother's and Grandmother's lace—that burned too. And just think—their jewels! (*Heavily.*) And then, all the dolls.

HILDA.   The dolls?

MRS. SOLNESS (*choking with tears*).   I had nine beautiful dolls.

HILDA.   And they burned also?

MRS. SOLNESS.   All of them. Oh, that was hard—so hard for me.

HILDA.   Were they dolls that you'd had put away, ever since you were little?

MRS. SOLNESS.   Not put away. I and the dolls had gone on living together.

HILDA.   After you'd grown up?

MRS. SOLNESS.   Yes, long after that.

HILDA.   After you were married, too?

MRS. SOLNESS.   Oh yes. As long as he didn't see them, then— But then, poor things, they were all burned up. No one ever thought about saving *them*. Oh, it's so sad to remember. Now you mustn't laugh at me, Miss Wangel.

HILDA.   I'm not laughing a bit.

MRS. SOLNESS.   Because, you see, in a way there was life in them too. I used to carry them under my heart. Just like little unborn children.

(DR. HERDAL, *with his hat in his hands, comes out through the door and spots* MRS. SOLNESS *and* HILDA.)

DR. HERDAL.   So you're out here, Mrs. Solness, catching yourself a cold, hm?

MRS. SOLNESS.   It seems so nice and warm here today.

DR. HERDAL.   All right. But is something the matter? I got a note from you.

MRS. SOLNESS (*getting up*).   Yes, there's something I have to talk to you about.

DR. HERDAL.   Fine. Perhaps we'd better go in, then. (*To* HILDA.)   Still dressed for climbing mountains, hm?

HILDA (*gaily, rising*).   That's right—full gear! But I won't be climbing and breaking my neck today. We two are going to stay quietly down below and watch, Doctor.

DR. HERDAL. Watch what?

MRS. SOLNESS (*to* HILDA, *in a low, frightened voice*). Shh, shh—for God's sake! He's coming. Just try and get him out of this wild idea. And then, do let's be friends, Miss Wangel. Can't we be?

HILDA (*throwing her arms impetuously around* MRS. SOLNESS). Oh—if we only could!

MRS. SOLNESS (*gently disengaging herself*). Oh-oh-oh! There he is, Doctor. We've got to talk.

DR. HERDAL. Is this about *him*?

MRS. SOLNESS. Of course it is. Just come inside.

(*She and* DR. HERDAL *enter the house. A moment after,* SOLNESS *comes up the steps from the garden. A serious look comes over* HILDA'S *face.*)

SOLNESS (*glancing toward the door of the house, carefully being closed from within*). Have you noticed something, Hilda—that the moment I come, she goes?

HILDA. I've noticed that the moment you come, you *make* her go.

SOLNESS. Maybe so. But I can't help that. (*Scrutinizing her.*) Are you cold, Hilda? You rather look it to me.

HILDA. I've just come up out of a tomb.

SOLNESS. Now what's that mean?

HILDA. That I've been chilled right to the bone, Mr. Solness.

SOLNESS (*slowly*). I think I understand—

HILDA. What do you want here now?

SOLNESS. I caught sight of you from over there.

HILDA. But then you must have seen her too, hm?

SOLNESS. I knew she'd leave immediately if I came.

HILDA. Is it very hard on you, that she keeps on avoiding you like this?

SOLNESS. In a way it's almost a relief.

HILDA. That you don't have her right under your eyes?

SOLNESS. Yes.

HILDA. And you're not always seeing how she broods over this business of the children?

SOLNESS. Yes. Mostly that.

(HILDA *saunters across the veranda with her hands behind her back, takes a stance at the railing, and looks out over the garden.*)

SOLNESS (*after a short pause*).   Did you talk with her quite a while? (HILDA *remains motionless, without answering.*) I'm asking, did you talk quite a while? (HILDA *says nothing.*) What did she talk about, Hilda? (HILDA *stays silent.*) Poor Aline! It was the twins, I suppose. (HILDA *shudders nervously, then quickly nods several times.*) She'll never get over it. Never in this world. (*Coming closer.*) Now you're standing there like a statue again. The same as last night.

HILDA (*turns and looks at him with great, serious eyes*). I'm going away.

SOLNESS (*sharply*).   Away!

HILDA.   Yes.

SOLNESS.   But I won't let you!

HILDA.   What can I do here now?

SOLNESS.   Just *be* here, Hilda!

HILDA (*looking him up and down*).   Sure, thanks a lot. You know it wouldn't stop there.

SOLNESS (*wildly*).   So much the better.

HILDA (*with intensity*).   I just *can't* hurt somebody I *know*! Or take away something that's really hers—

SOLNESS.   Who wants you to?

HILDA.   A stranger, yes. Because that's different, completely! Someone I never laid eyes on. But somebody I've gotten close to—! No, not that! Never!

SOLNESS.   But what have I ever suggested?

HILDA.   Oh, master builder, you know so well what would happen. And that's why I'm going away.

SOLNESS.   And what'll become of me when you're gone What'll I have to live for then? Afterwards?

HILDA (*with the inscrutable look in her eyes*).   There's no real problem for you. You have your duties to her. Live for those duties.

SOLNESS.   Too late. These powers—these—these—

HILDA.   Devils—

SOLNESS.   Yes, devils! And the troll inside me too— they've sucked all the lifeblood out of her. (*With a desperate laugh.*) They did it to make me happy! Successful! And now she's dead—thanks to me. And I'm alive, chained to the dead. (*In anguish.*) I—I, who can't go on living without joy in life!

> (HILDA *goes around the table and sits on the bench with her elbows on the table and her head propped in her hands.*)

HILDA (*after watching him a while*).   What are you building next?

SOLNESS (*shaking his head*).   Don't think I'll build much more now.

HILDA.   No more warm, happy homes for mothers and fathers—and droves of children?

SOLNESS.   Who knows if there'll be any use for such homes in the future.

HILDA.   Poor master builder! And you who've gone all these ten years and put your life into—nothing but that.

SOLNESS.   Yes, you might as well say it, Hilda.

HILDA (*in an outburst*).   Oh, it's just so senseless, really, so senseless—the whole thing!

SOLNESS.   What whole thing?

HILDA.   Not daring to take hold of one's own happiness. Of one's own life! Just because someone you know is there, standing in the way.

SOLNESS.   Someone you have no right to leave.

HILDA.   Who knows if you really don't have a right. And still, all the same— Oh, to sleep the whole business away! (*She lays her arms down flat on the table, rests her head on her hands, and shuts her eyes.*)

SOLNESS (*turning the armchair and sitting by the table*).   Was yours a warm, happy home—up there with your father, Hilda?

HILDA (*motionless, answering as if half asleep*).   I only had a cage.

SOLNESS.   And you won't go back in?

HILDA (*as before*).   Wild birds never like cages.

SOLNESS.   They'd rather go hunting in the open sky—

HILDA (*still as before*).   Birds of prey like hunting best—

SOLNESS (*letting his eyes rest on her*).   Oh, to have had the Viking spirit—

HILDA (*in her usual voice, opening her eyes, but not moving*).   And the other? Say what that was!

SOLNESS.   A robust conscience.

(HILDA *sits up on the bench, vivacious once more. Her eyes again have their happy, sparkling look.*)

HILDA (*nods to him*).   I know what you're going to build next!

SOLNESS.   Then you know more than I do, Hilda.

HILDA.   Yes, master builders—they're really so dumb.

SOLNESS.   All right, what's it going to be?

HILDA (*nods again*).   The castle.

SOLNESS.   What castle?

HILDA.   *My* castle, of course.

SOLNESS.   Now you want a castle?

HILDA.   Let me ask you—don't you owe me a kingdom?

SOLNESS.   If I listen to you, I do.

HILDA.   So. You owe me this kingdom, then. And who ever heard of a kingdom without a castle!

SOLNESS (*more and more animated*).   Yes, they usually do go together.

HILDA.   Good. So build it for me! Right now!

SOLNESS (*laughing*).   Is everything always "right now"?

HILDA.   That's right! Because the ten years, they're up—and I'm not going to wait any longer. So, come on, Mr. Solness—fork over the castle!

SOLNESS.   It's not easy owing you anything, Hilda.

HILDA.   You should've thought of that before. It's too late now. Come on—(*Drumming on the table.*) one castle on the table! It's *my* castle! I want it *now*!

SOLNESS (*more serious, leaning nearer her, with his arms on the table*).   What sort of castle did you imagine for yourself, Hilda?

HILDA (*her expression veiling itself more and more, as if she were peering deep within herself; then, slowly*).   My castle must stand up—very high up—and free on every side. So I can see far—far out.

SOLNESS.   And I suppose it'll have a high tower?

HILDA.   A terribly high tower. And at the highest pinnacle of the tower there'll be a balcony. And out on that balcony I'll stand—

SOLNESS (*instinctively clutching his forehead*).   How you can want to stand at those dizzy heights—!

HILDA.   Why not! I'll stand right up there and look down on the others—the ones who build churches. And homes for mothers and fathers and droves of children. And you must come up and look down on them too.

SOLNESS (*his voice low*).   Will the master builder be allowed to come up to the princess?

HILDA.   If he wants to.

SOLNESS (*lower still*).   Then I think he'll come.

HILDA (*nods*).   The master builder—he'll come.

SOLNESS.   But never build anymore—poor master builder.

HILDA (*full of life*).   Oh, but he will! We two, we'll work together. And that way we'll build the loveliest—the most beautiful thing anywhere in the world.

SOLNESS (*caught up*).   Hilda—tell me, what's that!

HILDA (*looks smilingly at him, shakes her head a little, purses her lips, and speaks as if to a child*).   Master builders, they are very—very stupid people.

SOLNESS.   Of course they're stupid. But tell me what it is! What's the world's most beautiful thing that we're going to build together?

HILDA (*silent a moment, then says, with an enigmatic look in her eyes*).   Castles in the air.

SOLNESS.   Castles in the air?

HILDA (*nodding*).   Yes, castles in the air! You know what a castle in the air is?

SOLNESS.   It's the loveliest thing in the world, you say.

HILDA (*rising impatiently, with a scornful gesture of her hand*).   Why, yes, of course! Castles in the air—they're so easy to hide away in. And easy to build too. (*Looking contemptuously at him.*) Especially for builders who have a—dizzy conscience.

SOLNESS (*getting up*).   From this day on we'll build together, Hilda.

HILDA (*with a skeptical smile*).   A real castle in the air?

SOLNESS.   Yes. One with solid foundations.

> (RAGNAR BROVIK *comes out of the house. He carries a large green wreath with flowers and silk ribbons.*)

HILDA (*in an outcry of joy*).   The wreath! Oh, that'll be magnificent!

SOLNESS (*surprised*).   Are you bringing the wreath, Ragnar?

RAGNAR.   I promised the foreman I would.

SOLNESS (*relieved*).   Oh. Then I suppose your father's better?

RAGNAR.   No.

SOLNESS.   Didn't he get a lift from what I wrote?

RAGNAR.   It came too late.

SOLNESS.   Too late!

RAGNAR.   When she got back with it, he was in a coma He'd had a stroke.

SOLNESS.   But go home to him, then! Look after your father!

RAGNAR.   He doesn't need me anymore.

SOLNESS.   But you need to be with him.

RAGNAR.   *She's* sitting by his bed.

SOLNESS (*somewhat uncertain*).   Kaja?

RAGNAR (*giving him a dark look*).   Yes—Kaja, yes.

SOLNESS.   Go home, Ragnar, to both of them. Let *me* have the wreath.

RAGNAR (*suppresses a mocking smile*).   You don't mean you're going to—

SOLNESS.   I'll take it down myself, thanks. (*Takes the wreath from him.*) And go along home. We won't be needing you today.

RAGNAR.   I'm aware that you won't be needing me permanently. But today I'm staying.

SOLNESS.   Well, then stay, if—you're so anxious to.

HILDA (*at the railing*).   Mr. Solness—I'll stand here and watch you.

SOLNESS.   Watch me!

HILDA.   It'll be terribly thrilling.

SOLNESS (*in an undertone*).   We'll talk about that later, Hilda. (*He goes, with the wreath, down the steps and off through the garden.*)

HILDA (*looking after him, then turning to* RAGNAR).   It seems to me you might at least have thanked him.

RAGNAR.   Thanked him? Should I have thanked *him?*

HILDA.   Yes, you absolutely should have!

RAGNAR.   If anything, it's probably you I should thank.

HILDA.   Why do you say that?

RAGNAR (*without answering*). But just look out for yourself, miss. Because, actually, you hardly know him yet.

HILDA (*fiercely*). Oh, I know him the best!

RAGNAR (*with a bitter laugh*). Thank him, when he's held me down year after year! He, who made my own father doubt me. Made me doubt myself— And all that, just so he could—

HILDA (*as if surmising something*). He could—? Say it out!

RAGNAR. So he could keep her with him.

HILDA (*with a start toward him*). The girl at the desk!

RAGNAR. Yes.

HILDA (*threateningly, with fists clenched*). It isn't true! You're lying about him!

RAGNAR. I didn't want to believe it either, before today—when she said it herself.

HILDA (*as if beside herself*). *What* did she say! I've got to know! Now! Right now!

RAGNAR. She said he'd taken possession of her mind— completely. That all her thoughts are caught up in him, only him. She says she'll never let him go—that she wants to stay here where *he* is—

HILDA (*her eyes flashing*). She won't be allowed to!

RAGNAR (*searchingly*). Who won't allow her?

HILDA (*quickly*). *He* won't either.

RAGNAR. Oh no—I understand everything now. From here on she could only be, shall we say—an inconvenience.

HILDA. You understand nothing—when you can talk like that! No, *I'll* tell you why he kept her.

RAGNAR. Why?

HILDA. So he could keep *you*.

RAGNAR. Did he tell you that?

HILDA. No, but it's true! It *must* be true! (*Wildly.*) I will—I *will* have it that way!

RAGNAR. But just the moment you come by—is when he drops her.

HILDA. *You*—you're the one he dropped. What do you think he cares about strange girls like her?

RAGNAR (*reflectively*). You suppose he's really been afraid of me all along?

HILDA. Him afraid? I wouldn't be so conceited if I were you.

RAGNAR.   Oh, I think he's suspected for a long time that I had it in me all right. Besides—*afraid*—that's exactly what he is, you know.

HILDA.   Him! Oh, don't give me that!

RAGNAR.   In certain ways he's afraid—this great master builder. When it comes to stealing other people's happiness in life—like my father's and mine—there he's not afraid. But if it's a matter of climbing up a measly piece of scaffolding—watch him take God's own sweet time getting around to it!

HILDA.   Oh, if you'd only seen him as I did once—way, high up in the spinning sky!

RAGNAR.   You've seen that?

HILDA.   Of course I have. How proud and free he looked, standing there, tying the wreath to the weather vane!

RAGNAR.   I heard that he'd once gone up—just that once in his lifetime. Among us younger men, talking about it—it's almost a legend now. But no power on earth could get him to do it again.

HILDA.   He'll do it again today.

RAGNAR (*scornfully*).   Sure—tell me another!

HILDA.   We're going to see it!

RAGNAR.   Neither you nor I will ever see that.

HILDA (*in a frenzy*).   I *will* see it! I *will* and I *must* see it!

RAGNAR.   But he's not going to do it. He simply doesn't dare. He's got this disability now, and that's it.

(MRS. SOLNESS *comes out on the veranda.*)

MRS. SOLNESS.   (*looking about*).   Isn't he here? Where has he gone?

RAGNAR.   Mr. Solness is down with the men.

HILDA.   He took the wreath over.

MRS. SOLNESS (*terrified*).   He took the wreath! Oh, God, no! Brovik—go down to him! Try to get him back up here!

RAGNAR.   Should I say you'd like to speak with him?

MRS. SOLNESS.   Oh yes, dear, do that. No, no—don't say *I'd* like anything! You can say that somebody's here—and he should come at once.

RAGNAR.   Good. I'll take care of it, Mrs. Solness. (*He goes down the steps and out through the garden.*)

MRS. SOLNESS.   Oh, Miss Wangel, you can't imagine how anxious I am about him.

HILDA.   But is there anything here, really, to be so frightened about?

MRS. SOLNESS.   Of course. It's obvious. Suppose he goes through with this seriously—and tries to climb that scaffolding?

HILDA (*thrilled*).   You think he might?

MRS. SOLNESS.   One just never knows what he'll come up with. He could easily do anything.

HILDA.   Ah, so you do think that he's—somewhat—?

MRS. SOLNESS.   I don't know what to think about him anymore. The doctor's been telling me so much now, and when I put it all together with one thing and another that I've heard him say—

(DR. HERDAL *opens the door and looks out.*)

DR. HERDAL.   Isn't he coming right up?

MRS. SOLNESS.   Yes, I guess so. In any case, I've sent after him.

DR. HERDAL (*approaching*).   But I think you'd better go in, Mrs. Solness—

MRS. SOLNESS.   No, no. I'll stay out here and wait for Halvard.

DR. HERDAL.   Yes, but some ladies are here asking for you—

MRS. SOLNESS.   Good Lord, that too? And right at this moment!

DR. HERDAL.   They say they absolutely must see the ceremony.

MRS. SOLNESS.   Oh, well, I suppose I ought to go in to them after all. It *is* my duty.

DR. HERDAL.   Can't you just invite them to move on?

MRS. SOLNESS.   No, that wouldn't do. Now that they're here, it's my duty to make them welcome. (*To* HILDA.) But you stay here a while—until he comes.

DR. HERDAL.   And try to hold him here talking as long as possible—

MRS. SOLNESS.   Yes, do try, Miss Wangel, dear. Hold him, as hard as you can.

HILDA.   Aren't you the one who ought to be doing that?

MRS. SOLNESS. Lord, yes—it's my duty, I know. But when you have duties in so many directions, then—

DR. HERDAL (*looking toward the garden*). There he comes!

MRS. SOLNESS. Oh, my—and I have to go in!

DR. HERDAL (*to* HILDA). Don't say anything about my being here.

HILDA. Don't worry. I'm sure I can find something else to talk to him about.

MRS. SOLNESS. And hold him, no matter what. I'm sure *you* can do it best.

> (MRS. SOLNESS *and* DR. HERDAL *go into the house.* HILDA *remains standing on the veranda.* SOLNESS *comes up the steps from the garden.*)

SOLNESS. I hear someone wants me.

HILDA. Yes, I'm the someone, Mr. Solness.

SOLNESS. Oh, it's you, Hilda. I was afraid it'd be Aline and the doctor.

HILDA. You're pretty easily frightened, I guess!

SOLNESS. You think so?

HILDA. Yes, people say you're afraid to go clambering around—like up on scaffolds.

SOLNESS. Well, that's a special case.

HILDA. But you *are* afraid—it's true, then?

SOLNESS. Yes, I am.

HILDA. Afraid of falling and killing yourself?

SOLNESS. No, not that.

HILDA. What, then?

SOLNESS. Afraid of retribution, Hilda.

HILDA. Of retribution? (*Shaking her head.*) I don't follow that.

SOLNESS. Sit down and I'll tell you something.

HILDA. Yes, do! Right now! (*She sits on a stool by the railing and looks expectantly at him.*)

SOLNESS (*tosses his hat on the table*). You know that I first started out with building churches.

HILDA (*nods*). I know that, of course.

SOLNESS. Because, you see, as a boy I came from a pious home out in the country. That's why the building of churches seemed to me the noblest thing I could do with my life.

HILDA. Go on.

SOLNESS. And I think I can say that I built those poor country churches in so honest and warm and fervent a spirit that—that—

HILDA. That—what?

SOLNESS. Well, that I feel He should have been pleased with me.

HILDA. He? Who's "He"?

SOLNESS. He who was to have the churches, of course. He whose honor and glory they served.

HILDA. I see! But are you sure that—that He wasn't—well, pleased with you?

SOLNESS (*scoffingly*). He pleased with me! What are you saying, Hilda? He who turned the troll in me loose to stuff its pockets. He who put on call, right around the clock for me, all these—these—

HILDA. Devils—

SOLNESS. Yes—both kinds. Oh no, I pretty well got the idea that He wasn't pleased with me. (*Mysteriously.*) Actually, that's why He had the old house burn.

HILDA. That was why—?

SOLNESS. Yes, don't you see? He wanted me to have the chance to become a complete master in my own realm—and enhance His glory with still greater churches. At first I didn't understand what He was after—but then, all at once, it dawned on me.

HILDA. When was that?

SOLNESS. When I was building the church tower in Lysanger.

HILDA. I thought so.

SOLNESS. For you see, Hilda, up in those strange surroundings I used to go around musing and pondering inside myself. And I saw then, clearly, why He'd taken my children from me. It was to keep me from becoming attached to anything else. Anything like love and happiness, that is. I was only to be a master builder, nothing else. And all my life through, I was to go on building for Him. (*Laughs.*) But that never got very far.

HILDA. What did you do then?

SOLNESS. First, I searched my heart—tested myself—

HILDA. And then?

SOLNESS. Then I did the impossible. I no less than He.

HILDA.   The impossible?

SOLNESS.   I'd never in my life been able to climb straight up to a great height. But that day I could.

HILDA (*jumping up*).   Yes, yes, you could!

SOLNESS.   And when I stood right up at the very top, hanging the wreath, I said to Him: Hear me, Thou Almighty! From this day on, I'll be a free creator—free in my own realm, as you are in yours. I'll build no more churches for you. Only homes for human beings.

HILDA (*with great, luminous eyes*).   That was the singing I heard in the air!

SOLNESS.   Yes—but His mill went right on grinding.

HILDA.   What do you mean by *that*?

SOLNESS (*looking despondently at her*).   This building homes for human beings—it's not worth a bent pin, Hilda!

HILDA.   You really feel that now?

SOLNESS.   Yes, because now I see it. Human beings don't know how to use these homes of theirs. Not for being happy in. And I couldn't have found use for a home like that either—if I'd had one. (*With a quiet, bitter laugh.*) So that's the sum total, as far, as far back as I can see. Nothing really built. And nothing sacrificed for the chance to build, either. Nothing, nothing—it all comes to nothing.

HILDA.   Then will you never build anything again?

SOLNESS (*animated*).   Why, I'm just now beginning!

HILDA.   With what? What'll you build? Tell me now!

SOLNESS.   The one thing human beings can be happy in—that's what I'm building now.

HILDA (*looking intently at him*).   Master builder—you mean our castles in the air.

SOLNESS.   Castles in the air, yes.

HILDA.   I'm afraid you'd be dizzy before we got halfway up.

SOLNESS.   Not if I went hand in hand with you, Hilda.

HILDA (*with a touch of suppressed resentment*).   Only with me? Won't we have company?

SOLNESS.   Who else?

HILDA.   Oh, her—that Kaja at the desk. Poor thing— don't you want her along too?

SOLNESS.   Ah, so she was the subject of Aline's little talk.

HILDA.   Is it true, or isn't it?

SOLNESS (*hotly*).   I wouldn't answer a question like that!
You'll have to trust me, absolutely!

HILDA.   For ten years I've trusted you utterly—utterly—

SOLNESS.   You'll have to keep on trusting me.

HILDA.   Then let me see you high and free, up there!

SOLNESS (*wearily*).   Oh, Hilda—I'm not up to that every
day.

HILDA (*passionately*).   I want you to! I want that! (*Imploring.*) Just once more, master builder! Do the impossible
again!

SOLNESS (*looking deep into her eyes*).   If I did try it,
Hilda, I'd stand up there and talk to Him the same as
before.

HILDA (*with mounting excitement*).   What would you say
to Him?

SOLNESS.   I'd say: Hear me, Almighty God—you must
judge me after your own wisdom. But from now on, I'll
build only what's most beautiful in all this world—

HILDA (*enraptured*).   Yes—yes—yes!

SOLNESS.   Build it together with a princess that I love—

HILDA.   Oh, tell Him that! Tell Him!

SOLNESS.   Yes. And then I'll say to Him: I'm going down
now and throw my arms about her and kiss her—

HILDA.—many times! Say that!

SOLNESS.   —many, many times, I'll say.

HILDA.   And then—?

SOLNESS.   Then I'll swing my hat in the air—and come
down to earth, here—and do as I said.

HILDA (*with outstretched arms*).   Now I see you again as
if there was singing in the air!

SOLNESS (*looks at her with bowed head*).   How did you
ever become what you are, Hilda?

HILDA.   How have you made me into what I am?

SOLNESS (*decisively*).   The princess shall have her castle.

HILDA (*jubilant, clapping her hands*).   Oh, Mr. Solness—! My lovely, lovely castle. Our castle in the air!

SOLNESS.   On a solid foundation.

> (*Out in the street, faintly visible through the trees,
> a* CROWD OF PEOPLE *has gathered. Distant
> music of a brass band is heard from behind
> the new house.* MRS. SOLNESS, *with a fur stole*

around her neck, DR. HERDAL, *with her white
shawl on his arm, and several* LADIES *come
out onto the veranda.* RAGNAR BROVIK *comes
up at the same time from the garden.*)

MRS. SOLNESS (*to* RAGNAR).   There'll be music too?

RAGNAR.   Yes. They're from the Building Trades Association. (*To* SOLNESS.) I'm supposed to tell you from the
foreman that he's ready to go up now with the wreath.

SOLNESS (*taking his hat*).   Good. I'll go down myself.

MRS. SOLNESS (*anxiously*).   What are you going to do
there, Halvard?

SOLNESS (*brusquely*).   I've got to be down below with
the men.

MRS. SOLNESS.   Yes, down below. Please, stay down
below.

SOLNESS.   Don't I always—as a normal rule? (*He goes
down the steps and off across the garden.*)

MRS. SOLNESS (*calling after him from the railing*).   But
you must tell the man to be careful climbing! Promise me,
Halvard.

DR. HERDAL (*to* MRS. SOLNESS).   You see, I was right.
He's forgotten all about that craziness.

MRS. SOLNESS.   Oh, what a relief! We've had men fall
there twice now, and both times they were killed on the
spot. (*Turning to* HILDA.) Thank you so much, Miss
Wangel, for taking hold of him like that. I'm sure I never
could have managed it.

DR. HERDAL (*roguishly*).   You know, Miss Wangel—you
have a gift for taking hold of a man that you shouldn't hide!

(MRS. SOLNESS *and* DR. HERDAL *move across to
the* LADIES, *who stand nearer the steps, looking
out over the garden.* HILDA *remains standing
at the railing in the foreground.* RAGNAR *goes
over to her.*)

RAGNAR (*with stifled laughter, dropping his voice*).   Miss
Wangel—do you see all the young people, down there in
the street?

HILDA.   Yes.

RAGNAR.   They're my fellow students, come for a look
at the master.

HILDA.   Why do they want to look at *him?*

RAGNAR.   They want to see him afraid to climb up on his own house.

HILDA.   So, that's what the boys want!

RAGNAR (*with seething scorn*).   He's kept us down so long—now we're going to see him have the pleasure of keeping himself down.

HILDA.   You're not going to see it. Not today.

RAGNAR (*smiling*).   Really? And where will we see him!

HILDA.   High—high up by the weather vane, that's where.

RAGNAR (*laughs*).   Him! Oh, you bet!

HILDA.   His will—is to climb straight to the top. And hat's where you'll see him, too.

RAGNAR.   His *will,* yes, sure—that I believe. But he simply can't do it. His head would be swimming before he was even halfway up. He'd have to crawl down again on his hands and knees.

DR. HERDAL (*pointing*).   Look! There goes the foreman up the ladder.

MRS. SOLNESS.   And he's got the wreath to carry, too. Oh, if he'll only take care.

RAGNAR (*crying out in astonishment*).   But it's—!

HILDA (*in an outburst of joy*).   It's the master builder himself!

MRS. SOLNESS (*with a shriek of terror*).   Yes, it's Halvard! Oh, my God! Halvard! Halvard!

DR. HERDAL.   Shh. Don't shout at him!

MRS. SOLNESS (*half distracted*).   I'll go to him. Get him down again!

DR. HERDAL (*restraining her*).   All of you—don't move!

HILDA (*motionless, following* SOLNESS *with her eyes*).   He's climbing and climbing. Always higher. Always higher! Look! Just look!

RAGNAR (*breathlessly*).   Now he's got to turn back. It's all he can do.

HILDA.   He's climbing and climbing. He's almost there.

MRS. SOLNESS.   Oh, I'll die of fright. I can't bear to look.

DR. HERDAL.   Then don't watch him.

HILDA.   There he is, on the highest planks! Straight to the top!

DR. HERDAL.   Nobody move—you hear me!

HILDA (*exulting with quiet intensity*).   At last! At last! Now I can see him great and free again.

RAGNAR (*nearly speechless*).   But this is—

HILDA.   All these ten years I've seen him like this. How strong he stands! Terribly thrilling, after all. Look at him! Now he's hanging the wreath on the vane!

RAGNAR.   I feel like I'm seeing something here that's— that's impossible.

HILDA.   Yes, it's the impossible, now, that he's doing! (*With the inscrutable look in her eyes.*) Do you see anyone up there with him?

RAGNAR.   There's nobody else.

HILDA.   Yes, there's someone he's struggling with.

RAGNAR.   You're mistaken.

HILDA.   You don't hear singing in the air, either?

RAGNAR.   It must be the wind in the treetops.

HILDA.   I hear the singing—a tremendous music! (*Crying out in wild exultation.*) Look, look! He's waved his hat! He's waving to us down here! Oh, wave—wave back up to him again—because now, now, it's fulfilled! (*Snatches the white shawl from the doctor, waves it, and calls out.*) Hurray for master builder Solness!

DR. HERDAL.   Stop! Stop! In God's name—!

> (*The* LADIES *on the veranda wave their handker-chiefs, and shouts of "Hurray" fill the street below. Suddenly they are cut short, and the* CROWD *breaks into a cry of horror. A human body, along with some planks and splintered wood, is indistinctly seen plunging down between the trees.*)

MRS. SOLNESS AND THE LADIES (*as one*).   He's falling! He's falling!

> (MRS. SOLNESS *sways and sinks back in a faint; the* LADIES *catch her up amid cries and confusion. The* CROWD *in the street breaks the fence down and storms into the garden.* DR. HERDAL *also rushes down below. A short pause.*)

HILDA (*stares fixedly upward and speaks as if petrified*).   *My* master builder.

RAGNAR (*leans, trembling, against the railing*). He must have been smashed to bits. Killed on the spot.

ONE OF THE LADIES (*as* MRS. SOLNESS *is carried into the house*). Run down to the doctor—

RAGNAR. I can't move—

ANOTHER LADY. Call down to someone, then!

RAGNAR (*trying to call*). How is it? Is he alive?

A VOICE (*down in the garden*). Mr. Solness is dead.

OTHER VOICES (*nearer*). His whole head's been crushed—He fell right into the quarry.

HILDA (turns to RAGNAR *and says quietly*). I can't see him up there anymore.

RAGNAR. How horrible this is. And so, after all—he really couldn't do it.

HILDA (*as if out of a hushed, dazed triumph*). But he went straight, straight to the top. And I heard harps in the air. (*Swings the shawl up overhead and cries with wild intensity.*) My—my master builder!